SPECTRAL EVIDENCE

THE RAMONA CASE

Incest, Memory, and Truth

on Trial in Napa Valley

MOIRA JOHNSTON

D0465463

HOUGHTON MIFFLIN COMPANY

Boston   New York   1997

For information about permission to reproduce selections
from this book, write to Permissions, Houghton Mifflin Company,
215 Park Avenue South, New York, New York 10003.

For information about this and other Houghton Mifflin trade and
reference books and multimedia products, visit The Bookstore at
Houghton Mifflin on the World Wide Web at http://www.hmco.com/trade/.

Library of Congress Cataloguing-in-Publication Data
Johnston, Moira, date.
   Spectral evidence : the Ramona case : incest, memory, and truth on trial
in Napa Valley / Moira Johnston.
       p.   cm.
Includes bibliographical references and index.
ISBN 0-395-71822-8
   1. Ramona, Gary — Trials, litigation, etc. 2. Trials (Child sexual abuse) —
California — Napa Valley. 3. Incest. 4. Recovered memory.   I. Title.
KF224.R32J64   1997
345.73'02536 — dc21   97-9026   CIP

Printed in the United States of America

MP 10 9 8 7 6 5 4 3 2 1

For Lee, with inexpressible love and gratitude

For Dotsy, whose spirit still sings and dances

*For my pal Vee, here is the "family" book
we had hoped to do together*

Contents

THE TRIAL

The Memory Wars

In Salem, Massachusetts, the locust trees were still bare in the bleak memorial park that honors those killed by the witch trials of 1692 — the twenty-five women, men, and a newborn hung, crushed, or dead in prison on accusations that they were inhabited by spirits of the devil. Innocents dead, at the hands of hysterical young girls, on the strength of spectral evidence, "that poisoned cloud of fantasy" that had stood as proof in court. This small yard of granite and worn grass challenged the human indifference that had permitted Salem's shame. The dead confronted you. You were forced to step on their cries, carved into flagstones, as you stepped into the walled space: "God knows I am innocent . . . Oh, Lord, help me! . . . I am no witch." On each crude stone bench that extruded from the rough granite walls was carved a name and date of death. John Proctor. Sarah Good. Rebecca Nurse. July 19, 1692. It was like sitting on their graves.

March 24, 1994. In California, Napa Valley girded for the courtroom battle that could change the course of the recovered memory wars, a baffling war that looked, to some, like that poisoned cloud at Salem. It was an unlikely field of battle, for this was paradise, after all, a place of feasts and vineyards, not lurid incest trials. But the network TV trucks gathering outside downtown Napa's hundred-year-old white frame courthouse betrayed the importance of the events unfolding that spring morning. As the pale celadon leaves unfurled on the vines that have made this one of the world's most celebrated and wealthy wine valleys, reporters from *People* magazine, the

New York Times, and — for the first time in a Napa jury trial — the international press filed into Courtroom B to report the proceedings. The family tragedy had hidden in the valley's shadows for four years. Now the Ramonas prepared to have the most intimate and degrading details of their lives exposed to the world's prurient gaze. They would become part of history in a way no family could possibly have wished.

Four years earlier, Gary Ramona, the chief of global sales and marketing at the Robert Mondavi Winery, had been charged by his daughter Holly with twelve years of rape and sexual abuse. She had remembered none of these events until a series of disturbing pictures in her mind revealed them to her when she was nineteen. As rumors of incest slithered from the cul-de-sac on Pinot Way south through St. Helena and into the winery itself, Gary Ramona lost everything: his wife, children, home, job, reputation, friends, money, and the almost-finished dream house on a hill. He was scorned as a pariah. Even if the trial were to vindicate him, the taint of "perpetrator" would cling to him for life.

For several years, daughters like Holly had been confronting their fathers, suing them and breaking from their families — the path to recovery, they were told. But the Ramona trial was different. For the first time, it would give a father the right to fight back in court against the therapist and psychiatrist he claimed had planted false memories of incest in his daughter's mind. For Holly's memories had blossomed under the care of a therapist, one of the many thousands of master's-level family therapists (MFCCs) who practiced in California. The rare act of granting a third party — not a patient — the right to sue a therapist was a chilling warning to the entire profession of psychotherapy. If Gary Ramona won, it would be a surgical strike to the heart of the international recovered memory movement; it would open the floodgates to lawsuits and force public scrutiny of, and perhaps wrenching change in, one of the most potent forces in American culture: the "talking cure." The ghosts of Freud and the founding fathers of psychoanalysis would also sit on the defendants' bench.

Robert Mondavi, who had loved Gary Ramona like a son, would be testifying on Ramona's behalf against his own two sons. Napa Valley was titillated by the promise of a juicy wine dynasty saga, but it was far more than the Mondavi name that drew attention. Since Holly's flashbacks, so-called recovered memories like hers had become fiercely controversial.

The basic issue was whether traumatic memories of repeated childhood sexual abuse could be totally banished — massively *repressed* or *dissociated* — from conscious memory and then, years or decades later, recovered as intact and reliable replays of events. These memories were a phenomenon that had gone "unremarked in the entire human record before the 1980s," according to Frederick Crews, former chair of the English Department at UC Berkeley and a prominent skeptic of both the memories and the Freudian theory that underlay them. They gave incest a special status not accorded experiences of the Holocaust, Vietnam, or the sight of a mother murdered — terrible traumas that were usually only too well remembered.

Holly's radiant belief in her memories was her proof. "My daughter wouldn't lie," her mother said. No one doubted her sincerity, but were the memories true? Behind a therapist's closed door, literal truth had never mattered as much as a narrative story, fact or fantasy, that gave insight and helped heal. A search for corroboration was deemed irrelevant, an insult to the victim. "I am a therapist, not a detective," one clinician declared. But suddenly proof mattered very much. For if a jury found Holly's memories true — if they believed that Gary Ramona did commit incest — it would be compelling support for the fear that a virulent epidemic of child abuse was indeed eating our families from within — that no father could be trusted.

If Holly's memories — and those of thousands of other young women — were false, a hysteria far wider than Salem's had taken hold across the land, a sinister extension of the preschool satanic sexual abuse trials of the 1980s. On the strength of children's fantastic accusations, they had convicted — without a shred of proof — dozens of teachers and parents who languished in jail with serial life sentences as *Ramona* began.

Soon the attorneys would stand and deliver their opening statements. They would place before the jury a provocative summary of the stories to be told over the next seven weeks. Listen alertly, the lawyers would urge, for in the ordinary lives of two beach-loving Southern California kids lie the templates for family patterns that would grow into tragedy. Somewhere in the conflicting stories of a family's rise to unimaginable success — and in the murky world of memory — lay the truth. Gary either did it or he did not. The truth would be elusive, ambiguous. There would be little hard proof. The most sophisticated memory science could not reliably distinguish a false from a true memory. But the jurors must find the most reasonable truth and reach a verdict.

And so must Napa Valley. Gripped by the trial, the valley watched, read, and debated in supermarkets, schools, and coffee shops. If *this* family could be struck, all were at risk. As the Ramonas were forced to bare their intimacies and secrets, their neighbors were somehow freed to bare theirs. Women who had kept incest secret for decades — fathers who had been accused — crept from the shadows of shame and spoke out. In his Sunday column, a local reporter confessed his sister's accusations against their father and the pain of having suspicion cling forever to his father's memory. The courtroom became a magnet for an extraordinary gathering of people bonded only by a sense of connection, at some level, to this case. No one was left untouched.

As the media carried the story across the nation and abroad, it became clear that the Ramonas, and the Napa Valley, were a microcosm of a country caught in a war many did not know had been declared. Beyond the personal war of each afflicted family was an epic war that had left thousands of families ravaged. It had challenged the most holy tenets of psychotherapy, created schisms within feminism and psychology, tested the justice system, launched the golden age of memory research, and exposed tragic flaws in the most privileged American families.

Prosperous families identified readily with *Ramona,* for recovered memories had emerged from America's golden communities. The Ramonas were chillingly familiar to men who had worked their hearts out to achieve material success for their families and to women who, like forty-eight-year-old Stephanie Ramona, were caught between old and new expectations for women's lives.

So many women had been touched by the issues raised in *Ramona* — child abuse, therapy, eating disorders, depression, feminism — in a friend, in a child, in their own lives. Given the sweeping range of definitions of sex abuse, from a "sexual look" to serial rape, what woman had not suffered some form of molestation or violation in her lifetime? So many college women, young wives, and professionals shared Holly's angst, her food and image problems, her discomfort with sex and men — if not the memories of abuse. For those struggling with emerging memories, Holly was a bright and hopeful lodestar.

Her memories had erupted into the welcoming climate of a culture conditioned to accept "repression," "the unconscious," and "denial," a culture in which therapists had become as accepted as family doctors, skilled listeners needed by a mobile culture cut adrift from child-hood friends, family, community, and other stabilizing institutions. Therapists today were also shamans delivering the miracle of relief from intractable disorders — depression, schizophrenia, mania, and anxiety — with a pill.

The memories had emerged, too, from a climate of national re-morse as the epidemic extent of child abuse and incest was at last being acknowledged. Incest was no longer seen as occurring to one in a million, as psychiatry textboks had claimed, but as a common crime — "the perfect crime." Embracing the slogan "Believe the child," even on bumper stickers, a compassionate America had easily, uncritically, extended that embrace to adult memories of abuse that had appar-ently slumbered since childhood. With the Franklin trial in 1990 — in which the recovered memories of a freckle-faced California house-wife named Eileen Franklin Lipsker convicted her father of the rape and murder of her childhood friend twenty years earlier — recovered memory became a riveting new phenomenon and "survivors" a heart-rending new TV talk show staple.

Half the states had rushed to change their statute of limitations, making it easy for women and men with recovered memories of even decades-old abuse to sue fathers, uncles, grandparents. A backlash began in 1992 when accused parents banded together to found the False Memory Syndrome Foundation. They named distinguished sci-entists to their advisory board and launched a tenacious campaign to educate the media and the public, to pursue justice through the law, and to get their daughters back. For the group that would turn up each day to support Gary Ramona — and for an estimated sixteen thousand accused parents — this trial was the turning point, the event that would convincingly expose the memories as sham, lay blame at the therapists' doors, and speed a return to reason.

But the memory wars had been fed powerful fuel when a branch of feminism had seized on these sensational memories as a political weapon in the continuing war on patriarchy. Influential feminists like Judith Lewis Herman, a psychiatrist at Harvard and at the Victims of Violence program at Cambridge Hospital, made incest a cogent metaphor for the repressive violence of the patriarchal system toward women, finding "commonalities . . . between survivors of vast concen-tration camps created by tyrants who rule nations and the survivors of small, hidden concentration camps created by tyrants who rule their homes." The incest perpetrator was the demon patriarch disguised as a regular dad. To these feminists, Gary Ramona was the personification of the enemy and must not win.

But not everyone in the women's movement warmed to this turn of events. As feminism's alliance with the recovered memory movement forced it into bed with politically languid "survivors," absorbed with their own pain and victimization as well as with abortion-hating Christian fundamentalists, some lost sympathy, and dissident voices began to surface. The social psychologist Carol Tavris wrote a withering critique of the popular survivor literature in the *New York Times Book Review,* "Beware the Incest Survivor Machine." The feminist author Anne Roiphe spoke out against man-hating in *Fruitful*: "The view of the world as a giant evil patriarchal system seems headed for eventual ridicule and oblivion . . . The patriarchal label is pasted over male fragility and diverts us from the rains of fearfulness and sorrow that fall equally on both sexes . . . Some men beat their wives . . . Some men lust after their daughters or attack strange women in elevators, but most men do not."

For men, *Ramona* focused the fear and confusion brought by recovered memories. For just as they were learning from women to be nurturing, affectionate fathers — sharing the parenting job, changing diapers — they were confronted with suspicion and attacked as incestuous rapists. By the time of the Ramona trial, fathers found themselves nervously measuring the tightness of a hug, fearful that giving a young daughter her bath and bouncing her on his knee could come back to haunt him, years later, as charges of sexual abuse — could turn a precious daughter into a stranger.

Disturbingly, the American home had become a dangerous place for many women and children. Some accused fathers were doubtless guilty. But in a nation of collapsing families, the paranoia growing around recovered memories was shattering any remaining trust between parent and child. And a crusade against incest based on uncorroborated memories risked diverting the focus from where it was desperately needed: on the real problem of child abuse.

No group had a greater stake in *Ramona* than psychotherapists. It was their worst nightmare, a third-party suit that thrust the profession into an ethical morass: How far did a therapist's — or any healer's — responsibility reach beyond the patient? How far down the chain of family and friends should, or could, a therapist foresee the damage that might be done by the private, trusting, delicate explorations of a clinical session? If this trial breached the sacred immunity of the thera-pist's office, all were fair game for lawsuits.

Yet there was no monolithic support for recovered memory among psychotherapists. The American Medical Association and American Psychiatric Association were preparing to issue cautions against en-couraging or believing these memories. "Good" therapists knew the fallibility of memory, the ease of misdiagnosis, and the dangers of trendy memory-dredging techniques. Incompetents, even those with empathy and good intentions, were wounding the entire profession at the same time the psychotherapist's territory was being shrunk by pharmacology and by a cost-driven managed care environment intol-erant of traditional long-term therapy.

The Ramona witness stand would reveal another point of stress in the profession: a struggle between clinical and research psychologists. Clinicians trusted what they learned from their patients; scientists trusted what they learned in their labs.

Clinicians who worked with repression, dissociation, and Freud's early theory that most adult mental disorders were rooted in the bur-ied sexual traumas of childhood had found a profitable new field in recovered memories. These therapists confidently claimed that, ban-ished by the traumatic stress of rape and betrayal, the memories that surfaced in the safe haven of the therapist's care were every bit as real as the battle atrocities suffered by survivors of Vietnam. But how could you trust recovered memories of abuse? "It's like a novel. In a great novel, you can *tell* if there's a central coherence," a leading champion of the theory offered.

Such words did not reassure one research psychologist, Dr. Eliza-beth Loftus. Clinical anecdotes and great literature were not enough. Show me proof, she challenged, that "repression" exists as anything more than a useful metaphor. On the witness stand, Loftus would sound the scientist's call that memory is malleable, reconstructive, suggestible, often unreliable, and easily implanted with false elements. Her voice was strengthened by new memory research which showed that memory is not located in a tidy archive in the brain, producing clear microfiches of the past; the memory of something as simple as a cup must be reconstructed from myriad memory centers. The broad outlines of remembered events can generally be trusted. But forgetting and remembering come in infinite forms and gradations. Distortion is intrinsic.

Science was finding scant evidence of the "robust" repression claimed for these memories or for Holly's kind of flashbacks. Yet with the potential for destruction, resolution was a matter of vital urgency. PET scans, which let us, for the first time, look at memory happening in the living brain, held the promise of breaking some of the codes of memory as scientists raced against an epidemic that might wrongfully be destroying lives.

Their work would increasingly find its way into court, for the memory wars were coming down to the legal system — to courts, to laws, to social policy. Attorneys, judges, and legislators watched the trial closely, knowing that they would face these complex and emotional issues again and again: Did these memories meet the scientific standard for courtroom evidence, or were they another form of spectral evidence, the invisible manifestations of the devil that had condemned Salem's innocent as witches? Was it right to put the protection of the potentially innocent — Gary Ramona — above the protection of possible victims of child sexual abuse? The reverend Increase Mather, president of Harvard College at the time of the Salem witch trials, had given a potent answer: "It were better that ten suspected witches should escape than that one innocent person should be condemned." It was the courts that had halted the witch trials. When the pointed fingers of the witch-hunt reached into his own home and charged his wife, Governor Phips ordered the courts to forbid the admittance of spectral evidence into the trials, the act that finally stopped the hangings.

Whether Gary Ramona won or lost, his case could not halt the memory wars overnight. With hundreds of lawsuits already filed, legal action would continue into the next century. Now women who had claimed memories were retracting them and suing therapists. And the conflicts that drove the wars were too deep — the scale of the political, professional, and intellectual investment just too enormous — for any one trial to summarily close them down.

But the fiercely opposed decision of a small-town California Superior Court to give Gary Ramona, a father and a third party, the right to sue therapists and to put memory to the test declared the courtroom the gateway through which recovered memories must pass before being dignified as acceptable evidence. Courts of law were a terrible place for the healing of emotional wounds. But, with *Ramona*, they were where the memory wars would be resolved, where memory would be examined with the rigor brought to the Scopes Monkey

Trial. And where common ground might, finally, be found on which a truce could be struck and families rejoined.

This is a story about both memory and truth. It is Napa's *Rashomon,* the classic Japanese tale that, in telling the story of a murder through the eyes of four witnesses, reminds us how very different our memories of the same events in our lives can be. It reveals how committed we can become to a truth that, even unconsciously, serves our purposes and protects our illusions. It shows us how we intuitively edit our "truth."

The stories of Stephanie and Gary Ramona have been forged, not just from lifetimes of normal remembering and forgetting — at best, crazy quilts of fact, hearsay, and fantasy — but also from the crucible of five years of reinterpreting their stories under the pressures of shock, disillusion, and legal expedience. It would be a miracle if either story conformed consistently, now, to "reality." The wildly differing reports of their sex life, for example, would serve each of them well in court — Stephanie's painting Gary's disinterest in sex with her as a clue to his incestuous interest in Holly; Gary's painting Stephanie's frigidity, rather than rape, as a source of Holly's sexual "uptightness" and fears. But these are the truths Stephanie and Gary stand by and, in large part, believe. Their early stories — Stephanie's, of violence and tyranny, Gary's, of the near-perfect family — hold the secrets to the source of the conflicts that, when the crisis came, exploded into irrevocable catastrophe.

For the Ramona family, the memory wars were felt as daily pain. Throughout the trial, they would be forced to reveal their most intimate moments. It would be unspeakably humiliating. Sadly, it is usually explosive public events that force us to look squarely at ourselves and face our flaws. Planes must crash before we seek fixes. But the insights gained — and the reforms that follow — are the redeeming aspects of America's tragedies.

True or false, Holly Ramona's memories and the poignant stories she would tell of the empty dinner table — of a family that never shared a meal or really talked — would reveal that Napa Valley's sunny suburbs had produced a hunger in its children not satisfied by its feasts. As the trial unfolded, Holly would force a shaken courtroom and a watching valley to look inside, to examine their own families. Everyone shared in the desperation that had built, unseen, within a smiling cheerleader at St. Helena High. True or false? Twelve random Napa citizens would arrive at the best verdict they could. But a psychologist in Napa summed up the sadness and compassion that would haunt the valley long after the trial: "We've deified our chefs, but starved our children of nurture."

If the perfect family was vulnerable, we all were.

A PERFECT FAMILY

1

A World of Women

Until she was seven, Stephanie Ramona was raised in a world of women. "Maybe that's why I'm funny about men. I never know how they feel," she says from the shattered landscape of her marriage. Her father had died in the fiery skies over Indochina in June 1945 — six weeks after her birth, ten thousand miles from her crib in California — as Japanese bullets found the skin of a slow-flying amphibious PBY and brought down a spirited young California Icarus. Red-haired and boyishly handsome, Walt Vogelsang had dreamed of returning home to train as a football coach and of seeing his new daughter. In a terrible irony, he was on his last bombing mission before being furloughed home, just two months before the end of World War II.

Six weeks premature, Stephanie Joan weighed just three and a half pounds at birth. Placed in an incubator, she was kept from her mother's ample breasts and warm arms for six weeks. But Betty Vogelsang would "put a bow in my hair, dress up, and go see her." Stevie, as she called the infant, had eyes so big they called her Betty Boop, and under the jaundiced skin she had her father's fine-boned face. At just twenty-two, Betty had become both mother and father. She had few resources, but she was determined to protect little Stevie from harm, from need, and from life's pain. As she watched her daughter's exposure by the trial as a helpless trophy wife, Betty worried, "I think I overprotected Stevie, did too much for her." If so, it was circumstance and the best of intentions that led Betty to forge a ring of security around Stephanie, which may have screened her from some of life's lessons, and a bond between mother and daughter no man could ever fully breach.

Armed with California's peacetime optimism, a high school diploma, and a shorthand course, Betty got a job as a secretary at C. F. Braun, an engineering firm in Alhambra. She moved into her mother's small house in Monterey Park, one of the towns that had grown up to serve the citrus groves that still carpeted the idyllic San Gabriel Valley, east of Los Angeles.

The orange groves became Stephanie's playground. The abandoned Victorian homes, replaced by subdivisions after the war, were her haunted houses. From the shade of the groves the child watched the black smoke of the smudge pots, lit to fight killing frosts in late winter, darken the sky. She scarcely noticed a new kind of cloud blowing in from Los Angeles, choking the trees, beginning to hide the view of the San Gabriels. It was called smog. Stephanie witnessed the transformation of one of the most beautiful and productive agricultural regions on earth into the sun-kissed consumer culture that still defines America abroad. When Covina's Eastland Mall opened, she saw the birth of the American shopping mall.

Stephanie's first memory is of the beach, of a tiny girl chasing pigeons and trying to shake salt on their tails. She loved to head down the freeways with her mother, aunts, and cousins to the broad, tawny beaches of Orange County. They'd drive to Huntington Beach and farther south through the farms of Anaheim, where Walt Disney was building his Magic Kingdom, to Newport and Balboa. For Stephanie, the beach has "always, always been where I can walk . . . and put both feet on the ground, and think . . . and get my head together. Standing on the beach with the sand and the sky and the ocean, it looks so simple."

Her aunts were not career role models, but they schooled Stephanie in loyalty, practical jokes, and the family stories. Her mother was "the life of the party. A Pollyanna, she was always happy," says Stephanie. But Betty had moral lessons to teach. She sent her daughter to the Presbyterian church. And, catching her in a lie, sent her to her room trailed by what Stephanie recalls as "the most horrible words I've ever heard: *'I'm so disappointed in you,'*" and left her to sit in silence with her guilt.

Distressed when an aunt gave Stephanie a loose Hawaiian muu-muu, Betty taught her the classic look that would become her style for life. A tailor's daughter, Betty knew the quiet worth of beautifully made clothes and passed on to her daughter the maxim: Buy few items, buy the best, and they'll always be in style. Being perfectly turned out in clothes of quality and structure may also have been a kind of moral armor against the tenuousness of life for a widowed mother — and against a humiliating difference Betty had felt as a child. Stephanie loved the fact that her grandmother was quarter-Cherokee, the matriarch who had come to Pasadena from Kansas in the 1920s. She could still see her grandmother drying her hair in the sun, her hands working the waist-length dark fall, combing it, braiding it, wrapping it around her head. But for Stephanie's mother "it was hard to be part Indian. Kids thought Indians were the enemy. They were bad." At seven, Betty had screamed at her mother, "You're a savage!" as she wrung the necks of chickens and turkeys.

Betty married Walt Nye, an engineer and fellow employee, when Stevie was seven, and they moved to a house in a new subdivision carved from the fields of Covina. "You remember *The Donna Reed Show*? That's what my mother was. Before my father would come home, she'd take the baths, she'd fix up." Betty quit work but, addicted to self-improvement, kept taking courses.

Stephanie yearned for Walt's attention, but her new father would closet himself in his dark den and drink. Stephanie, who so loved the buzz of big family gatherings that she still turns on the TV just for the noise, found herself in a house that was hushed: "He was very silent. A loner." She chalked it up to Walt's experiences in the war, where he had been in Darby's Rangers, a commando group like the Green Berets. "I used to figure he'd seen a lot and . . . that it had affected him." He tried to be a father, took her fishing, riding, and hunting for the biggest Christmas tree in the world. "But I would never go up to him. Except once, when he . . . gave me a spanking . . . and I got on his lap and said, 'Now you're my *real* father.' But he didn't respond. I stopped reaching for hugs."

Walt stayed home when the women went to the beach. As surfing gripped California's young, Stephanie began to go off with her friends. In a bedroom papered with pictures of Sandra Dee, Stephanie pulled on her two-piece bathing suit and joined the surge to the beach in a "woody," the wood-paneled station wagon that was the surfer's status symbol. At Huntington Beach, home of the modern surfboard, she loved to carry her board down to the water; it was a small, fast board the boys put together for her from a $50 kit.

"But I was not good . . . and have the scars to show . . . I'm not coordinated . . . I was very shy and extremely small. I was always the last one that everybody picked on the team," says Stephanie, revealing the self-criticism that pervades her sense of herself as a child. School did little to bolster her self-esteem. "He could spot the weak ones," she says of the eighth-grade teacher who caught her passing a note between two girls and tore her apart in front of the class. "From then on, he would humiliate me in front of everybody, even when I knew the answer. I stopped raising my hand." Contracting mononucleosis in high school, she fell behind in math and dropped it. In English class, however, she got the scrap of praise that remains a highlight of her high school years. "But I was going down in English. It was probably boys," she says on reflection.

As boys were entering Stephanie's life, Betty's ten-year marriage to Walt ended in divorce.

Named for the snowy peak that looms over the valley, Mt. San Antonio College opened in 1946 in Pomona to accommodate the flood of families moving to the area. Stephanie entered "Mt. SAC" in 1963 with vague dreams of being an architect. She had read Ayn Rand's *Fountainhead* and admired its architect-hero, Howard Roark. How great it would be "to be able to build your dream house on a hill." She didn't talk about ambitions, though. People might think she couldn't do it. There was only one goal she would admit to as she entered college: "I just wanted to have kids." She signed up to major in psychology.

Stephanie still felt backward and shy, but boys saw a fragile beauty, a tiny-waisted body, a head of curly dark hair. She loved to laugh and was genuinely sweet and ladylike. An entire fraternity came over one night and toilet-papered her house, a tribute to her popularity. The Toastmasters Club talked her into running for Homecoming Queen and coached her to perform as Snow White in front of the school. The crowd went hysterical when she forgot her lines, but she didn't like it: "I didn't win. I had no business being there. I'm sure they regret it now!"

She has an image of Gary Ramona walking down a hill at school:

"He was with a group of girls, and I remember watching him. He seemed very carefree, and I liked that." But her very first sight of Gary was at the library. "I was running for Homecoming Queen and I remember going through the library doors and there was Gary and his friend Joe Strader just waiting for me. They'd open up both doors and bow. They'd bow!"

Gary began picking her up after classes. They'd sit on her steps at home and talk. "At first he was just a good friend . . . I thought he was kind of a silly guy, kind of a pest." But the man who would become a master salesman made the sale with his smile. Gary always had a smile on his face. He made her laugh, and he gave her attention. "Gary was the opposite of my father. Gary had a zest for life. He gave me excitement. Maybe it was something that I didn't think I was capable of doing myself . . . I needed someone to do it for me."

Gary was "the absolute opposite of what my mother wanted for me," Stephanie says now. Betty found him "rough. He'd do things all wrong. He had a great smile, but he laughed too loud." But Betty could see how her daughter, so quiet, would be attracted to Gary's outgoing personality, how she might like his dark Italian looks. Opposites attract. And, clearly, Stephanie was very attracted to him. "At first he pursued me. He was jealous." Then the tables turned. She was jealous of another girl he'd taken to the hills. "I think he was sexually active. I thought he was a normal, healthy boy . . . until it came to *me*. He never tried anything with me." She was known as "Nye-eve" in those days. "However, if Gary had tried, I probably would have," says Stephanie.

Her virginity was very important to him; they talked about it in the car one night. "It was important that I had never 'done anything.' He didn't just mean intercourse; he didn't want anybody to have even touched me." At the time, a lot of men were that way about the girls they married. She and Gary petted some, but technically Stephanie remained a virgin. A virgin who had never had a drink. Disbelieving, Gary took her to the home of his friends Scott and Mickey Evans and fixed her a 7-Up and vodka. Stephanie had a few sips and thought, "Oh, my God, what's going to happen to me?" She didn't like the taste, and he didn't push it. He was protective and respectful. "That was it," Stephanie reflects. She had fallen in love.

But her mother was perturbed as she listened to Gary and Stephanie doing their homework together in the kitchen. Gary would say, "I see that people could fall in love with several people — there's not just *one* person out there." Betty would shake her head. "He was saying, 'You better marry me or I'll find somebody else.'" This could manipulate a girl who was not as confident as she could be. "Stevie always thought Gary was right. Always did what he said."

This extended to her appearance early on. Even before he knew her well, Gary started buying her clothes, which her mother made her return. He had a generous streak. But Stephanie suspects now that it had more to do with his wanting to control her, to remake her into his image. "He wasn't wealthy at all. He had this thing about class — the word 'class' would just infuriate him. Yet I think he wanted certain things in life." And he wanted Stephanie to be a reflection of those things. "I didn't wear hose. I was kind of a tomboy. He would tell me that young ladies should wear hose. I'd say back at him, 'Well, no one else does.' But it's interesting that later, you saw me wearing hose." When Stephanie jumped in the car one day without any makeup, going to see some friends, Gary was furious. When they got home, he ordered, "'Don't you ever go out of the house again without makeup . . . *ever* — it's unacceptable.' I admit it, I don't think I was ever natural looking. But how bad can you *look* at twenty?"

Gary started pressing Stephanie to marry him. Vietnam hung over them, and she suspected that he wanted to marry now so that he could avoid being drafted. "He was so scared to go into the service. And at that point I thought I loved him. I didn't want him going any more than he wanted to go. But I wasn't ready . . . I was having fun." She said no. They'd argue. "And Gary kept getting angry." But she wasn't prepared for two scenes he would later deny — along with most of her other stories of lies and violence. Reconstructing her confused memories, Stephanie says, "We were sitting in his car," talking about the Vietnam War, "and he'd asked me to get married. He was nervous, and I remember he kept hitting his hand against the window. I think it shattered . . . I was scared. The next time, his hand was taped, and he told me — I don't know if it's true — he'd fractured his hand by doing that . . . We had the same argument, and he did it again, the same hand." This time he didn't break the window. But the violence shocked her.

Yet she capitulated. They planned to elope to Las Vegas. They would keep it quiet, Gary promised. "We'd tell our parents later and have a regular wedding to make my mother happy." Why did she decide to marry him? "I'd *like* to say I was doing it as a favor to him, but I don't think anybody's *that* good. I didn't want anything to happen to him. But these feelings were for *me,* not for him. I didn't want to lose him."

Stephanie had to sneak her turquoise wedding dress out of the house. Scott and Mickey joined them for the elopement and would be their witnesses. Stephanie told her mother she was going hunting. They left for Las Vegas at six in the morning. "Just outside of Las Vegas, we stopped at a gas station. I went in to change my clothes. When I came out, Gary was in a daze . . . I said, 'Look, if you don't want to do it . . .'" She'd offered him an out, but he still seemed dazed. "Let's not do it. I don't want to," Stephanie snapped.

Gary was galvanized into action, and he went into the gas station and changed. Stephanie can't remember the name of the wedding chapel, Cupid something. They had a license but no rings, so they borrowed Scott and Mickey's. Stephanie felt panic yet went through the motions, giggling and crying "during the whole thing." Gary still seemed dazed as they heard the formal words: "I now pronounce you man and wife." They went to Denny's for dinner, and Gary had her back home at her mother's by six that night.

She tells of catching him in his first lie the day after they got married: "It was the first time . . . He made it sound like I was crazy and didn't know what I was talking about." He had agreed they'd keep the marriage secret; they'd live apart at first, then have a proper wedding. "And then it changed. The day after we got married, he showed up on the front porch telling me, no, I was going to move in with him *then* and we were going to tell our parents." It was as if the agreement didn't exist. "I'm a wimp and you can take advantage of me — unfortunately, that's the way I am . . . But I don't like to be lied to." She confronted him: "You said we were going to keep this quiet so nobody would get hurt." They had a terrible argument, and she declared, "I'm not going. *I'm not going.*"

"That's when he hauled off and hit me . . . On the side of my face with the back of his hand. He cut my face with his school ring." No one had ever struck her like that. "I was devastated. I ran into the house and covered my face. My mother came into the hall as I was walking through, and I hid my face and went into the bathroom to clean up. I couldn't tell her."

Stephanie wanted an annulment, but she also wanted to help Gary stay out of the service. Her ambivalence became moot when an aunt spotted the listing of their marriage in the Vital Statistics column in the newspaper, and word raced through the family. But Stephanie stayed with her mother for several more months, the marriage unconsummated. Gary would take her to the local hangout, In-N-Out, for hamburgers and pressure her to move in with him. Gary had ceased showing affection the day they married; he seemed a different person since that day. "But I loved being with him," and she succumbed. She knew Gary would look after her as her mother had from birth.

The Ramonas started their life together in an upstairs apartment in Glendora. A few months after they got married, Stephanie quit school to get a job. They needed the money, but it wasn't a sacrifice, for Stephanie lacked her mother's impulse for learning. She got a job as a receptionist and mail room and teletype clerk at C. F. Braun, where Walt Nye worked. After her mother's divorce, he had dropped out of her life, but she had never stopped wanting his love. When she suddenly saw him in the hall one day, he walked right past her. "He just said 'Hi' like I was just anybody." He had treated her like a stranger, and she broke down, crying.

Nor was marriage bringing the affection and security she craved. Gary had been "a great kisser," but the kissing had stopped. Both of them tried awkwardly to discuss the issue during the first months of marriage. But having sex was a bigger problem. They had tried once before living together and it hadn't worked. Stephanie thought that in time it would just come naturally. She couldn't be the first bride to face this. "I mean, those were times when there were more virgins."

But intercourse had become a huge issue. Six months after they eloped, the marriage was still not, technically, consummated. "Gary was gentle. He was *too* gentle," Stephanie recalls. "He had no problem with an erection. We'd get to the point where he would put his penis right to my vagina, but he wouldn't go any further. He didn't push. He didn't do anything. He kept saying, 'It's not time. You're not ready.' And I remember thinking, 'God, what time's the right time?' I remember so vividly making a comment, 'Shouldn't we be doing something?' And I wanted to . . . He was a sexy man.

"I always thought it was me . . . Maybe I'm not big enough — this is how stupid I was . . . I think I was nervous with Gary. But I have to say that I was more curious than anything. I think if he'd tried, we could have." A few weeks later she went to a gynecologist, who gave her a pelvic exam and said, "There's no problem. Go home and have a drink. Tell Gary to have a drink, too." For a girl who didn't drink, it was a formidable order. "That night, I had a drink — I don't know if Gary did. And it *worked!*"

Once they had crossed the threshold of penetration, "he was good. I enjoyed myself . . . I always had orgasms. Throughout the whole marriage until, of course, the end, I will say — and it's tough because it's just complimenting Gary. I'd love to tell you he was selfish — but he always took care of me first . . . Maybe I'm crazy, but I loved it."

Her daughter's confidante, Betty was relieved there was nothing wrong. But what bothered her about the incident with the doctor was the passive obedience it revealed in her daughter. "Gary *let* her go to a doctor — *let* her! Imagine, he had to give her permission."

The first year or two of life together were stormy. Stephanie recalls eight to ten incidents of violence. Once Gary hit her because a hair appointment had made them late for a party. In another rage, she remembers, he kicked his foot through a door. The decisive event was when Gary socked her in the stomach so hard she had to go to a doctor.

She had felt insecure about Gary's staying out late and feared he'd found someone else. He admitted he sometimes played pool with Scotty and the guys, but he would laugh off her fears, melt down her anger. He *was* working hard, studying and taking classes after doing construction all day. But a few times she'd fitfully protested the late nights; she'd called Scotty to move her back to her mother's, loaded up his truck, then changed her mind.

With the fist in her stomach, however, Stephanie had had enough. "I turned around and piled everything I owned, which wasn't much, and put it in the car and left him and filed for divorce." She took the dog with her, went back to her mother's, and, she reports, got a restraining order against Gary — an order Gary claims never to have received. Stephanie most feared for Prince, the mutt they'd got free at a gas station, for Gary seemed to have a love-hate relationship with him. "Gary called my mother's, threatening to come and get the dog — not *me*." That hurt.

This was their longest separation, several months. "I didn't want her to go back to Gary," says Betty, "but Stevie said she had to because 'I'd be a failure.'" The couple reconciled when Gary promised he would never hit her again. Stephanie arrived back at their apartment, expecting Gary to greet her, and found that he'd moved to a smaller place. With Gary, she was always being caught off guard.

Once they were back together, Betty was supportive of the marriage. She never forgave Gary for a crude comment he made about her large, and Stephanie's small, breasts. Laughing, as always, he'd said that Betty was a Jersey cow while Stephanie was evaporated milk. "But he had improved so much. He was a learner, he worked at it. I admired him for that."

Gary's parents were supportive, too. Tony Ramona, Gary's father, had a wonderful laugh and a tender heart. When Stephanie and Gary first got married and didn't have any money, he'd sneak twenty dollars to Stephanie and make sure his wife didn't know. Stephanie always felt a chill from Gary's mother, Garnet Ramona — partly jealousy, she guessed. When she was dating Gary, and was at his house before they went out, Garnet would yell at Gary to go and get his jacket, then pull Stephanie aside and tell her she'd gotten lipstick on his collar. "She'd say, very quietly, 'How shameful.' What was I doing with her son? Then Gary would come out and everything was fine."

In 1967, two years after their marriage, Gary began his career as a salesman, taking a full-time job with a citrus juice distributor, Vita-Pakt. He was a natural. After all, he had always been able to sell Stephanie on forgiving him. The violence seemed to have passed. Stephanie loved him. And, Betty knew, "no family's perfect."

Stephanie started to think about getting pregnant. She had tried to ask Gary about having a baby but doesn't remember his ever saying yes or no. "I was ready. I was excited. I was pregnant the second month I stopped the Pill." If Gary shared her joy, he didn't show it. "It wasn't like you see on TV." Several months later, Stephanie quit her job at Braun.

When labor pains began on August 15, 1970, Gary was visiting his mother in Costa Mesa. The pains weren't as grabbing as she had expected, but Stephanie timed them and knew that she should think about getting to the hospital. She was in San Dimas, forty minutes from Huntington Memorial Hospital in Pasadena. Gary was over an hour's drive south. She called Gary and urged him to come home. He recalls being home in about an hour. But Stephanie says that after two hours, she called again. The pains were getting stronger, closer. "You're overreacting," he kept saying. Baffled, she called her own mother to take her in.

When Gary arrived, after her second call, he was furious to find Betty there. Stephanie thought, "This is crazy," and pleaded, "Gary, we have to leave." "I'm not going until your mother leaves. She's not going to the hospital with us," said Gary. "But couldn't she go — she's here anyway?" Stephanie begged, seized by growing contractions. "No, absolutely not," he snapped. Stephanie "was livid" as Betty left; then Gary took a shower. "A forty-five-minute shower — I watched the clock." This was a ritual cleansing, like the showers he always took before they were going to make love. It was strange, like the episode early in their marriage — which Gary denies — when he told her she should douche every three or four days, as his mother did, and took her to the drugstore to get supplies.

"As he came out of the shower, I said, 'Gary, we're going.' And, you know, he got out his camera first . . . He kept taking a picture every time I had a pain." The pains were now hard and getting closer. "He had to stop at McDonald's and get a Coke. He had to buy more film . . . To this day, I don't know what that was."

After twenty-four hours of labor, Holly Ramona was born.

Holly gave Stephanie someone she could safely hug. Holly was cuddly and soon hugged back. Physically, she was all Gary, and she had his great smile. Gary also had a new preoccupation: a possible job with a little winery in Napa Valley, Robert Mondavi.

The carpet of vineyards had turned to a harvest patchwork of red, rust, and yellow when Stephanie drove through Napa Valley with Gary for the first time. He had insisted that she join him on the trip to the interview. "I don't know why, because I just sat there like a bump on a log." Yet Mondavi did everything he could to put them at ease. He took them to lunch, applying no pressure. "You don't have to move up right away. Just take your time," he offered. Gary loved the challenge of the big Southern California market and didn't want to move north any more than Stephanie wanted to leave her mother and the beaches. Mondavi put them up at the Silverado Country Club, the area's only world-class resort in the calm before the storm of tourists found Napa Valley, when the best restaurants were still in the homes of a handful of winemakers.

Stephanie had no objection to Gary's selling wine. She didn't personally like to drink, but wine was just another product, like orange juice. What was important was that the job would let them stay in Southern California. Within three days of their visit to Napa, Gary was hired.

Pregnant with her second child, Stephanie wore a bright red dress for courage when the Mondavis flew her north with Gary for the winery's Christmas dinner at the Copper Kettle in St. Helena two months later. Seated at a long table, she met the family that would become as important to Gary as his own. What was she doing here, she wondered, if she couldn't even drink the product? It hurt her throat and stomach as it went down, and her heart started doing funny things. Moreover, wine didn't fascinate her the way it did the Mondavis. But Robert's younger son, Tim, put her at ease. Still in college, with long hair and unmarried, he was, she thought, so cute, so nice. He *talked* to her.

She met the elder son, Michael, and his wife, Isabel, who had installed the Ramonas at the private Meadowood Club in the hills east of St. Helena and invited them to drop by their apartment in Yountville to pick up some wine and wineglasses. Stephanie was particularly taken with the graciousness of Marj, Mondavi's wife. It was a nice family. And yet she thought she sensed something between Mondavi and his sparkly special events director, Margrit Biever, who attended the dinner with the husband who had brought her to Napa from Switzerland as a military bride years earlier. On the drive back to Meadowood, Stephanie felt pleased with her first Christmas party as a Mondavi winery wife.

Early in 1972, the Ramonas moved to Diamond Bar, a new community in the hills twenty minutes south of the valley towns where they'd grown up. Kelli was born that spring. Stephanie was twenty-seven and Gary twenty-eight. They had caught the wave of the longest unbroken economic boom in California's history. With a loan from Betty, from the sale of her house in Covina, they had the down payment on a brand-new house. Diamond Bar was the Promised Land to its residents. Built above the brown carpet of smog that lay over San Gabriel Valley in the rolling hills of an eight-thousand-acre ranch, it promised the mystique of the old Spanish *rancho* era with modern suburban amenities.

What Stephanie wanted was a safe street with neighboring playmates for Holly and Kelli. Number 2107 Holly Leaf Way was on a cul-de-sac, a one-story white stucco ranch house with a shingle roof and a garage on the left, its yard still raw. But Stephanie knew Gary would fix it up and build a pool.

The living room had a cathedral ceiling and wall-to-wall carpet. Its sunken conversation pit had built-in plush velour sofas in an L shape around the fireplace, which you could see from the kitchen and family room, like a fire in the middle of a cave. A step led up to a dining room, which looked out on the backyard. Beyond a tiny room that would be Gary's office were the bedrooms, off a long hall. With the master bedroom at the back, Holly and Kelli would share the one closest to Gary's office. Stephanie could see the bunk beds.

On the day of the run-through with the real estate agent before moving in, Gary and Stephanie were in the house by themselves and he hugged her — the first time she ever remembers him doing this when no one else was around. Then he told her that this day he was the happiest he'd ever been in his life.

"Am I shallow because I think of that as the best time of my life?" Stephanie wonders now. A friend she'd worked with at Braun, Shary Quick, lived just a few doors away. Good friends bonded by children close in age, the two women shared the years. They helped each other as their children were born. They played tennis, went shopping, drank coffee at each other's houses. They went to the beach and the club, walked the kids to the bus stop, and stood there to chat every morning and again in the afternoon. With money still tight, they babysat for each other's kids. They traded recipes from Betty Crocker and *The Joy of Cooking*. Shary shared her recipe for cheddar cheese pinwheels with Stephanie.

Children defined the days, the pattern of life. Since it was a new community, the mothers started their own nursery school, Tiny Tots, hiring a teacher and taking turns helping out. On the cul-de-sac, both Holly and Kelli were known to be quiet and shy. In Shary's opinion, it was a shyness that went beyond holding back at a party and then joining in. But since when was it a problem to have darling, well-behaved kids? Stephanie thought. She kept the girls turned out in matching outfits with crisp ribbons in their hair, ready to meet Gary at night when he got an office twenty minutes from home. While a nation of mothers read Dr. Spock, Stephanie didn't feel the need; she had no philosophy of child rearing. She didn't need any. Her kids "were good, *too* good."

Her memories are of normalcy, of Holly's playing dolls with Kelli and watching *The Brady Bunch* and *The Partridge Family,* of their playing with the neighboring boys on the cul-de-sac and the high school kids next door. Holly had trouble paying attention in school and with reading comprehension, and she was absent a lot with kidney and bladder problems. But she had a best friend, Maureen Gonzalez, from kindergarten to third grade at Evergreen School, a memory Holly valued because, she said later, "I don't think I ever had another best friend." At Christmas, the girls would get their parents and grandparents up at dawn, if they could, to open the mountain of gifts. In the bedroom Holly now believes was a scene of incest, Kelli slept in the top bunk because Holly was afraid of heights.

There was a flurry of anger from Gary when Holly couldn't learn to ride a big bike. But Holly remembered only one spanking, which was, admittedly, for being a brat. Father and daughter went horseback riding, visiting his parents, and once to a wedding. For a year Gary took Holly to Indian Princesses, a version of Girl Scouts where the men dressed like Indians and helped the girls make crafts.

Diamond Bar was also a world of couples. Joan and Bill, Shary and Mike, Stevie and Gary. In fours or sixes, they did things together: New Year's Eve parties, surprise birthday parties, and barbecues. Together, they waited in line to see *American Graffiti*. Fathers would play Santa Claus for one another's Christmas parties. They had family and other friends — the Ramonas did business entertaining — but their lives revolved around Diamond Bar.

Although black girls became Pasadena Rose Parade princesses, civil rights scarcely sent a breeze through the Ramonas' lily-white enclave. Nor did "women's lib" or Vietnam. Though the war was officially over when the Ramonas put down roots in Diamond Bar in the early seventies, the nation was still raw from the experience as the vets came home. Where her mother had pushed pins around a map, following her husband's flying missions in World War II, this war was an abstraction to her daughter. In this conservative community, Shary recalls, "Of course, we thought Jane Fonda was doing a terrible disservice to the country."

After the turbulent first years of marriage, things were settling down with the Ramonas. Stephanie was running Gary's office at home, answering forty phone calls a day and arranging his wine tastings. Gary would hire her friends to serve wine and cheese at Diamond Bar's clubhouse and in private homes. The young winery was still low on funds, so they washed wineglasses in bathtubs. Stephanie glimpsed the glamorous side of the industry when she bought a new dress and entertained customers with Gary or joined the Mondavis at elegant events.

Stephanie connected with the business not through wine but through her affection for Marj Mondavi, Robert's wife. Together they went to Disneyland and then to Hawaii. Always a little insecure, Stephanie sensed some secret nervousness in Marj. But, with her hair in a chignon, her clothes beautiful and simple, Marj was an elegant lady with not a phony bone in her body.

Gary had always been intense, but he had become such a hard worker that Stephanie was always worrying that he was going to have a heart attack. He'd work late into the evenings for Mondavi and on the college courses he was taking at Fullerton State. At home he was building a pool, landscaping, repairing. Stephanie never pulled a weed. If something had to be fixed, if she had a flat tire, either Gary would do it or she'd call him for permission to get it repaired. She'd watch Shary put up wallpaper without help, marveling at her capability. But, then, did Gary ever clean the house? she reflects. A few times he surprised her when she woke up after a dinner party and found the dishes all done. "I had come from my mother, went to Gary, and — I'm not proud of that — he just took care of me."

Gary was good with Stephanie's family. The terrible flare-up between her mother and Gary at Holly's birth had not been repeated. Living now near her work in Orange County, Betty came over less often, mostly when Gary was out of town, but Gary took Betty with them to Hawaii, where she helped babysit. All the parents would come over for the holidays, and Gary welcomed Stephanie's relatives, seventy or eighty of them, to Holly Leaf Way for the traditional Christmas Eve gathering. Stephanie still found Gary's mother, Garnet, to be cold.

They felt so safe on their cul-de-sac. They never locked any doors, never worried about their children's safety. Stephanie would look out the window at the gang playing on the street, Holly and Kelli in their sleeveless romper dresses with strawberries on them, certain that she and Gary were going to live happily ever after. She would eventually look back on these years as a lie. But at the time she thought, she says now, "Oh, I had no problems."

Under her surface happiness, though, Stephanie was worrying — about Holly. Holly had pulled back. At about a year and a half, when they were moving to Diamond Bar, her behavior had changed. Suddenly, she didn't like to be hugged. Stephanie remembers going to hug her and being pushed away. Holly just didn't like any close contact. Stephanie still played the hugging game with the girls: she'd hold out her arms and say, "Who loves Mommy?" and both children would come running into her arms to be swooped up. But she hugged Holly in a different way now, a little bit softer.

Gary would pick her up, but she would never go to him. Kelli was not initiating hugs with her father, either. Stephanie winced as she saw both girls hold back from their father. Gary was so outgoing, but they didn't like his power hugs. When he came home from a trip, they would stand back. When Holly didn't want to go places with her father, her mom would tell her, "You spend time with your father. He's your father." Holly didn't want to hurt his feelings, but she dreaded it.

Stephanie noticed that Gary had begun to take more of an interest in Holly when she was about a year old, just at the time she began to pull back. He hadn't seemed too interested when she was very small, like most men, Stephanie guessed. But by the time Holly was a year and a half, Gary was eager to watch her and would light up at the sight of her. Cute, Stephanie thought. Holly was the firstborn. But she felt sorry for Kelli, being ignored, when he would take Holly out to see the jackrabbits at night and leave Kelli behind. "There was no one who knew this family who could not have seen that the favoritism was extraordinarily toward Holly," says Shary. She knew it broke Stephanie's heart.

But Holly had problems Stephanie knew nothing about until years later. A high school girl, a neighbor, would say, "Let's play Mom and Dad," and, on the bed, get on top of Holly and bounce up and down. Holly didn't know what it meant but felt something was wrong, felt ashamed. Stephanie wonders now if the withdrawing, the shyness, and the obedience that made her kids, especially Holly, too good were partly fear of things they couldn't tell her. Were they scared little girls trying to please?

There was also Holly's health. The child shuttled steadily to the pediatrician's for a series of chronic minor problems during the early years at Diamond Bar. She was diagnosed with constipation when she was three; it hovered like an albatross wherever they went. A day at Disneyland with Holly and Marj Mondavi was punctuated by long visits to the toilets, with Marj waiting patiently on the curb. Holly was afraid that bowel movements would hurt. She had stomachaches and bladder infections. She would point to her vaginal area and tell her mother her bottom hurt. Dr. Klink never reported any signs of sexual abuse when he examined Holly. "But I don't think they were looking for that," Stephanie reflects.

Holly's medical problems led to a series of invasive procedures. There were enemas. Medical records say "enemas 3 or 4 times a week," numbers that would be vigorously debated in the trial when enemas were suggested as a cause of Holly's traumatic memories. There were insertions of a rectal thermometer. In 1977, when Holly was seven, doctors at Children's Hospital inserted a long tube, a catheter, into Holly's urinary tract to perform a voiding urethrogram, trying to solve the mystery of the bladder and urinary tract infections. The doctors and nurses showed her the catheter and explained the procedure as Holly hugged her teddy bear, but she was nervous. The doctors had suggested anesthesia, but Stephanie had resisted, fearful of overmedication. "When I went to pick her up, she was in a little dressing room," huddled and alone. "She had her teddy bear and she was waiting for me and she looked, I mean, gee, she . . . I picked her up." Holly was such a passive child that it was hard to tell how traumatized she was. But Stephanie felt guilty for years afterward.

Holly was put on her first diet at the age of six months: Stephanie took an ounce out of her bottle to return her weight to normal limits. It was not, in Stephanie's memory, until Holly's sophomore year in high school that she dieted again. Yet medical records show that a diet was recommended at age two because her growth charts showed her distinctly shorter and heavier than average.

Stephanie remembers nightmares too. She would hear Holly call out in the middle of the night, and she'd jump up and go to Holly's room. "Gary would be there at the bed, saying, 'Everything's okay. She just had a nightmare.'"

Stephanie was still never sure Gary loved her. Although his behavior was better than the first few years, Gary still stayed out late. And there were bizarre incidents. The phone call at 2 A.M. saying, "Your husband's been picked up by the police. He's in jail for messing with a woman at a bar," was a practical joke, Gary explained, laughing, when he got home. There were the blondes at a party saying they'd met Gary. When Stephanie asked, "Were you fooling around?" he'd laugh and tease her until she started giggling. Why hadn't she really confronted him?

The day after a party at a neighbor's, Stephanie did confront him with the wife's report that he had said several times, "I want to f—— you" — she couldn't say the word. He simply wouldn't comment. They got into an argument and, she says, Gary got her up against a wall and had his hands around her neck. "Don't! The kids will see us!" Stephanie gasped — a scene Holly remembered seeing. Holly, huddled in fear on the sofa, heard and saw several of the fights. In one fight, Gary put a fist through the wall of their bedroom. Embarrassed because Tim Mondavi was coming to stay with them, Stephanie made a joke by tacking a note next to the hole: "Gary was here." Prince, the dog, was still a source of fights. Gary kicked him.

Stephanie would talk to Shary about Gary's behavior. "She'd get ticked off — angry," says Shary. But she always made excuses for it. He was studying late at school and entertaining for Mondavi. She had seen him have to sit around with a restaurant owner until two in the morning. "She always thought he was working. She believed him. She loved him," recalls Betty, who had finally come to think that Gary was a pretty great person. But several times Stephanie did rebel and moved briefly to Betty's apartment with the girls. "But he used to cry . . . Sometimes he'd sit down on the floor next to Holly's bed . . . and he'd cry. And I'd think, 'Oh, my God, how can I do this — taking his whole family away?' And I'd go back."

Stephanie threatened to withhold sex. She had no complaints about their sex life at the time: "He still didn't want to do much with me. But when we made love . . . I enjoyed myself." But there were times he didn't come home until two, three, five in the morning, when she'd threaten that she wouldn't go to bed with him the next night. Then he would come home from work and her knees would get weak. "His smile — I just loved his smile. I'd just melt."

Yet there was no intimate affection or talk between them. "He was a different man inside and outside the home." When he walked out the door, he was a lovable teddy bear who would hug up a storm and even kiss her on the cheek. At home, she'd sit on his lap. He would talk about wine but wouldn't tell her his problems. "He's protecting me, doesn't want me to worry," she recalls thinking. Stephanie considers the very happiest times of their twenty-five years of marriage when she and Gary would go to McDonald's. There, over a Big Mac and fries, she had him all to herself. She also treasured the times they drove up to Napa. "In the car he'd talk to me. I got to talk to him . . . He couldn't jump out."

She never felt she really knew Gary. But did he know her? When she showed him her feelings, he wouldn't respond, and she learned early on "you don't really tell your problems to Gary." You don't assert your opinions. If she did, Gary somehow made her feel stupid. "It was always like I was bringing home a bad report card and feeling awful."

What had started with hose and makeup grew into a pattern of put-downs and critiques. Her breasts were too small. Her hair was a problem. When she washed it, it was curly and out of control. In the humidity of Hawaii it went bananas. Over the years, she developed a system of straightening with a broad iron, and she experimented with streaking and dyeing until she could present the flawless blond mane that appeared in court. But in Diamond Bar, she wore scarves on bad hair days. Home movies show Stephanie in fitted bell-bottoms, her hair in ponytails over her ears, with a body as petite and slim as a model's. But she watched her food, working constantly on keeping up her figure, exercising. Trying to be what Gary wanted her to be.

The beach was the only place Stephanie felt free to be herself, comfortable with her frizzy hair and her huge appendix scar. She often went there alone, free from Gary's critical gaze.

Gary encouraged her to go while he babysat. "Even while he was working and going to school, he worked his days so he could watch the kids. 'Go shopping, go do what you want,' he'd say." Stephanie noticed it because "it wasn't a Gary thing." He could be fun with the babies, but he was too busy to pay them much attention. As Holly became a more interesting toddler, however, he was constantly pushing Stephanie to get out. "What a good father," she thought.

Yet Stephanie recalls several incidents that stayed in her mind, no more worrisome then than some unanswered trivia question that nags at you.

Once, when she left to go to the beach, Gary was in the kitchen, dressed and cooking. About ten minutes down the freeway, she turned back to get her towel. She saw Kelli, left out again, playing in the courtyard wearing a thin summer nightgown. Angry, she grabbed the child by the arm to take her inside, pressed the handle, but found the door locked. It was never locked. She rang the doorbell. No one came to the door. As she was heading around to the back, Gary opened the door wearing white undershorts. "Why would he have his pants off?" she remembers thinking. "He must have spilled grease, or something." But she didn't pay much attention.

Where was Holly? Eating at the table? Gary had been making pancakes for the kids. And why had Kelli been left out in the yard? "I should have said, 'This isn't right. There's something wrong with this. Tell me, Gary, why was this door locked?' I should have pursued and pursued." But she did not. It hadn't disturbed her. She was in a hurry to get to the beach. "Why is it that women don't listen to themselves? Don't listen to little things?" she wonders now.

There were also the sheets, another of the incidents Gary would dismiss, later, as Stephanie's fantasies — or lies. She recalls it distinctly. She'd come home, walked into the master bedroom, and found the sheets off the bed. Holly didn't have her underpants on. Gary was standing by his dressing room. "What happened to the sheets?" Stephanie asked. "They're in the wash," he said. "Well, that's a first," she cracked. When she got the wash out of the dryer later that day she saw Holly's pants — they could have been Kelli's — the shorts that matched a little sundress. "Perhaps Holly was just playing and skidded," she recalls musing. She didn't question it or even think about it. Yet she never forgot. It was something about Gary's attitude, a look in his eyes. Nothing — not Holly's chronic problems with "down there," not the sheets or locks — led her to suspect sexual molestation.

The disturbing incidences remained just that, not connected by a pattern. Holly had never complained to her mother or grandmother about any strange acts. She seemed to be on good terms with her father, her grandmother thought. Incest at 2107 Holly Leaf Way? "I wasn't looking for it," says Stephanie. What mother, then, would be?

At the beach she could think, recognize a vague dissatisfaction with her life. She'd lie in the sun and wonder, "Am I going crazy? Is there something wrong with me, feeling this way? I'm not accomplishing anything." She read I'm O.K., You're O.K., hoping it would help her figure out her feelings. Maybe a job would make her feel more useful. But what could she do? She had discovered the stock market after they were married and was crazy about investing with the limited funds they had. But how could you turn that into a job, with a houseful of small children and almost no math? When she brought up working, "Gary said, 'No, no, no.'" Then she became pregnant with their third child.

In the spring of 1978, the idyll was coming to an end with Gary's graduation. The Mondavis had let him stay in Southern California until he got his degree, but they had promoted him again and again. Now they wanted the Ramonas to move north to be near the winery, in Napa Valley. Stephanie told Gary that she would not move unless he promised to start coming home at night and end his favoritism toward Holly. He promised he would.

"Gary wanted the biggest graduation party in the world . . . He was so proud of what he did, and he should have been . . . He wanted tuxedos, a sit-down dinner at a banquet room, very elegant. We didn't have that kind of money." Stephanie did the best she could. She staged a surprise party at home, fully catered. Michael and Isabel Mondavi flew down and gave Gary a watch. His uncle Frank came, and so did his beloved grandfather.

Betty hated to see Stevie move away. But she wanted her to go to prove to herself that she could be on her own. Betty *knew* that her daughter was stronger than she thought she was. But she worried that she and Stevie had been too close, and that her daughter still did what Gary said. Napa would be good for her.

In front of everybody, Gary gave Stephanie a string of pearls. He put them around her neck and said, as she remembers it, "Thank you for sticking with me and seeing me through it." She didn't expect a gift, and was moved to tears. It was *his* accomplishment. He'd done it himself. "In hindsight, I think he may have been trying to win me over for all the late nights. He could have won me over easily if I could have had more of him."

In Hawaii that winter, Stephanie felt a flush of happiness as she watched her three little girls playing, topless, with Gary in the sand, laughing as the surf spilled over them. Holly was eight, Kelli six, and Shawna a toddler. Holly's problems and her own frustrations were so small compared to this larger picture of her life she saw here at the beach. Stephanie saw the photo she wanted and set it up. She asked them to hold hands and walk down the beach, away from her. It saddened her that they wouldn't take Gary's hand without her urging, but it turned out perfectly. Three suntanned little bodies, bare feet traced in the sand, holding their father's hands. She has tried to tear the picture up and throw it away, but she cannot, for it represents the perfect family she thought they had been.

2

The Birth of a Salesman

The palatial hilltop home he lost when his life crashed could scarcely have been imagined by the Gary Ramona who began his boyhood in the rural outskirts of Los Angeles — in the Orange Grove Trailer Park at Grand and Cyprus Avenue, five miles from downtown Covina. Shoulder-to-shoulder on postage-stamp lots, each trailer was ringed by a white picket fence with a mailbox out front; a cement patio shaded by a metal awning bloomed with pots of geraniums, brave efforts to replicate suburbia. The table was too small to hold much more than the Christmas turkey, and a few bells and stars hung on the varnished wood-veneer walls. But the young Gary, moving a fork full of turkey toward his mouth, was a Norman Rockwell image of a happy boy.

Years later, Stephanie would speculate that Gary's upbeat personality — his tendency to paint everything perfect — was a shield from some suppressed pain from his childhood, something sinister, she implies. However, there is no evidence. If Gary's later concern for appearances was rooted, partly, in a sensitivity about the boyhood trailer, he hid it behind his laugh and the smile that shines from his earliest pictures. The toothy smile of a nine-year-old blazed as visiting family from Ohio gathered proudly around Gary and his accordion. Starting at the age of six, he took lessons and played until he was fourteen. In a full-sleeved white satin shirt, his hair brushed back, spit and polished, Gary held his shiny Sylvanir accordion across his chest, the arc of white keys echoing his grin. A natural performer, he played "Lady of Spain" and "The Beer Barrel Polka" in concerts and parades.

The love of music came from his Italian roots "back east" in Ohio, Gary's birthplace in 1944. Each summer, he and his parents went back to his grandfather's home in Euclid. Accompanying himself on guitar and harmonica, his grandfather, who had emigrated from Italy at six- teen, would sing Italian songs. At the daily dinner table, a huge family was fed from his grandfather's garden. With the food lover's tender recall of every herb and tomato, Gary rhapsodizes over his grand- mother's cooking — the chicken broth soup . . . and the gnocchi! "To- day it's a gourmet dish, but it was peasant food."

His grandfather had been a mason until an accident crushed his back, and Gary's father was a skilled machinist, proud of his precision in making parts for airplanes and nuclear submarines. Gary inherited both his father's tools and his square-jawed, olive-skinned good looks. The Italian Ramona genes overwhelmed his mother's German blood. With her fine, pale features, delicate bone structure, and quiet style, Garnet looked more like a fragile houseplant than the hard-scrubbing laundrywoman her mother had trained her to be. She did light factory work throughout Gary's childhood.

Garnet's mother had taken in laundry from the neighbors to help support her large family. As a child, Garnet would pack up the clean laundry, meticulously ironed and glowing clean, and deliver it by cart all over the neighborhood. At the trailer park, she did wonders with an old roller washing machine. "Even at eighty, my mother has great pride when she washes clothes. She has her own way, her own style," says Gary. In the laundry tubs of his grandmother's basement in Ohio may lie the source of Gary's lifelong respect for "clean," which Stephanie would come to see as obsessive and even perverted. For Gary, "clean" may have been a metaphor for the pride of the poor.

In Ohio, he learned life lessons. He learned that work was fun. "An uncle and I might paint trim together. Then we would wrestle and play football," he recalls. They would fix cars, then go to the lake. He learned that there was always time for talk. His grandfather's power- ful hand gripping his, they would walk to a little ice cream parlor on the corner for black walnut ice cream. Then they would continue around the block, stopping house-to-house for a little chat. The future salesman was learning to shmooze from a master. Education came from Uncle Carmen, who put himself through dentistry school while raising a family. *"Get the degree, Gary. Get the degree. It's the one thing they can't take away from you,"* he impressed on the barefoot California boy.

But Gary never took school seriously as a kid. There were pals, bikes, orange groves. The groves were the site of fierce wars as the boys sent barrages of oranges through the air like the arrows at Agincourt. The thick white fogs produced by irrigation and humidity offered smokescreens. Caught up in games, they glimpsed the glory of their playground only through the eyes of occasional tourists, who stood in awe before their first orange trees.

The one event from his childhood that seems to have vanquished the smile and moved Gary to heartbreaking memories, as vivid and detailed today as forty years ago, was the death of his horse. When Gary was ten, his father had traded a debt he was owed for a half-Arabian polo pony, Sandy. He rode her in the Glendora and Covina parades. He helped pay for her stabling by taking groups for rides. They would take moonlight rambles over the hills to Glendora City, get pizzas, gallop back through a fabulous valley filled with oak trees, and camp out. When the Ramonas moved to a house in Charter Oak during Gary's sophomore year in high school, the boy built a corral for Sandy. She died there when he was fifteen. Her jaw locked; she became listless and could no longer feed. When her legs collapsed under her, they put her in a belly harness and strapped her up to keep the weight off. Gary learned later that a nail driven deep into the frog of her hoof had caused a lethal infection. But for three weeks, helpless, he could only watch her die.

He compensated by working hard — paper routes, lawnwork, odd jobs for neighbors. He worked for restaurants — doing dishes and bussing tables — and pumped gas and fixed cars, saving for college.

Gary entered Mt. SAC, the local junior college, in the fall of 1963. He was nineteen, almost a man of the world, when he met Stephanie. He was working as a carpenter while going to Mt. SAC, doing casual construction with his boyhood friend Scotty Evans mostly in the summers and going to school full-time. When he first saw Stephanie Nye, she seemed different from the other girls. "When I met her she had dark brown hair. . . . I liked very much Steph's look. She had a very nice classic look. It doesn't mean that Steph would not wear Levi's or Bermuda shorts from time to time. But she dressed more traditional, much more conservative than most other girls.

"She was also very naive. She wanted to have fun and many times didn't know exactly how to go about it. She couldn't sort of loosen up." There was "a kind of unsureness in her . . . a little standoffish-ness," Gary's pal Scott agrees. But Gary thought Stephanie was "a beautiful lady," reserved and shy but fun to be with. They did simple things: went to movies and school dances, studied together. And, of course, there was the beach. Two or three times a month they'd take Harbor Boulevard down to Huntington Beach and have a hamburger and Cokes at Zack's. Gary called her Steph.

Perhaps her uneasiness about men and her tailored, proper style was a reflection of her mother's attitude, Betty Nye's "very tight, con-trolling approach," the young men recall speculating. "But Gary was real good about kidding around with her," Scott observes. Gary won her over, too, with his industriousness. Carpenters in the booming tract-building trade, he and Scotty did framing, rough-framing walls, laying plywood sheeting on floors and ceilings, putting in trusses. They did "piecework," which was paid by the foot. "The more you got accomplished, the more money you made. We didn't sit around the union hall; we went out to the site to get jobs." At the end of the day, Gary focused on school, where he had switched his major from drafting to business. For Gary, "finishing my college education was not an issue." He was beginning what would become a thirteen-year slow march toward his B.A. degree, dropping out for whole semesters and taking night classes for years while working at a full-time job.

When Gary and Stephanie had been dating for a year and a half, they increasingly talked of marriage. Gary was not a militant pro-tester, but he knew that marriage might help him avoid the Vietnam draft. He angrily denied Stephanie's claim at the trial that, when she resisted marriage, he smashed his fist twice on his car window. "I've never broken my hands — my finger, my wrist."

Gary has only vague memories of eloping to Las Vegas on April 4, 1965. He recalls feeling stage fright and thinks the ceremony took place in the late afternoon; he drove Stephanie back to her mother's that night. Gary was twenty-one, Stephanie was twenty. They had both wanted a proper wedding later, Gary claims, and it was the fam-ily's discovery of their wedding — not his flip-flop on the promise — that led them to start married life together sooner than planned. He recalls clearly that the marriage was not consummated for many months.

It soon became clear that they had very different approaches to adult life: Gary armed with can-do energy and practical competence; Stephanie overprotected, with few life skills or experience of success.

"I've quit school, Gary," he recalls Steph's telling him one day when he came home from work. He knew she was adjusting to marriage, but when he found out that she didn't even bother to sign out of her classes — that she would get *F*s instead of Incompletes — he was distraught. You had to keep the door open so you could go back. "Whatever you do, Steph, don't get *F*s." He couldn't bear it that Stephanie would jeopardize something so precious. As two very different personalities faced an early test of will, Gary's forceful encouragement may have overwhelmed Stephanie's weaker ego, triggering inaction as a defense. She did not act on his urging. In this very early test of power, Stephanie won.

"It probably wouldn't have bothered me so much if it wasn't that she always had to be so close to her mother," says Gary, concerned that Betty catered to Steph's incompetence by making a big deal about anything Steph did. "There's nothing wrong with complimenting, you know. But it's not the real world. Out there, you don't get a pat on the back every minute just because you tie your shoes right." When the first test came — when she needed to clear up her grades — "she wasn't able to do even this small thing for herself." Gary was sad, but he loved her. He didn't force her.

Gary also thinks he felt Betty's influence haunting their nuptial bed. "In the first six months, Stephanie could not have intercourse. Or she *wouldn't* have, let me put it that way. She was so tight. I mean, she was like a board. It was just impossible for her to relax." Some of it could be a result of her upbringing, he guessed. "Her mother does not have a high regard, as I see it, for men. And it wasn't, okay, all of a sudden, 'Let's have sex.'" She was a virgin and needed time. "There was the foreplay . . . We kissed, I fondled and masturbated her." Stephanie was *interested* in sex. "But any penetration — finger, penis, or any penetration — was just impossible . . . Even her facial expressions would tighten up, and she would simply pull away," he would tell a jury nearly three decades later.

"Once the penetration was done, then she could relax, and there was no difficulty climaxing. The bottom line is, I thought I handled it rather well. I never pushed her. Never made her feel uncomfortable about it. We took our time and just slowly worked at it." For Gary, intercourse wasn't everything. As far as he was concerned, they had good sex with or without actual penetration. He felt strongly that it was not intercourse that consummated a marriage. He loved his wife.

Yet he admits to one — only one — act of violence against Stephanie. "We were having an argument. I was upset, she was upset, and I said, 'I've had enough of it,' and I hit her in the stomach." Stephanie left; it was their longest separation — roughly two months. But not just because he had hit her. Because of "major differences . . . There were times when I was in construction I would be shooting pool and would sometimes get in at seven or eight o'clock — sometimes I got in later. That was, unfortunately, part of my immaturity at that stage." But then Stephanie got upset about innocent things. And, in fact, Gary says, she committed a few violent acts herself. She threw a hamburger at him when they were driving. And once, alone at Gary's parents' house, she threw a knife at him "and it stuck in the cupboard door . . . We had our differences," Gary admits, "minor mutual tussles . . . But there wasn't any violence to speak of."

Unlike the other separations, this had been mutual. Gary had asked her to leave, and he moved to a smaller apartment. This time Stephanie had filed for divorce. "We . . . started going to a marriage counselor; but Steph was uncomfortable having to talk about her family and stopped." As always, she melted, and the marriage went on.

The year 1967 saw the birth of a salesman. Once he was married, Gary saw that construction wasn't "good security for my family. I might work for two, three months, and then the job would be completed. Then I'd have to go out and find another one. If it rained, I was down for a day or two." Friends urged him to think about the sales business, and in the classifieds, he found an ad for a salesman at Vita-Pakt Citrus Products, in Covina. "I went and interviewed. I had no sales experience whatsoever." He called back four times. Finally "they said, 'This guy's . . . persistent. We'll hire you.'"

He started with Vita-Pakt in 1967 while Vietnam was raging and flower children flocked to San Francisco for the Summer of Love. Gary's battleground was every supermarket in his territory — Vons, Safeway, Luckys, Ralphs, Boys, Hughes. Tropicana was the major competition, the enemy. For the first year and a half he merchandised, trying to increase sales by expanding the displays of his products, winning shelf space from the competition. The secret was to expand your "ends and facings." He'd spread out his citrus juices, frozen fruit bars, his Don the Beachcomber cocktail mix, so that more of it faced the customer. You won more "ends" — the end of an aisle, where the traffic was — by personal contact. "I'd be in the store at seven o'clock in the morning, before anybody else, and these people would say, 'Hey, here's a hustler,' and they would always give me a little extra space." He was getting fifty-case, hundred-case ends. He was promoted out of the merchandising trenches to the executive sales force, and Don the Beachcomber became his account. In just one year, Gary drove a ten-thousand-case increase in Don the Beachcomber cocktail mix. "*One year!* It just took off."

Don the Beachcomber released the salesman in him. "Oh, I loved it . . . I worked well with people . . . I treated them with a lot of respect. They always treated me great." But the thrill came from seeing sales go up. "It felt good, like when I'd finish a day with ten walls up, or knew I was eighty percent done. I'd feel the satisfaction of 'I achieved this today.'"

Now that Gary was meeting the public, Stephanie wanted him to look good. She had great taste and started going with him to pick out his clothes. His career was on the move but, after four years of marriage, Gary and Stephanie still didn't have a house of their own. And a baby was coming.

Gary had been "one proud man" when he learned Stephanie was pregnant. Driving her to Huntington Memorial for Holly's birth, he "took pictures, tried to keep it light, to lessen Steph's anxieties." But he felt trapped in a ritual that excluded him, that didn't make sense. Stephanie wanted all her children born at the hospital where she was born, even though it was a forty-minute drive from their house and there were perfectly good hospitals ten minutes away. What hurt Gary most, though, was that Stephanie wanted to have her mother there for the birth. He felt slighted. "This was our moment, Steph's and mine. It was our intimacy. It was our time," he recalls thinking. It wasn't anything he ever held against Betty or Steph; he wasn't angry. It was just a hurt. Right from the first. Even before they had children, he felt that Steph would rather have her mother there than have him there. "It's like you're — what do I want to say? — you're *expendable*."

But he loved Stephanie dearly, and he had dreams for his small family: a house in one of the beautiful new subdivisions in the hills, above the smog belt. He was restless to move but didn't have the money for a down payment. They fixed up Betty's house when she prepared to sell, raising the sale price, and Betty offered to lend them $5,000 cash for a down payment on their first house.

Gary was restless, too, with Vita-Pakt. As Holly was born in the summer of 1970, a career move was in the air. His success with Don the Beachcomber had caught the attention of Fred Franzia, the distributor for Robert Mondavi, a new winery north of San Francisco. As Franzia got to know Mondavi and saw the potential, he called Gary: "I think you should interview."

Gary "barely knew the difference between red and white." Who were they, this little Napa Valley outfit? He interviewed with Mondavi's national sales manager, Dick Russ, and learned that Mondavi was selling only thirty-three hundred cases a year in Southern California. He checked around. "Everybody had good words to say about them. They were real small, but they were up-and-coming in the fine wine business." He interviewed again.

Before he made any career change, though, Stephanie had to be comfortable with it. Not only did she not enjoy wine, but she also seemed to have an issue with drinking because of her stepfather and several other relatives who had drinking problems. Gary took Stephanie with him to look over the Mondavi winery.

After picking up a car at the San Francisco airport, they drove north into Napa Valley on the two-lane highway and spotted, midvalley at Oakville, the Spanish-style stucco belltower and arch that would become an international symbol for Napa Valley wines. Gary was greeted by Bob Mondavi and his son Michael and given a tour. In the lab, they talked in what seemed to an orange juice man a foreign tongue of brix, backbone, limousin oak, varietal character. But what captivated the salesman was the production line, the big silver fermenting tanks, the almost empty barrel room, and the vast, sunny Vineyard Room for tasting events. They had a lot more capacity than they had sales and were ready to grow.

Bob Mondavi shared his goal with Gary: "to be able to rub shoulders with the great wines of the world." This was audacious. The little winery was leveraged to the hilt, largely owned by a Canadian brewer, Molson's. The French ruled the wine world, New Yorkers sneered at California wines as the "low end," and beer and booze owned the mid-American market. But Mondavi aimed for something even more audacious. "I believe we can do half a million cases — a million! And still hold quality. But I don't talk to a lot of people about it," he told Gary, "because it scares them off."

It didn't scare Gary. He saw in Mondavi a sense of quality that he had always admired. "When I finished cement with Ray Lyons, when I pounded nails, my mother's laundry — it was quality . . . There was always a pride."

He didn't yet comprehend the momentum of the boutique wine movement being spearheaded by a handful of visionaries crushing grapes in sheds, garages, and minuscule wineries in Napa and Sonoma. But he sensed he was catching a wave at the perfect moment. "I knew in my heart that I could really go out and be part of this — that I *wanted* to be part and parcel of this." Here was something that really had a future. Robert Mondavi, the prophet of Napa Valley wines, had found the salesman for his dream.

Gary spent his first month as a lowly "cellar rat" on the winery bottling line, learning the business from the ground up. But he was able to glimpse a world he had never seen before. Margrit Biever — chatting with guests in several languages — was setting up the winery's art shows in the Vineyard Room and staging the summer concerts at which famous jazz musicians would perform and the lawn would be spread with blankets and picnic baskets. Gary felt the feverish atmosphere of experimentation as the explosive sparks of science and art came together. That Mondavi believed, even during those hand-to-mouth days, that it was as important to build a home for art shows, concerts, and dinners from the world's great chefs as to build a home for crushers, barrels, and fermenting tanks told Gary that this product had a civilizing mission.

Gary saw, early on, that what Mondavi was really selling was the good life, an idea whose core was the dinner table, where wine, food, and family converged. If Gary could blend into his sales pitch the marriage of peasant simplicity with elegant refinement he had glimpsed at a harvest lunch at the Mondavis' home and in the winery's art shows, he could move the product. From his garage in Diamond Bar, Gary loaded wines into a Mondavi company car and hit the road.

In 1971 the L.A. Basin was the largest potential market in California, the second largest in the United States. Both Bob Mondavi and his elder son, Michael, had made their battle orders clear. Gary was to conquer the market with three ideas. That Napa Valley's wines should take their place with the best in the world. That a bottle of wine should sit on every dinner table as part of daily life. And that a premium winemaker could be big and still be good. Mondavi wanted to surpass two other well-known family wineries, Mirassou and Krug, in quality, reputation, volume, and net profits.

Gary's first target for Mondavi was the one he knew best, supermarkets, which in California were permitted to sell wine. Wine or orange juice, you had to win ends and facings. Gary had no cheap jugs of reds and whites to sell. He had varietals, grapes few had ever heard of — Zinfandel, Cabernet, Fumé Blanc, Chardonnay — a dozen kinds that would shrink to a few as Napa Valley discovered which ones it did best. You could sell, but not taste, wines in a supermarket. So Gary hired housewives who would come in, nicely dressed, to serve cheese and crackers next to the wine and explain to shoppers what wine went best with steak or chicken. He turned the ends of aisles into tiny vineyards, bringing in cuttings from the vines and selling them for ninety-nine cents.

He seized every opportunity to set up wine tastings — anywhere, anytime, in Southern California. "There was a time I was doing four tastings a week in the evenings." In an exclusive new development of $400,000 homes opening in Orange County, he talked the builders into sharing open houses on Friday and Saturday nights; they'd bring in the people to look at the houses, Gary and his staff of Stephanie's friends would hand them a glass of wine. "It was great exposure."

Lloyd and JoeAnna Jenkins were building a wine cellar in their home in Arcadia and were seeking out new California finds. Gary set up wine tastings for them, and they dined out with the Ramonas. Lloyd became Gary's financial adviser, and Gary did him wine favors. "With his personal style of marketing . . . what he was doing was recruiting an additional sales force. We sold a lot of wine for him," Lloyd recalls. But JoeAnna hastens to add, "Our friendship was not intentionally cultivated to help him sell wine."

Gary worked the major hotels and restaurants. In his first few months on the job, he learned that the Century Plaza in Los Angeles, a major account, was threatening to take Mondavi's wines off their list because of a supply problem. It was time to try the high-risk salesmanship he'd learned from Bob Mondavi: he would treat a customer to a lavish lunch, uncork his own Cabernets and Chardonnays, then put the best French wines on the list next to his own and let them speak for themselves. "Give me six months — that's what I ask," Gary told the Century Plaza's general manager, "and I'll see personally that you're taken care of . . . Then, I want you to taste two or three other wines that I want on your wine list, and if they're better than what you have on your list . . ." The Century Plaza expanded its list of Mondavi wines. "We were doing fifty, seventy-five cases a month — one account! It was just fantastic."

Meanwhile, the *L.A. Times*'s powerful wine critic, Robert Balzer, had become the Pied Piper of California wines, luring people to the adventure. In the spring of 1972, he gathered the best California wine-makers, thirty or forty of them, at the Buena Vista Winery in Sonoma and staged a blind tasting of their own wines — no labels were visible. He called it the Vintners Tasting. Mondavi's '69 Cabernet won. "This wasn't just Bob Mondavi saying it's great wine. It was his peers who made it number one. *Very* powerful. . . . Our Cabernet was flowing out of the stores, you couldn't believe it." Mondavi's early goal of surpassing Mirassou and Krug was being achieved. Soon Gary was made sales manager for the Southwest, covering all the western states and Hawaii.

From day one, Gary had been able to translate Mondavi's message into sales. "People don't drink bricks and mortar, they drink heart and soul . . . I took the heart and soul of Robert Mondavi . . . and marketed and sold the whole organization around his philosophy." No one worked harder than Gary Ramona. "No one ever told me when to go to work and when to come home." And the Mondavis made him feel part of the family. As the Mondavi name pulled ahead in prestige during the seventies — as Gary became pivotal in executing the dream — he became, as Bob would laughingly say, "my adopted son."

Maggie Haswell's eyes were always doing a motherly scan of the cul-de-sac from her house across the street from the Ramonas', watching her own boys, watching the others. She watched Gary come home from work, the girls waiting with "ribbons in their hair, dresses sashed. Those kids looked perfect every single day." Gary would drive up to the house and Holly, especially, would rush to him, saying, "'Hi, Daddy, hi, Daddy.' He'd hug them, and they'd hug back." Weekends, he happily put on his carpenter's or barbecue apron. He shared land-scaping projects with the men in the neighborhood, and they played tennis together, helped one another build walls and plant lawns of dichondra. Gary was there for the birthday parties on the clubhouse lawn at Diamond Bar, for the miniature train ride at Knott's Berry Farm, for the trips to San Diego's Sea World and the zoo. He took Holly and Kelli to an Indian Princesses' overnight at a lodge in the snow at Big Bear. Like Stephanie, he'd look back on these years as the happiest of his life.

The Diamond Bar years were studded with trips to the beach. They'd take day trips to Huntington Beach, sheltering the girls under an umbrella while Stephanie and her mother baked in the sun. For a week or two in the summer, they rented a place on the beach at Newport or a little house on Balboa Island, where the quaint cottages had become fashionable.

Balboa was a place where Gary could kick back. "Give me a week, and . . . I didn't want to go back." It was also a measurable achievement, like selling fifty cases of wine. He had to save to afford it, but it gave him pride. Stephanie loved the little shops, the hanging baskets with geraniums and bougainvillea, the beach. They'd take the dime-a-ride ferry to Newport to see the Balboa Pavilion, glittering at night with lights like a great ship at sea. They'd rent bikes or a motorboat, take the kids to the Fun Zone, line up at Sugar and Spice for a frozen banana — a treat that lost its innocence as Holly's memories turned bananas into phallic symbols.

The home movies and snapshots of that period record an All-American family. The grandparents were always there for outings and birthdays, Betty and Garnet coiffed and dressed up, even for Disneyland. There are images of two little girls in matching sundresses and sandals in the Bahamas, in Hawaii — of Gary's picking up and hugging Holly and her sisters. Pictures of Holly at the beach at the age when she claims incest was occurring show her smiling, waving, and having fun. There was a certain shyness, her father recalls; the water would splash on her face too much and she would back off, a little cautious. But she was a happy kid, a big ham.

"It doesn't mean we were perfect . . . and didn't have our differences. But I'm telling you, we had a very good family life," Gary reflects.

A pediatric nurse who worked the night shift at Children's Hospital in Orange County, Maggie Haswell was more alert to signs of abuse in a child than most mothers in the neighborhood. She also worked with battered children several decades before the problem was widely recognized. "If you did a psychological test on abused kids, they will not draw happy faces. They draw sad faces." Holly Ramona drew happy pictures. That's what happy children did, Maggie knew.

Holly had Gary's features, complexion, build, and smile. Was

Holly, in a way, special? "Yeah, in the sense of being our first child," Gary admits. "But was she getting preferential treatment? Was she loved more than Kelli, more than Shawna? No. Not at all." Many times, when he came home very late in the evening, he would go in to say good night to them — Holly on the lower bunk, Kelli on the top. "I'd kiss them good night and pat them on the head. There were times when I'd tickle them on the knee or the funny bone. Or sometimes I would read them a book."

Gary was very aware of Holly's physical problems — the constipation, the bladder problems, the cystourethrogram that left Stephanie blaming herself for years. But doctors were her sphere. She ran the routine, the children, the schools, the doctors, the enemas. Stephanie worked for Gary part-time the first few years at Diamond Bar, but she was primarily a homemaker. Gary put an extension of the office phone in the kitchen, "where she spent a lot of time with the children, which I thought was great. She could come and go" on the office job "as she chose . . . Stephanie did what Steph wanted to do."

To Gary's chagrin, she had never cleared up her grades and still had no thoughts about returning to school. He would bring it up occasionally, but she wasn't interested. It also hurt him that she resisted trips in the summer to visit his relatives in Ohio. Stephanie wanted to go to the beach instead or to Hawaii. Luckily, the children got to know Gary's grandfather before he died because he traveled the circuit each year, visiting each of his children for several months at a time. But the girls grew up knowing few of his relatives. He never really pushed the issue, though.

Stephanie ran the discipline. "On occasion, they'd get a little mouthy and start challenging a few things, and Stephanie would say, 'You can't let them get away with that.'" She set the tone of very little drinking in their home, and the Ramonas rarely had a glass of wine or a drink at home unless they were entertaining. "I gotta tell ya, there is no way that I would ever be watching our children if I was drinking. Steph was paranoid on drinking," he says.

Stephanie fed the children, although he saw little of that. He left too early to join them for breakfast and, still studying nights at Fullerton State, rarely returned before the girls' dinner. He'd often make a snack for himself, sometimes his favorite rigatoni and tomato sauce, and eat alone. He knew Stephanie had erratic eating habits. She'd brag about eating a dozen doughnuts in a sitting; she loved sweets. Yet, look at her: she was always slender. But she would not eat what Gary called "substance . . . She wasn't into a lot of athletics, so that was the way she would control her weight." He only learned later that Stephanie did not eat with the girls.

The Ramonas' eating patterns were largely a product of the suburban way of life: commuting, children busier with activities than any previous generation, fast food. The irony was, the more successful Gary was for Mondavi, the less time he had to do the very thing he was promoting: to make the dinner table the heart of the civilized life.

He made time to babysit, happy to let Stephanie go to the beach. But he has no recollection, he says, of the scene that Stephanie claims nagged at her all those years: coming home from the beach and finding the front door locked. The doors at Holly Leaf Way were always open — even the garage, where Gary stored fifteen to twenty cases of wine. There were regular doors, sliding doors, windows all over the house. Stephanie's keys opened every door in the place. "This was Diamond Bar. We were in a cul-de-sac. There wasn't much crime. The kids had toys around, the backyard and front . . . Steph was home ninety-five percent of the time . . . The house was never locked if we were around."

Nor has he any memory of the day when Stephanie claims to have come home to find the washing machine going with a load of sheets and a pair of Holly's underpants while the child ran around bare-bottomed. "I scrubbed floors for her. I washed windows. I've vacuumed. I may have thrown clothes into the washer-dryer." But this scene was as crazy as Steph's accusation, after a party, that he'd said he wanted to fuck a neighbor's wife." These incidents simply never happened.

In 1976 Gary moved out of his office at home, reclaimed the garage that had been a warehouse for wines, and opened an office for Mondavi in Placentia, a twenty-minute drive west of Diamond Bar, just a few blocks from Fullerton State. The commute lengthened his already sixteen-hour days.

If timing is a factor in success, Gary's was extraordinary. As he was opening the new office, nine thousand miles away in Paris one of the pivotal events of modern wine history was unfolding. A busload of Napa Valley vintners was touring Bordeaux, lunching at a château, when they received the results of a bicentennial wine tasting in Paris.

A number of California wines had been blind-tasted against the most prestigious French wines, with the French themselves doing the tasting and judging. Two Napa Valley wines — Château Montelena's Chardonnay and Stag's Leap Wine Cellars' Cabernet — had won. For the French, it was an appalling rout. Napa Valley wines had, at last, arrived where Mondavi had always preached they belonged, "in the company of the best in the world."

Ironically, Mondavi's own wines had not been entered in the tasting, but the sensation of the event cast its magic on all of California's premium wines, and Mondavi took off with the rest. He had started national distribution in 1975 but, until the Paris tasting, few in New York had heard of Napa Valley. The Midwest had not yet heard of wine. While he pursued the national market aggressively, Mondavi was making plans to take on the world in 1977, the year after the Paris tasting. But first, America. Gary, who was already covering all the western states and Hawaii, was being groomed to take over national sales.

Still highly leveraged to his partners, Mondavi needed more volume, more sales. Gary went after a huge new market for Mondavi: the lower-priced wines. The winery took a popular-priced line of wines Bob had started producing in modest amounts at Oakville, bottled it under the new RM label, and sold it as generic red and white wine. The first year they sold sixty thousand cases and in three years increased it to ten times that. "Bob white" and "Bob red" went national in 1980 and would grow, over the next decade, into the most successful "popular premium" wine in the nation.

As his world expanded, Gary saw Stephanie's shrink to chronic fear that he would be unfaithful to her. He called her from Caesars Palace, in Las Vegas on a business trip, to share the excitement of the kid from the trailer park staying in the Frank Sinatra Suite. He could sense her freeze up as he told her about the penthouse, the extravagant bar, the grand piano, the mirrored bed. Why, he fretted, was Stephanie so paranoid about other women that she got steamed up even when he worked late at school? After the Caesars Palace incident, he found it was best not to share his trips with her.

Gary began to see a pattern. Throughout their marriage, when she was miffed, Stephanie had always shown her anger by withholding — like canceling out on something she'd promised to do. Gary gave Stephanie her due. Many times she went out with him on tastings and entertained customers from all over Southern California at their house. But he began to realize that this withholding was her way of getting back at him, of showing her independence. Passive resistance was not Gary's way. "You can't communicate. I'd just as soon put all the cards on the table and then move on." It all went back to her relationship with Betty, he suspected. When Stephanie was growing up, she and her mother would be at odds with each other and might not talk for a week, she told him. She would just hold it in, her way of showing strength.

She used the same withholding in their sex life. He was used to her saying no or "Why can't we just snuggle?" or "Wake me up early in the morning. It's the best time for me." But one area in their marriage bothered him deeply: the initiation of sex. "It was only two or three times in her whole life" that Stephanie was the one to "initiate the issue of sex. *Two or three times*. And I complimented her, because it was great. It was fabulous . . . Those few times, it was as if she almost *had* to have sex . . . I guess where she was the aggressor is every man's dream. You want to feel not just that *I* want, but that *she* wants. That makes you feel good, okay. It makes you feel attractive. Wanted. Sexual." Her lack of initiation hurt him.

"How come you don't want to?" he asked her.

"I couldn't take the rejection if you said no."

"Tell me one time I *ever* said no, Steph," he said.

It was interesting, he thought; those few times were always when they were on a trip. At home, Stephanie had rituals that inhibited sex. "You got to make sure the miniblinds are down, that the TV was up loud . . . that the water is running, that the door is locked." In their entire marriage, they had rarely had intercourse as often as once a week. There could have been years as seldom as half a dozen times. "But Steph never complained about our sex life."

When Gary got his B.A. in 1979, the winery's pace was accelerating. The family was completing the buyback of the winery and would at last be free of outside control and operating constraints. Gary had been promoted to national sales manager before he graduated; Mondavi had launched exports a year earlier. The winery's world was growing, and Gary's with it.

Now that Gary had graduated, Stephanie could no longer refuse to move to Napa; that had always been the deal with the Mondavis. Gary flew his family to Hawaii for two weeks after graduation, planning to move north in the spring of 1979. He had been rewarded with the largest sales responsibility Bob could give him: world sales manager and vice president. The Mondavis were calling him home, to headquarters.

3

The Family Table

Gary had wanted to buy a huge house in the rolling, rural outskirts of the small city of Napa. Stephanie preferred to be closer to the down-home blue-collar county seat that sat separated, culturally, by a Great Divide from the wine country upvalley. It was more like the towns she'd known in San Gabriel Valley as a child, with things close by. But they both agreed on a house in St. Helena, the hub of upvalley. Less than a mile west of its turn-of-the-century Main Street, the new house on Pinot Way was on a cul-de-sac.

Life in St. Helena was not very different from that in Diamond Bar. The house was far bigger; shaped like a *U*, it had redwood siding and glass-walled wings facing each other and onto a wooden deck that led to the pool. This time, the Ramonas were able to hire one of the top landscape designers in the Bay Area to design terraces down to the pool and three gazebos for entertaining. But Gary still ran the actual building — landscaping, pool, and the new barbecue.

The girls could ride their bikes or walk to school. Even Holly, though shy, had adjusted easily. Stephanie joined Meadowood Country Club and befriended a group of neighborhood women, bonded by children and the cul-de-sac, as she had at Diamond Bar. The "mother network," as the children called it, tracked their movements with the efficiency of a military warroom.

But in some significant ways it was not Diamond Bar. Stephanie's home was in Bob Mondavi's valley. The winery was just down the road, in Oakville, an almost daily reminder of Gary's other life and of Stephanie's obligations. Marj Mondavi had been replaced by Margrit Biever, who had married Bob quietly in 1980, shortly after the Ramonas moved to Napa. Their romance had survived years of living apart in the same small valley while each struggled through a difficult divorce, with Margrit feeling daily hostility from Bob's sons, Michael and Tim, who were loyal to their mother. The Mondavis' love affair seemed to confirm the vineyardists' truism: grapes that are stressed by marginal climates and soils produce better quality. Their struggle to be together had forged an extraordinary partnership, with Margrit expressing Bob's cultural goals for wine as fully as Gary expressed his sales goals.

Stephanie was being forced to confront the larger world as Gary's job became global. Within two years he would take over all of marketing as well, making him one of Mondavi's most powerful executives. In 1980, when the Mondavis took a small group of the senior winery "family" on a grand trip to Europe, Stephanie was invited. It was her first time abroad, her first glimpse of "a big, wide world out there."

Gary had never minded that Stephanie would not even fake an interest in wine on these trips. But Margrit, who had planned the trip, felt it was a hostile message, an insult to Gary and their hosts. Bob would be giving a university course in wine at Romanée Conti, and Stephanie would go shopping or stay home, Margrit noted. Isabel would always have a glass of wine in front of her, but Stephanie would push her wineglass back in a great restaurant and order Coke. She carried a bag of Oreo cookies with her on the bus. Coke and Oreos! To Gary, it was just Steph.

He was insulted, though, when he thought his wife was flirting. At dinner in a storybook lodge in Westphalia, Stephanie was seated next to a man who had been openly flirting with her. Gary loved the gemütlich spirit — pewter gleaming, logs blazing in a fireplace tall enough for a man to walk into — as Bob declared to his hosts, "I'm not going to show you how to make sauerkraut and potatoes. I want to show you the *best*," uncorking his wines for the feast of smoked trout and dark breads of the region. Margrit dismissed the flirting as innocent; European men pay attention to pretty women. But Gary's jealous anger became so obvious that one of their party walked him out of the room to cool him down. Stephanie remembers the events that unfolded when they returned to their room as one of the worst nights of their marriage. Gary kicked her out of bed, called her a slut, and ordered her to go and shower. His irrational obsession with cleanliness had always plagued Stephanie, but he had never behaved like this before. Scared and crying, she showered and returned to bed. Again he kicked her out and told her to take a shower, she remembers vividly. "I was filth. I was dirt."

When she came back, he seemed to be asleep. She lay down on the floor and, when she was sure he was asleep, quietly, frantically, searched his pockets. She had no money and she needed credit cards; she had to go home. "I *wanted* to go home," she recalls, still chilled by the memory. Then she slumped with the futility of it. Alone, in the middle of the night, escape seemed overwhelming. If she asked for help, no one would believe her. No one would help her. She crept back into bed.

Gary admits that he built to a rage as he watched one of the German hosts attending flagrantly to his wife — and Steph letting him. He liked to clear the air, and he let her have it, he says. He had been humiliated by her behavior, he told her — everyone was embarrassed. Then he let it go and fell asleep. Stephanie's story simply didn't happen.

Back in Napa, Stephanie now had Margrit to measure herself against — and fall short. As Bob's wife, Margrit was arguably the most powerful woman in Napa Valley. But she radiated her own power, independent of Bob. Stephanie was both admiring and intimidated. At one of the first Mondavi dinners she attended, Stephanie watched Margrit cook at home for maybe ten people, speaking German and French to her guests as she chopped and stirred. She set her own table. With a gift for crafts and painting, she was an artist at combining sheafs of yellow mustard and plum blossoms picked by the roadside, dried leaves, and naked grapevines into stunning centerpieces. Then she served dinner herself.

Stephanie was more comfortable with the younger Mondavi women, Isabel and Dorothy, Tim's wife. Any intimidation she might have felt at their being Mondavis was diluted by their also being, like herself, women raising a family; their children shared classes with Stephanie's, and the women chatted together outside the school.

Stephanie tried to improve herself, to be what Gary and the winery expected her to be. She took a wine appreciation course at the old Farm Center on Lodi Lane, struggled with French lessons, and worked on her appearance. Gary's six-figure salary gave her credit cards for every good department store from Orange County to San Francisco as well as a brand-new Mercedes. She worked on her hair to get it smoother, more chic — still a battle. She drove to a favored hairdresser in Walnut Creek an hour away and had Gary arrange to give him a special tour of the winery. She occasionally sat in on the Great Chefs of France program Margrit staged at the winery, feeling too shy to do more than listen. But she was entertaining for Gary at home, learning how to cook and serve elaborate, multicourse dinners. With an extra barbecue set up, she would entertain up to a hundred people seated at tables around the pool.

On the surface, Stephanie was living a marvelous life. She traveled all over the world, shopping in Hong Kong, Tokyo, Singapore, London, while Gary did business during the day. She always felt rushed getting the girls' lives covered while she was gone; Tony and Garnet had moved up to the valley shortly after Gary and Stephanie, and they stayed with the girls. Stephanie was meeting movie stars and celebrities at Mondavi concerts and dinners and on trips: Natalie Wood and Robert Wagner on a sunset cruise in Hawaii, Danielle Steel at the Mondavis' home, Ann-Margret in Las Vegas. Winery dinners were dotted with the rich and famous and an increasingly international guest list.

There were evenings when Stephanie felt she was living a fairy tale. One was the black-tie launch for Opus One, the new winery created in 1984 as a joint partnership between the Mondavi winery and Mouton Rothschild (one of the most famous châteaux in Bordeaux). The event was held in the grand foyer of the San Francisco Opera House, and Margrit had sent word through Gary, "Tell Stevie to really dress up." "Gary took it seriously. He took me everywhere to try all these fancy dresses . . . It was so important to him." At I. Magnin in Southern California she found a strapless powder blue dress with a short bubble skirt. But Gary rejected it, angry that she had picked it without him. "So back we went to I. Magnin and I got one that was *very* expensive," a long, black dress with a short ivory satin jacket. Very simple. Very elegant. "This is where Cinderella lost the glass slipper," she thought as she and Gary descended the stairway, moving through a glitter of chandeliers and marble, announced like royalty. "It was wonderful."

In 1981 the vintners launched the ultimate image-maker, the first Napa Valley Wine Auction. In a long weekend of gala activities, the wineries competed to offer the most enchanting hospitality — Greek feasts, famous chefs from New York or New Orleans, opulent vineyard picnics in oak groves. As Gary shmoozed with customers from all over the country — the crowd fanning themselves with paddles under a sweltering tent in a heat wave — a liquor dealer from Syracuse,

New York, bid $24,000 for a single case of the first vintage from Opus One, the '79. It was still in the barrel and wouldn't be bottled for two more years. The highest bid of the auction, he had paid $333 a glass.

As Napa's sheen and glamour grew, a handful of people were aware that four stunted vines in a vineyard in Rutherford, a few miles north of the Mondavi winery, had been diagnosed, in 1980, with the dreaded scourge: phylloxera. The tiny root louse, a nematode barely visible to the eye, had swept through American and French vineyards in the late nineteenth century, destroying them. The Cabernets and Chardonnays that had made Napa Valley famous had been grafted to AXR rootstock developed to resist the infestation. But the tenacious louse had breached AXR's immunity. All seemed normal in Napa Valley, however, as the deadly disease silently attacked and killed.

Only Holly Ramona and a few of her friends knew that, by eighth grade, Holly had begun to worry about her weight. She was constantly asking her friends, "Have I gained weight? Can you tell?" Her mother tried to reassure her. But no one guessed the seriousness of the disease taking hold in Holly. To the casual observer, she was a normal teen. She had moved on from *The Brady Bunch* to the soaps and loved *Days of Our Lives*. She had outgrown her problems in reading comprehension by the fifth grade and became a serious student from sixth grade on. Her life was full of the requisite lessons: piano for ten years, riding, and ballet. But by eighth grade, Friday nights were hard for her, because other girls were beginning to date. But not Holly or her friends, the shyer girls. Although they would go to the school dances together, she felt lucky if she was asked to dance even once.

Holly was becoming very private about her eating habits. Occasionally she would eat a whole box of cookies at once. The erratic family eating pattern collaborated with her new habit. Unseen, Holly could raid the pantry for cookies, potato chips, and Reese's peanut butter cups. Yet, as she blew out her candles at a birthday pool party, the girl in the red-and-white-striped bathing suit with the engaging smile was lean and well proportioned, with an adolescent's knobby knees and elbows. Looking, today, at a picture of Holly at the party, her mother says, "Oh, my God, did I miss it? Was she anorexic?"

Sometimes before she went to bed at night, Holly would be swept by a sudden fear of a snake entering her body "down there" — her vagina. She had always been afraid of snakes. And worms. She couldn't bear weeding the garden for fear of worms. She had seen a live snake on display at school in third grade and was horrified.

Holly started pulling away, choosing to be by herself. She told no one about the cookies. "It was a humiliating part of myself. I never made the decision not to tell. I just didn't." Guilt and shame were becoming her companions. By the end of the school year, Holly had started restricting her diet. By then she had made a pact with herself that, even if she grew taller, she would never allow herself to weigh more than she weighed then.

As a high school freshman, she learned about bulimia in health class — how people would eat an enormous amount and throw it up by forcing themselves to vomit, use laxatives, or exercise to excess. But she didn't worry she might be bulimic. Twenty cookies at a time was scarcely bulimia. And throwing up was so gross.

Gary fulfilled a dream in 1985 when he took the whole family to Europe, including the two grandmothers. Travel and education were the greatest things he could give his daughters, he felt. Neither Betty nor Garnet had ever been abroad, and Gary loved being able to play host to them all. Betty, Garnet, and the girls flew to Bordeaux via Paris. Gary and Steph met them there after VinExpo, the international wine show in Bordeaux that had become a showcase for California wines, largely because of Gary's promotion of the California wine and food pavilion. Then all seven of them piled into a minivan with their seventeen suitcases. For four glorious weeks they toured France, Italy, and London, eating together three times a day. "How many people can honestly look you in the eye and say that they had four weeks straight with their whole family?" he reflects.

"Gary loved to be able to provide for his kids and his wife," the winery's public relations director, Harvey Posert, recalls observing after spending a relaxed day on the beach with the Ramonas on that trip. Gary took such enormous pleasure in what he could do for his family, Margrit confirmed, always talking about his girls, so proud of their accomplishments. Perhaps there was a little Italian macho, some showing off at times. But it was Margrit's nature to look compassionately under the skin. She had been raised multilingual at the crossroads of Europe; Gary had not, and it made a difference. He had come from such humble beginnings and had risen so high; he wanted to do things right. He had such a hunger for self-improvement. "He spent money, but always in the quest for the best." He never showed off with his clothes, though, she noted. The Mondavi men were peacocks — Bob had a London tailor, Brioni shirts, Italian sport coats. Her picture of Gary is in his navy blue jacket and gray slacks, sometimes polyester, working with distributors and restaurateurs in the Vineyard Room. "Good, loyal Gary."

At home he was losing his privacy. As the girls entered junior and senior high, they would crash in his and Steph's room with their sleeping bags and food and curl up and watch TV. They were always coming in unannounced. He would come home and find Stephanie stretched out in the bathtub, her pubic area modestly covered, and the three girls sitting on the edge of the tub. But he didn't feel comfortable letting the girls see him dressing, so he started locking the bathroom door when he took a shower. When Steph objected, the girls taught her to open it with a bobby pin. But as their lives got busier, he saw less and less of them. For a while, he tried to get home at five-thirty so that they could eat together, but there was no way he could say to Bob and Michael in the middle of a meeting, "Thank you very much, fellows. I've got to get home for dinner." And the girls' lives were getting so busy that they seldom ate together at home and, as a family, almost never.

Margaret Mackenzie, a medical anthropologist, professor at Oakland's California College of Arts and Crafts, and former nurse, would soon sound an alarm about the decline of the family meal in America. "Children from affluent households may be suffering from emotional deprivation because of the isolation and loneliness of which the absence of shared meals is one signal," she would write. Increasingly, statistics showed that fewer and fewer households ate together regularly as a family. Explanations abounded: divorce, working mothers, commuting, the collapse of "community," television, family structure in a state of flux.

The importance of the shared meal would be echoed by Margaret Visser, a classics scholar. One definition of a family, she reminded us, is "those who eat together." Seeing the American family meal reduced to a hit-and-run affair of thirty minutes, maximum, eaten largely in silence, she speculated, "Where families spend less and less time together, removing dinnertime talk may well be a serious deprivation; it takes away what was scarce in the first place."

Bulimia and childhood obesity, too, were increasing with the decline of the family meal. "When meals are eaten socially, we are constrained by our manners toward moderation," said Leann Birch, a psychologist and child food expert at Penn State. Rules of the culture are taught at the table. Eating alone loosens constraints, permitting the snacking that leads to obesity; it accommodates the secret bingeing and purging of the bulimic.

As restaurants became virtually the only place families ate together, observers wondered if they were evolving into the family table for our age. They are certainly "intense food-sharing enterprises," anthropologists agreed. But except for a burger at McDonald's, American restaurant dining was not essentially multigenerational; nor was it like the boisterous family feasts of Gary's Ohio childhood. To visit the restaurants of Napa Valley was, largely, to see the generations divided.

At restaurants and winery events, Stephanie looked poised and chic. But it was a facade; she was as insecure about her body as her daughter. Gary still pointed out that her breasts were too small, her bottom and thighs too big. Lying in bed after winery events, he critiqued her. At nearly forty, Stephanie had a body most women would envy — well proportioned, beautifully maintained, and above all slim. Yet she felt an unattractive slump of pear-shaped hips and sloping shoulders, inadequate without shoulder pads. She was standing by the sink in the kitchen one day in her shorts when Gary said in alarm, "What's that on your leg?"

"God — what, where?" Stephanie thought. "Is it a black widow or some terrible growth?"

"There, on your legs," Gary insisted.

It was cellulite, tiny puffy pockets that bubbled almost imperceptibly under the smooth skin on her thighs. He wanted her to have liposuction. She refused. But she stopped wearing shorts.

Worse than feeling fat, Stephanie felt invisible — like a stand-up cardboard prop at events when Gary steered her around by the elbow, introduced her to groups of people, but never let her stay long enough to speak. She started reading *Time* and *Newsweek* to try to educate herself, but her friends Jean Sawday and Karen Maestas felt Gary was not pleased. Even though he claims otherwise, Stephanie felt he rebuffed her plans to take some college courses and preferred her to spend time building a wardrobe.

"Images were very important to Gary. But I also played my part in it," Stephanie admits. "I love to shop . . . Maybe I felt that all I *was* was my appearance." With enough surface beauty, perhaps she could defy invisibility. But her close friends felt Gary had turned her and the girls into decorative props against their will. Karen had observed that Kelli seemed very unhappy about having to wear a form-fitting Mandarin-style dress to greet guests at an Asian theme reception at home for her father's salesmen.

Her friends resented, too, that Gary required Stephanie to go to the winery dinners, then delighted in humiliating her. "If she made any comment at dinner, he would counter it by saying exactly the opposite to make her look stupid," Karen remembers thinking as Stephanie let out some of her feelings on their morning walks. Karen feared the control that Gary had over her. And he never once thanked her for all the entertaining she did for him and the winery. But in Stephanie's eyes it was she, not Gary, who fell short. "Yes, I had to go to these events — was required to cook and entertain," she admits, "but I didn't complain to him about it."

Stephanie's smoldering resentment flamed when Gary, looking for his car keys, dumped the contents of her purse on the bed and left them there. "It didn't matter, because I didn't matter. I didn't exist." When she saw the scattered mess, raging inside, she picked up a stack of his papers and hurled them all over the floor. She wondered why she hadn't done it before. Gary has no memory of the scene.

Mothering was where Stephanie felt confident. The girls were fine — active in school, sports, lessons, Girl Scouts, and friends. Their lives were all running on such full schedules that there was not much time for the kind of talking she'd experienced growing up with all the women, but she felt she was good friends with her daughters. The closeness in the Ramona family was among the females, as it had been in Stephanie's childhood. She was touched to see the girls do loving things for one another. When Shawna's rheumatoid arthritis kept her from cutting her steak in a restaurant, Kelli very quietly cut it for her. They were basically normal kids who camped out in the backyard, put on dress-up shows for their grandparents at Christmas, and charged the family ten cents to watch their water ballet. They played their own rapacious variant of Monopoly, "the business game," their ruthlessness amusing the neighbors as they bought and sold the rooms in their home and buildings all over town. Their mother taught them the art of practical jokes: Tabasco in Grandma's coffee on April Fool's Day, toilet-papering six of the neighbors' houses at prom time. The girls heard Stephanie and Betty laugh over stories and gossip about the aunts and uncles in Southern California. But Stephanie could tell them none of Gary's family stories. She knew nothing about his family. It was not until his father, Tony, died in 1982 that the stories came out, for Tony's brothers and one of their wives came to the funeral. They reminded Stephanie of her own family — crazy, loud, and fun. They started talking about the old days, Gary's summers as a kid, the musical uncles. It was the most she had ever heard.

Stephanie wished the girls felt closer to their father. He certainly gave them things — whatever lessons or equipment they needed and a four-week trip to Europe in 1985. "But let me tell you, it wasn't relaxed," Stephanie says. "It was always, 'We're going to have fun now.'" They would sit in a restaurant in Paris, Gary charming the sommelier while the women and girls sat, slumped, looking as if it were the Last Supper.

Shawna remembered just one time, on a Christmas trip to New York in 1987, when she and her father had fun. Excited about the pogo ball she got for Christmas, she and her dad went pogo balling up and down the hallways of the Plaza Hotel. "It was neat because we did something improper. And it was okay. He kind of expected us to not really act like kids, to get excited or act dumb like kids normally do when they play. I felt like he was relaxing and letting his guard down. I was surprised that he could do that," she says.

Stephanie's vague dissatisfaction would focus itself, from time to time, in her suddenly deciding to leave Gary, as she had early in the marriage. Once she packed the girls into the car and drove as far as Yountville, ten miles away. But, losing heart, she turned around and told them, "We're going to be leaving soon," alerting them to be ready and quiet when the time came, making them conspirators in the hovering plot. "But 'soon' would never come," recalls Holly.

It seemed to Gary that he could give Steph the world and her restlessness would only grow. She had never made a secret of wanting to move back south, even though he always offered to bring Betty north to be near them. "We'll have your mother move up. She's a good secretary," he urged. To keep Steph from worrying, Gary happily helped with Betty's travel costs, rent, and a small car. But he knew that Steph's discontent was deeper than concern for her mother.

Steph would say wistfully, "Gary, you're so successful. You do everything well."

"Steph, you can do anything you want to do. You really don't have any restrictions other than what you put on yourself." Gary was extremely proud of Steph; she was stylish and beautiful, a truly good person, a wonderful mother to his children.

How about starting a business? Gary suggested. Stephanie loved jewelry, and when she discovered, on her first trip to Hong Kong, how cheap things were, she got Gary excited about helping her get set up. He invested $20,000 in the Hong Kong jewelry business and watched her flush with excitement when she discovered, buying pearls in Hong Kong, that she was good at bartering. "She was like a little kid." But he laughingly reminded her, "Remember, they've been doing this a long time . . . and they're always going to make money on you." He didn't mean it as a put-down; he just wanted to help her learn the tricks of the trade. Like merchants on the Silk Road, they returned from the Orient laden with pearls, lapis lazuli, and black onyx, which Stephanie had made into necklaces, bracelets, and earrings. But if she was serious about it, there had to be some profit. Gary urged, "Go out and call on a few jewelry stores" meaning to give advice, not criticism. In the end, Stephanie didn't sell much jewelry beyond her circle of friends, and the business bogged down.

She worked for a while in real estate, but it led nowhere. Why didn't she try decorating? She had great taste. If she got a job, that was fine, he told her, but she had to realize that she wouldn't have the freedom she had now to be with the girls, to visit her mother, to play tennis. What about volunteering? They always needed people to work on charity things, he said. It sounded to Stephanie as if he was discouraging her from getting a job.

To Gary's distress, Stephanie seemed to be bypassing opportunities for herself, just as she had since she dropped out of school with Fs. She rarely attended the Great Chefs cooking school at the winery. When she did, Margrit noted, it was as a silent observer. She'd sit in her classic double-breasted green silk blazer, a very pretty woman, Margrit thought, and becoming more attractive. She dressed beautifully, and she'd changed her hair from the Gypsy look to a smoother style with a blond streak. It was the generational difference that kept Stephanie aloof from her, Margrit guessed.

Gary began to feel that Stephanie was again expressing frustration by withholding. He had been tolerant. But by the mid-1980s, his wife was avoiding winery events more and more. "Steph, we get invited to Michael and Isabel's and you don't want to go, I don't have a problem. But I do have a problem if you say we're going, they're having a table place set for you, and you decide not to go at the last minute," said Gary, upset. It was embarrassing. It was inconsiderate. If she did go, she'd find a woman she knew, and they'd huddle and talk about children and women's things. And yet, Margrit marveled, "Gary never said one negative word about Stevie, never, *ever*. He loved her. He had her on a pedestal like a goddess."

He saw Stephanie's problem as being within herself. He saw the old insecurity in her fury and hurt feelings when he planned to take Holly on brief trips without Steph — to visit colleges back east on one of his business trips and to take Holly and her friends skiing during a Mondavi sales meeting at Tahoe. The girls' departure for college was approaching. He thought, "It's a time bomb ticking."

Finally Stephanie stopped attending winery events. Fed up, she says, with eighteen years of mandatory appearances, with Gary's undermining critiques, with feeling voiceless and invisible, she simply quit. "I guess I was feeling my oats and, all of a sudden, I put my foot down," she says, as her women friends cheered her on.

Returning from a trip to Chicago, she and Gary were driving home from the airport on Highway 29, and as they reached the winery in Oakville, she suddenly saw big signs tacked to all the telephone poles, STEVIE IS TURNING 40, all the way home. Her friends had put them up while she was gone, a show of affection that overwhelmed her. The next day, Gary took her out on the ruse of looking at some vines while the three girls set up a surprise party. They had done it all themselves — a barbecue and french fries, everyone dressed like the fifties. They played relays. "It is one of my happiest memories. Anytime with my children is a happy memory."

The Ramonas' sex life was not so happy. Coinciding with her fortieth birthday in 1985, intercourse with Gary ended, Stephanie claims. She feared that Gary was having affairs. Maybe he wasn't interested in her any longer. "Gary, why am I not attractive to you anymore?" she dared to ask him. His ambiguous answer was, "I loved you." What did that mean? At forty-two, Stephanie went through menopause, for her a nonevent. She had a few days of furious hot flashes, but before she could accustom herself to them, both the flashes and her periods were over. Just like that. What should have been the freest time for them sexually she found the coldest.

Bob Mondavi turned seventy in 1984. He had the energy of a twenty-year-old, traveling around the world with Margrit Biever, promoting wine, sneaking a week of skiing or sailing for themselves here and there. But Gary saw a growing unease over the unspoken question: Could the business survive Bob's absence? On the surface, relations between Gary and Bob's sons were excellent. But Gary felt tension between himself and Michael because of his special relationship with Bob, and he wasn't sure what would happen to him if Bob retired. Perhaps it would ease things, he thought. The boys would be running the company and would no longer be vying for their father's job. But which son would run it? They couldn't both be number one.

No one had forgotten the feud twenty years earlier between Bob and his younger brother, Peter. It had destroyed the family partnership at Mondavi's Krug winery and forced Bob out to start again on his own; his mother took Peter's side as the rivalry exploded into a sensational trial in a Napa courtroom. A battle over dynastic succession as Bob fought for a place at Krug for his sons, it had also been a battle between two very different men over differing visions — Robert the ambitious prophet for wine, Peter content with more traditional wine-making goals.

Bob's sons had been given different jobs: Tim, the winemaker, Michael, the manager. No disputes had yet exploded into destructive sibling fights. But the tension was there, and Bob was always watching. In 1985, he bought a neighboring winery, Vichon, so that he could expand in Napa Valley without hurting the image that premium wineries should not be big. But the perception was that he bought it for Tim, to relieve some of the competitive tensions with his brother. The Mondavis had hired Barry Grundland, a Napa psychiatrist, to work on the family dynamics. He had helped some well-known vintners through difficult times, and was, so to speak, therapist to the stars of Napa Valley. At Robert Mondavi, he was given extraordinary access to the soul and workings of a family company that, though high-profile, still guarded its privacy. Grundland attended meetings of the management council and board, traveled to the East Coast for sales and marketing strategy meetings. Senior executives were encouraged to see him on issues relating to the winery's human issues — that is, Michael and Tim — and he met with Gary several times.

By the mid-1980s, the edge was off Napa Valley's wine "miracle." Competition had grown intense, and in a valley that had never needed to advertise, marketing was suddenly a matter of survival. It was not clear to everyone that, in this less forgiving business climate, Gary's natural talent for sales would continue to translate into rocketing success. "Maybe he overcompensates by working harder and harder," Margrit Biever speculated, for he was a workaholic. But the almost spiritual way in which Gary executed Bob's passion and vision in the marketplace, she felt, made up for anything he might not have or anything a Harvard MBA might bring to the table. "What they lack is the *passion*." The numbers spoke for themselves: higher sales and profit every year. Gary was still the best.

By 1985 there had been two more outbreaks of phylloxera: one in a Napa vineyard, the other in Sonoma. The news was sketchy, but more cases would be identified after the torrential floods of February 1986. Phylloxera was undeniably back in the valley. Yet it was still only spoken of in whispers. Stymied, the elite viticultural school at UC Davis had not declared it an emergency or even a danger; nurseries were still selling, and wineries still planting, the vulnerable rootstock AXR. But vines were dying. Wherever phylloxera struck, the vineyards had to be ripped out and replanted, at a cost of $20,000 an acre. It could not only drive smaller, less profitable wineries and growers out of business, but it could also hurt the image Mondavi and his competitors had fought so hard to build. Would tourists in search of wine and beauty come to a blighted valley?

Other forces were attacking the wine industry as well. A neoprohibition movement had launched a moral assault on all drinking; the carnage on the highways had spawned MADD (Mothers Against Drunk Driving); and every winery had to post a warning at the entrance to the tasting room that pregnant women should not drink because of the risk of birth defects. Furthermore, America was going on a fitness craze, and the glass of wine over lunch was being replaced by Perrier water.

To rebut these forces, Gary helped Bob Mondavi develop and

launch an educational program to send on the road nationwide. Gary also planned an aggressive strategy to carry Bob's message to Orange County, the most affluent wine market in California; he would build a wine and food center in Costa Mesa. It was an expensive investment, as wine economics grew tighter, and there was some resistance at upper levels of the winery. But Gary won Bob's enthusiasm and support, and the center would open in 1989. It was Gary's baby. Greg Evans, Mondavi's chief financial officer, feared it was not a good idea.

Like her father, Holly was highly motivated to become the best at anything she did, especially if — like cheerleading or learning to read — it didn't come easily. She made the varsity tennis team in her sophomore year after working on her game with her father, who practiced with her four or five times a week. By high school, she was teaching tennis and beating her father. "I became more competitive," says Holly. "No one likes to lose." She also beat Gary in a cross-country race at the winery. Holly was made president of the ski team in her senior year; her dad joined her in the Sierra for the father-daughter ski weekend. When possible, Gary drove Holly and her sisters to practices and Girl Scouts, attended concerts, and shared car-pooling duties.

As Kelli and Holly grew into their teens in the mid-1980s, their differences, disguised under identical dresses as small children, became more pronounced. Kelli was popular, as Gary had been in high school. She got grounded once for running with the wrong crowd and had to pull up her grades. She played three instruments in band as well as the "in" sport, volleyball. She was nominated for Homecoming Queen; with PRINCESS KELLI bannered across a convertible, she sat with her tuxedoed escort and waved to the crowds in two parades while Gary's video camera whirred.

Holly was noticeably shy and innocent for her age. When she was in junior high, her mother gave her a short lecture on the facts of life, explaining that "the male puts his penis inside the woman's vagina, and that's how babies are made." It left Holly feeling that the sexual process was "pretty gross. I'm never going to do anything like that." Her sexual maturity came late; her menses did not begin until she was sixteen. She knew what a crush felt like but hadn't experienced sexual impulses and didn't know what "fondling" was, she later said. She was the perfect babysitter. When she was fourteen, the Kellys, neighbors down the street, hired her once a week. Each time she came in the door Maggie Kelly felt relief. "She was just the kind of sweet, smiling, nice girl you wanted babysitting with your children." They always overpaid her, and Stephanie would send her back to return the extra.

By high school, it was as if Holly was missing some of the building blocks of experience that most kids learn as they grow up, reflects Karen Maestas, Stephanie's closest friend — odd gaps, Karen later believed, that came from Holly's blocking out most of her childhood. Yet Holly was not the kind of kid who got teased. "She was a liked person. I don't remember anybody being cruel to her. Everyone was happy when she tried out for cheerleading," says Jean Sawday, another close friend and neighbor. But a cheerleading photograph shows Holly self-consciously pulling her sweater down.

Feeling ugly didn't happen overnight, however. "It wasn't like one day I woke up and said, 'Today I'm ugly.' It was just kind of always there," says Holly about her deteriorating self-image and her growing preoccupation with her weight. By sophomore year, she would go swimming in her clothes, not a bathing suit, because she felt so uncomfortable about her appearance. She wore baggy sweat shirts and warm-up pants.

Diets had become a way of life. Holly had begun fasting by ninth grade, afraid she was overweight. During this period, between ninth and tenth grade, Holly woke up one morning and remembered a dream she had just had. "The dream was, I was about ten or eleven. We were in the house in Diamond Bar . . . on the floor in the den . . . He was wearing shorts and a T-shirt . . . I was there. My two younger sisters were there in the background and he wanted us to touch him. He was asking us to rub his feet and to kiss his legs, and then he would do the same to me." She awoke upset and disturbed and saying to herself, "Don't ever have that dream again. Don't ever think about it." Normally, she did not recall her dreams. This one she had always remembered.

The pattern of fasting became more intense. From the end of her freshman year to the middle of her sophomore year, Holly would starve herself to the point of fainting. "Sometimes I would go for three days," she admits. She never said a word to her mother about her weight or her diets. But Stephanie saw, and wanted to know more. She took her daughter to Dr. Baldwin, their pediatrician since the move to

St. Helena. When Stephanie tried to ask questions "he'd say, 'You're not listening. I asked you to stay out of it. This is Holly's business.'" She was so offended that she grabbed her purse and walked out. Flustered, Holly followed her out, crying, but she wanted to stay. "I was very interested in what he had to say."

By the summer of her junior year Holly had joined Weight Watchers. Using her mother's small white kitchen scales, she started one of its rituals, weighing her food. If she used the packets of chocolate and vanilla Slim Fast her mother kept in the cupboard, she canceled them out by gorging on other food.

Gary spotted Holly weighing her food — he saw Steph and Holly together weighing every lettuce leaf — and was distressed. Yet she kept gaining weight. This couldn't be a healthy way for a young girl to live. Margrit Biever saw the two women going through the weighing ritual, with little breasts of chicken pounded and scraped of every bit of fat or skin, and shared Gary's concern. When she was a child in Switzerland, the table had been the center of family life. Everything, feelings as well as food, was shared there three times a day. The food was so good — the roasts and dumplings and puddings — and the table such a happy place that, at lunch, you talked about what you were going to have for dinner. For her, "dining is sacred." How incredibly sad, she thought, to see this child and her mother so stripped of the pleasure of food that, for them, food was an enemy.

Gary told Stephanie that he was worried about Holly's gaining weight and planned to talk to her about it. "Gary, that would be very hard on her. Please wait. I'll talk to her," Stephanie pleaded. "If you don't, I'm going to," he replied. She took Holly for a walk and discussed her preoccupation with weight. "If it means so much to you to lose weight . . . why don't you just let me help you with a diet and then you can get it over with," Stephanie suggested impatiently; it should be easy for a disciplined child like Holly.

"Holly looked fine to me," her mother claims. Yet Stephanie would never be able to explain why she committed an act she would forever regret. Holly had been jumping on a trampoline in the family room, and women's magazines and photos of models torn from them were spread out on the floor. Stephanie picked up one of them and taped it to Holly's bathroom mirror. She just left it there, with no comment.

Holly knew she was privileged. She had been to Europe, New

York, and the Bahamas. She had been given every lesson she could want. Neither parent helped her with homework, but tutors were there for algebra, physics, chemistry, if she began to fall behind. Her parents gave her a new BMW for her sixteenth birthday. Her dad took her to brunch at the Silverado Country Club, and when they came out, there was the car, wrapped with a huge bow. Her dad always said she could go to any college she wanted. She couldn't understand why she was so unhappy.

Holly was going to the senior prom, her only date during high school; several of the local children had talked a tall, cute neighbor into taking her. Gary took movies as they prepared to leave. The film shows a matronly Holly in a white two-piece dress with big sleeves and shoulders, smiling, a little self-conscious, as she pinned a boutonniere on a slim, very handsome blond boy. No one guessed that the big smile that had been Holly's signature since babyhood was, increasingly, a charade, an effort. The prom, her mother's friends feared, had been "miserable" for Holly. Her date had gone his own way at the dance — he dumped her once they got there, Holly's friends observed.

"It was in her senior year that I definitely knew something was wrong with my daughter," recalls Stephanie. Holly would stay in her room a lot. She'd always done that, but now she didn't want to be around kids, even her own friends. They'd ask her to go places, but she'd refuse. Holly never spoke of what was wrong. Stephanie searched her face. "Her eyes were dead. A mother sees it — *her eyes were dead.* And then she'd change and be okay, and I would look at her and think, 'Oh, she's all right. It was just my imagination.'"

Holly needed therapy, Stephanie told Gary when they were in Orange County on a business trip. He wouldn't talk about it, but there were tears in his eyes as he paced back and forth. "'There will be no therapy. *There will be no therapy,*'" Stephanie recalls him saying as he pinned her against a wall at the Westin Hotel, a memory Gary does not share. "Why *didn't* I get her into therapy? I should never have listened to Gary."

When Holly had a yeast infection her senior year, Stephanie took her to the family physician, Dr. Thomas Stiles. He came out to see Stephanie in the waiting room, she recalls, took her by the arm, and asked, "Has anything ever happened to Holly? Has Holly ever been molested?" He couldn't do an internal exam — he hadn't been able to get near her genital area. He had never seen a patient so nervous in all his years of practice, he said. Alarmed, Stephanie took Holly aside and asked her "and she said no." But the disturbing word "molested" had been planted in Stephanie's brain.

Through her senior year, as Holly's secret eating binges grew like a virus, taking over her life, she did not know that she was following the familiar and dangerous path from anorexia to depression and bulimia. Her weight had fluctuated all year. At times it had been as low as 120 pounds. By the summer of 1988, as she prepared for college, it had risen to 155 pounds. She was barely five-foot-four.

As Holly left for her freshman year at UC Irvine, she heard her mother say, "Continue your education so that you won't be in the same place I'm in now, without an education, without much knowledge." She called home every day at first. She was in a dormitory and liked her roommate, Tiffany, and she kept her grades up, with a 3.0 GPA the first few terms. But Holly had carried the depression and bulimia with her to Irvine. That fall she sent Grandma Ramona a videotape of greetings for her seventy-fifth birthday. Her script sounded rehearsed, her voice artificially lifted for the occasion: "Happy seventy-fifth birthday. I wish I could be there . . . I'm having fun at college . . . I'll see you in December."

Holly was confronted by two very different models — her father's competitive love of excelling and her mother's frustration with the traditional homemaker role and "gilded cage" glamour of her life. The tortured pattern unfolding in Holly's life would be explained by many theories over the next few years. But it would also prove to be a prototype for a theory being developed by two East Coast psychologists: that the current epidemic of "disordered eating," depression, and anxiety among young women was a single syndrome caused by the conflict of this mismatch between parents. But theory was meaningless to Holly then; she was increasingly a hostage to uncontrollable compulsions.

The impulse to binge began at college after the Christmas break. At a stop at McDonald's, Holly had started with pancakes. She bought doughnuts and other food at a supermarket, but she didn't want Tiffany to see her gorging in their room. Instead, she went to her grandmother's apartment in Irvine to eat while Betty was at work. It was there Holly tried purging for the first time. She stuck her finger down her throat and tried to throw up, but it didn't work. Afterward she felt sick, overstuffed, and took Pepto-Bismol to calm her stomach. She continued to use Betty's apartment as her sanctuary for binges, which increased to once a week, leaving before her grandmother got home at night. Although her father was building his wine and food center just a few miles from Irvine, she could never tell him how troubled she was when they met. She told no one.

That spring, Holly became even more obsessively concerned with calories. She would limit her eating to 500–600 calories a day and exercise into a lather for two or three hours. Then she would force-feed herself like a French goose being fattened for the kill. She was able to keep her grades up and ended the year with As and Bs. But she was unhappy at Irvine and confused about why. She convinced herself it was because there was no football team, no school spirit. It was boring. She thought of applying to UC Berkeley, but after one look at the application forms, she decided it wasn't worth the effort. Energy for daily life was getting hard to come by.

Holly hit bottom in the summer of 1989, after her freshman year. She had a job as what her father laughingly called a "crystal engineer" in the Vineyard Room at Mondavi, washing dishes and clearing tables. She glimpsed the exquisite three-course lunches being served to showcase Mondavi's wines while, for her, food had become a secret purgatory. The binging continued. She would wait until Kelli and Shawna left the house before eating — always by herself.

It was on a day off from Mondavi that she first successfully purged. She had driven, alone, an hour south on I-80 to the Concord Mall in the East Bay. Awash in an ocean of consumer bounty, a hundred stores spilling over with things to buy, this starved nineteen-year-old began to eat. Buying doughnuts and muffins, she ate and ate. Normally, her discomfort with the crowds and her anxiety about men looking at her and thinking she was ugly would have driven her away. But she was too focused on her cravings to care. In thrall to a depression she didn't know she had, her emotions were dulled. She was vaguely aware of "I shouldn't be eating this" — she had been an obedient and compliant child too long to fully repress the guilt and conflict. But she couldn't stop. Caught in the humiliating cycle of guilt, shame, and secrecy that is the life of the bulimic, she would only later be able to say, "I think purging was the only way I knew to get all of my emotions out . . . I did not consciously make that decision. But . . . it kept progressing." Leaving the mall, bloated and full, she bought more food from a supermarket nearby. She arrived home in the evening and began to eat in the kitchen. She thinks Kelli came in and said hello, but she remembers nothing but the eating. She ate doughnuts, frozen yogurt, cake, bread, peanut butter, cookies. "I had eaten so much that it was almost natural; it halfway just happened . . . I remember going to bed. I drank a lot of water. I went into the bathroom. I felt sick. I leaned over the toilet. I put my fingers down my mouth and threw up."

For someone viewing Holly and Napa Valley simultaneously, the contrasts are unbearably poignant. As Holly's lonely despair deepened, the valley's stylish abundance was increasingly celebrated.

The decade since the family's move in 1979 had been the Golden Age for Napa Valley wines. By the late 1980s, Napa's beauty and cachet had made it so desirable that the cost of vineyards and homes had soared. The valley was becoming a weekend retreat and full-time home for the wealthy. Distinguished wineries and champagne houses from France, Germany, Spain, and Italy bought up property, formed partnerships, built their own wineries — reluctantly paying tribute to this upstart wine region in California. New winery buildings that had no discernible architectural roots in Napa's culture or history were rising incongruously — a spectacular Etruscan temple, a recreation of Monticello, slate-roofed French châteaux, a monastery converted to a winery–cum–modern art museum — all fighting for brand identity in a valley that now had two hundred wineries.

The domestic hospitality that had been Napa Valley's best advertisement was going professional. Winery wives, on the road as part of the marketing team, became too busy to cook. Though Margrit Biever continued to cook some of her own dinners, catering had largely taken over for entertaining. The humble pleasures of food and wine were being lost to competition and image.

At the same time, an American cuisine was emerging in triumph over rich French sauces and fat-larded pâtés. The movement had started an hour's drive south, in Berkeley, with Chez Panisse, the restaurant that expressed Alice Waters's commitment to the growing, preparing, and sharing of good, fresh food and her belief that "the table *is* community." The Mondavis had nurtured the movement; Margrit's cooking schools shifted from the Great Chefs of France to the great chefs of America — Jeremiah Tower, Paul Prudhomme, Wolfgang Puck. Fresh produce, local foods, and the flavors of the many cultures contributing to America's palate were served at the stylish restaurants popping up along Highway 29. Mondavi had largely achieved his goal: the marriage of fine food and American wine had, at last, been consummated.

The Ramonas' life echoed Napa Valley's showy success. Gary's power and responsibilities had expanded steadily; he was now one of the six men who sat on the management council, the group that ran the Mondavi winery, in addition to running sales and marketing worldwide. In July 1989, Gary and Stephanie broke ground for their dream house. Set on twenty-eight forested acres high in the hills west of St. Helena, there would be a tennis court, a pool, and the stable, white fences, and horses Gary had wanted since his horse had died. A spectacular home for his family, a place to entertain the wine world — this house was the culmination of his life.

Stephanie had been looking for property, mostly as an investment. A Realtor took her to look at the site, but it was just trees, rocks, and one big hill. Climbing to the top to see the view of the valley, she stumbled over the rock pile and thought, "Who would ever buy this?" She'd feel so isolated. But Gary's enthusiasm carried the day.

Gary was the first to seize on the idea of a massive showplace; for Stephanie it was too big, too far from town. But his excitement was contagious. Here was something creative she could do. She had never forgotten *The Fountainhead* and its architect-hero, Howard Roark. After interviewing a dozen architects, the Ramonas hired Sandy Walker, from San Francisco. Gary knew what he wanted, a house that echoed Margrit and Bob's spectacular hilltop home, which had been featured in *Architectural Digest* and shot from a helicopter for *Lifestyles of the Rich and Famous*. He wanted large, gracious spaces for entertaining and radiant-heated limestone floors. He would have expanses of beige Italian travertine, although Stephanie thought hardwood looked warmer. The girls' bedrooms would be tiny, but the entryway would hold four tables of eight for dinner parties. There would be a magnificent kitchen with a fireplace and the warm Tuscan colors Margrit had helped them choose — a kitchen for large-scale entertaining. Margrit suggested that Gary turn the loft into his office — his tree house.

Yet, as Sandy Walker gave Stephanie a voice in the design, her interest grew. It was she who wanted the living room a little bigger and who loved the pyramidal skylight in the center, which opened up to the stars like the winery's Vineyard Room. She could see herself sitting in her bathtub, looking out to views of the valley.

Just when his full attention was needed at work, Gary became his own contractor. "He *loved* building," Walker observed, as Gary spent more and more time at the house site. But so had several other senior executives who'd built houses, Gary knew — Michael and Tim Mondavi, Cliff Adams. You were encouraged to use your secretary to help, to take some time off, to take out a loan through the winery.

The forces that had been building through the 1980s were hitting the wine industry. For the first time, per capita consumption of wine in the United States declined in 1988 and was continuing down in '89. That year, UC Davis's phylloxera task force finally sent out an urgent press release to "DISCONTINUE PLANTING AXR #1 ROOTSTOCK" and declared phylloxera an epidemic. Mondavi would need capital for replanting as well as continued expansion; it was buying another small winery and a vineyard nearby.

It was becoming known that if you wanted Gary, you'd find him at the house. Michael was frustrated when he couldn't reach him, but he was still producing record sales and profits each year. He felt secure, part of the Mondavi family, appreciated in all sorts of ways. His base salary of $280,000 plus investments and benefits would gross him $600,000 in 1989. He was opening the Costa Mesa center that October. A month later, at Bob's urging, he added the running of the Vichon winery to his duties — a job he had vigorously resisted because it was Tim's.

As Gary spent more and more time at the house, Stephanie began to worry. He had told her, she recalls, "If Bob Mondavi ever kicks the bucket, we're in trouble." He often made comments about Bob's being closer to him than his own father, that he was as close as Bob's own sons. She hoped Gary was not overconfident and feared that, with Bob Mondavi gone, the sons might kick him out.

Margrit Biever smelled trouble in the marriage, not the winery. She was surprised that Stephanie was never there when she went up to the house. But he and Steph wouldn't be building a house together if things weren't good between them, Gary said firmly to himself. After dropping out for a few years, she had lately become more willing to attend events. He had chalked up much of her restlessness of the last few years to "the change." That was over. He felt he was making an effort, cutting back on travel now that he had such a large staff and making his trips less hurried so that he could spend more time with Steph. She seemed to be enjoying planning the house with him; they'd drive up to make decisions. Although Stephanie claims now that intercourse had ceased, Gary did not admit that their sex life was in crisis. Steph was still uptight sometimes, as she had always seemed to him, he noted, but an intercourse count had never been his measure of their sexual pleasure.

As the building of the house progressed through the summer, a subtle metamorphosis was occurring in Stephanie. As she watched "the most beautiful home I've ever seen in my whole, entire life" emerge from the architect's plans and the rocky land, she was coming to terms with herself. "It was that last year when I backed away from winery functions. I learned that I missed them. You take things for granted, and then you stay away awhile and say, 'Wait a minute, I really like that.'" She started going again, and it felt good "because it was my decision," on her terms. She would even go to events by herself when Gary was out of town, something she had never done before.

People had always told her that she was better and stronger than she thought she was. "Maybe I started tuning Gary out and listening to them." "The kid is strong," Betty thought as she watched her daughter emerge. "She was so independent that I loved it. She had been all along. But as a mother, sometimes you're so close to it that you don't see. You just worry." After all the years of concern that she had overprotected Stevie, "it made me feel I had done something right."

Gary had played his part, too, Stephanie had to admit. He was home more, and when they did travel, he wasn't filling his days as full and was spending more time with her. He had been supportive when she was going through her traumatic experiments with hair color, playing out her restlessness in every shade of blond. She was helping with the decisions on the house — on tile, colors, bedrooms — and was beginning to look forward to living and entertaining there with Gary.

Sandy Walker knew that one person, usually the wife, dominates in building a house, and it was clearly Gary's house. "Stephanie had great ideas, and I don't think Gary in any way bullied her, but he had so much energy and enthusiasm it might have appeared that way to her." Yet to Walker, the Ramonas appeared to be "in sync" as a couple, enjoying jokes together.

Yet Stephanie remembers some disquieting events. Six or seven times, she had found unexpectedly locked doors at the St. Helena house; Stephanie dismissed them as "just the kids fooling around." There had been the perplexing time when, Stephanie recalls, she had picked up a *Playboy* magazine from the back of the toilet and photographs of Kelli and Holly had fallen out. There was the image of Holly's screaming when her dad hugged her, then pushing him away. She filed these fragments in the back of her mind with the incidents at Diamond Bar.

And she remembers more lies: Gary's saying he was at the office working when he wasn't — his car wasn't there — and coming home silent. Betty knew about the sex problem but thought it was more Stephanie's beginning to assert herself than a real marriage problem. "If Gary did have affairs," says Betty, "he was always discreet. He never embarrassed Stevie in public." Betty had been gratified when Gary said to her one day, "She's always a lady. I am so proud to take her anywhere." Betty felt that he had always tried to divide the women — Holly and Kelli, Garnet and Betty, Stevie and her mother — and saw it as the lack of confidence she had seen in him from his earlier, rougher days. There was nothing sinister in a lack of confidence. On balance, says Betty, "I thought Gary was a pretty great person." Stephanie felt that "the only thing that had to change was our sex life. But I thought Gary would work on that." She had no plans to leave the marriage. As her mother had said years before, "No family's perfect."

4

Flashbacks

One night in August 1989, as Stephanie arrived home from a winery reception, Kelli and Shawna ran to tell her, "Holly's throwing up." She found her oldest daughter vomiting in the bathroom. "Mom, I have the flu," Holly said.

"Oh, I'm sorry, Holly," Stephanie said, handing her a towel. But the alert mother did not hear Holly get up and vomit during the night, the familiar pattern with the girls' flu. Two days later, Stephanie was putting on her makeup in her dressing room when Holly came in, looking very strange. A mother's intuition made her ask, "Holly, is anything wrong? Do you have something to tell me? Were you forcing yourself to throw up the other night?" Stephanie felt sick as she saw in Holly's distraught face that she had struck a chord. Holly was afraid to tell her mom or dad for fear that they would think less of her, but she blurted it out: "Yes, Mom. It wasn't flu. I . . . I think I have a problem with food. I think that maybe I need some help." She wanted therapy but didn't want her father to know. Don't tell him, she pleaded.

"Well, maybe it will go away," Stephanie suggested to her daughter, thinking perhaps it would disappear if they waited. But Holly binged and purged again the next day.

Two or three days later Holly went to her mother again. "It's getting worse. It's not going away. I'm really going to need to get some help." This was not a family of pill poppers; it did not like depending on shrinks, doctors, or medication. Holly, Stephanie, and Betty all shared a certain stoicism about healing yourself and not complaining.

But Holly cried for help. With that plea, the Ramona family tragedy was set immutably in motion.

From Gary, Stephanie had learned about Dr. Barry Grundland, the winery's therapist, and she asked Gary to call him about Holly. "I think she's bulimic," explained Stephanie.

Depression and bulimia. These were the diagnoses suddenly hanging like a dark cloud over the Ramona family. Grundland thought an antidepressant drug might help, but Holly needed supervision and probably therapy. He suggested that, since she'd be returning to Irvine in a few weeks, she contact the university's student medical services.

Her daughter's health overriding her distaste for medical intervention, Stephanie flew to Orange County before the school year began to find a therapist for Holly. She didn't go to the Irvine campus, as Grundland had suggested; through her aunt Barbara O'Connell, who worked for some psychologists, Stephanie was led to someone reported to be a specialist in eating disorders, Marche Isabella. Isabella's office, the Irvine Family Psychological Services, was right in Irvine. Still wishing Holly could control her bulimia herself, Stephanie called her in Napa and said impatiently, "Why can't you just stop?" Holly was binging every other day at this point. "I couldn't communicate to her why it was difficult for me to stop," Holly recalled in depositions. "She didn't understand the dynamics of addictions." Stephanie personally interviewed Marche Isabella. Isabella had the letters MFCC after her name, certifying that she was one of California's twenty-three thousand marriage, family, and child counselors. Stephanie knew nothing about her credentials — Isabella, in fact, had little special training in eating disorders — but found her warm and likable.

Stephanie asked Isabella about bulimia. Several years of therapy was the treatment for eating disorders, she said. She was evasive about the causes of the bulimia until she met and evaluated Holly, but Stephanie pressed her. "There's got to be *something* that causes this." Here, their stories diverge on what would become a critical legal issue: Who was the first to bring up the subject of molestation? Isabella recalls that Stephanie asked if Holly might have been sexually abused; Stephanie claims that Isabella brought up the issue as she cited some alarming statistics about eating disorders. Some studies, she said, suggest that 70 to 80 percent of bulimics have been sexually molested. The data chilled Stephanie. Here, again, was the molestation issue raised by Dr. Stiles well over a year earlier. Isabella added that about

60 to 70 percent of her own eating disorder patients had been sexually abused.

These statistics, strongly suggesting a connection between bulimia and childhood sexual abuse — controversial and unsubstantiated, yet spoken by an authority figure during the family's very first contact with her — would open Marche Isabella to charges of professional irresponsibility and malpractice. Yet if Stephanie had been the first to wave the red flag of molestation, the charge of suggesting and implanting the idea of abuse would shift, at least partly, to Holly's mother.

Stephanie came home upset but with a sense of mission. She might be a submissive wife, but, as her mother had observed, "Stevie's a tiger when it comes to her children." Sitting at the kitchen counter, she asked Holly if she had ever been molested. Holly became red in the face and mumbled, "I think so, yes." Although Stephanie has been ambivalent over whether Holly actually said yes, her reply somehow confirmed for Stephanie the suspicion that had floated since Holly's senior year in high school. She took Holly to dinner and raised the issue again, this time offering the names of some of the neighbors as possible perpetrators. Holly rejected the names, but she was visibly upset. As they were getting into the car, her mother finally asked the big question: "It wasn't your father, was it?" Holly looked straight ahead and, in a flat tone, said, "No, no." On this disturbing note, she went back to college for her sophomore year.

In bed watching TV, Stephanie recalls telling Gary of her fear that Holly had been molested. She couldn't believe it as Gary looked at her, looked back at the TV, and said not a word. It could have been one of the neighborhood children, she suggested, possibly Kathy, the high school girl. He responded, "That's a shame," as blandly as if she'd suggested that Kathy had burned the girls' toast.

She asked him again, urgently, "Gary, are we going to do something about it?" and heard Gary burst out angrily, *"Steph, just leave it alone."* Leave it alone? The specter of sexual abuse meant not only possible damage to her daughter, but it also called into question the one thing Stephanie believed she had done well: mother her children. She pushed Gary on it as he left for work. Again he ordered her, "Leave it alone," and slammed the door.

She confided her fears about Holly to Karen and Jean. Do something, they urged. Find out who did it! But Gary had told her to leave it alone, she told them. They thought about it, and both guessed Gary. "Even before Stephanie knew for sure, I'd told my husband," says Karen.

But Gary denies that this was the moment Stephanie told him that Holly could have been molested. He claims it wasn't until months later that she brought it up.

After Holly left for Irvine, Stephanie asked Gary to call Grundland again, this time so that she could go and see him herself. "Tell me about bulimia. Did I cause it?" Stephanie asked at their first session in September, ready to blame herself but pleading with Grundland, obliquely, to help her understand her role.

"Help me help my daughter," Stephanie begged him at their second two-hour session several weeks later. Correctly sensing that she was also saying, "Help me with myself," Grundland began to draw Stephanie out about her own background. When she described her childhood as being just fine, he said, "I think there's more. Something you're repressing." At the next session she told him about Walt Nye, the drinking, the rejection. As the discussion began to focus on her own life, Stephanie realized that she was stumbling into an unfamiliar and frightening place — herself. She wanted to explore further and wished Grundland wasn't also seeing Gary professionally. But she didn't want to stop. She had become interested "to see what makes me tick."

On September 5, Holly had her first meeting with Marche Isabella. As their discussion ranged over a number of issues, she asked Holly if she had ever been sexually abused. "I'm not sure," Holly recalls saying, as Marche also told her that most of her patients had some type of abuse. She reported to Steph that she liked Isabella and that they were exploring the family dynamics. What she did not tell her mother at first was that Stephanie herself was the subject of discussion. Holly brought up her feelings of resentment about her mother's slimness, her obsession with clothes. Marche said that when a parent was too concerned about her appearance, a daughter might model herself on that body image; she thought this was a problem for Holly.

Gary came under scrutiny, too. Holly told Marche that her father gave her indirect "fat" messages if she ordered dessert in a restaurant with a look that said, "Should you really be having that?" He had also tried to bribe her to diet with tennis rackets and trips. As Holly described her father's controlling nature, Isabella violated the rules of good therapy by sharing her personal history with her patient. She told Holly that she'd also been raised by an Italian father. She too had been bulimic. She understood.

Holly's bulimia was getting worse, though, in spite of therapy. As Holly recalls, "The weeks varied. Sometimes I could . . . make it through a whole week and be good, and other times I would have three days and not be good." Nervous about having to give a fifteen-minute presentation in French in front of her class, she binged and purged the day before. Isabella sent Holly to an endocrinologist to check her metabolism; he did not prescribe Prozac, the drug Holly says Dr. Grundland had mentioned to her the previous summer. Holly was as resistant to medication as her mother and grandmother; she wanted to feel in control of her emotions.

Isabella suggested she join the therapy group she ran, a group of roughly a dozen women from eighteen to forty. All had eating disorders, and some had been sexually abused as well. "Why not just go and give it a try?" she urged. Holly joined.

Stephanie didn't pry. This was Holly's private business. But Holly began to tell her mother, over the phone, some of the issues that were coming up in her sessions with Marche Isabella. She had thought of suicide, she said, and Stephanie's appearance was an issue. Stephanie shook, hardly hearing, as the complaints spilled out: the shopping, the clothes, the makeup, always weighing herself as a measure of self-worth. If Stephanie was causing something, she wanted to know, to get to the bottom of it and get Holly better. But it pained her to hear things she wasn't proud of.

Stephanie flew south around Thanksgiving, beckoned by Holly to join her and Isabella to discuss Holly's issues; she returned to Napa weeping, needing the consolation of Gary's hugs. Holly had confronted her mother: "I'm getting messages from you that I don't understand . . . Why would you hang a picture in the bathroom of a model that I should look like?" Why was she so preoccupied with dress and appearance? Why did she spend so much money on clothes? Stephanie reeled as the barrage went on. Why had she dressed Kelli and Holly in identical outfits? Why did she make comments about Holly's personality? Her parents, Holly felt, wanted her to get a new personality, to be more of an extrovert. "You and my father both want me to be something different than I am," she charged. "No, Holly, no, that's not the case," Stephanie responded, reassuring her daughter as she had throughout her life. "I think you look terrific." But Holly railed back, "*I can't be you.*"

Stephanie was overcome with guilt. Searching for explanations for her behavior, for her obsession with appearance, she volunteered to Holly that maybe it was her own lack of self-confidence — an insecurity that might be connected to her stepfather's drinking. Holly was amazed by her mother's confession. To her, her mother looked like Linda Evans, the glamorous TV star of *Dynasty.* She had never known, until then, that her mother had a problem with self-confidence.

When Holly came home for Christmas, Betty observed Gary giving her a power hug. "He held her so tight, so long," she remembers, "that Holly's face was agonized. It was uncomfortable, and I said, 'Hey, ease up.'" On Christmas morning, there was the usual pile of presents under the tree. Betty and Garnet were there as the girls came down, as always, in their nightgowns. During that vacation, there had been a moment when Holly had sat frozen in place as she and her father were in the living room. Her father had stared at her in a way that disturbed her — in a way, she thought, that was more how he should be looking at her mother, in a *sexual* way. She kept the event to herself when she joined her mother and Betty for a few days in Palm Springs before she returned to school.

It was in the car on the way to Palm Springs, with her mother driving, that Holly had her first flashback. It was the middle of the day, she recalls, and "it is like a freeze frame . . . The first ones were very quick, a couple of seconds." The image was of her father's hand on her stomach. "I am lying down . . . I see his hand on my stomach or toward my chest, and it's his right hand and the thumb is spread apart . . . from the other fingers. . . . It's down . . . I only see my stomach and the hand and there's no nightgown in between," she would describe later. There was no context — no room, no other people. She could not see her father's head. The little girl she saw was five, six . . . maybe eight. She could tell by her hair and how she looked that it was a very young Holly at Diamond Bar. She was shaken. But she remained silent.

Holly had had the same experience thousands of young women, and some men, were having across America: flashbacks, visual images — memories, they would insist and believe — of events from their past. With that two- or three-second experience, Holly joined an epidemic of women who, beginning in the late 1980s, would shake the nation with their disturbing reports of incest memories recovered, whole and intact, from decades of total repression. These sensational memories would often start modestly, as had Holly's, then grow more lurid, often evolving into monstrous acts that stretched beyond the possible or credible. From memories of a father's errant finger to the baby-killing atrocities of satanic cults and alien abductions, they would rampage through the psychotherapy community and the courts and onto the daytime TV talk shows. Striking unprepared parents with the shock of an earthquake, the young women made their accusations public, they claimed, as a way of healing their emotional wounds and as a voice for abused children who could not speak for themselves. Believing their memories, increasing numbers sued their parents.

The terms "flashbacks" and "memories" were interchangeable. Holly believed her flashbacks *were* memories. But while to Holly these memories were unique and personal, she described them with a "survivor" vocabulary that would become clichéd and repetitive as best sellers like *The Courage to Heal*, the seminal book by Ellen Bass and Laura Davis, spread the dogma and the language of the sexual abuse survivor movement. In early 1990, however, critical thinking was not being applied. "They are *my* memories," she would say possessively.

Holly described the experience many times: "It is a memory of an earlier event." It was a visual image, and once she had seen it, she could conjure it up again, intact. "I can see the flashback when I choose to as it was when I first saw it, so it's something that stays with me." Being able to "resee" her memory made it more believable to Holly. Memory scientists knew that "rehearsing" a memory reinforced and strengthened it, but they were also learning that rehearsal gave more conviction, a greater sense of reality, to even *a distorted or imagined memory*. This new research seldom reached a family therapist, however. "The only difference I can make from a memory is that I remember . . . that it was longer ago than something that happened yesterday," said Holly, "and I don't always see as much movement as I would with a memory of me going to the store yesterday and what I thought and what I did. It is more like a freeze frame of something I remember." She did not remember any events that led up to, or followed, the freeze frame.

At first she did not tell her mother or Betty or even Marche Isabella, for she feared that she wouldn't be believed or would be thought crazy. By mid-January she found the courage to tell Isabella about her father's "sexual" look at Christmas. Over the next few weeks the flashbacks began to pop, like light bulbs being switched on.

She was lying in bed in the apartment she'd moved to in Irvine when the second flashback came: "I am in my room in Diamond Bar," in her bunk bed. "There is a sheet up over me. My father is sitting by the side of the bed. I remember the pink lamp on the light in my room. His hand is rubbing my upper thigh on the inside and I was feeling frozen and I couldn't move." She could see her own face and her hair "halfway pulled up . . . some hair in a half ponytail." Holly could see her father's face.

She was in bed again when the third flashback occurred: "I am in my bed in Diamond Bar in my room. It is nighttime. I'm lying down. My face is scared. I'm pushing my father away and his head is somewhere between my legs, and my face is scared and wants him away . . . I remember looking at the top of the bunk bed. That's all that I can remember."

As the flashbacks came, Holly's bulimia continued to worsen; the binging was out of control. In January she increased her sessions with Isabella from once to three or four times a week, trying to manage the eating, trying to handle the flashbacks, so that she could concentrate on her schoolwork and go on with everyday life. She wished she could quit therapy, to get away from the memories, but knew she needed help. She went, dutifully, to a psychiatrist in Isabella's building for a psychological test, but she felt uncomfortable and left before medication could be discussed. It would be suggested, during the trial, that she left because the doctor reminded her of her father.

She went diligently to group therapy. In the waiting room before group one day, one of the women told Holly that she had been given sodium amytal, a hypnotic sedative popularly thought to be a truth serum. She had taken it to uncover memories and the questions asked by her therapist had revealed sexual abuse. Holly was intrigued. She wanted her flashbacks to stop; she wanted to prove her memories wrong. If sodium amytal could help, she would take it. She discussed the drug with Isabella. Yes, it could help uncover hidden memories, but she felt that Holly didn't need it now. "Your memories are com-

ing. You'll remember when you're ready to remember." Holly let it go
for the time being.

The second time Stephanie was called south to meet with Holly and
Isabella, in February, Holly revealed more of the memories she was
having. She told her mother about the look from her father that had
made her uncomfortable at Christmas, a look Isabella had labeled
"emotional incest." It was a term she later admitted making up. However, it was already the title of a book in the proliferating sex abuse
literature being avidly consumed by young women like Holly, who
had read *The Courage to Heal*. It encouraged them to think about
sex abuse as the source of even the vaguest and most general symptoms — and to trust their memories. Holly told her mother that she
had remembered Gary's rubbing her leg, and she showed Stephanie where — about at the knee. This hardly seemed like a sexual
touch to Stephanie, who "thought there was nothing to be real upset
with at that point." Holly remained silent about the more graphic
flashbacks.

But she told her mother something she had never forgotten about
Kathy. The high school girl had put Holly on the bed, got on top of
her, and pumped up and down in imitation of intercourse, playing
"mother and father." Kathy's name had crossed Stephanie's mind late
the previous summer. Hearing this story, she was appalled and punished herself with thoughts: "God, what trauma had this been for my
child? Where was I? I watched them so closely. I screened sitters so
carefully. Kathy was a next-door *neighbor!* How could I not have
known?"

She flew home, weeping with worry and a sense of failure, again to
be consoled by Gary. He made no comment, she says, when she told
him about Kathy. It was nearly six months since she first mentioned
her fears of molestation, and he was still passive. How could a father
not care, not want to get involved?

Holly's flashbacks continued. One morning, standing at the bathroom sink, she saw herself struggling with her father as he held her
arms up. In another fragment, she was walking into her father's bedroom. In another she was lying down with her father's hand over her
mouth. She couldn't see his face but explained that "I knew my father's hand." She was in bed again in her apartment when she saw, for
several seconds, a picture of her father, naked, holding Prince, the

family dog from Holly's earliest memories. Holly would later describe this image in detail: "I'm in my parents' bedroom . . . It is daytime. My father is standing in front of the mirror. I can see the back of him and he has no clothes on. He's holding the dog by the two front paws up against, toward, the front of him. There is a dresser in front of him and a mirror, and there's a light from outside." She couldn't see if her father was having sex with the dog. In a flashback a few days later, she lay on her parents' bed as her father held Prince and the dog's penis moved toward her.

Another time "I'm in my bedroom in Diamond Bar. I can see the top of the bunk bed. My father is on top of me. I see his back and he doesn't have any clothes on, and he's sliding over me and his shoulder . . . I, I feel his shoulder, and I want him to go away." It was now clear to her that her father had molested her.

Holly feared that from some buried midden in her mind she was recovering fragments of real events. Glued together, they forced her to rewrite the story of her life. If they were true, her childhood would be a lie. This was not terrain she wanted to explore. Pray God let these images stay buried and not be real! She must be going crazy. Let her be crazy.

In their phone calls, Holly was giving her mother more glimpses of what she was remembering. At this point she had had six flashbacks, increasingly sexual and specific. She finally came out with the words her mother had been dreading: Holly *knew* she had been sexually molested. She said she had had a flashback of her father's body on top of her. She had not yet reported penetration, but . . . Sick at the words, at the image, Stephanie called her mother in despair. Neither could accept it. "It *couldn't be*," Stephanie said, weeping. Betty agreed. "No, no, it *couldn't be. It couldn't have happened.*" Yet Holly would never lie. As Betty thought about it over the next few days, she began to accept that it could have happened. Struggling past shock and denial, Stephanie came to the same terrible conclusion. It *could* be Gary.

The memories were still coming. Stephanie dreaded the call that would show Gary in the act of raping Holly. In Napa Valley, winter was putting on its most colorful show of the year: a coat as green as Ireland dressed the hills. Flowering plum trees exploded overnight into blossoming balls of pink popcorn along roads and driveways. In the vineyards, blazing yellow mustard cloaked the stark, pruned vines that would soon push the first tender shoots of the 1990 vintage of Napa's famous wine. In the shadows of the glassy, high-tech corporate megaliths of Orange County in Southern California, Holly Ramona's flashbacks would soon culminate in an image of incestuous rape, and she would make the call that would shrink Stephanie's sense of beauty to a nub and narrow life to a black hole — that would destroy a family's trust.

In late February, as Holly drove from school to Newport Beach, the freeze frame came. It was daytime in her parents' bedroom. "I was lying down. I see the reflection of the light off the sheets, a lot of white light. My knees are up and spread apart. My father's penis is in my vagina and I can see his face and his chest, and his arms are up past my shoulders, and I remember his eyes were kind of glazed."

Holly had known for weeks that it was her father. She had now seen him naked. They had been such a modest family; she had never seen Gary get out of a shower or drop his towel as he dressed, never seen him change into his bathing suit. A nineteen-year-old college girl, she had had no boyfriend, no sexual encounters — she had no brothers. Until her flashbacks, she had never seen male genitals, except perhaps in paintings. She had only seen her father undressed in her memories. Now she had felt his penis inside her.

Holly felt a need to confront her father, to ask him to take responsibility for his acts, to apologize and get psychiatric help. Confrontation was being encouraged in the self-help books as well as by therapists. Marche Isabella, too, suggested it would help heal her wounds. But the damage it could do to the family began to haunt Holly. First, she must confirm her memories, so she was determined to have sodium amytal. She needed to tell her mother about her plans, reassure her that the sodium amytal was "for me to feel more comfortable with my memories so I could later confront my father," and hope she would understand and support her.

The dreaded phone call came from Holly on a Sunday evening in late February of 1990. Stephanie took the call in her bedroom. Holly was sobbing as she tried to speak.

"Mom, I have something to tell you. Will you still be my mom? Will you love me? Will you believe me?"

"Of course, Holly, yes, but what? *Tell* me."

"Mom, I'm sorry, I'm sorry . . ."

Stephanie couldn't stand it. "Holly, just spit it *out!*" she snapped.

"I had another flashback. He put his you-know-what inside me."

"Where was *I*, Holly?" her mother demanded, accusing herself.

"I don't know, Mom."

When Stephanie called her mother, sobbing out of control, and said, "It's Gary," Betty simply said, "I know."

Stephanie Ramona's daughter had just told her that her husband, the man she had lived with for twenty-five years — the man she still slept with — had committed the most terrible crime against a child, an act for which inmates will kill a fellow prisoner. He had breached a taboo that in this culture ranked with cannibalism, even though the violation of the taboo was being revealed as epidemic.

Stephanie did not think of asking Gary if it was true. She did not ask Holly. She had no need to. Why would Holly lie? She had everything to lose. "I would have loved for Holly to be crazy. I would have given my eyeteeth for it not to be true . . . Because to believe my daughter means that I, as a mother, have failed." Stephanie agonized, thinking, "I wasn't there to protect my children." But she believed everything Holly said. "I know my daughter. She wouldn't lie . . ."

Suddenly dozens of pieces, small events Stephanie had put in the back of her mind over the years, fit. "It did make sense. It was like putting together a puzzle and . . . the pieces fit." Holly's story of Gary's guilt would explain Holly — the bulimia, depression, stunted social development, chronic childhood ailments, fear of vaginal exams. The pulling back from her father. With that call, Gary died in her mind. She knew that she would be forced to take the action that would bring her marriage and her family to an end.

Stephanie's next thought was: "Where am I going to hide Shawna?" her youngest daughter. Kelli would be leaving for college soon, but Shawna was only twelve. Stephanie had never seen Gary touch the kids. But if he had been capable of this . . . She would never leave Shawna alone with him again.

She then thought about survival, for she would have to leave Gary. She called her neighbor Karen Maestas to come over; she had to start hiding some things at Karen's. While she waited, she tucked her feet under her on the sofa and looked out the window in the family room. She appeared to be a fine-boned forty-four-year-old in sleek blue jeans and flawless makeup, a petite beauty whose smoothly sculptured blond mane of hair was a symbol of the chic, meticulous dress and grooming that were her signature. But inside she was in turmoil, thinking that it was good-bye to everything. It was good-bye to somebody she had looked up to almost as a father, and good-bye to a way of life beyond her dreams: Europe, Tokyo, New York — the world. Anything the girls needed or wanted — educations, cars. The glamour and excitement of winery events, where she could be Cinder-ella at the ball, feted by the most famous chefs in the world. The half-million-dollar salary from the Robert Mondavi Winery. The house that was rising in the hills.

"But the hardest is giving up the dreams," she thought mournfully. "Not just for myself, but the dreams I had for my children . . . To get their educations. Grow up to be happy . . . trusting individuals. Get married, have children." Now, what would their lives be? This man had stolen their childhood, their future.

On March 1, Stephanie talked with Dr. Barry Grundland. She must tell the girls immediately, he advised, or Child Protective Services might think she was in collusion with Gary. She picked Kelli and Shawna up at school, took them home, and forced herself to explain the situation to them. "Holly has said that your father . . . that your father had sex with her." There was no reaction, not even a shocked look on other faces. They didn't want to hear any more. Stephanie hated asking the next question: "Have either of you had memories? . . . Has your dad ever done anything to you?" They both said no. Grundland arranged for Stephanie to meet with a divorce attorney, Vic Fershko, in Napa at five-thirty that same day. The divorce was set in motion.

In Irvine, Marche Isabella had suggested that Holly confront her fa-ther. Holly had seized on the idea and made it her goal. If she was to heal, her father would have to "own" the damage he had done. But she also knew that with every new memory, the stakes got higher for her family. They could be torn apart. She had to make absolutely certain that her memories were accurate and true before she con-fronted her father. Isabella still resisted the sodium amytal, but if Holly was determined to take it, she felt they should do the interview before the confrontation.

"Mom, this is *my* issue to confront him on," Holly insisted to her mother by phone, claiming the right to be the one to face her father. Stephanie was angry. It might be Holly's issue, but it was *her* husband, *her* daughter, *her* divorce, and she wanted to confront Gary. "I'm going to divorce him," she said. Holly wasn't surprised. Her mother had always been telling the girls, "We're leaving," sticking them in the car and driving as far as the next town, then having a change of heart. This time, though, Holly believed her.

Gary Ramona holds his firstborn, Holly, outside their home in Southern California a few months after her birth on August 16, 1970. *(Courtesy Gary Ramona)*

Gary Ramona and his wife, Stephanie, are all smiles as his career soars with the young Napa Valley winery he joined in 1971. *(Courtesy Gary Ramona)*

A charming child, Holly already suffers from small but chronic health problems later blamed on sexual abuse. *(Courtesy Gary Ramona)*

A cheerleader at St. Helena High, Holly is hiding weight worries that will develop into bulimia. *(Courtesy Gary Ramona)*

The Ramonas celebrate the European launch of Opus One in 1988 at Château Mouton Rothschild, Robert Mondavi's French partner in the joint wine venture. Gary heads Mondavi's global sales and marketing. *(Courtesy Gary Ramona)*

A Napa Valley Christmas. Grandmothers Betty Nye
(LEFT) and Garnet Ramona watch the girls open gifts.
(Courtesy Gary Ramona)

Holly's comfort in petting the family dog later casts doubt on her recovered memory of bestiality. *(Courtesy Gary Ramona)*

Gary would show these family videos to the trial jury as evidence that Holly led a normal, happy childhood. *(Ramona family videos)*

The infant Holly reaches for her father.

Holly, five years old, in Hawaii.

With Grandmother Ramona.

Holly's pointed finger later charged Gary with rape.

New York, New York!

Senior prom.

This frame from a home video catches the sad truth: food has become an enemy for Holly, here at her high school graduation poolside party. *(Ramona family video)*

For defense attorney Bruce Miroglio, the dinner table is the center of family life. Here baby Celia "does her day" while her father and siblings listen. *(Christie Johnston)*

"Mom, *please* don't file until after the sodium amytal interview and until I'm able to confront my father," Holly pleaded. "He raped *me,* not you."

Upset about Holly's wanting to take a drug, Stephanie turned to Barry Grundland for reassurance while Holly, upset at her mother, called Marche Isabella.

"Mom wants to tell my father. *I* want to tell my father. Please call my mom."

Isabella advised Stephanie, "Stevie, this is a tough situation. But Holly wants to talk to her father. She's adamant. It's *hers!*"

"Let Holly make the decision," cautioned Grundland.

Stephanie wasn't really angry at Holly. It was not Holly but Gary who had stripped her of her voice over the years. She had let him. Stephanie gave in to her daughter.

With the issue of incest now inescapable, the need to verify the rape had grown urgent, Isabella felt. Stephanie was becoming explosive. "This family is ready to blow up," Isabella told Grundland as they discussed the potential violence of the confrontation. Grundland recalled another family confrontation in Napa that had ended in a murder.

Stephanie had secretly gotten hold of Holly's childhood medical records; Holly's urinary tract infections could have been caused by intercourse. Isabella felt that Holly should now have an internal exam, her first, as a way to try to corroborate her memories. On March 1, a gynecologist, Dr. Stephanie McClellan, examined the convulsively sobbing young woman. Holly Ramona's fear of the pelvic exam was the most violent she had ever seen in the many thousands of exams she had given. It was the hymen she wanted to check for traces of sexual abuse. Using a small speculum, she opened the vaginal cavity very gently. The hymen in a child or virgin is normally a tightly puckered ring at the vaginal opening. It looks a little like the top of a drawstring purse, pulled tight, with the ruffling almost closing the opening to the vagina. With intercourse and childbirth, the neat puckers stretch, becoming flaccid and uneven. Holly's, in one spot at the bottom, had lost its tight ruffling and was stretched — a minor posterior separation.

It was not conclusive. The separation could have been caused by the repeated penetration of a penis. But it could also have another, more innocent cause: falling on the bar of a bicycle or horseback riding. Tampax. Masturbation. Hymens are not all built the same. She was twelve years too late to know if she'd been raped. The labial region is so forgiving; rips and tears repair themselves and vanish swiftly, often leaving no trace of violence. Reflecting on Holly's panic, Dr. McClellan thought, "I don't know if she's been sexually abused. But something awful has happened to this girl. Her reaction is not healthy."

The same day, Isabella asked Holly to draw a picture of the snake she feared would enter her vagina at night, the snake that would still be there even when she turned and moved and closed her legs — a recurring terror she had had since junior high. Holly drew a snake's head that was impossible not to interpret as an erect male phallus. Isabella scribbled notes as Holly described a horrifying scene: "Flash of sheet flying, I'm fighting, it's dark, someone is holding my arms. . . . I think I can see his face, it's fuzzy, feel constrained, something white . . . stripes, summer night . . ." Isabella interspersed her own observations with Holly's words. ". . . knew it was her father, fear of what he was going to do, nightgown up toward his [sic] neck, don't like his skin touching my skin, I don't like his smell or aftershave, feel his body heat . . . his hands on the mattress behind her shoulders . . ." It was the story of a small girl experiencing the most terrible violence. To Isabella, Holly's words, her drawing, cried incest and rape.

That afternoon, with the results of the internal exam and Holly's sketch in hand, Isabella set up an emergency conference call with Grundland and Stephanie in Napa. Isabella had resisted the sodium amytal interview, but no longer. She and Holly were now determined to carry it out for final confirmation, "to ascertain the truth of the matter," Stephanie would later state in a court document. Both wanted to schedule the sodium amytal as soon as possible, then proceed immediately with the confrontation.

Isabella talked to Dr. Richard Rose, a psychiatrist who rented space in her office, to discuss the drug and the confrontation. "Holly wants to talk to her father, and I want to verify this is completely accurate," she said. Rose urged that the confrontation take place in his hospital, Western Medical Center, where the staff and guards would guarantee safety. He agreed, too, that if Holly was an appropriate candidate, he would conduct the sodium amytal interview himself.

Holly leaped at the plan. Compliant, obedient, she had hidden her opinions and her feelings all her life. Quiet and studious, she had tried to meet her parents' expectations. But she had been uncomfortable with her father as long as she could remember. They had never really talked, and she had much more than rape to tell him. She was ready.

She called her father's secretary, Marcia Santos, and said she wanted her father to come down to Orange County to meet with her and her therapist. "It's very important and I need to speak to him." The meeting would be within the week.

"Gary, Holly called and wants you to come down to meet with her next week," Marcia reported when he got back to the office. He had been up at the house that March morning, making plans for the travertine slabs that would soon spread over the floor like the smoothly raked sands of Southern California beaches.

"Great! Clear my calendar, check the time and place, and I'll be there," he told her, as he always had for important events with the girls. Concerts, graduations, birthdays — whatever. He was thrilled to get the call. Stephanie had been called down several times to talk about Holly's eating problems, and had come back distraught. The last time she was upset by Holly's report that a teenage neighbor might have molested her years ago. Stephanie was hurting and crying, and he'd held her in his arms and tried to console her. "That's Holly's problem, not yours, Steph. You've been a fine mother." This was Stephanie's first mention of molestation, Gary claims. He felt, If Kathy did this years ago, what could you do about it? If you were able to find her, what would you charge her with? Gary did not believe Holly had been more seriously sexually molested, by anyone. But then Stephanie had closed up and said, "I'm not really supposed to talk much about it." If she wanted to talk about it, he was there. All she had to do was ask.

Gary was frustrated at being out of the loop, as he had been ever since Steph had discovered Holly's bulimia. "Don't talk to Holly about her bulimia, Gary," Barry Grundland had said. "It would just put more pressure on her." That made some sense to Gary, and he agreed. Yet if family dynamics were part of the picture, as Grundland had indicated, how could they cut him out? He had always struggled with feeling excluded from Betty, Steph, and the girls. Now he was being excluded from his daughter's illness. "You'll have your time one day," Stephanie kept assuring him. He tried hard to comply.

But he was feeling increasing anxiety. He had learned enough about depression and bulimia to know they were dangerous. They could damage your health and even lead to death. There was also the specter of suicide. Gary hadn't seen Holly since Christmas. The last few weeks, he'd noticed — and mentioned to Steph — that Holly's calls home had virtually stopped. She usually called every day or so, and he got a chance to say hi. It wasn't Gary's nature to shut up and wait, especially with his daughter at stake. If there was a problem, his salesman's instinct was to make the call and keep making it. He loved Holly; he loved all three girls dearly. There was nothing he wouldn't do for them, and it was driving him crazy. Now Holly had called him.

Could she bear the waiting, Stephanie wondered. The sodium amytal interview was tentatively scheduled for the week of March 12, pending Rose's return from vacation to evaluate Holly; she hoped to confront her father the day after the interview. Until then, Stephanie had to endure a charade of normalcy. For nearly two more weeks she had to keep making decisions about the house, keep going up the hill with Gary.

Stephanie watched him warily as they climbed into the pickup truck for a trip to the house. The road was steep and full of serpentine twists; the cliffs that fell away on the downhill side had always scared her. Still a rough construction road, it had turned to slippery gumbo in the late winter rains, and the truck kept getting stuck. "Gary, this makes me really nervous," said Stephanie, trying to sound nonchalant so that he couldn't read her real thoughts. He stopped the truck, looked at her, and said, "So get out." She knew he was trying to intimidate her. Bleating back in her "silly me" voice, she said, "No, no. But just be careful, Gary." They drove on, and as they got to the house site at the top, Gary drove right to the edge of the cliff. As Stephanie climbed out into the mud, she glanced over at the truck; it seemed to be sliding toward the edge of the cliff. Her first thought was, "Ah, this would be wonderful. He'll go off the cliff." She had never been a hater and could hardly believe she was having these thoughts. She was the wimp of the world. What had this horror reduced her to? But then she reacted and yelled, "Get out of there, Gary, you're going off the cliff!" He'll think I care about him, she feared, but also racing through her mind was, "Oh, my God, if he goes off they're going to think I murdered him."

As a workman came up to help free the truck from the mud, Stephanie passed through the walls of the time warp in which she now lived and stepped onto the unfinished floors of the most beautiful house she had ever seen. Like a sleepwalker, she made decisions with Gary on the flooring and the color of the stucco. None of it mattered; just a few days from now, the house would become an empty shell.

On the way down the mountain the skidding was even worse. When Stephanie begged Gary to be careful, he ordered her, "Walk!" and opened the door, daring her. Her stubbornness — the native stubbornness that had shown itself mostly, in the past, as passive resistance — asserted itself. "Fine, I'll get out," she said as she climbed out and stalked off, trying to maintain her straight-backed defiance in the mud. Gary pulled the truck over behind a tree and just watched her, then started driving toward her. As he got fairly close, he revved up the motor as if he were going to run her down. "That's Gary. Being funny. Trying to scare me. He knows he can laugh me out of anything." But she could see his face, and he wasn't laughing. It wasn't that kind of joke. His face had a look that scared her. "He's testing me to see if I know. If I even flinch, he'll know I know," she thought, her heart pounding. She whirled around and planted her feet apart firmly in the mud, stuck her fists on her hips, and dared him. "He won't kill me. Gary's too smart for that. But I don't know what he's capable of." As he continued to move toward her, she planned her strategy: "If he comes too close I'll roll over the edge." But she didn't flinch. She had tried to avoid his eyes all the way up so that he couldn't pick up anything. Now she looked straight at him through the windshield, her eyes locked on his. For one of the first times in her life with Gary, she stood and held her ground.

Much of her hope for her marriage lay in this house. At first it had seemed too big, too isolated. She loved a flat, safe cul-de-sac. But it had grown to be the symbol of maybe really sharing their lives, of finally being the perfect couple everybody thought they were. It had been the symbol of a new strength to stand up, positively, to the power of the winery and the Mondavis in their life, to share Gary with his other family on her terms. She had planned to go on entertaining for Gary here. Even sex, she had been sure, would get better here. She loved this land, and she knew she would never see it, or the house, again.

"You're going to have to live with your father for a week or more. Can you do it?" Stephanie asked Kelli and Shawna separately or together — she can't recall. How could you ask children to live a lie like this? But they both said yes. Stephanie also told them that she was going to file for divorce.

No matter what Holly learned from the sodium amytal, it wouldn't affect Stephanie's decision. "I was divorced the day my daughter told me." It was over. He was no longer the Gary she thought she had known; that person had died in her mind. She had had no serious plans to leave Gary. But it was something that had been rumbling in the distance, like thunder on the horizon. With the disturbing reports from Holly these past weeks, she could feel the storm moving toward her. Holly's call had forced her to come to a decision about a marriage and, perhaps, a life she had never quite been able to confront.

To protect Shawna, she felt, she must get custody. But Gary might try to take her, her attorney warned. Well, then, she would have to be ready to leave the country and take Shawna and Kelli with her. She began secret preparations to escape. She went to K mart and bought three suitcases. They had plenty of luggage in the house, but if Gary noticed any missing, he'd know something was up. He was watching her, she felt. She found the passports — she knew where Gary kept them. She grabbed clothes from closets, packed the suitcases, and stored them at Karen's. She hunted for personal papers and assembled the money she would need to get out of the country. Her aunt Eva gave her $10,000; her mother flew up to give it to her in cash. Her friends raised $5,000. She put the money in an account she opened in her own name at the Bank of America.

What if Gary tried to kidnap Shawna before she could get her out of Napa? Hunting for a safe haven, she ran into a woman downtown she scarcely knew — someone Gary would never find — and arranged to hide Shawna there if Stephanie suspected he might do something dangerous.

It was at night that she confronted her failures as a mother and faced her guilt. She would lie awake wondering, dredging and sifting the past for clues. "Maybe I missed something with Holly. Why didn't I pick it up? What was wrong with me?" Sworn to secrecy by Holly, she crawled into bed at night with the man she believed had molested her oldest daughter — and who might have molested her younger daughters as well. She had always wanted more of him than he had given her. He was not a monster, however; she had seen his good sides. She had been powerfully attracted to Gary since the first day she saw him on the Mt. SAC campus in San Gabriel Valley, when she was eighteen. She wept as she thought of the smile that could still make her melt. Oh, he was Mr. Charm, and she realized there was a side of him she still loved.

Then she'd see the image of a terrified little girl, flailing, her father's hand clamped over her mouth as he closed in to rape her. She would feel overpowering rage, hate so violent and visceral that she couldn't believe herself capable of it, this woman who had been meek and forgiving all these years. She had known he was capable of lies, of controlling, of violence: he had struck her early in their marriage. She had seen him overtaken by anger and strange, irrational behavior. Perhaps he had always been sort of a Jekyll and Hyde. But in Stephanie's mind he was now no better than a murderer! He had murdered their lives, and she wanted him jailed. She would put him in jail. She didn't believe she would ever trust a man again.

"Mom, how long do we have to play this charade?" Kelli demanded one night. The girls felt such conflict. Shawna still loved her father, but she wanted him excluded from the family, she told her mother as she burst into tears. Kelli had started taking Shawna out for dinner every night and coming home late to ease the strain of sharing the house with Gary. Stephanie pleaded to Marche Isabella by phone, "I can't stand it any longer, goddamn it. My kids can't stand it. I've got to get out of this. *Get me out of this house!*"

The confrontation was set, finally, for March 15 — just a few more days. Holly called her father's secretary again and gave her the date. Holly knew he would be there.

For Gary, Thursday, March 15, was perfect. He was already scheduled to fly down on Wednesday for an event at the new wine and food center in Costa Mesa, just minutes away from the meeting with Holly the next morning. It would eliminate the chance of getting delayed by fog or traffic if he tried to fly in that morning. Holly and Steph had got a little upset the times his work had made him late for things. He would not let that happen this time.

5

Confrontation

The night before Gary left for Orange County, Stephanie lay in bed with him, pretending to be asleep. There was an old movie on TV about a rape case, an innocent man accused. She could hardly stand the irony. She didn't dare move, afraid Gary would hear her swallow. At the end of the movie, the voiceover urged viewers to make a phone call — for information about rape — and gave the number. Gary picked up the phone and she thought, "Oh, my God, he's calling there." But he was just picking up his messages from the winery.

"So he knows," Stephanie thought as Gary left the house the next morning, the day before his meeting with Holly. They looked at each other, and he gave her a kiss. Gary had stopped kissing Stephanie when they got married. Even if he was leaving for Europe, he didn't kiss her. This was not a kiss to go down to Southern California and be back in two days. It was something only a wife would know. It was good-bye. Stephanie wanted to say so many things. She wanted to know why, not if. She wanted to talk to her husband. But she had promised Holly. "I never got to say good-bye."

On Monday, March 12, Holly was admitted to Western Medical Center to be evaluated by Rose before the sodium amytal interview was scheduled. The young woman was more seriously ill than any of her family, or even Holly herself, fully understood. She was suffering from major depression; her bulimia had worsened, with bingeing and forced vomiting alternating with sieges of obsessive exercising; and her weight was fluctuating wildly. Like her father, she could cover her feelings with a dazzling smile. But she was weepy, scarcely able to concentrate, and had suicidal thoughts. After about forty minutes with her, Rose declared her an appropriate candidate for a sodium amytal interview. He wasn't sure that it would be of any value in confirming memories so many years after the events, he told Holly. The results could be very uncertain and cloudy. But "her mood was one of desperation," and he would do it, he said, if she was determined to proceed.

On March 14, Holly lay in her hospital room in shorts and a T-shirt while her grandmother Betty, who lived nearby, sat in the waiting room. At 2:30 P.M., Rose injected Holly with 600 milligrams of sodium amytal at a rate of 100 milligrams per minute. She could feel herself becoming drowsy, losing awareness. As she reached the cusp of unconsciousness, the doctor began the interview: "Holly, try to recall the events you've been worried about, that you've been talking to me and Marche Isabella about. Try to remember events you're having trouble remembering." The same scenes she'd been describing to Isabella in therapy poured out freely. She spoke in the voice of a small child but with an adult command of words. There was no audiotape or video camera to record the session. They did not routinely use either.

One new incident emerged. Her father had raped her, Holly said, and afterward sat on her bed crying, pouring out his feelings as he never had before. He told her that he had had affairs with other women and that her grandmother Garnet Ramona had been raped by her brothers. The interview was over. The soporific overwhelmed Holly, and she fell deeply asleep.

Stephanie sat by the telephone in Napa, waiting for Isabella's call that it was over and that her daughter was all right. "It's finished. Holly's okay . . . It was rape," Stephanie heard when Isabella called late that afternoon.

Stephanie's close friend Jean Sawday immediately drove her the half hour south to Napa to catch the bus to the San Francisco airport. On the way, they stopped at Fershko's office for Stephanie to sign the divorce papers, to be served as soon as Gary returned. Jean then picked Karen up and they drove to Stephanie's house; they had keys and instructions to clear the house of everything Stephanie cared about — clothes, tapes — for she was afraid Gary might come back and destroy her things, lock her out — who knew? Jean and Karen stuffed everything into huge plastic garbage bags and — in daylight, watched by neighbors — loaded them into Jean's Jeep Cherokee.

A sweet elderly neighbor lady came out and asked, "Is anything wrong?"

"Well, yes," Jean replied as they drove off.

Stephanie was met by her mother at the Orange County airport. Her worst fear had been that she might run into Gary in Orange County, where he would also be spending the night. But she knew the terrible days of stress, of secrecy and deception would soon be over.

When Holly woke up the next morning, she was dizzy, and her arm felt too heavy to move. She was so tired she didn't want to get up, but the nurse urged her to walk around. She could only dimly remember any of the interview. The only words she remembered saying, over and over, were: "He put his you-know-what inside me," and Isabella's saying, "What is his you-know-what?" prodding until Holly said, "His penis."

After breakfast, as Isabella went over her notes with Holly, telling her what she'd said under the drug, Holly feared, as she had since her memories began, that she may have lied. Anxious, she asked Rose if this was possible. He was reassuring: "Usually you need to be trained to lie under sodium amytal, Holly, and given my experience and my analysis of you during the interview, you were not lying." She asked Isabella for reassurance. "You have to be trained to lie under it," she said, reflecting that over the painful months of unfolding memories, Holly had been consistent; she had never tripped herself up. The nurse who attended her before and after she was given the drug asked her outright, "Holly, are you lying?" She had said, "No, I'm not." For Holly, the interview had confirmed the worst.

Rose came by to make sure she was strong enough for the meeting with Gary. She still felt woozy, but she was able to move around. She had carried her breakfast tray back to the kitchen. What were her goals for the meeting? "I had hoped that my father would admit to what he has done, apologize and say, 'I need to get help, and I will get help,'" she would say later. In her eyes, what he had done would still be wrong. But she didn't hate him as much as she sometimes thought she should; she still had feelings for her dad. She might never want a relationship with him again, "but if he worked on what he needed to work on, it might lessen the chances . . . that it could happen to some-one else."

"Can you handle whatever happens at the meeting, Holly?" Rose asked her. "Yes," she said. He could see no reason for her not to go ahead with the confrontation.

About ten o'clock, Stephanie and Betty arrived at Western Medical Center. Betty would wait. Stephanie briefly visited her daughter, then joined Holly and Marche Isabella in the small meeting room where the confrontation would take place. Still dizzy, Holly was trying to focus on what she would say to her father. Taking control of events between them for the first time in her life, Holly was focused on what his reaction would be and on what she wanted to achieve. Stephanie sat in the next chair, holding Holly's teddy bear, and waited for Gary to walk in the door.

Gary faced the day of the meeting feeling optimistic. As he closed up the event at the new Costa Mesa center about ten-thirty Wednesday night, he knew it had gone well. This was the dream house he had built for his other family. Walking to the parking lot, he passed the small demonstration vineyard, the Japanese sand and rock garden, cascades of bougainvillea and a Bufano sculpture. The center was just half an hour's drive from the trailer park in Orange Grove where he grew up, but he had traveled many worlds away. On March 14, 1990, he thought he had it all.

Gary was on the road in a rented car by nine the next morning. He was to meet with Holly at eleven o'clock and wanted to check on the location first to be sure he wouldn't be late. He drove by Western Medical Center, a three-story, fairly modern-looking gray building, then found a hotel with a restaurant and had breakfast.

He made a few calls and glanced over the morning paper: reunification talks in Germany and Gorbachev promising more reform in Russia. Trouble in Orange County — oil spills on the beaches, Vietnamese gangs growing, the widening of I-5 causing congestion. Sneak preview for *Pretty Woman*. Beirut. Oliver North. An item in Today in History: On this day in 44 B.C., Julius Caesar was assassinated, betrayed by Brutus and Cassius and his nobles as he walked, unsuspecting, into the forum.

It was a perfect day, sunny and warm. Gary entered the medical center and waited in the high-ceilinged lobby for twenty, twenty-five minutes, before inquiring where he could find Marche Isabella's office. He was told that he should have entered at the back of the building.

He walked down a long corridor to a small reception area and waited again. Impatient, he paged Isabella. A door opened, and there walking toward him was the woman he'd been hearing about for six months, the gatekeeper to access to Holly. A slightly plump, pink-cheeked woman in her late thirties or early forties, with curly blond hair, she was not pretty but what you might call feminine and motherly looking — definitely not chic and trim like Steph.

She introduced herself, and as he said, "I'm Gary Ramona" and reached out his hand, she turned away and started down a hall to the left of the reception desk.

"How's Holly doing?" Gary asked, as they walked down another hall to the right.

"Holly's been in the hospital . . ."

Hospital! "What's she . . . ? I'm her parent. No one told me. I didn't know."

"Holly's fine. She wants to meet with you," Isabella said briskly, cutting off his questions.

She opened a door, peeked in, and closed it. She opened the next door, to a small, windowless room crowded with a sofa and chairs, and ushered Gary in to the shock of his life. There was Steph! She was sitting, dead serious, holding a teddy bear. What in hell? She hadn't said a word about being at the meeting when he kissed her good-bye in Napa the day before. Why hadn't she mentioned it? She could have flown down and stayed with him. Her hand was out, touching Holly's leg. Oh, my God — Holly. She was slumped on the sofa, one leg tucked under her, wearing a shapeless sweatshirt and bermudas; she looked dazed, spaced out, glassy-eyed. She stared right past her father as he patted her knee and said, "How are you doing? It's good to see you." She looked up, expressionless. As he sat down in the chair Isabella directed him to take, opposite Holly, his mind was desperately racing, trying to process what was going on.

Isabella seated herself in a chair almost in front of the door and said, "Gary, I think you ought to know that Holly's been in the hospital since Monday."

He got it. Suicide. His eyes flashed full of tears. *"Oh, my God, now my daughter's going to tell me she tried to commit suicide."* He had to compose himself. *"I can't do this to Holly . . . breaking down, and put more guilt on her."* He stood up and said, "I'm going to step into the corridor for just a minute."

"Sit down," Isabella snapped.

"You're not going anywhere, Gary. Sit down!" Steph ordered, hurling the teddy bear to the floor. "Don't do this to your daughter."

Do what? What was this? My daughter's been in the hospital since Monday, and no one's said a word to me. This poor kid tried to commit suicide. If he pushed the issue of stepping out of the room, it would just make it worse for Holly. Increase her guilt.

He sat down as Isabella turned to her and said, "Now, Holly, you wanted to tell your father something."

Holly, talking like a robot in a dead monotone, started reciting a list of hurts and grievances, a litany Gary had no idea of. "You are selfcentered . . . You only think about yourself and your job. . . . You haven't read anything about bulimia, have you?" There was no anger, no smile. Then she tore his heart out. *"You were never there when I needed you . . ."*

"No, no, Holly, that's not at all how it was," Gary objected silently as the list went on. "That doesn't mean that I wasn't there on frequent occasions because I was traveling . . . But we played tennis. We were in Indian Princesses. We went to McDonald's . . . to the ice cream parlor, the beach."

She paused.

"I don't understand, Holly. What are we talking about here?" he asked.

Then she came out and said it: *"You raped me."*

Gary gave an involuntary gasp, as if he had been socked in the stomach. "What? Holly, that's not true!" He looked at Isabella and demanded, "What the hell is going on here? I did not do this."

Isabella was prodding his daughter: "Now, Holly, tell your father about how, when he would come home at night in Diamond Bar . . ." Holly was silent. She seemed drugged and looked at Isabella in a puzzled way. So Isabella went on, to Gary: ". . . when you'd come home at night from work, you would go into her bedroom and you would put your hand on her thigh in a sexual way."

"What do you mean — 'a sexual way'? Where was Kelli? Where was Steph?"

"She was out playing tennis or getting her hair done."

"This is at *night?*" he burst out, disoriented in a world that had just turned upside down. "Nobody's *home?*"

Then Isabella said, "Holly, tell him about when he would take you into his bedroom at night and" — speaking to Gary again — ". . . you would lock the door and you'd put her on your bed. And you took her nightgown and put it up and you stuck your penis in her vagina."

"Yeah, and it hurt her so bad you had to put your hand over her mouth," Steph blurted out.

"Steph, I'm telling you, this is not true."

"And then, afterward, you sat on the side of your bed," said Isabella, "and you were concerned about your mother, that her two brothers had raped her."

He was overwhelmed. "I don't know what's going on, what the hell you people are talking about. But I'm telling you, this is not *true!*" Raping his daughter . . . when she was five? The girls slept in the same room. Slept in the same bunk bed, one on top of the other. "Where was Kelli?"

They didn't know. They didn't need to know. Descending on him like the Furies, Steph and Isabella told him, "We have proof."

"What proof? How could you have proof of something that didn't happen?"

They'd explained that they'd given Holly sodium amytal. "It's kind of like truth serum in the movies, and it can get to information that's hidden," Isabella told Gary. "You have to be trained to lie under it."

"I'll take it. I'll take it to prove to Holly I didn't do this. I want to take it," Gary choked out, his tears spilling helplessly.

The two women drove on relentlessly with their proof. They had doctors' records. "She had kidney and bladder infections. The only way you can get this infection is with outside skin contact."

"You're blaming me for my daughter's urinary tract infections?"

"We also have the gynecologist's report, and it shows she was raped . . . We know that Holly wasn't lying because she talked in baby talk."

"Are you telling me a five- and six-year-old is saying I stuck my penis in her vagina?" Gary challenged. Holly was silent.

As he struggled to grasp it, he gathered he had been accused of an act of rape that had emerged from this sodium amytal interview.

"How come I don't have any memory of any of this?" he demanded.

Isabella asked, "Have you ever drunk so much that you could never remember?"

Steph was primed. "What about when . . . we went over to this house, it was some business people, and . . . do you remember this?" she said.

"Sure I do," Gary said as he finished the story: "We had a nice dinner, there was wine and champagne. Afterward a fella got on the table, he was dancing, and he fell off. And you and I decided to leave, got into our car, and drove back to our place together." Steph looked at Isabella, shocked. If this was to have been her proof of his blank, blind drunkenness, it had backfired.

What about Holly's memory? If these terrible things really happened, he demanded, *how could Holly not remember until now?*

"Sodium amytal takes away resistance to repressed information . . . of incidents that, on a subconscious level, you have chosen *not* to remember because *the emotional pain is too great for you to deal with*," Marche stated with the supreme confidence of the prophet who holds the tablets of wisdom.

Stephanie had been somber at first, but he could see she was shifting to rage. Her body became stiff-legged and rigid the way it did when she was very angry. The two women began to demand a confession.

"It's really important to Holly. Don't think of yourself. Don't be self-centered." Confess, for Holly's sake.

They railed for confession not once, but five, six, seven times. Overwhelmed, tears pouring down his cheeks, he pleaded over and over, "I'm telling you . . . there's nothing to confess."

Holly collapsed and was helped from the room by two orderlies, standing outside the door. As Isabella left the room to attend to Holly, Stephanie said to Gary, "I want to talk to you." She appealed again and again for him to confess. "Get help, Gary," she pleaded.

"Steph, I didn't do it."

"I don't want you going home. You're not to go home. Go stay with your mother. You need to be with somebody."

"I'm not to go home?" Dismayed, uncomprehending, he struggled for words. "I'm going to have to go and get some clothes."

"Fine. Pick up some clothes. But you're not to go back to the house."

The meeting was over, said Isabella when she came back to the room. Gary stood accused of incest, banished from his home and his daughters, guilty without trial. "No one ever asked me one question. After twenty-five years of marriage, Stephanie never asked me, 'Gary, did you do it?' There wasn't one second where they even considered my innocence. Not one second." That's what he could not believe, not accept.

He had moved from the world he knew — one of success, family, the American Dream — into a world where he was out there on this point, all alone, and didn't want to live. A powerful image from his Ohio summers as a boy flooded his mind, an experience so strange and out of the ordinary that he never forgot it.

He was sitting on his uncle's porch at the lake; it was a dry and sunny day. Suddenly, as he watched, the sky started boiling and went black. Thunder and lightning moved toward him, and he could hear the rain approaching. It came right up to him, over him, and kept moving. But for that amazing moment — he'd never experienced it before — sheets of rain pelted one side of the porch while it was dry and bright on the other. Yesterday he had one life, in the sun, and all of a sudden that life had just dissolved into blackness.

Unable to tell the front from the back of the hospital, he asked an aide to point the way to the parking lot as he stumbled out to find his car.

Gary Ramona's free fall had begun.

DISCOVERY

6

A Family Falls Apart

Leaving the hospital on Friday, the day after the confrontation, Holly looked up at the sky and said something Stephanie would never forget: "Mom, the sky doesn't look so blue, and the trees don't look so green anymore." Stephanie looked. They didn't. Nothing looked the same. She had no words to comfort her child. What can you tell your kid after she's been raped repeatedly by her father — "Yeah, you're right, everything's dirty"? Stephanie felt useless. She put her arm around her daughter, and they walked to the car.

Maybe it had been a smoggy day. But even Napa's spring green looked gray now. Suddenly, Stephanie was seeing abuse in the faces and eyes of children she encountered in town, in church, at school. No one was safe or immune. No one could be trusted. Her memories had turned dark and dirty. Her own innocence was gone. It was crazy; how could she still have been an innocent at her age? But here she was, still true to her nickname — "Nye-eve."

Shopping for groceries in downtown St. Helena, she thought, "I can't, I *can't* push the cart down the aisle," feeling panic as she kept running into people she knew. When they stopped and talked to her, she'd think, "They know. They know. Everybody can tell what I've just found out. Everybody knows." She felt ashamed. How could this have happened? "How can I face them?"

She asked Barry Grundland. He told her, "Stevie, you continue to push that cart down that aisle."

One thing still threw her about Gary's guilt. "It's weird, but at the same time that Holly remembers the abuse, sex with Gary was okay — it was very good. I enjoyed myself," she told Grundland. How could that be? She'd heard it was supposed to be the opposite, an idea spread by Judith Lewis Herman's book *Father-Daughter Incest*: "Implicitly the incestuous father assumes that it is his prerogative to be waited upon at home, and that if his wife fails to provide satisfaction, he is entitled to use his daughter as a substitute." Stephanie thought, "Maybe I'm crazy, but making love with Gary was, in some ways, even better" during the years of Holly's memories. Yet she believed Holly. The other pieces fit.

Gary, of course, thought she'd run south to her mother, but she would stay here in the valley. Shawna and Kelli would stay in school. They would all walk the daily gauntlet and endure it. "Hold your heads high," she told the girls. "We didn't do anything. *He* did." But in her room at night, when she thought Shawna was asleep, Stephanie would cry.

"Mom, you think I don't know, but I know," Shawna said to her.

"Cry in front of her, Stevie. It's best," said the therapist Shawna had started seeing.

Alone, she tried to talk up her spirits: "I will not let myself feel humiliated. I didn't do anything wrong. But more than that, my kids did nothing wrong. If someone asks me about it, I'm going to tell them about it. With my daughters standing there, we're going to talk about it openly in this valley." Part of her just wanted to confront everybody and scream what had happened to Holly in this so-called paradise.

Stephanie suspected, however, that she would pay dearly if she spoke out. This was not her valley; it was Mondavi's, and, through him, Gary's. She feared Gary would punish them relentlessly. He would deny that he had threatened her when they were alone after the confrontation, but she was sure she had heard him say, "If you tell one soul, you will be sorry I laid eyes on you."

But how could she keep the incest secret when it was the basis of everything that was happening? It had permeated her initial divorce declarations, even before the confrontation. Her fears for her daughters were behind her plea to the judge to grant her sole custody and deny Gary visitation rights, to order Gary to stay two hundred yards away from the girls' school and home, and to restrain him from making any contact with his family. Insinuations of incest crept from the court papers in her reference to Gary's "unpredictable and explosive temper" and in her concern for what he might do when he was confronted "by some very highly sensitive issues dealing with his relationship with our three daughters" — issues she would not share with the court unless forced to do so. Gary had stolen their dreams, but she would fight for whatever she could retrieve of the material remains of their future and urged the judge to order the sale of the new house. Much of her security lay in that house. Stephanie feared that if Gary moved in, it would become a fortress from which he would fight his family until they broke.

Her worst fear was that Gary would fight for custody of Shawna. When, almost immediately, he acquiesced to her requests for custody, child and spousal support, and the sale of the house — and did not push for visitation rights, she did not trust or believe him. She wanted him jailed. But Stephanie couldn't sue; she wasn't the one who had been raped. By the first of the new year, 1991, laws in California would dramatically extend the time span within which a recovered memory victim could sue. Holly, at nineteen, was safely within the frame of the current law: she could sue her father in a civil suit. But she could only prosecute him criminally if she were still a minor, under eighteen. If Gary had abused Shawna, though — if she had memories of abuse — then Shawna could sue. Shawna had told her mother of disturbing dreams about a Raggedy Ann doll touching her in places she didn't like to be touched. Stephanie suspected Gary had abused his other two daughters, too.

As Gary Ramona left the confrontation on March 15, he moved into unfamiliar territory. With Holly's words "*You raped me*" driving like glass splinters through his head and heart, he stumbled out of the hospital, found his car, and got on the road. Through a blur of tears, he hunted for a pay phone. All he knew was that he was going to the airport, he was getting the hell out of there, and he had to call Barry Grundland. "Barry, I've got to see you tonight," he said.

"I expected your call," Grundland responded. "Six-thirty."

Gary was stunned. His own therapist had apparently known the confrontation was coming and hadn't told him. Somehow he got to the airport. Calling on thirty years of a salesman's experience, a thousand passages through airports, Gary returned his car and caught a flight to Sacramento. He stalked the aisle like a caged wild animal. Five or six times during the flight, he went to the emergency exit at the back of the plane, ready to pop the door and "just go." He was going nuts. He forced his head back in the seat and gripped the armrests. At Sacramento, he picked up his car and headed for Napa; then the transmission went out. He called his old friend Larry Graeber to come pick him up.

Gary had to tell someone. He and Larry had been close for twenty years; they had followed the same job path, selling orange juice and then moving to Mondavi. Gary had been there for Larry when his child drowned in an accident; now he needed Larry. "What I'm going to tell you, I don't want you to tell anyone, including your wife." Larry promised, listening in disbelief. Then fear hit him, for himself as a father: "Oh, my God, Gary, I'm going to have to watch it. From time to time our kids get in bed with us." He drove Gary to the house so that he could grab some clothes and get his pickup. He went to his mother's house on Daffodil Drive. "I need to stay here for a while," he told Garnet. He didn't have the heart or the time to tell her the whole story just then. He left to see Grundland.

"If ever there was a time when you'd think about hitting the bottle, this would be it," he thought. But he couldn't even drink water. "Devastated" didn't begin to describe how he felt. He'd been accused of the most heinous, perverted crime; he couldn't feel any lower, any sicker. If a truck ran over him, he wouldn't care. He wouldn't feel it. The most humane thing would have been for someone to just put a gun to his head and pull the trigger.

"I wasn't allowed to tell you," explained Grundland, Gary recalls, at the start of their ninety-minute session. He had been walking an increasingly delicate line, seeing all the Ramonas. Gary blurted out the accusations, urging Grundland to give him sodium amytal so that he could prove to Holly that he didn't do it. "I'll take it, damn it, if this is truth serum." He was shocked to hear Barry say, "It won't do you any good, Gary. Sodium amytal has no validity whatsoever to do anything in regard to truth. It's not reliable. I haven't used it. I don't know anyone who does." Then why had it been used on Holly? And what about the charge that rape had caused her urinary tract infections? They could as easily have been caused by her playing in a sandbox, wiping the wrong direction, or dirty hands, Grundland explained. But this had been their proof! Finally he told Gary that Stephanie was leaving him. "You need a good divorce lawyer, Gary. I know one in San Francisco," Eugenia Magowan. Gary would be served the next day by a sheriff. Stephanie was taking pity on him by serving him not at the winery, in front of his colleagues, but at Grundland's office.

Sitting at his mother's kitchen table that night, Gary tried to explain what had happened. It was a hard, hard thing to do. Garnet, in her late seventies, had always looked fragile, but she came from strong German immigrant stock, and her spirit showed in her response: she was angry. "This is craziness," she said, indignant. Still, Gary could not bring himself to tell her that she, too, was involved — that Holly believed her grandmother had been raped by her brothers. Uncle Bill. Uncle Lester. Holly had never even met them, and Lester was dead. Now they stood condemned as rapists.

The next day, Gary went through the motions of work, but in the middle of a management council meeting he couldn't stand it and left. He walked into Michael Mondavi's office and broke down. "Stevie's divorcing me," he said. He could not bring himself to speak of the incest charge. Michael hugged him. "What can we do?" Gary thanked God for his other family, the Mondavis. His work with them was where, for twenty years, he had found much of his identity; it was where, now, he knew he would find his compass, his sanity. Later that afternoon, he drove to Grundland's office to be served with divorce papers, then Larry drove him to San Francisco to meet with his lawyer.

When he woke up the next morning, he was back in the sun for that first fraction of a second, feeling the old resilience. But then the heaviness engulfed him, and he felt too leaden to move. "He's burying himself in what he knows best, wineries," said Scott Evans's new wife, Peggy, as they arrived as Gary's guests at the Taste of Life, a gala benefit at the Costa Mesa wine and food center. Gary couldn't avoid the party; he had coordinated the event, and a friend's wife had headed the committee. A black-tie American Cancer Society benefit auction, it was, for Scott, "a real great evening. Dancing, different restaurants' food booths all around, the wineries pouring their wines." Michael Mondavi and his sister, Marcia, were there, and sports stars were among the eight hundred people partying under a huge tent on the lawn. Scott felt almost guilty having a good time because he knew Gary was devastated. He marveled as he watched Gary being a great host, a good sport.

Scott was one of the few people who knew what he was going through. Gary had told him about Holly's allegations as the two men walked near the beach by the Marriott before the party. "It was just like they did open heart surgery on you without any medication. Just stuck their hand in there and pulled your heart and guts out and threw them on the table and you're gasping for breath," Gary said, trying to explain. Scott stood by him but confided to Peggy later, "Gary is the only one in the world who knows for sure." "He is innocent until proven guilty," snapped Peggy, who would make no effort to keep her twelve-year-old daughter from him.

Sometimes it was as if it was happening to someone else. At the party, people came up to him saying, "Boy, Gary, this is absolutely magnificent"; meantime, his family was in shambles. It was so lonely, with all these people he knew saying hello, complimenting him, while inside he was feeling so humiliated, not knowing if they knew. Since March 15, Gary had thought a lot about suicide. The thing that stopped him was that there was no way he was going to allow himself to go to his grave until he had an opportunity to prove to his daughters that he was innocent.

His obsession from the first was to keep the lines of communication open, to talk to Holly, the girls, Steph. To find out what had happened and set it right. Barry Grundland was trying to set up a meeting with the girls, but Stephanie was thwarting him. Gary began a series of ten, twelve, fifteen calls to Rose, who had administered the sodium amytal. In the coming weeks he would make three separate appointments to go in and talk to the doctor about taking sodium amytal himself, but all were cancelled by Rose's office. Rose finally returned a call; Gary called back, and he said that he would not meet with him.

Gary told Rose, "Both Steph and Holly requested that I meet with you."

"I cannot and will not talk to you about Holly, and you can't become involved in her therapy. There would be [a] conflict," Rose claims he replied.

Through Marche Isabella, Gary had been able to set up another meeting with Holly for the next Monday, March 19. He flew south. As Gary tells the story, Isabella ordered him, "Sit down by Holly," as he entered her office. She then told him to move farther from Holly, so he got a pillow and put it between them. Then Isabella told him to move to a chair. He was experiencing the sensitivity of what therapists called boundary violations, a language he had not yet learned.

"Marche," Gary said, "the reason I asked for this meeting was the fact that in the Thursday meeting, you did all the talking. I want to hear my daughter tell me what is going on."

Holly looked to Isabella for help. She took over again, repeating Holly's "visions" — Gary refused to call them "memories." The rapes had switched from nighttime to daytime since the previous week.

"Are you saying that it's in the middle of the day, all of a sudden I get some sex urge . . . Then I go out, call Holly in, take her into my bedroom, and rape her?"

Again, Holly looked to Isabella, who seemed to be her voice.

Building her case for Gary's guilt, Isabella moved to her next item. "Gary, you have to understand, I know what it's like to be raised with an Italian father who controls everything." You don't talk back. She was "really into this issue about the Italian father and these dictators," he saw, amazed.

For Gary, the leitmotif that would flow through depositions and hearings and testimony and trials for four years began here. In fact, however, by 1990 the theme of the overcontrolling father was already well established in the incest literature and in the offices of many psychotherapists. Judith Lewis Herman, the feminist psychiatrist whose Harvard credentials gave academic credibility to the recovered memory movement as it oozed from a foggy intellectual swamp in the 1980s, wrote in *Father-Daughter Incest* in 1981 that "the locus of the problem is the patriarchal father, dominating the home with absolute authority and free to view his children as his personal possessions." Herman's book may also have been read by some of the thousands of young Hollys as a manifesto for abandoning the blood family: "If incestuous abuse is indeed an inevitable result of patriarchal family structure, then preventing sexual abuse will ultimately require a radical transformation of the family."

As the far-ranging scope of child abuse was recognized in the 1980s, said the social psychologist Carol Tavris in *The Mismeasure of Woman*, "to the feminist writers, these facts were evidence that incest and other forms of child abuse were not the aberrations of a few sick men but the results of a system that endows men with the sense of entitlement to control and abuse women and children." The men who allegedly molested, she said, were almost always "the symbols of patriarchy: the father, the father's wealthy friends, the judge . . . the psychiatrist, the company president, the priest." Marche Isabella's Italian father easily became a metaphor for the overcontrolling perpetrator already in the literature, compounding, in the minds of the Ramona women, the connection between Gary's domineering style and Holly's incestuous rape. The theme would flourish and grow. It would flow from Stephanie's lawyer during the divorce hearings and from the mouths of attorneys as the dominant argument for Gary's guilt in the trial four years later. *Controlling* would be seen by Stephanie's women friends, as they looked back for clues, as Gary's overarching trait, compelling evidence that he was a rapist.

Gary's gut response to Isabella's charge was, "In most Italian families, the *women* certainly run the roost!" Where was her proof, he challenged Isabella, that Italian men had a corner on control over German or Asian men? Isabella leaned back, resigned to his denial. "Okay."

"On Thursday, you brought up this drinking issue," Gary went on, addressing the suggestion that perhaps his blind drunkenness explained incest he couldn't remember. "Steph was paranoid on drinking. Two or three of her aunts were alcoholics . . . I gotta tell you, there is no way that I would ever be watching our children if I was drinking. We hardly ever drank at home."

"Gary, I was just trying to give you an out."

"I don't need your outs!" he hurled back.

Trying to pump life back into a meeting he felt was slipping away, he asked Holly what she'd meant by her "concern for Shawna." "Are you jealous of Shawna because I've been able to shoot baskets with her a little bit more now? I've been able to take her places more?" Holly sat back, silent, offended, and angry. The meeting was over; it had been as futile and destructive as the confrontation. And Holly wasn't getting better; she was to be readmitted to the hospital that day, he was told. As Rose's hospital notes would state, Holly had "begun reexperiencing intermittent self-destructive ideation, severe impairment of self-esteem, feelings of guilt, and intense desire to binge and purge again."

Stephanie saw Gary appear from the meeting as she waited for Holly by her car. She walked over to him, seizing the chance she had been denied earlier to confront him. She had been sure when he leaped up with tears in his eyes and tried to leave the confrontation that he knew he'd been caught. But it could all stop right here; this is where the whole nightmare could end if Gary would care about Holly and confess. Holly still loved her father, Stephanie claimed. "She just wants you to admit it to her. Gary, I've lived with you. I know." Of course he denied it. He railed again that Holly's claim was a concoction of lies. Then, for some reason, Stephanie thought of something Holly had said under sodium amytal — that Gary had confessed to having an affair. She didn't know why it mattered now, but she asked, "Did you, Gary?"

"Someday I would like to sit down and talk to you about it," he said, leaving Stephanie confused, the question unanswered.

It was as if Holly were no longer his daughter. Gary was beginning to suspect, as he drove away, that Marche Isabella and her quack therapy were the source of this nightmare. After the confrontation, the women had used a tactic of isolation, Steph permitting him no communication with his daughters, Isabella and Holly reinforcing it. It was a brainwashing technique. He had seldom tried to put feelings on paper, but on March 29 he sent a brief note to Holly, ostensibly to give her income tax information and her auto license sticker. It was really a plea for contact. At the top he wrote and underlined, "*Love You Always, Dad,*" and told her, "I called Marche's office but she will not talk with me. Holly, please let's talk. I love you very much! Maybe we could meet with Barry Grundland. If not in person what about a phone conference between us." Gary would send a stream of notes, little gifts, calls. They would vanish into a void or be sent back. But he would keep doing it, keep making the call.

Next he put his hand over my mouth and forced his penis inside me. He called me his special little girl and told me that this is what you do to special little girls. After he raped me, he talked about not wanting to loose [sic] his mother and about an affair he had. I remember his smell and his skin and I hate them both. I can see the after noon [sic] sun coming in through the window . . . The last thing I see is my father sitting by the side of the bed with his face in his hands. I'm coming off the bed, looking at him. I'm wearing a blue dress with white poca [sic] dots . . .

These were not words spilled out under sodium amytal or scribbled by Marche Isabella in therapy sessions. Holly, sitting in her hospital bed twelve days after the confrontation, was writing a seven-page letter to her father, speaking about him rather than to him, as if trying to avoid his eyes. A nurse made a cryptic record of the event: "She wrote her father a letter which is helping her process." The little girl who rarely expressed opinions was finally speaking out.

Basically, I avoid having any type of relationship with guys. I'm too scared and I don't feel as if I can trust them. If anything reminds me of my father whether it be a look, smell or a gesture, it makes me sick. I end up projecting my feelings about my father onto the other person . . . It's changed the way I feel about myself too. Deep down inside, past the smile and the person who says everything's OK. I've always hated myself . . . I love my father but I hate him too I hate him for what he did to me and how it's torn my family apart. I don't think anything will ever make the pain go away completely. Sometimes I wonder how someone I looked up to and loved so deeply could hurt and betray me so much. Sometimes I wonder if he really ever loved me at all. I wish I could make it all go away and that we could go back to being a "normal family," but no matter how much I try, the memories are always there.

The desperate girl who had wandered through the mall on a bulimic binge, unable to feel, was now identifying the links between the incest and her problems. "In most of the popular counseling and survivor groups, progress in therapy is defined as the recognition of these links," says one medical anthropologist, Dara Culhane. "You are 'more healed' when you come to understand that most of your problems result from your having been a victim of sexual abuse."

. . . The abuse has also effected [sic] how I use food and the way in which I look at myself. There were times when I'd diet excessively sometimes not eating for days or surviving off of two to three hundred calories a day along with exercise that sometimes lasted up to two hours or I'd exercise for 30 minutes every hour. I didn't want my father to look at me; I didn't want to develop breasts. Sometimes I get angry and I eat excessive amounts of food and then I throw it up. Other times I get scared and I just eat and gain weight for protection. Who will look at me if I'm fat and ugly? Sometimes I don't eat at all because feeling hungry is better than feeling the pain. I know it's my fault that I do these things but . . . it's the only thing I knew how to do in order to survive and feel safe. Sometimes I feel so weird and messed up inside I think I'd be better off if I just wasn't here and then I wouldn't have to deal with any of this. But I don't think that any more. Life has gotten better and I'm making progress.

Writing this paper is a lot like purging only I don't have to put my fingers down my throat to do it. I think purging was the only way I knew how to get all of my emotions out.

Holly was processing the new perception of her life forced upon her by the memories. Her letter joined a sea of narrative, of journals, letters, poems, pouring forth from thousands of young women, transforming the mute pain and desperation of their memories of abuse into meaning. The process of rewriting your own life story — of creating a new reality in which you could portray yourself as a tenacious survivor rather than a helpless victim — was so powerful that it was giving birth to a whole new therapy movement, "narrative therapy." These stories "are narratives that provide a unifying theme to organize the events of our lives. They attempt to be true, but they are rarely the whole truth and nothing but the truth," said Tavris in *Mismeasure of Woman.*

For Holly, writing her letter was a courageous act. But by this time the style and format of therapy writing had become so stereotyped and repetitive that almost every word and every subsequent step in Holly's "process" was predictable from the proliferating self-help survivor literature or the stories told by other "survivors." The psychologist Christine Courtois, in *Healing the Incest Wound,* recommended reading, first, the less emotional writings, then moving on to first-person accounts and poetry, searching for stories that matched the victim's own. She encouraged the reader then to write an uncensored letter that would not be sent, a letter "not encumbered by style, tone, emotional censorship, or guilt." Isabella encouraged Holly's writing as "a typical therapeutic tool for dealing with pain." In Orange County, a hothouse of experimental, New Age therapies and several thousand therapists, the idea of writing as part of the healing process was in the air to be absorbed, like secondhand smoke.

Holly didn't address the letter to her father but sent it to her mother along with a hesitant note, asking her to use her judgment about when her father should see it. Stephanie read it to Gary in Grundland's office — both were still seeing Barry — but refused to relinquish it to him. In the last pages, Holly revealed her course of action.

. . . I don't want to be controlled by my father anymore. He can't just destroy my life and walk away. Being raped is a very degrading experience. He took away all of my pride, dignity, and self-respect. I'm taking my life back. I'm taking what belonged to me back. I have the power now to stand up to my father . . . now I have the power to make sure that this never happens to me again. I didn't have that power when I was five years old . . . but the process of standing up to my father helps me feel like I'm in control again . . . I hope it will also help other people who have been abused, by letting them and the rest of society . . . know that any type of abuse is wrong and that the victims have a right to defend themselves . . . I'm not out for revenge

*or to destroy my father. I just want to get on with my life. I can't deal
with him any longer. I need to move on, to break all ties with him and
this is the only way I know how . . .*

She had put her father on notice that she was cutting any cord that
might still bind them together. Suing him had also crossed her mind.
At times, Holly still had doubts that her memories were true. But with
every telling, with every act of commitment to them, they would become more vivid and her belief in them would deepen. As leading
memory scientists knew so well, the repetition and rehearsal strength-
ens memories — false ones, true ones.

Twice hospitalized for depression and bulimia, Holly had still not
been given — or been willing to take — any antidepressants, although
Grundland had discussed it seven months earlier. She was given none
"due to the patient's rapid response to in-patient psychotherapy
alone," wrote Rose in his first discharge notes. Holly's characteristic
discipline and smiling compliance had served her well. She had been
"encouraged to work intensively on her depressive problems," and
"in an honest and intense manner" she had. Rose's notes, though,
reveal the assumptions that underlay her care: Holly's bulimia "had
apparently resulted from sexual molestation experiences . . . a sodium
amytal interview was carried out for the purpose of uncovering suppressed memories of the patient's episodes of molestation . . . which
successfully helped her remember specific details . . ." Rose wrote his
first discharge notes for Holly from memory, in fact, months after
her discharge, reminded by an administrator who'd spotted the omis-
sion. That oversight would prove to be more serious for Rose than it
seemed at the time — far more than just sloppy procedures. It would
make him vulnerable later in court. For whether or not the late note
reflected lapses in memory over the months, the words reflected Rose's
belief in the causal connection between sex abuse and bulimia — and
in the power of sodium amytal to wake true memories from their
slumber. It also narrowed the search for other explanations.

Another element was at work in Holly's treatment: the "Christian
connection," there from the first day of therapy. Marche Isabella had
gone to Christian colleges, majored in Christian education, and, in her
practice, saw a "large Christian population." The Christian connection surfaces persistently through the recovered memory phenomenon, a setting in which a disproportionate number of abuse memories
have blossomed. Carl Sagan, the late, great astronomer and social

thinker, identified the Christian connection in false memory, particularly in satanic ritual abuse. "A significant number of those touting the peril of rampant Satanism in America . . . turn out to be Christian fundamentalists; their sects explicitly require a literal devil to be meddling in everyday human life," he said in *The Demon-Haunted World*. "The connection is neatly drawn in the saying, 'No Satan, no God.'" Holly had not reported memories of bloody satanic rituals, but in the hospital she was put in the psychiatric wing run by one of the New Life Treatment Centers, a contract management company whose literature claimed to "integrate Biblical principles with the highest quality clinical care and treatment methods" and to "emphasize consistent use of God's word as the primary resource of strength and understanding." For the fundamentalists, that word was a more trusted resource than science and literal truth. New Life provided a pastor at the hospital for spiritual counseling. Growing numbers of fundamentalist pastors had become full-blown therapists — and were exempt from needing a license to practice. Charged with implanting memories that grew into the satanic, pastors were being sued by recanting young women.

In the mainstream, bulimia was being successfully treated with drugs like Prozac or Xanax together with cognitive therapies, but New Life viewed eating and sexual disorders as compulsive addictions. Its brochures, available to every patient, taught that 6 to 12 percent of the American population were sexual addicts, of whom 80 percent had been sexually abused as children — figures that mean, conservatively, that twenty million sexual addicts who were sexually abused as children walk our streets. Like MFCCs such as Marche Isabella who dealt with bulimia and clinical depression, New Life's personnel may well have been motivated by compassion. But as groups like New Life seized the huge opportunity created by the incest survivor movement — as private clinics sprang up across the country — the profit motive must also be considered. "New Life is a marketing ploy," Gary Ramona had heard. And Holly was still sick.

This time, Holly was released from the hospital after eight days. On March 27 the notes reported: "Discharged ambulatory with belongings. Patient left with mother in auto." The bill at Western Medical Center, $14,000, was paid by her father's insurance. Within two months, Holly was in such bad shape, and so humiliated by her weight, that she could not bear to go home for the summer. She risked suspension from UC Irvine for plummeting grades. By mid-July she asked to see Richard Rose about an antidepressant, ready, at last, to try one.

It was not an Easter week like those of the past, with beaches and Disneyland. Shawna and Kelli had not seen Holly since the drama of memories, sodium amytal, and the confrontation. They needed to hear it from Holly directly, Stephanie felt, so she suggested that, this Easter vacation, the girls meet with Holly and Marche Isabella.

"I was sexually abused in Diamond Bar," Holly told her sisters in Isabella's office on March 11, 1990. She described her father's sexual touches and the experience of rape she had stitched together from her memories. "The purpose of the meeting is for you to understand what has happened to Holly," Isabella told the girls. She told them about repression, explaining that "you don't remember things until you're ready — that Holly had probably remembered much later because her repressed memories were too painful to handle until then." Both Holly and Isabella confirmed to the girls the connection between sexual abuse and bulimia, with the therapist repeating the statistic that 80 percent of bulimics had been sexually molested.

When she asked the younger girls if they had any memories of abuse, Shawna told about her scary dreams of a Raggedy Ann who was "coming out of my closet or door, and a child's voice saying, 'I am coming in your bed now. I'm coming now.'" The voice would turn mean and evil when she said no, and "something" would touch her under her arms, and she cried. In another dream, she walked into her parents' bedroom; her dad's blow dryer was going and he turned toward her, a towel wrapped around his body, and when he dropped it and looked at her, Shawna turned away and tried to scream, but nothing came out. They could be just dreams or signs of something else, Isabella told Shawna. But she suspected sexual abuse.

It was decided that the family would contact Gary only through Holly; Stephanie had lost power again to her daughter. But the five of them, the Ramonas and Betty Nye, emerged with solidarity behind Holly, a family of women again. Shawna told Betty, "Holly was brave to make this stand, when she didn't know who we'd believe." Asked if she had any doubts, Kelli said, "I have no doubts. Holly had no reason to lie. She knows what has happened to her . . ." They all stayed at Betty's for Easter week, Kelli and Shawna sleeping on the floor.

The girls returned to Napa true believers. Gary, however, would later view this meeting, when its details spilled out in depositions, as the next step in the brainwashing of his family as they barricaded themselves behind Holly's imaginings, further isolating him.

After the meeting with her sisters, Holly and Isabella both filed reports of possible molestation of Shawna and Kelli with Napa's Child Protective Services. For Isabella, it was mandatory if she suspected child abuse; for Holly, it could mean protection for her sisters and set an example for other children. When a caseworker asked Kelli and Shawna to come in for interviews, Shawna recounted her dreams, but Kelli had no memories to tell. The caseworker told the girls, and told Stephanie separately, that with no specific reports of sexual molestation, there appeared to be no basis for charges. Yes, there had been boundary violations by their father, in her opinion. But they weren't enough to charge Gary Ramona with a criminal act. Even if Raggedy Ann was a metaphor for real events, dreams would not stand up in court. The agency told Isabella, in its report: "We need more information from her memory to be conclusive molestation." The case, and Stephanie's hopes of jailing Gary, was closed. But her fears for the girls were still alive.

7

A Mother Knows

Gary needed a good criminal lawyer. "If you really want the best, I know one," Eugenia Magowan advised him. He agreed. "They didn't just accuse me, they convicted me guilty and want the rope around my neck." Who knew what could happen? Steph was pushing: Was there something with Shawna? With Kelli? She might go for criminal charges. "If I have to go this route, I wanted to make sure I had the best." Magowan took him to a colleague, Ephraim Margolin.

Gary was "at probably the lowest I'll ever be in my life" as he entered Margolin's third-floor office overlooking the palm trees of San Francisco's Union Square. Margolin was the man to lift him up off the floor. A senior defense lawyer who had argued appeals to the U.S. Supreme Court, he was considered an attorney's attorney by his peers in the defense bar. He had represented judges, seventy of them, before the Commission on Judicial Performance. His father, a Polish philosopher and Zionist, had sent his wife and son to Palestine in 1936, before he himself was sent to a concentration camp (where he wrote a book later published in seventeen languages). At fifteen an officer in the Israeli underground, Ephraim became secretary to Menachem Begin, then a parliamentary candidate, and read philosophy and literature at the Hebrew University in Jerusalem before moving to the United States in 1950 to study constitutional law at Yale. He wrote articles for philatelists' journals, taught law at UC Berkeley's prestigious law school, Boalt Hall, and belonged to a men's group that discussed philosophy instead of their inner warrior selves. He had defended the underdog since heading the ACLU's legal committee in Northern California in the early sixties. With a thick head of gray hair that rose to a satyr's tuft on top and steel-rimmed glasses, Margolin was a social activist who fought the "barbarians" who, he had learned as a Jewish boy in Europe, always threatened civilized freedoms. "I am on the side of people who are very, very frequently falsely accused," he later said.

Margolin observed the man in the dark suit sitting opposite him. Ramona was slightly overweight — but, then, weren't we all. He listened to Gary. Probably not terribly sensitive, he mused. With his Polish-Israeli accent, Margolin says, "My first reaction, the one thing that did not sound right: he described his marriage as a happy marriage. I thought to myself, 'If you have a happy marriage, and then your wife suddenly serves you with papers, then you are either very insensitive or you live in a different world from the wife.'" But, then, if the divorce was strictly his wife's reaction to the terrible shock of her daughter's report of incest, maybe he had had a happy marriage. Margolin knew that very frequently people come to lawyers to solve other problems, not legal ones. He told Gary, "There are a lot of problems that cannot be solved by the law. You come to the courts only as a last course. The only people who benefit are lawyers.

"First issue, Mr. Ramona, is there criminal exposure?" Could he be criminally sued? Under the current statute of limitations, Holly would have had to complain either before she was seventeen, when a guardian could have brought suit, or within one year afterward. So, Margolin advised that no criminal charges were possible. He was safe there. If Child Protective Services charged molestation against the younger daughters, Shawna and Kelli, however, there could still be trouble.

He questioned Ramona closely that day, and on several subsequent occasions. "And I became, gradually, more and more unhappy with the wife." Margolin's experience was that bulimia could often be traced to the mother's behavior. So, he guessed, the mother here had a very powerful reason in this case to shift the blame, if there was blame. He began to see her as a self-indulgent, opaque woman who would have gone along with this marriage, who knew how long, until she had the excuse — and the money. They had been drifting apart, he speculated, and she had used the daughter in order, finally, to confront what she didn't want to see — the selfish motives that had kept her in a crippled marriage. But a bad marriage was not raping your daughter. Was there rape? There was always something behind dysfunction, but it was not necessarily sexual, in Margolin's view.

Was this man guilty or innocent? At first, Margolin reserved judgment. Despite popular belief, in his experience there was no such thing as a preconceived profile of a pedophile: people were people. But it was more likely that somebody who was abused would become an abuser, just as it was unlikely and unbelievable for someone to commit what Ramona was charged with without a history of doing it over a very long period of time and to many people. Where was Ramona's history? In Ramona's version of events, at least, there was none of the familiar pattern of the perpetrator. "At first I had no perception of him. Then the perception hardened, and it ended with a man to whom dirt was done. Dirt he did not deserve."

Stephanie called Gary to say that Child Protective Services had found nothing substantial enough for criminal charges. Since no abuse had been found in Shawna and Kelli, Margolin told Gary, "You don't need a criminal lawyer." Perhaps there was no longer the threat of criminal action. But from his numb state, Gary was beginning to formulate a response: his own action against the therapists.

"Could I sue?" he asked Margolin.

The short answer was no. "You can't sue therapists. They owe you no duty" — no legal or ethical responsibility to someone who is not a patient — and the chances were remote that a judge would permit such a case into court. Stubborn, indignant, Gary would continue to demand — to Margolin, to everyone from whom he heard the same thing — "What do you mean, there's no duty? You mean people can come out and accuse you, destroy your family, and you can't do anything? This is crazy!"

"Gary, you want your children back. You want vindication. If you turn to the courts, it may cost you everything you've got and it's going to perpetuate your pain . . . In my experience, there are no winners. The only thing that's left is scorched earth." Margolin discouraged him from suing for a host of other reasons as well. For one thing, he couldn't get the records he'd need, Holly's medical records. They were all confidential.

But Gary saw Margolin as a lifeline — the kind of cultured European, like Margrit Biever, who aroused a poignant reminder in him of the culture and education he had missed. This was a man of quality, he sensed. A mentor. "At $400 an hour, I am an expensive friend," Margolin said. Gary pleaded with him to keep seeing him. He wanted to build a legal team and wanted Margolin to head it. But Gary would be best served by someone who practiced civil cases, Margolin told him, because civil law is different from criminal law, the case material is different. "You've got to understand, you're in a *major war.*" Gary extracted a promise that Margolin would continue to consult. "I believe Ephraim sort of took me under his wing," says Gary.

This formerly high-flying executive was, indeed, a broken bird. He did not need an attorney as much as he needed someone to talk to, Margolin sensed. He had lost everything. He was trying to make far-reaching decisions for his life. He had no girlfriend, no close colleague with whom he could discuss these things. In defending murderers, Margolin had skated on the edges of psychiatry for a long time. "I may have quite a bit of insight, but I am not a licensed psychiatrist." He sent Gary to the best psychiatrist he knew in San Francisco, Wolfgang Lederer.

Lederer was cut from the same cultured European cloth as Margolin. The author of an unpublished book on Thomas Mann, a psychoanalytic work, *The Fear of Women,* and a psychohistory of Hans Christian Andersen, *The Kiss of the Snow Queen,* he combined a professorship at UC's Langley Porter Institute with an active practice. In his mid-seventies, he seemed the classic therapist, with his Viennese accent and distinguished head of silver hair brushed back from a strong, square face dramatically scored by two thick strokes of black brow. After thirty-nine years of practice, Lederer saw quickly that this was an emergency. Ramona was stunned and acutely depressed. The anger had not yet surfaced.

Like Margolin, Lederer responded to Ramona's story of a happy family life with skepticism. This man did not seem to think he had marital problems before March 15, when his wife told him not to come home. Lederer heard a different story: a difficult sex life at the beginning and for the last year and a half of their marriage. A wife who apparently thought he could do nothing right and was never happy with him as a sex partner — a wife who complained about his absences yet, when he was home, complained that he was underfoot. Ramona did not blame himself. The problem was *her* reluctance in sex. Yet he never blamed her, either. He never talked of fault. Like Margolin, Lederer suspected that Stephanie had wanted to divorce him all along. His treatment plan was to cure his depression and get him healthy again. He saw no symptom that he was treating a sexual deviate. He encouraged Gary to keep trying to see his family, to work it out peaceably. He gave him a prescription for a tranquilizer and agreed to see him on a weekly basis.

He also told Gary about *The Crucible,* Arthur Miller's play about the Salem witch trials of 1692. The hysteria in the Puritan seaport had jailed two hundred people and hung nineteen before being exposed as a tragic delusion, even though backed by a sincere and pervasive belief in the biblical reality of witches. Miller had written the play in 1951 as a caution against McCarthyism; hysterical sightings of the communist "devil" were destroying lives just as spectral evidence of the devil had destroyed lives in Salem.

Gary had to plead ignorance, something that always embarrassed him. He had never heard of Salem, but he bought and read the play, riveted. It lifted him more effectively than therapy to connect with an event in which, almost exactly three hundred years earlier, delusional fantasies had condemned the innocent. In America! He had opened a page on some persisting themes of history — zealotry, superstition, and the paranoid hysteria of crowds. Suddenly he saw links among the Inquisition, Hitler, Salem, McCarthyism, and recovered memories of incest, stunned that he might be part of this history. "To think we haven't even learned from that yet. Still leading people to death on . . . their own preconceived idea . . . Then it becomes the *Bible.* Irrationally. Without using common sense, or without investigating." Could Holly's memories be today's spectral evidence?

For a brief moment in June, Gary felt as though a butterfly sat on his shoulder. He had finally achieved meetings with his daughters. First, with Holly in Orange County, where Gary heard no openness on Holly's part to hear him out or even consider his innocence. The interchange left Holly feeling, she told Marche Isabella, "ripped apart," with nothing but anger for her father. Then, with Grundland and all three girls in his office in late June, Holly and Kelli presented Gary with their school expenses. "That isn't what we came here to discuss," he pleaded, hoping they would talk about their feelings. Shawna and Kelli confirmed their belief in Holly, citing the sodium amytal as their proof. "You hurt Holly," said Shawna, breaking his heart. The meetings had failed.

If they wouldn't listen to him, perhaps his family would listen to the experts he was finding. The potential links between Salem's and his own experience goaded Gary to intensify the research into bulimia and sodium amytal he had begun the day of the confrontation. By talking with people, combing bookstores, running computer searches at the UC Davis library, he found the experts and contacted them. At the University of Minnesota, he got in touch with Dr. David T. Lykken, the author of *A Tremor in the Blood: Uses and Abuses of the Lie Detector.* From him Gary learned that back in the forties, sodium amytal may have been considered "the royal road to truth," but it had since been found unreliable. As a memory drug, Lykken told him, amytal was so outdated that finding recent studies would be difficult. Gary flew to Eugene, Oregon, to see Dr. Jean Rubell, the head of the Anorexia/Bulimia Association, based on the University of Oregon campus, and learned more about Holly's illness.

He sought out Dr. Charles Marmar, a trauma specialist and research psychiatrist at UC San Francisco, and Dr. David Spiegel, a hypnosis expert at Stanford. With Gary keeping himself out of it so he couldn't be accused of bias and manipulation, both scientists agreed to see Steph and Holly. But neither Holly nor Steph would talk to them.

Gary still loved them dearly. Making a sale took time; sooner or later they would listen. But the anger Lederer had not seen at first was beginning to surface. Early, tentative suspicions about Marche Isabella's therapy were firming into outrage. "What made me so angry with the Marche Isabellas of the world is that it took me a whole lifetime and twenty-five years of marriage to build a wonderful family and a great career, and in less than six months, a stranger can do this." Gary Ramona felt himself becoming invisible, a nonentity. Still too emotionally limp to take the offensive, he continued to comply with Margolin's warnings not to sue.

Stephanie didn't have to tell her closest friends that Holly's memories had pointed the finger of sex abuse at Gary. They guessed. Since the previous fall, when Holly began to suspect she had been molested, they had worried and wondered, "Who?" When Stephanie and Gary rushed south in March, with Holly in the hospital, and Stephanie suddenly filed for divorce, it seemed obvious to some. Karen Maestas had already figured it out and told her husband weeks before Holly told Stephanie it was Gary. "It was years of events. When you put them all together, it made sense," says Karen.

"It was a deep dark secret for a couple of years," says Karen. Jean Sawday says, "Karen and I and our husbands were the only ones that knew and later, when the stuff came out, our kids. We told them they couldn't tell anybody." Kelli and Shawna were initially told to tell no one. But you had to have someone to talk to. Stephanie would have gone crazy without her friends. She needed them, trusted them not to talk. It kept her sane to be able to confide in Karen on their morning walks. To talk to Jean. No one had ever seen Gary lift an incestuous finger toward any of his daughters — or a finger of abuse to any other child. But to them, that was only proof of his slyness.

As friends examined their memories of Gary's behavior, his need to show off, manipulate, and control, it fit everything they'd heard about the perpetrator. "It's so obvious, just so obvious. At first, you feel heartbreak — these kids are like our own kids — then almost sick that you didn't notice something to stop it," says Jean. "But he was the world's best salesman. I can see how he snowed Stevie. How he snowed everybody." The past now reeked with irony. Karen recalls how, every time Stephanie was really upset, she would say, "'Well, there's one thing about Gary. I know he loves his children.' She used to say that all the time. 'He loves his children.'"

"God, did he *ever!*" says Jean.

Stephanie began to suspect a conspiracy between Gary and Barry Grundland — that the man who held everyone's secrets, who pulled everyone's emotional strings, had warned Gary about the confrontation. It had not been an ambush, as he claimed, she feared. When Gary leaped up early in the March 15 confrontation and tried to leave the room, Stephanie was sure that the only surprise had been her presence — that he and Barry had both lied. In this climate of fear, she saw Robert Mondavi's power as omnipotent, and she came to believe him capable of doing anything he wished for Gary — save him, punish her — with the snap of a finger.

As word spread, friends rallied around Stephanie and the girls. Jean was a rock. Strong and athletic, an avid golfer, she even looked the bodyguard to Stephanie's blond fragility. Stephanie's oldest friend from high school, Petra Bray, came and stayed with her for several weeks during the summer. Stephanie told another friend, Lois Swanson, that Holly had said Gary raped her. At Lois's, another friend asked, "How's Holly? I've heard rumors." "She's doing fine, considering everything," Stephanie responded. "You know, it's hard to just stop loving somebody, just like that." Hard for Holly, for herself. One friend, Leslie Wright, had heard the news through the children and said, "I'm praying for you, Stevie. Could I come over and pray with you one day?" Stephanie later named at least eight more friends she told.

One man used to shake his fist at her when she was driving downtown. But from most people it was: "What can we do for you?" "Even people who were still keeping an open mind, people I didn't know well, were so helpful to me. Inviting me here and there, inviting me and Shawna." Her mother had warned her that sometimes single women were left out. But if there was a party, her friends would even send their husbands to get her. "Maybe women aren't jealous of me. I don't know. I would never, ever mess with someone else's husband — never." The generosity meant a lot. Stephanie was feeling so down on people — Gary, attorneys, the system. It kept her belief in people alive.

The girls' friends joined this protective ring. Each girl was permitted to tell one friend. Shawna told her best friend, who gave her total support. "She just lets me talk and say what I want to say." "Kelli wasn't the one to talk about it, even to her friends," says Jean. She was an extrovert like her father, but the most private. She kept the pain inside, yet word got out.

As other classmates and friends gradually learned about the rape, they exhibited fierce loyalty. "Kelli had some pretty terrific friends," says Karen. "If anybody had said anything, they would have jumped right down their throats with the truth . . . I think the same kind of feeling came over them that I had, of 'That's it. That's what's wrong,'" says Jean, "not 'Oh, it couldn't be Gary,'" adding that her husband, Chuck, had always believed Holly and never doubted Gary's guilt. There were doubters in the valley, though — husbands and wives who, hearing rumors, preferred to keep an open mind. Maggie and Brian Kelly, who had used Holly as a babysitter, agreed with their daughters at the family dinner table that they must condemn no one without proof.

But Stephanie didn't hear the doubts. From the day Marche Isabella first told her about the bulimia and sex abuse statistics, her own gut belief in her daughter's memories echoed from the solid wall of friends around her. As Stephanie and her friends would say many times — as they would embroider on the internal banner they flew for Holly — "*a mother knows.*"

The yellow mustard of late winter gave way to the lavish green of spring in Napa Valley. As summer approached, the grapes fattened and colored on the vines. White milk cartons and plastic sleeves protected the fragile shoots of new rootstock, planted to replace the strain that had fallen to phylloxera. But something just as insidious was spreading underground — rumors of incest. With loyalty and emotion instead of proof, Stephanie, her friends, and their teenage children were quietly spreading the accusations that could bring Gary Ramona down, unwittingly planting the seeds of a witch-hunt.

The rumor was creeping into the winery. Stephanie had told Anna Graeber about Holly's suspected molestation the previous November while Anna was doing Stephanie's nails, part of her job with Mary Kay cosmetics. Several Mondavi executives and their wives knew, Gary's close colleague John Lawson and his wife, Renee, among them. "Gary's wrecked Holly's life," Stephanie had told Mickey Theisen, the wife of Gary's friend Bob, over lunch, but she had said nothing more. In the fall Stephanie had told Dorothy Mondavi, Tim's wife, about Holly's molestation and bulimia. She loved Dorothy as a fine and beautiful mother — admired both Dorothy and Isabel, Michael's wife, for the solid, human touch they brought to the winery. But neither could know who had done the molesting. It could mean Gary's job — and her security.

Dorothy first called Stephanie in March, just after the confrontation. She called "I don't know how many times" again. "A mother knows," she said, as she asked Stephanie if Gary had done something to one of his daughters. Finally, when Dorothy called and said that she had guessed, Stephanie said, "Yes, Holly has said Gary had molested her or raped her, and it's true." Stephanie was chilled to hear that Dorothy had told Tim.

Stephanie asked her, "Do Michael and Isabel know?" and thought Dorothy got teary-eyed as she responded, "Stevie, I'm sorry," suggesting that they did. Stephanie had always been fond of Isabel, but when Kelli took a call from her, she just couldn't call her back. Kelli urged, "Call her back. She'll think that I didn't give you the message."

Hearing Stephanie crying as she finally returned the call, Isabel said, "Stevie, are you okay?"

"I'm scared."

"What of?"

"I can't tell you."

"Stevie, I just called you for lunch."

"We can't have lunch, and don't call me."

Isabel called Barry Grundland to ask what was wrong; he said, "Listen to Stevie. Don't call her."

Stephanie was being hurt and offended by other rumors. Gary's mother, Garnet, had reportedly spread a rumor, while having her hair done in San Diego, that Stephanie had run off with her tennis instructor. Then Isabel told her she had heard that Stephanie had been out to dinner with a man nobody knew. Later — without asking her directly about Gary's molesting Holly — she said, "Are you going to move?" "No, we didn't do anything wrong. Gary did . . . My kids don't want to move. We're staying right here," Stephanie snapped back.

She was shaken when Bob Mondavi called right at the beginning, wanting to talk to Gary. But apparently he knew only about the divorce. "I wanted to tell Gary that I'm supporting him all the way, to take off some time to get his personal life together if he needs it," he said. Stephanie gave him Gary's number at his mother's.

Marcia Santos, Gary's secretary, had called Stephanie at her mother's when they were all south for the confrontation to ask, "Is Holly okay?" "Yes," she said. "Oh, thank God. I thought it had something to do with Holly," said Marcia, relieved. Stephanie said, "Marcia, it has everything to do with Holly," then hung up. The two women continued to talk in innuendos. Later, Marcia asked Stephanie, "If I knew, would I hate working for Gary? Are you telling me *I don't want to know?*" "Yes, you don't want to know . . . But it's important that you stand by Gary," said Stephanie, hoping Marcia would maintain her loyalty and her silence.

Gary wasn't talking to anybody, but he finally told his mother about Holly's vision under the amytal that Garnet had been raped by her two brothers. Garnet was outraged. "How in hell could anybody ever say anything like that? It is absolutely not true. Where could they *get* something like that?" she demanded, her tiny body rigid with anger.

But Gary challenged her five or six times over the next weeks: "Mom, you're not doing me any good if you don't tell me." The belief was out there that incest ran in families. Steph was rattling the threat of criminal charges. He had to know. But, deeply hurt, Garnet said over and over, "Where could they get something like that?" Otherwise, he told none of his relatives — his stepsisters, his uncles and cousins. "I took a very hard stand not to talk about it until I had my day in court." His family would come to their senses. They must. The word "incest" would ruin him just by association. No one would care if he was innocent. The moral blot would stain him forever.

He had to tell Lloyd Jenkins, his accountant. It was tax time, and with the divorce, his financial picture would change dramatically. He made Lloyd promise not to tell his wife, JoeAnna.

Larry Graeber was the only one he had told at Mondavi, and he trusted Larry totally. He couldn't tell Bob Mondavi. This craziness would be cleared up once he'd got his family to listen and his three daughters knew the truth. The Mondavis need never — they must never — know.

Divorce had become the organizing principle of life, the structure of law the armature on which the tattered remains of the Ramona family were hung. With the first hearing on March 19, *Ramona v. Ramona* was born as a divorce case on the court calendar. The courtrooms of Superior Court judges Champlin, Fretz, and Snowden in the shaded hundred-year-old white frame courthouse in Napa would become as familiar to the Ramonas as their home had been. The courtrooms would be the scene of three separate trials as the issues of property, support, and custody were fought. Stephanie had cited "irreconcilable differences" as the cause of the divorce. With California's community property law, it should be a simple division of assets, everything split in half. "All I wanted out of this was a divorce. Half of what was mine," says Stephanie. But driven by the underlying issue of incest and perceived betrayal on both sides, the disposal of every cent and stick of furniture would be fought to the death in what became the longest and most bitter divorce battle in Napa's history.

Discovery — the uniquely American process that permits both sides in a lawsuit to demand full disclosure of any and all relevant information — was triggered the moment Stephanie Ramona filed for divorce. It would be triggered anew with each lawsuit Stephanie and

Gary filed and cross-filed against each other. Through the legal process of discovery, privacy became a poignant memory.

As this new phase of life began, Barry Grundland's office became a neutral zone where the couple could meet without violence to sign checks and make decisions on the unfinished house; Stephanie felt they must finish and sell it.

When she walked into that office for the first time after the confrontation to meet Gary, she snapped at him, "Get up and get out of that chair." She didn't even want to sit in that particular chair; she just felt she had to do something, some kind of spontaneous power play.

"Huh?" said Gary, shocked.

"Just get out of that chair. I'm sitting there."

He got up and moved to the chair she usually sat in.

Fueled by the adrenaline surge of survival and fear, Stephanie had found a new assertiveness, flexing muscles of independence, trying out her voice and reveling in it, like a child. "I was concerned about money, but I knew I could do it. Sometimes, when you don't have a choice, it's easier," she says.

Later, she recalls, Gary called her on the phone and said, "Look, I don't know what you're going to do. You can't do anything. You don't know anything . . . All we have is $300,000 in the bank, and that's our retirement."

"Don't worry about it. It's my worry. I'll do it," she responded, and hung up on him. She now thinks "he was just trying to knock me down or to scare me." As discovery began, "I found out we had a lot of money. Plenty of money." The Ramonas were worth millions.

Gary's first deposition was on June 13, 1990. A man whose only previous brush with the law had been throwing a July Fourth firecracker out of a car — who had never told his best friend, Scott, how much money he earned or how well he was doing — was forced to dump everything on the table. So far, the divorce had been gentle with him. His legal costs had been only $5,000. He still owned both houses. His job poured half a million dollars a year into the family treasury. He was still naive about the process as Steph's attorney began to interrogate him.

Gary was edgy and impatient with the questions, with his life being reduced to dollars and cents: cars and clothing bills, the financial details of his life at Mondavi — salary, stock, house loans. The personal wine cellar he had been collecting since he joined Mondavi in 1970 would be valued at $48,000. The cost of the pool, the gazebo, the value of his homes. He reported that he had paid $160,000 for the house on Pinot Way, that he and Steph had agreed on a selling price of $575,000, and that it was for sale. Just the week before, he had listed the new house with Chuck Sawday. It was just a smokescreen, Stephanie feared; she knew Gary wanted to move in and hold that prize.

Gary sat in the office of Stephanie's attorney, Roger Lewis, on the second floor of one of the restored Victorians that had survived the demolition ball in Napa. He knew he would grant custody of the children to Stephanie. As long as he could get visitation rights to see the girls freely, his concession to Steph on this point might help keep quiet the rumors in the valley that could further devastate the family. The Mondavis continued to be incredibly supportive as the house and the divorce took their toll on Gary's ability to focus. He felt safe with this family.

Gary was five days from receiving a shock from the Mondavis as devastating as Holly's charges had been from his blood family. Yes, he had been distracted with the divorce and the house. He was spending two or three hours a day on the house and running back and forth to lawyers with papers. He knew he wasn't functioning at his best, but he was having a superb spring at Mondavi. The family had praised him for the five-page color foldout tribute in the May issue of *Wine Spectator,* the spread he had orchestrated for the wine auction in June. His name did not appear in the tribute, nor should it, he felt. The family was still the best marketing tool he had; they were the magic. The financial year just ending showed profits at historic highs. "I took this company [as part of a team] from under thirty thousand cases to doing about three million cases in wine annually, from under $1 million in gross revenue to just under $120 million in gross revenue — from one winery to four wineries." He had never asked for a raise. No one had ever told Gary his performance was anything but exemplary.

He felt his problems with the sons were under control. Knowing Michael's sensitivity about Gary's closeness to his father, he had tried to stay away from Bob as much as possible the last few years. With Tim, there was still a tension, created when Bob installed Gary over Tim to run Vichon the past November.

But rumors of incest gave a new edge to the old tensions. Tim and Michael had learned about Holly's charges from their wives and told Bob, who was shocked. In twenty years Gary had never lied, and he did not, for a second, believe it was true. From the first moment, Bob was clear and unswerving: "I support Gary. He is innocent. This rumor is not to be considered in any dealings with Gary." He reported it to his daughters-in-law, Isabel and Dorothy, worried that their fears as mothers and their friendship with Stephanie would lead them to lose perspective. He dropped by Dorothy and Tim's one day, and, with Tim present, had one of several emotional talks with Dorothy. "At the beginning, she said we should have no one working for the winery with these accusations," Bob recalls. "But I made it clear that the accusations were not proven, and any judgment should be withheld completely," he argued. Isabel, also, "made it very clear that Gary should not be associated with the winery, and I made it very clear that I didn't believe it at all." The rumors were just that, he argued again and again.

Bob Mondavi had never before heard a word of criticism about Gary Ramona. Nor had Bob Theisen, who had worked with Gary and Larry Graeber for nine years. Gary was a great salesman and would drive his points home, but he was never dictatorial. Now, however, there were rumblings, and criticisms of Gary began to float through the rough plaster halls of Napa's most famous winery. For some, negative thoughts that may have been harbored for years were now unleashed by the rumors. For others, Gary may have become a lightning rod for anxiety over the market. The wine industry was in a sales slump, and pressure on the industry and serious attacks on wine were coming from several quarters. The Mondavis were trying to catch up to the "fighting varietals" wave, and sales was Gary's responsibility.

A change in attitude toward Gary took over the inside group. "He's just not tracking," said Greg Evans, the chief financial officer since 1983, viewing him with a finance man's eyes. "He was not tracking on budgets." Evans urged him to install a financial person to take better control. But Gary "wasn't responsive to suggestions for change . . . I think for a while Gary probably understood where Bob wanted to go as well as anybody. I think he took on Bob's lavishness to some degree, which, depending on how you looked at it, was either extravagant or — for a company that did no advertising — simply a marketing expense." Bob's self-termed "crazy projects" often ended up being very shrewd business deals. Opus One had proved successful and would pay off in the long run. But was Gary's judgment as good as Bob's? To Greg, the classic example was Gary's promotion and development of the Costa Mesa center. Greg did not support it. "I thought we would be better off bringing people up to the vineyards as opposed to having another Vineyard Room in the middle of this corporate park. L.A. is really a place people want to leave to go up to Napa." But at a special board meeting to approve the cost, Bob had announced that he was behind Gary all the way, thought it would work, and urged "Let's go forward," silencing any opposition. The center was a beautiful place with an amorphous mission. It was not "a profit center."

"We all love Gary. He is part of the family," Michael said. Outwardly, they all agreed that Gary should be supported and presumed innocent. But both sons still harbored a deep sense of displacement by their father's bond with Gary. Bob felt Gary was still there and available whenever he wanted him. "He was busy selling, and that I understand," Bob would say when Gary couldn't be reached. But that spring, Michael's impatience began to erupt over Gary's inaccessibility. He couldn't reach him. He wouldn't return calls, Michael fumed. But he knew Gary got his messages. The pickup times were recorded on the phone.

Gary had joined a small family company; he now ran global sales and marketing for a $200 million corporation — which would, within two years, go public on the stock exchange. Gary was a good businessman, most thought. He analyzed problems well. But complaints were now heard that perhaps he lacked the marketing sophistication, the delegation and organizational skills, for today's marketplace. Great salesmen were not always good managers. Perhaps to some, Fullerton State B.A.'s were not Harvard M.B.A.'s. A number of the Young Turks thought Gary did not have a good sense of his own limitations — that like the young bond trader of the 1980s in *Bonfire of the Vanities,* he felt invincible.

Gary Ramona was, in fact, extremely vulnerable. The words "allegations of rape" were never used. "To the family's credit, I never heard anyone say that Gary probably did this or Gary is guilty of this," says an insider. But a quiet case was building against him. The issue of Gary erupted several times at board meetings, where Bob "made it very clear that it was not to be part of any decisions we made." But Tim and Michael, senior management, and the board became convinced that Gary's job needed serious reevaluation. The company, always evolving, often called on consultants to help structure changes. The decision was made to hire Price Waterhouse to do a review of all senior sales and marketing management over the summer — not just of Gary, but of other executives as well. It was to be evenhanded.

They could dance around it, but the board members knew they were dealing with a delicate moral and political issue. The idea of rape within this family company was difficult even if it did not involve a virtual member of the family. Previously, an employee had been convicted of child abuse, and he had been kept on as a rehabilitative gesture. But Gary Ramona was one of the most powerful, visible stars in the management firmament, with great customer relationships all over the world. What damage would the rumors do? "At the board level, it got to be one of those subjects of conversation that you develop some euphemisms for," says a senior executive. "You'd hear about 'Gary's issues' or 'Gary's problems.' No one said they thought Gary was guilty. They'd say, 'We don't know whether Gary's been involved or not, but his effectiveness, level of trust, and rapport with people in the business is going to be a real problem.'" The proposal was made to put him on a six-month paid leave of absence. It would give him time to resolve the personal problems that were distracting him from his work, and in January he would return with full power and pay.

Did the incest have any bearing on this decision? It was doubtless driven by genuine feeling for Gary's personal needs at the time. Bob himself publicly defends it: "We discussed the accusations at the board meeting — we *knew* it — but it was not the purpose of the leave of absence, it was not the basis of anything we did." But the need to rationalize a painful moral decision can shape corporate memory as surely as it shapes an individual's. And the concern over Gary's inadequacy in the new world of wine marketing took on a ring of conviction as it was argued by Mondavi's board and management council over the coming months and years.

Bob was profoundly torn. In their hearts, both he and Margrit believed the leave of absence was an excuse to remove Gary from the winery. Bob didn't want to let him go. But he had made the decision six years earlier to turn over the management of the winery to his sons. The process had begun fitfully. "They didn't think I gave them full charge . . . One would go south, one would go north." Just in the past year he had removed himself to the role of chairman and given Tim and Michael full executive power as partners. They were beginning to work as a team; in fact, they were doing "one hell of a job." The continuation of the family wine dynasty meant much to Bob. "The only way they can learn leadership is by making their own mistakes." Michael's self-confidence had grown tremendously, Bob felt, through Mike's activity in the Young Presidents Organization. And Mike and Gary had been agreeing more the past few years. If he started second-guessing and intervening, it could undermine the delicate balances of power and personality that were finally being achieved.

Bob feared he and his sons would be head-to-head about Gary, that Mike and Tim would not fight for him as Bob would have. The three men respected one another's points of view. But already it was clear that the sons stood with their wives in the opposite camp from their father. Bob had ceded power to his sons and was being outvoted. On June 10, the board directed that a leave-of-absence letter be written for Gary Ramona. Michael would sign it, but all three Mondavis would present it to him.

On June 18, Gary spent all day in meetings at the guest house in the hills of the vineyard estate in Yountville where Bob, Tim, and Michael had built their homes, a five-minute drive from the winery. A rambling California bungalow, it had been restored and decorated by Margrit in a fresh and comfortable country style. Toward the end of the day, a discussion began about the need for talks with various executives about remuneration. With the market generally softening, they were not anticipating any salary increases this year. Gary was enthusiastic about a salary freeze. Let the top executives lead the way. He picked up no undercurrent, no red flag.

As the meeting was ending, Bob said, "Tim and Michael, I think we should meet with Gary for a few minutes."

"Sure, where do you want to meet?" asked Gary, anticipating a continuation of the salary discussion.

"Why don't we meet just outside."

The four men strolled to a picnic table and benches under a tree in the small garden. As they sat down, Michael prepared to hand Gary two sheets of paper, a letter, but before Gary could read it they wanted to read it to him. Gary cannot remember who said it — "Gary, we're putting you on a leave of absence."

His head pounded, his eyes filled with tears as they read to him. He heard only snatches of the words: "We have a hundred percent faith in you . . . and look forward to . . . growing together over the next twenty . . . sabbatical to study the wine industry . . . changes in the market, project the next ten years . . . open and full communication with anyone at the winery. However you will have no responsibility or authority . . ." He heard Tim and Michael making comments. He heard Bob constantly inserting his reassurances that he was part of the family, that they would maintain his salary. "This leave and sabbatical reflect our commitment to you as a person and our belief that your renewed energies and intellect are essential elements to the future of our company and family," they read. As he sat there, Gary was no longer functioning. He just listened.

"Are you done?"

One of them started to say something else. "Are you *done?*" Gary choked out, cutting him off.

"Yes."

"Okay, I'll see you." He took the letter and wandered toward his car, crunching the gravel of the driveway as Bob called out, "You're going to be at my birthday party, aren't you?"

Gary drove to his mother's, scarcely able to see the road, trying to assess the shock of this bomb going off in his face. "I've never had a negative review. We've just finished the most profitable year in the history of the company." He knew the answers were not to be found in the balance sheets. Holly's allegations had found their way to the heart of the organization. From within the winery, the snake had struck.

At his mother's, as he fumbled to get dressed for Bob's party, he knew that this was the first of a number of steps the Mondavis would take to try to distance themselves from him and protect themselves legally. The pain was even worse than what he had felt at the confrontation with his daughter and Marche Isabella. Then, a stranger had been the messenger. He didn't blame his family. He believed that, as they learned what Isabella had done, they would reconcile. But this blow had been struck by the Mondavis themselves. For the second time, a family had abandoned him. Again, no one had asked him a question — not one question.

Gary drove up the twisting mountain road to Bob and Margrit's hilltop house, the house he had visited so many times to strategize with Bob, for dinners and parties, always welcomed like a son. The reception was under way. Cloth-skirted tables with Margrit's flowers and candles were set out around the interior pool, a few steps down from the expanse of marble where thirty or forty guests were sipping Mondavi's own sparkling brut reserve and nibbling from trays of hors d'oeuvres. Margrit and Bob were making the rounds, welcoming guests: Margrit hugging and releasing her squeals of enthusiasm like a sunburst into each little group, Bob with the kiss on both cheeks he'd learned from Baron Rothschild for the women. Gary saw Greg Evans and Cliff Adams and said hello to a few people, feeling sick. He asked Margrit to please take his name off the seating chart; he couldn't face dinner. He went over and toasted a happy birthday to Bob. Gary knew Bob was loyal to him, would always be loyal to him. He loved this man, and he knew Bob loved him. The two men hugged, an aging king and the beloved champion he could no longer protect, caught by fate in a gathering tragedy. Gary left.

"When you come to work on Monday and are told that *Gary Ramona* is taking a sabbatical for six months, everybody knows it within thirty-eight seconds," says Harvey Posert, who reported to Gary as director of PR. "Then the rumor of incest began to pop up." Bob Mondavi watched, horrified and helpless. "It just spread like wildfire."

8

The Christmas Present

Darn it, Holly's going to have a real birthday. Betty was determined. "I felt so sorry for Holly." Her twentieth birthday was coming up on August 16. Holly had moved in with her grandmother at the end of her sophomore year, in May. "She was staying with me and I only had one bedroom. The poor kid was sleeping on the sofa and she was so good." She worked so hard, did what she had to do. Always worked and helped pay her way. And she didn't complain. Betty wished she would sometimes. Betty's niece Barbara O'Connell had got Holly a part-time job in a psychiatric hospital — billing, filing, using computers, managing. It was a scheme concocted by the aunts to help her learn how to run her own practice when she became a therapist. They loved Holly at work. They loved her at Unisys, where Betty was a senior secretary, whenever she came by. They saw her, as Betty did, as the most honest kid in the world. They believed her. They invited Betty and Holly to things, to little parties, dinners.

But there was hostility out there, too. It hurt Betty that, with most people, the first response to Holly's story was: "Her father worked so hard all his life. He lost everything." They never thought about the children, about Holly. And she was amazed at the number of friends who now came to her with their stories of molestation. She had had no idea how many women out there were holding secrets or how sheltered she and Stephanie had been. She didn't worry about Kelli. Kelli was widely capable. Heading off to the University of Colorado, she'd be taking business courses, qualifying as an aerobics instructor, studying to be a private investigator, having fun with her friends. But Holly's life was so lonely. She had good days, bad days. She could seem strong, but the vulnerability inside pained her grandmother. She was so distrustful.

But so was Betty. Gary had destroyed her capacity to trust. He was evil. She had always been tolerant of his trying to divide and separate the women in the family, trying to control, because she thought it came from his lack of confidence. Now she saw sinister purposes, and she hated him with a ferocity that scared her. Happy Betty, who loved to laugh, play craps, and, in her sixties, still had New Year's slumber parties with her pals, had stopped laughing. Her Pollyanna nature had been transformed into "I hate, I *hate*."

As soon as Holly was asleep the night before her birthday, Betty started decorating the apartment. "I got this big balloon with the legs on it and put it right there by her so she'd see it when she woke up. I put streamers and balloons all over the house. I had to do it so quietly." As Holly stirred in the morning, Betty cried out, "Surprise! We're going to Catalina!" The night Betty and Stevie's father celebrated their engagement, they had sailed to Catalina with a bunch of friends. It was full of good memories; maybe they'd rub off on Holly. They took the ferry across to Balboa and had breakfast at Britta's, the cute little café that was their favorite. At nine A.M., they boarded the huge catamaran that raced across the surf to Avalon, the tourist town on Catalina. They stayed outside on the deck, Holly's long hair streaming in the wind. "It was so neat," so nostalgic for Betty. At Avalon, they toured the little shops, escaped the tourists by taking the tram up to see the live buffalo, and took the catamaran back in the late afternoon. Betty was thrilled. Holly had loved it. "She was so shiny about the boat ride."

There was little "shiny" in Holly's life. It was a life bounded by her depression, her flashbacks, and her therapy. Marche Isabella's sketchy notes of Holly's office visits recorded her decline at Irvine. *July 25: From A & B student to C & D student.* Holly's grades were a measure of her deterioration since leaving the hospital the second time. A habitually good and disciplined student, she had been put on probation at the end of the spring quarter when her grades dropped and her GPA plunged from 3.5 to 1.7. She was going to summer school to catch up and working an extra job as a high school counselor so that she could make a little money; at $7.25 an hour, she made $580 a month. She felt like a hooker, having to ask her father for money. For the first time she was not spending the summer in Napa. Her father was in the valley, and she didn't want to see him. But in a letter to her mother she said, "The major reason I don't want to go home is because I've gained weight . . . I don't even like to see my family when I've gained weight because it puts pressure on me."

Betty loved Holly so much, but there began to be some friction between her and her granddaughter. Betty understood. After living with Gary's controlling for so long, Holly was reacting. Belatedly, she was exercising her assertiveness; at times she was *over*controlling. She would do things her way and was very sensitive to anybody suggesting anything, Betty observed, walking on eggs. As Gary had in his meetings with Holly, Betty was discovering the sensitive geography of boundary violations. After church on Sundays, Betty would be "so careful not to suggest brunch. I wait for her to suggest. She is finally determined to run her own life."

Holly had had "issues" with her grandmother since the first months of therapy. Betty had given her the third degree, Holly reported to Isabella, being protective of her daughter and angry at Holly for bringing up criticisms of her mother. Her grandmother had continued to "violate boundaries," Holly reported, but by the summer she was confronting Gram, setting her own boundaries. She was frustrated with her mother and feeling anger — a familiar pattern for young women recovering memories of incest. Isabella scrawled in her notes: *Realizing she's angry with her mother for not protecting her.* Holly was suspicious that her mother *had* guessed something was going on and not acted. Why had her mom not been the "strong one for me" while Holly went through the trauma of remembering her abuse? Her mom was getting upset and dumping on Holly, stirring things up for her and her grandmother.

Part of her frustration with her mother and Gram was their opposition to her lawsuit. Holly had been on an emotional roller coaster since May over suing her dad. As early as May 2, Isabella had recorded Holly's decision to press charges. She had first seen a lawyer in mid-May, finding Robert Marc Hindin's name by calling a lawyer referral service. Isabella noted the reasons Holly wanted to sue: *Stop sexual abuse of another child. Stand up to him. Don't want him to get away with it. She feels she gave up something as a little girl against her will . . . he will be forced to pay money against his will. Has to be accountable.* But she felt ambivalence that paralyzed her from acting. A note recorded: *Teary, feeling the loss of her dad.* By July 11, she was still debating whether to go to court.

During the months of indecision, Stephanie and Betty were a persistent chorus of opposition. All along, Betty warned Holly not to sue. "Do you know what you're getting into? You know your father. They'll tear you apart." Stephanie said the same thing. But Holly argued that she had to do it, at the risk of her own privacy and safety. There were other kids out there she must protect.

On July 24, Richard Rose put Holly on Prozac. Isabella noted: *Much brighter affect. Sleeping better. Not as depressed.* But Holly was still bombarded by flashbacks, and they were no longer freeze frames. "As time went by, after the sodium amytal, I would get bits and pieces with much more motion than before, and I began to be able to see a complete picture . . . to put a sequence of events together." August 23: *Memory of father, oral sex — penis in her mouth, age 5–7. Parents' bedroom.* Holly hardened her determination to sue. She told Isabella about a fantasy she had had of being more powerful than her father.

Holly, too, was frightened of her father and for her family. A lawsuit could bring down his wrath. That summer she wrote her mother: "Maybe this is one of the most selfish letters you've ever received. Maybe your [sic] getting angry right now. I know you're concerned about Shawna . . . about what people will think . . . I don't want to hurt you guys just so I can make myself feel better . . . I realize that I'm not going to come out of this whole thing with everyone thinking what I did was good or right. Some people will think it's very selfish and that I only did it for the money . . . But I don't want to sit on the sidelines, I don't want to play the victim's role. I want to fight back."

On August 28, her mother capitulated and joined Holly in her lawyer's office in L.A., where Marc Hindin delivered a lesson on sex abuse law. Holly had been specifically aided by a California bill effective on January 1, 1987, allowing victims to sue within three years of majority age in cases of abuse by a household or family member. At the moment, she had one year left in which to sue. But early in 1991, the statute of limitations was further liberalized to accommodate the groundswell of childhood sexual abuse victims wanting access to the courts and would be dramatically extended: California would permit women (and men, too) with recovered memories — as well as people who had always remembered their abuse — the right to sue *after discovering the psychological damage done by the abuse.* Having seen the principle work for asbestos victims, Mary Williams, a Northern California attorney and champion of access to the courts for victims of childhood sexual abuse, pioneered this "delayed discovery of injury" in California. Her goal had been to give access to women who had never forgotten their abuse but only belatedly made the connection between it and their symptoms as adults. "But in practice, the courts and judges tended to find it easier to understand the delay, and thus to permit it, if the victim claimed to have repressed or otherwise forgotten the abuse itself," says a disappointed Williams. Delayed discovery would permit Holly to sue up to eight years after her majority or within three years of discovering her damage, whichever was later. Leading a wave of change that would subsequently reach more than half the American states, California's new statutes would let you sue until you were sixty, eighty, ninety!

The climate for Holly to sue was almost irresistible, for lawsuits were being encouraged by the survivor movement. Judith Lewis Herman supported the young women who came forward to fight incest through lawsuits in her 1992 *Trauma and Recovery:* "In refusing to hide or be silenced, in insisting that rape is a public matter, and in demanding social change, survivors create their own living monument." Suing had the appeal of martyrdom. Mary Williams was quoted in *The Courage to Heal* as saying that after a lawsuit, "a lot of my clients also feel a tremendous sense of relief and victory. They get strong by suing . . . The legal system is so important to the American consciousness. If you can take it to court, there's a way in which you symbolically get vindicated that doesn't happen in any other way."

Still Holly held back. Gary's attorney would later accuse Holly of delaying until the new house had been sold and her mother had her share of the money in the bank — that Holly had held back for money. But Stephanie would claim in an emotional outburst in a deposition that Holly delayed because she, her mother, kept warning her, "Don't do it." "Yes, I was . . . worried — I'm not proud of the fact, but about money, about everything." But mainly it was the guilt and the fear. "I should have protected her and I didn't. I was her *mother,*" Stephanie would admit, in tears. She would try to protect her now: *"Don't sue. I don't want you doing it. You don't know your dad."*

In late August, Stephanie picked up her telephone messages and shook with fear. The voice sounded as if it was coming from a car phone. Shawna heard it, too. It was a growling sound, like that of a lion or some other animal. The sounds were unintelligible until the end, when through the guttural growl she could make out the words,

"Fuck you." She told Anna Graeber, Jean, and Karen, unable to say the *F* word. She thought it was Gary.

Stephanie's fear of Gary had been growing over the summer, for other frightening things were happening. Kelli believed that she and her best friend were being followed by a very scary-looking man in a blue car. Was it a private detective? Several times they ran into an ice cream shop to hide. Or he would sit in front of their house. Holly and Shawna both had feelings they were being followed. Stephanie would come out of Grundland's office and there the man would be.

One hot day in August, Stephanie and Gary were standing next door, in front of Charlie Piazza's house, signing papers. She recalls telling him about a paper she had lost, and Gary was smirking and laughing. She had always loved his laugh, but this arrogant, uncaring . . . She fired off, "How can you smirk and laugh and act like that when you have raped our daughter?" Gary was silent, waiting. Charlie was working in the garden nearby, hearing it all. As soon as Charlie went inside, Stephanie recalls Gary threatening her: "If you don't shut your mouth, I am going to shut your mouth . . . *permanently,* so no one ever hears it again."

Stephanie learned that he had changed his address in the winery's telephone directory from his mother's to the dream house. His agreeing to sell was a ruse, she feared; he *was* going to move in. The cost of finishing the house was escalating out of control — Gary kept going to court asking for hundreds of thousands more, draining the pot of resources, trying to hurt her, she believed. Using the house as an excuse, he had suddenly, in September, slashed her monthly payments from $5,100 to $1,400 without asking the court; she'd had to borrow from her aunt and friends to pay her bills. With no savings, she hid $2,000 in a baking soda box in the refrigerator as a fallback for food. Paying for the new house had been systematically reducing her style of living since 1986; she no longer even had a housekeeper once a week while Gary earned half a million a year. "It's the control. If he takes the house away from the family, then we'll buckle. We'll be in trouble, have to move into a shack. He thinks I'll put pressure on Holly. Kelli won't get an education . . ." Stephanie needed a new lawyer, one with no ties to Gary. Before her legal troubles were over, Stephanie had as many lawyers as Elizabeth Taylor had husbands.

Friends were saying that she needed "a stronger, better lawyer" to blast Gary out of the new house. Led to Sandra Musser in San Francisco, Stephanie prepared to take all her legal papers and dump them on Musser's desk. The brio she had exhibited the first few months was collapsing, drained by her fears, the lawyers, the emotional issues with Holly, and the money going, going. She was nearly ready to crack.

The Saturday before meeting Musser, Stephanie was sitting on the floor at home surrounded by papers, weeping as she tried to organize them, when Karen and Jean came through the door and said, "We're taking over from now on." They had offered before, but "I didn't want to ask for help. I didn't want to dirty them." Finally they just came in and said, "That's it. We're going to sit down, work together, and get it organized." And they did. "I think I probably wouldn't be here today if they hadn't walked in that door that day." They went with her to meet Sandra Musser. When the lawyer said, "Tell me the story," Stephanie burst into tears. "I was a basket case."

"She was a very dominating, domineering type. She just takes charge," one of Stephanie's several subsequent lawyers would say about Sandra Musser. Musser went immediately on the offensive, filing a restraining order against Gary on November 9, citing his past violence, the "chilling telephone call," and his threat to "silence" Stephanie permanently. In a declaration of expenses, she argued that the house had careened "way over budget and behind schedule," a pattern of vindictive profligacy that would destroy Stephanie's future and her children's health, welfare, and education.

On that day Musser also filed a sealed affidavit, a secret document describing Holly's accusations of incest against her father. It was this devastating abuse, the document argued, that made it "crucial" that Holly be financially able to get therapy (she paid for her own Prozac) and finish college. Stephanie knew that this document contained dynamite that could demolish Gary's — and therefore her own — future if it were to become public. But she was fighting for her children's future, fighting for the financial support he should freely give.

Musser guided Stephanie firmly through her first depositions for the divorce in the office of Gary's lawyer, Eugenia Magowan. On November 16, sitting across the deposition table from Gary, Stephanie dumped her financial story onto the table — her dozen credit cards, her Meadowood membership, two hairdressers, her passion for music tapes and purses, the $20,000 she had already paid her lawyers. Nervous and stumbling over the questions, she said, in defense of why she still spent a pathetic few dollars each month on flowers for the house, "I buy them to make it happy." Stephanie told a poignant story of the failed jewelry business. "I think I still have some pearls left."

As the depositions continued on November 30, the mood was taut. The new house had a buyer. Escrow was closing; the questioning was punctuated with the drama of phone calls and papers rushed in and out for signing. The real estate market had crashed. The house had been put on the market for $3.8 million; it was being sold for $2.3 million — a fire sale. But it had to go through. "If this falls apart, it falls on you," Musser said, glaring at Gary as tension built to the closing of the deal by the end of the day. The house netted the Ramonas $565,000 in liquid assets.

"Was Prince red or brown?" Holly asked her mother on the phone. Oh, God. Prince had been their dog in Diamond Bar. Stephanie knew what the question meant. Holly had had another flashback.

By late fall, Isabella's notes showed a disturbing progression of Holly's memories, from a benign hand on the thigh ten months earlier to, by the end of October, bestiality — sex with an animal. On October 30 she recorded: *Remembers a picture or a flash of father naked holding the dog's legs and fears he was having sex with the dog.* On November 13: *Talking about bestiality father did to her and with their male dog.* Holly saw herself as being between five and eight years old, an obedient little girl, performing an act of oral sex with the dog. She had always felt dirty and wanted to shower after her flashbacks, but there was no shower that could purge her of the disgust she now felt. As she flew north with Betty for Thanksgiving, she had told Isabella that she was filing a civil suit against her father by mid-December. With the flashback about Prince, any lingering indecision about suing vanished. Holly was ready to make him pay for what he had done, to hold him accountable.

Stephanie faced the desolate news about the dog. She knew that Gary had lost interest in her the last few years of their marriage. Intercourse had ceased, and she was sure he'd had affairs. That was hard enough to face. But when she got Holly's call about Prince, she went to Grundland, shaking, and said, "I guess it's hard to realize and to figure it out that your husband really may, quite frankly, have preferred a dog or a child to you."

The five Ramona women gathered on Pinot Way for Thanksgiving, their first without Gary. Kelli drove in from Colorado, where she was a freshman. They kicked off their shoes as the women in Betty's family used to; it was a women's world again. "The family is so much happier now, so much more relaxed without Gary," Betty observed. For Stephanie, it was "a silly, laughing, happy time. People could say we tore the family apart. No, that's wrong. Someone tore away from the family." The five women *were* a family.

For the gregarious salesman, the isolation forced on Gary by the sabbatical was hard. It had stripped him of contact and purpose. An industry report he was supposed to do was simply make-work, in his opinion. He was grateful when Michael Mondavi invited him to a major wine event, the Wine Experience, in San Francisco in late November. He felt alive again.

Gary took a break from the Wine Experience about five-thirty or six and returned to his room at the Marriott to pick up his messages. He was always checking in for messages.

"I hear you're into dogs now, huh," a woman said. It was Steph's voice. He listened to it two, three times. He couldn't believe what he was hearing, just couldn't believe it. To think that your spouse, whom you spent twenty-five years with, could call you up and leave this sick — and she was obviously sick — message. It was not the same woman. "This was a very disturbed, distorted sick person." Gary had no idea what it meant, but he could guess. What bothered him most was that she believed it had happened, but he still could not feel anger toward her; it wasn't her fault. He pressed Ephraim Margolin again about a lawsuit against the therapist; again, the lawyer discouraged him.

At a divorce hearing in a Napa courtroom on December 10, Sandra Musser launched another withering barrage of declarations against Gary. He heard the same theme Marche Isabella had planted: the overcontrolling man. In a plea for spousal support, Musser argued: "Husband insists on continuing to control his wife . . . Wife alleges that husband exercised demeaning and wrongful control over their children and over her. She seeks to terminate her marriage and to extricate herself from his control. He has employed every device to continue to exercise control over wife . . ."

Then she announced the existence of the sealed affidavit filed by Stephanie on November 9. "Blackmail," Gary exploded, when he

read the sealed document in Judge Champlin's chambers. He saw that
they had wanted him to see it. It was filled with "absolute lies" — the
charge that Holly had been raped, that Steph was "advised" by Child
Protective Services that he'd molested Shawna. Lies! She and Sandra
Musser clearly still believed the sodium amytal interview to be the
very heart of their evidence of his guilt: "In order to ascertain the truth
of the matter and to assist Holly in coping, her doctors administered
sodium amythol [sic] and questioned her. Under this drug Holly recalled three instances where she was raped by her father. Subsequent
examinations of Holly and of her childhood medical records are consistent with Holly's statements under sodium amythol [sic] and her
flashbacks." Steph had signed it.

For nine months Gary had tried to get his family to meet with the
top psychiatrists in the country. "Look," he'd offered, "you go in and
meet with them first. Or we'll go in and meet as a family. However you
want to work with this." He couldn't get them to budge — even to
listen. He had been soft on Steph, chalking up her behavior to gullibil-
ity and naiveté, accepting what Isabella told her to think, doing whatever Musser told her to do. The anger Wolfgang Lederer knew would
finally come had erupted.

Gary read the document as a blatant threat: either you acquiesce
to our financial demands or we're going to open this document. Any
secrecy had already been badly breached. Chuck Sawday, who had
sold the house, told Gary he had discussed the charges with his
wife, Jean, and felt caught in the middle and wanted to stay out of it.
Karen Maestas and her daughter had betrayed themselves by their
rude behavior. There had been a humiliating incident in downtown St.
Helena when, coming from Chuck's office after signing some papers,
a winemaker friend spotted Gary as he left a restaurant and came up
to shake hands. As he reached out, Gary saw the man's stepdaughter,
a friend of Shawna's, "go berserk" at the end of the block. It was
just a kid being loyal, Gary knew. But if the teenage network knew,
their parents did. In late summer he got a call from Reno, from a
Mondavi distributor who was a good friend. "I've heard a number of
nasty issues. But I want you to know, Gary, I don't believe this.
You have a friend," he said, inviting him up to Tahoe to relax if he
needed a break. What chilled Gary was that he said he had heard
the rumor from a Mondavi district manager who worked directly
for Larry Graeber. It was all over the wine industry! His career was
already "going down the tubes." "The hell with you," he decided.

"They were holding over my head the publicity of going public with the allegations," thinking he'd fold. "You want this public? It'll be public!"

Knowing Ephraim Margolin would say "You can't sue," Gary aggressively sought out other lawyers. One in Sausalito also discouraged him. Again he heard, the therapists owed him nothing — no duty; he could not get Holly's medical records. Gary set up an appointment with an attorney in Southern California. Whatever further advice lawyers gave him, Gary had set his course: he would sue Holly's therapists.

One of the few people who encouraged him was Lederer. He agreed with Gary that a lawsuit might get Holly back — that if it was established that Marche Isabella and Richard Rose had wrongly supported Holly in her memories, it might reawaken her doubts. There was no proof her memories were factual. Like Margolin, Lederer did not think Gary was guilty; Gary needed to clear his name. With a lawsuit, there was also a chance for reconciliation with Holly. There could be none if he confessed to molesting her just to please her.

Lederer continued to treat Gary for stress as his career at Mondavi moved into its final stages. Through the fall of 1990, the Mondavis were boxing him in. Michael had canceled the industry study he had been assigned and ordered him to have contact with no one but himself. He was now fully isolated from the winery. His two secretaries, Teresa Speck and Marcia Santos, had told him that rumors were going around. Tim told him that the executive committee knew about the allegations of incest and that the winery people had already made up their minds — about his guilt, Gary assumed.

Old friends were closing him out. For months, Larry and Anna Graeber had continued to see him and have him over. Then Anna went on the warpath, trying to oust him from the winery. "The Graebers came to my office . . . and seemed to believe the story about sodium amytal," Bob Mondavi says, "and I made the same statement about 'no judgment without proof.'" Tension grew between the two men as Larry was caught between his wife and Gary.

There were no more invitations from Isabel or Dorothy Mondavi. "The wives believed so strongly in Gary's guilt. And Dorothy was even more forceful than Isabel," Margrit heard from Bob. Why were the wives so adamant? "They were jealous of Bob's always bringing Gary out and saying, 'My adopted son.' And Bob would listen to Gary while he didn't listen to his sons. That I understand. But the women —

I now realize the women were much more sensitive to that than I realized. They were predisposed to be anti-Gary. And then, when this came along, it was just like manna from heaven. It was the women who marched into Bob's office."

"It was the *wives,*" Bob says, "who infected their husbands with the myth about sodium amytal," the rumor that poisoned the climate for Gary as much as anything. "They referred to it as a truth serum and were devastated by its implications. I knew it wasn't true. But when that stuff came out, it had a demoralizing effect on the whole organization . . . It had an effect on their wanting to work with Gary, especially in sales."

In early October, Gary and several senior executives met at the guest house to discuss the preliminary findings of the confidential Price Waterhouse report on management. It was a devastating indictment of Gary's performance. Gary and Larry Graeber had dinner that night at a small Mexican restaurant on Napa's Main Street, Rio Poco. Gary denies he discussed the highly confidential report with Larry, but word was out that he had. Gary stood accused of violating secrecy. Larry was now also trapped between the Mondavis and Gary. The Graebers cut off contact completely. As Gary read the draft report at a later meeting, he believed he had been set up, and he fired off his riposte, pages of justifications and denials of the charges.

Simultaneously, Gary was stripped of his rank — told in a memo from Bob Mondavi on October 11 that he would not be returning to his old job after the leave of absence, as promised. On October 12, a manila envelope marked Confidential was delivered to his mother's home with the final Price Waterhouse report. He knew there would be no job for him at the winery after this withering critique.

At the highest level, termination had been secretly decided. "I don't agree with it," Bob said, agonized. "It's a bad judgment. I've told them they shouldn't take the allegations under consideration at all in making decisions, but subconsciously, this damn thing hangs everywhere." He wondered later why Gary had delayed so long in telling him directly about Stephanie's allegations. When they finally met in November, it was too late for Bob to do anything but lament the course of events. Bob said he had heard that Gary had molested all three daughters. He told him of the hours he'd spent trying to convince Isabel and Dorothy why he didn't believe the allegations, which, Bob said, they had heard directly from Steph.

When Margrit felt the end coming, she had to take a stand. She pleaded for Gary to Mike, with Bob and Tim in the room: "You know, in this country, of which I am a member, you're innocent until you're proven guilty." Mike was evasive, but Tim spoke up and said, "Margrit, you may not realize it, but I was the one who pulled the rug out from under Gary." Since Mike had seemed more competitive, it surprised her that Tim had made the final hard decision; it was Tim asserting himself, she guessed. But "after that, I never brought it up again . . . Only God knows what really happened. There must have been things in that family that were bizarre," Margrit speculated. "I think that Holly was a girl with a feeling of some rejection, possibly a lot. And then, the imagination plays a big role. There may have been lots of things between the siblings, too. *But I just don't believe Gary molested his daughter. To my dying day, I will not believe it.*" As Margrit watched the winery closing him out, she thought, "There's a squadron out there, but there is not one person who has emerged that equals Gary . . . The other ones, they come in, and they are good. And some of them are loyal. But none of them is Gary. None of them."

As Christmas decorations filled the boutiques and streets of St. Helena, it fell to the winery's powerful attorney Cliff Adams to dance the final ritual round with Gary Ramona: offers of other jobs, none of which he could accept, and they knew it. To Gary, it was all a charade, humiliating offers of diminished jobs out of the way, out of the valley. The crowning insult was to be offered the invisible job of managing the Costa Mesa wine and food center, his own crown jewel — a job valued at a fraction of Gary's salary. "The job isn't big enough for Gary," Bob argued. Gary was assured he'd earn his current salary, but he would have to agree to an intolerable clause — that he could be terminated "without cause." It required a response by the end of February. Gary read it as an ultimatum: "If I had signed, I would have given up all my rights. It was just a paper trail they were creating to cover getting rid of their embarrassment without liability."

At one of a series of little meetings with Greg Evans, the chief financial officer, and Cliff Adams, Gary was appalled to hear Greg make the comment: "You have to understand that you've been a bad boy, and Michael and Tim are punishing you." Punishing! Was he serious? Twenty years of contribution were being repaid by his being punished like a little boy? Then, from Cliff Adams he heard, "Gary, if I were you, I wouldn't put up with all this. And first, I'd get myself the best lawyer I could, and I'd sit down and negotiate a deal with Bob Mondavi, and I'd leave town."

As Christmas approached, Gary was paying his mother $500 a month for a room in her modest house on Daffodil Drive, and she was buying the groceries. Another family was preparing to spend its first Christmas in the house that was to have been the ultimate achievement of Gary's personal dream. Margrit and Bob loyally urged him to come to their annual Christmas party, but the usual invitations from other friends were gone. He sent the girls cards and gifts but expected no response.

Karen Maestas had Stephanie and the girls for Christmas. Jean was having sixteen for dinner and knew the Ramonas would be very uncomfortable with the crowd. Karen was just having her family. "Do we have to dress up?" Stephanie asked. With Gary, she and the girls always had to be picture-perfect. Karen said, "On Christmas Day — are you kidding? Wear your pajamas if you want. All we do on Christmas Day is watch movies and have dinner. Open presents and turn the movie on. Watch a movie before dinner and one after dinner." No rush, no dress code — it sounded like heaven to Stephanie.

As she and the girls left to go home Christmas night, she said to Karen, "This is the first really happy Christmas I've had."

On New Year's Eve, in Orange County Superior Court in Santa Ana, Holly filed a lawsuit against her father, charging sexual abuse. He would not be served with papers until January, but she had given him the only present he would receive from his family that year. In filing, the discovery rules required that she release her medical records to lawyers and participants on both sides of the case. Isabella's notes, hospital reports, Holly's letter to her father — all would be exposed by the adversarial glare of discovery. These were the records that would enable Gary to sue the people he believed had destroyed his family and his life.

9

This Thing Called Repression

The first criminal trial involving recovered memory — the George Franklin murder case — was about to begin in October 1990. Twenty years earlier, an intense police investigation had not found a shred of evidence tying George Franklin to the murder of eight-year-old Susan Nason. Yet a jury would find him guilty, solely on the basis of the memories his daughter had massively repressed for those twenty years, then recovered in lurid detail.

Eileen Franklin Lipsker, a red-haired Southern California mother of four, had been in her suburban family room, her five-year-old daughter, Jessica, sitting at her feet, drawing, when the memories first came.

Now. Now. Mother's and child's eyes met . . . at exactly that moment, Eileen Lipsker remembered something. She remembered it as a picture. She could see her redheaded friend Susan Nason looking up, twisting her head, and trying to catch her eye . . . She remembered Susan, just four days short of her ninth birthday, sensing George Franklin's attack and putting up her right hand to stave him off. Thwack! *Eileen could hear the sound, a sound like a baseball bat swatting an egg — the worst sound of her life.* "No!" *she yelled inside her head.* "I have *to make this memory stop."* Another *thwack.* And *then quiet. Blood. Blood everywhere on Susan's head.*

Recovered memories such as Eileen's were a new phenomenon. They were a new experience for the two expert witnesses in the Franklin case, Dr. Lenore Terr, a psychiatrist and nationally respected child trauma expert in San Francisco, and Dr. Elizabeth Loftus, a University of Washington research psychologist who was famous for having in-

troduced memory science into the courtroom as evidence. Although
Terr also did rigorous field research, the two women personified the
wide gap in the profession between the subjective experience of the
clinical therapist in her office and the scientific findings of the research
psychologist in her laboratory.

Terr and Loftus personified, too, the clash over Freud that was
thundering through psychotherapy. In 1984 the psychoanalyst Jeffrey
Moussaieff Masson declared in *The Assault on Truth* that Freud's
abandonment of his seduction theory — the theory that adult hysteria
has its roots in repressed but very real sexual abuse — was an act of
betrayal to the terrible truth about childhood sex abuse. This betrayal,
Masson claimed, had led to the faulty belief that these hysterias were,
instead, sexual *fantasies* based on repressed Oedipal conflicts. Freud
had recanted, Masson believed, in a "failure of courage" in order to
be accepted by his conservative medical colleagues and a patriarchal
European society that denied the existence of child abuse and incest.
With the earlier Freud a model for today's recovered memory therapist, Terr and Loftus would be taking this debate into the courtroom
as they defended and attacked the truth, or fantasy, of Eileen Lipsker's
memories.

When Terr received a call in the spring of 1990 from the prosecuting attorney, Elaine Tipton, to testify to the authenticity of Eileen's
memories, she could say confidently, as she would in the Ramona trial
to the question "You believe in the existence of repressed memory?"
"Yes, I do. I see them and I've studied them." She had long studied
children's memories of traumatic events. Yet, in roughly forty jury
trials, she had never seen them recovered like this.

Loftus was willing to accept repression, too — but just show her a
proven case. She worried that "what Freud intended as a free-ranging
metaphor had been captured and literalized." She was sure Eileen
believed her memories. But a man was being charged with murder.

Terr had developed a new diagnosis for child trauma. It was not
yet formally accepted by her profession but would be published in a
journal as she entered the Franklin case: Type I and Type II traumas.
Type I trauma victims, she said, were children who had suffered a
single traumatic event. Their memories were incandescently clear;
they never forgot. Type II was the repeatedly traumatized child, the
child who repressed memory as a mechanism to endure the repeated
horror she was helpless to stop. "But when repression lifts, the memo-

ries may come back relatively intact." Terr had examined Eileen Lipsker and found her a convincing Type II.

Terr was facing a conundrum, as Loftus saw it. If, as Terr argued,
single traumatic events create clear, detailed, and long-lasting memories that children do not "deny away," how was Eileen able to push
the memory of Susan Nason's murder — certainly a singular and traumatic event — out of her conscious mind for nearly twenty years?

"I study memory and I am a skeptic," stated Loftus, a veteran
of more than two hundred trials. Explaining the fallibility and suggestibility of eyewitness testimony with articulate charm, she deftly
stripped the jurists of one of their most cherished myths, that memory
was reliable: "The 'drawers' holding our memories are obviously extremely crowded and densely packed. They are also constantly being
emptied out, scattered about, and then stuffed back into place." She
continued to be fascinated by the power of suggestion to distort and
alter memory, to sneak, through suggestive questions, false elements
into memory, like a "Trojan horse."

Loftus came to the case with her skepticism given a sharp new
edge by her own stunning experience with recovered memory: thirty
years after her mother's death by drowning in a swimming pool, she
was told by an elderly uncle that it was she, Beth, who had found
her mother in the pool. "The memories began to drift back . . . I could
see myself, a thin, dark-haired girl, looking into the flickering blue and
white pool. My mother, dressed in her nightgown, is floating face
down . . . I start screaming." Memories now flooded of police cars,
lights, the stretcher with a white blanket tucked around her mother's
body. Suddenly Beth's life was explained — "my obsession with memory distortion, my compulsive workaholism, my unfulfilled yearning
for security and unconditional love." The rich blossoming of her
memories ended with a call from her brother three days later. Sorry,
her uncle had been wrong. It was Aunt Pearl who found the body.
Family members corroborated it. A scientist observing her own reluctance to relinquish the "crisp colors and narrative drive of my invented story-truth," Loftus had experienced the powerful tug of false
recovered memories.

As both women testified in the Franklin trial, the clinician's
compelling anecdotes overpowered the scientist's memory lessons.
Though forbidden by the judge to say if she believed Eileen's memories, Terr shrewdly told Eileen's story in heartrending hypothetical

terms, ending with her statement that such memories *"would very likely — would probably most likely be repressed."* On the other hand, "Loftus's testimony spoke to memory but not to childhood trauma," Terr noted with satisfaction. As Tipton hammered home the point that repressed memories don't fly by the same rules as ordinary memories, Loftus began "to sense the power of this thing called repression."

On November 30, after only eight hours' deliberation, the jury returned a verdict of guilty. Denied evidence until the last minutes of the trial that Eileen could have learned all her details of the murder from newspapers, the jury had believed her memories. George Franklin went to jail for life. His daughter became a celebrity survivor: she wrote a book; Shelley Long played her in the TV movie.

The Franklin trial sent the recovered memory movement soaring. The writings of several prophets of childhood incest and sexual trauma awareness — Terr, Diana Russell, Judith Lewis Herman, John Briere, Masson, Alice Miller, Bessel van der Kolk, and the multiple personality gurus Bennett Braun and Colin Ross — were beacons leading the emerging incest survivor movement toward a newer genre: an outpouring of best-selling self-help pop therapy books that married incest awareness and recovered memories to New Age feel-good jargon.

It is hard to overestimate the influence of books like *The Courage to Heal* on the growing "survivor" audience. Offering lists of universal symptoms, a sensual lesbian love scene, along with reassurances that feeling more pain after your memories is the path to healing, the book became a comforting daily road map for troubled young women. Dog-eared copies of Renee Fredrickson's *Repressed Memories* became "the companion you need on your healing journey." The theme of incestuous flashbacks reached out to a literary audience as Jane Smiley's brilliant *A Thousand Acres* won the Pulitzer Prize and as the novelist Sylvia Fraser shared her memoir, *My Father's House*. Although Fraser offered no corroboration of incest, the dramatic force of her writing was convincing.

Loftus had left the Franklin trial as the underdog, determined to be better armed in her next joust with repression. She was eager to find an answer to the question constantly asked of her: Why would patients want to incorporate into their life history such brutal and painful memories if they weren't true? At a conference shortly after *Franklin* she posed the question to George Ganaway, a psychiatrist at

Emory University and one of the few urging caution about recovering memories of abuse. "What would motivate people to see themselves as victims and portray their loved ones as cruel and uncaring?" Ganaway explained, These "memories impart a feeling of importance and specialness, even a sense of adventure. A patient may have felt deprived or ignored as a child, or perhaps felt unexceptional because nothing exciting or unusual ever happened to him . . . Their elaborate pseudomemories help them to feel special and worthy of a therapist's attention, even fascination."

Gary Ramona was out of town when a sheriff arrived at the door of his mother's house on January 10, 1991, to serve him with Holly's lawsuit. He felt a chill when his mother told him, but he thought, "I don't have anything to run from. I'm going to go down to the police station and pick up whatever they want to serve me." He went to the second floor of the county building. "When I gave my name I could just sense this sort of disgust." He had already learned what it was to be a pariah: "You're in a world all by yourself. You start going around town. There's a little buzz going on, people looking at you, other people who won't have anything to do with you. It is so lonely . . . There were times when you'd just have to . . . pull the strength from wherever and you just look them in the eye and continue to go on."

The worst moment for Gary, though, came two days later. He was driving on Spring Street near the house on Pinot Way and saw Shawna, but when he blew the horn, she ran and hid in the bushes. "I couldn't believe that here was my daughter who actually, literally, ducked down, ran into the bushes, and hid from me . . . How could she go from a daughter who would help me take things to the trash in our truck, to working up on the hill, to me teaching her how to drive — playing tennis, all these things — to, all of a sudden, having this hysteria? How could her mind change so?" Until then, he hadn't fully grasped how Shawna's mind had been poisoned by Stephanie, as well as Marche Isabella. Stephanie said to Gary, "I've told Shawna that she is never to get in the car with you. Ever. That she should run the opposite way."

He had been holding back, even though he had determined in December to force the issue of custody of Shawna. But now he believed she was being harmed by lies and by isolation from her father. He would go for joint custody as well as a lawsuit. In his declaration, he would cite the scene on January 12: "Respondent honked his horn. When Shawna recognized Respondent, she ran and hid from him . . . Wherefore, I pray that the court order . . ." The flourish and formality of legal language could not begin to express the emotion behind the declaration — the image of his child running from him like a frightened fawn.

He returned to Margolin. "There was a day when Gary Ramona walked into my office and told me, 'My daughter Holly has just sued me.'" That changed the game. For almost a year Margolin had tried to keep Gary from litigation. He had argued the issue of duty. He had argued the financial cost. "You have no idea how much money you will have to spend" — three, four hundred thousand dollars, perhaps more. "But once you get into a megatrial like this, the whole concept becomes meaningless because you have several lawyers working. Before you know it, there is a whole industry around that." Gary would face adversaries with deep pockets. "The moment you sue a hospital — or, for that matter, the psychiatrist or therapist — you face insurance money. And that simply means that you have to be prepared to spend another million dollars that you may not have."

Above all, Margolin had always argued the human cost. "You don't gain the love of a family by suing, Gary."

But Gary had reached a point of no return. "He was angry. He was at a breaking point." It had never been the difficulty of a third-party suit that had distressed Margolin; that had always excited him. If there is a wrong, you find a way to respond to it. If there is no law to do it, then you create a law. He himself had helped create the law that would directly affect Holly's efforts to sue her father. In 1978, in *People v. Shirley,* he had successfully argued before the California supreme court against the courtroom use of testimony taken under hypnosis and, by analogy, under hypnotic drugs, like sodium amytal, which were known to produce both true and false information.

As he examined the material flowing from depositions, Margolin became more convinced of Gary's innocence. "This was rare for me. I have a skeptical bent." Gary's story of Shawna's running from him confirmed for Margolin his early view that Stephanie had played a poisonous role in denying Gary access to his children. Far worse, in spreading the word that he was a child molester, she had become "an extremist, a true believer," a state of mind alarming to a Polish Jew who, as a child, had escaped the Holocaust. Of course a mother would tend to believe her child. And it's not that he thought Gary was perfect. "I suspect there were other reasons why he was losing his job, including the Mondavi changing of the guard. But, without question, the wife gave them the excuse." As Margolin saw it, Stephanie had egged on Holly's beliefs in collusion with Isabella. "I think between Holly and her mother, they warped the other two and deprived them of a father who may not have been sensitive, who may not have spent as much time as they wanted with them, but who was still a very good provider and who cared for them very deeply."

Margolin suspected the daughter was now suing because, with the divorce and the uncertainty of his job at Mondavi, Gary had told them there would be less money to go around, and she was moving to claim it for herself. The time had come for a self-defensive counterattack. Margolin could have fought this case with commitment, but he was in the middle of a major corruption case and couldn't take it on.

For Gary to win, he must first prove that he was not a molester, had never raped his daughter. But, Margolin knew, "we live in a culture of accusations and sex panic. In the final account, it will be very hard for a jury to disregard a statement of a young woman when she says, 'My father raped me.' Very difficult," he told Gary.

Margolin wanted him to go with the best attorney around and thought of his old friend Richard Harrington. Margolin had met Harrington on the opposing side of a divorce case, a case they had settled in a rational way. "The swashbuckler lawyer, the Rambo lawyer, is not my idea of lawyering. I found in Dick a very kindred soul." In the late sixties and early seventies, they fought causes together on behalf of public schools and against the Vietnam War.

Though from different backgrounds — Harrington was a Missouri boy with a Harvard degree — the differences had blurred over the years, and they now belonged to a men's group that had evolved into "the Greek agora." Margolin knew Harrington's mind; he would be drawn to this case. Margolin briefed him, but Harrington had to meet Gary before he would agree to take it on.

Harrington, when Gary Ramona met him in Margolin's office that January, looked every inch the dapper Irish gentleman in a navy pinstripe three-piece suit, unkempt wisps of white hair curling over his collar. But he used his words like a shillelagh.

"Tell me what took place at the meeting March fifteenth. Okay, now, you're in the room — who's there? Who spoke first? What did Isabella say?" Gary tried to tell him, tried to pour it out, but Harrington would cut him off. "Wait a minute. What did *she* say?" "This man lacks personality, he's abrasive," were Gary's first impressions. "Richard Harrington absolutely drove me for thirty minutes. He wanted facts, the answer to his questions. I wanted to give him the whole story . . . to tell him what went on, and it's 'Okay, okay, who spoke next? I didn't ask you what Marche said, what did *Holly* say?' . . . And he kept grilling me, and grilling me. I was so frustrated." Gary got emotional, crying as he tried to explain. He wished there were a switch he could "just turn off and forget." Then he reminded himself, "He wants to know me. He wants to know whether I'm telling the truth." At the end of the half hour Harrington said yes, he'd take the case.

Since the attorneys still believed it would be impossible to sue the therapists, Gary would sue Stephanie for slander, which would permit them to attack the therapists indirectly and shut Stephanie up at the same time. That was fine for now. But Harrington glimpsed a possible way of suing the therapists directly. The key was Gary's confrontation with his daughter and Marche Isabella. Perhaps because Isabella had invited Gary to come to that explosive event, they did owe him a duty. Perhaps.

That same January, just a few miles from Boston, Dr. Harrison Pope, chief of the Biological Psychiatry Laboratory at Harvard's McLean Hospital and an associate professor at Harvard Medical School, took a phone call from some man named Gary Ramona. Gary had come across a copy of Pope's book *New Hope for Binge Eaters* and was trying to learn more about bulimia. He explained about his daughter, her bulimia, therapy, an amytal interview, and accusations of sexual abuse. He needed information and didn't know where to turn; his daughter's therapist wouldn't talk to him or return his calls. Pope was busy, however, finishing an academic paper. He gave Ramona the name of a psychiatrist in Southern California and said good-bye. As he hung up, he said to his colleague Jim Hudson, "I've just had the most remarkable call," and resumed his work.

But as Gary's story sunk in over the next fifteen minutes or so, he realized, "Good heavens! I can't live with myself unless I call this poor man back and find out what has happened to him." His secretary tracked Ramona down through Information, and he called back and said, "Mr. Ramona, would you please tell me that whole story again, in chronological order." "As he told the story again in more detail, the enormity of what had happened came over me and I said, 'Something, something has to be done. I simply cannot sit on the sidelines and not somehow get involved with what has happened here.'" Pope was already speculating: "Could the image of sexual abuse be false?" He'd seen delusions as part of bulimia. He was growing more intrigued by the minute and was eager to meet Ramona. "You name the time and place and I'll be there," said Gary.

Harrison Pope and Gary Ramona met at Orange County's John Wayne Airport on February 6, 1991. Pope was in California to testify as an expert witness in a case. Wiry and hyperactive, he was more than usually energized by the chance to evaluate Gary. "I was still unsure of whether he really did it or not, and I wanted to check him out and see what kind of man he was. My question, as we walked round a playing field and through the neighborhood, was to look at him and ask myself, 'Is it actually possible that this man would have raped his five-year-old daughter?'" For an hour and a half the two men walked along the immaculately landscaped streets of Irvine Industrial Park. "He struck me as a rather normal and ordinary man. There wasn't anything particularly unusual or bizarre about him at all. But that, in and of itself, does not prove that someone is not guilty. But then, toward the end of our walk, he played me a message from his answering machine which he had on his cassette recorder. It was a message he had received from Stephanie saying words like, 'Hey, Gary, I hear you do it with dogs, too.' When I heard that there was an accusation about sex with animals, the preposterousness of the accusations began to grow on me."

Pope's response was typical: the taboo against bestiality, like incest, had been deeply imprinted. But did it exist in Napa Valley? The Kinsey Report's claim, in 1948, that up to 7 percent of American men had had "animal contacts" was probably as overstated as its incest numbers were understated. Bestiality had flourished in mythology, from the northwest coast to the gods of ancient Greece. Real acts of bestiality had been reported from Herodotus to Kinsey; Freud wrote about "sexual relations with animals."

But there was scant evidence in America's cities and suburbs. "There are no brothels or underground markets to sell animals for sex," no solicitation on the Internet, no "mutual support, advocacy, or even self-help," as there are for pedophiles and other sexual minorities, reported the 1994 encyclopedia *Human Sexuality*. With bestiality so broadly proscribed — forbidden by the Bible, traditionally punished by death for both human and animal, and outlawed by most of the United States — why has this not led to more of the forbidden activity, as prohibitions typically do? The reason, the encyclopedia conjectured, is that "All animals, in fact, preferentially mate with their own species."

Pope said later, "As I watched other people form their opinions about the case, it was often the dog that finally tipped people over the edge to say, 'Wait a minute. This is ridiculous.'" Reviewing what little he knew of Holly's symptoms, the more it sounded as if all of them were the stereotypical symptoms of a depressed and bulimic young woman, one with a treatable disorder.

Pope and Jim Hudson had established a "large biological beach-head in suggesting that eating disorders might have a biological base." They were the first to discover and publish the finding that antidepressant drugs were effective in treating bulimia nervosa. When they presented their evidence at a meeting of the American Psychiatric Association in May 1983 that eating and other mood disorders — depression, obsessive-compulsive disorder — may be caused by the same biochemical imbalances, and that those imbalances run in families, they got "an outraged response." The genetic basis of bulimia is still debated, as is the proper balance between drugs and therapy in treating it. Yet the successful use of antidepressants for bulimia followed their report.

After meeting Gary, Pope had still not decided to take up his cause in the unfolding lawsuits. He flew back home, "hit the books and read everything that had been published in the whole world literature about childhood sexual abuse and eating disorders."

At her depositions in Eugenia Magowan's office in San Francisco on the afternoon of Monday, February 4, Stephanie learned that Gary was filing for joint custody of Shawna. "He slapped it right in front of me. The one thing I was fearing most. He was going for it." It had already been a horrible afternoon; her attorney, Sandra Musser, had tried to pry support from Gary for Holly's therapy. Musser had snapped out "Objection!" and shut her up when Magowan asked her, right out, "Mrs. Ramona, do you think your husband is a good father?" When Magowan asked, "Do you believe your daughter Holly needs psychiatric therapy at this time?" Stephanie answered limply at first. "Yes. She's bulimic, and she says that her father raped her." Then the mother lion in her roared and she cried out, *"She's bulimic, and she was raped many times."*

Stephanie then had to sit and hear her own lawyer reduce her powerful feelings about Holly's rape to nothing as Musser said, "Counsel, it does not matter for the purposes of our litigation . . . whether Holly was in fact raped or Holly *believes* she was raped. Under either set of circumstances, she needs therapy." Stephanie's ears pounded. Whether Holly's memories were factual was "immaterial"! Musser went on, "More particularly, if it is *false* — she's in greater, maybe, need of therapy than if it's *true*." She had to do this, Stevie knew. But she hated it. Hated her naming the possibility, for whatever legal reason, that Holly's memories could be false.

At the end of the depositions, Gary had his back to her, smirking and laughing at her, she felt. Furious, Stephanie walked by him and lashed out, *"How does it feel to be a baby raper?"* The day left her shaken and frightened. Gary was out to get them.

Stephanie had already told her friend Renee Lawson that she was worried about what Gary might do if the *Napa Valley Register* got wind of the lawsuit and wrote a story. "I was afraid for our safety." She called Captain Lonegran in the sheriff's office to find out if Gary had been served with Holly's lawsuit. He had, she learned from the woman who fielded her question. "What I'm calling for is to find out if something like this — my daughter suing her father for rape — would come out in the paper," she asked hesitantly. She was given the number of the *Register*. When she called and asked someone there the same question, she was transferred to someone in the newsroom, then transferred again. "No, if your daughter filed and lives in Southern California, it wouldn't come out in Napa. Not to worry," she was told. But then the reporter started asking questions, and Stephanie used the word "rape." She identified herself, Gary, Holly, the Mondavi winery, and gave addresses — said that Gary had already been served. She pleaded that he call her if they were going to do a story but felt very nervous as she hung up. She called Renee and said, "Uh-oh, I have a feeling they may have taken a report on me." Increasingly frantic, she called back the *Register* and demanded, "Did you take a report on me? Because, if you did, it's not right. That was not why I was calling. If you did, tear it up." "But nothing is going to come of it . . . It goes in a file . . . We get phone calls from jealous wives all the time."

Gary heard it quite differently. His secretary Teresa Speck told him that Steph had called the *Register*, wanting them to run a story about the allegations. Teresa's husband, John, worked for the paper and had learned of the call. Then Gary received a call from Harvey Posert, the head of Mondavi's public relations. The *Register*'s senior wine writer, L. Pierce Carson, had called Posert about the call from Stephanie, wanting confirmation. Posert had handled it delicately, he assured Gary. He hoped there would be no story.

When Stephanie went to the *Register* to let the world know that Ramona's daughter had sued him for incest, that was it for Gary. He called Richard Harrington. On March 12, 1991, Gary signed and filed in Napa Superior Court *Gary Ramona, Plaintiff, vs. Stephanie Ramona and Does 1 through 10, inclusive, Defendants. Case No. 61698. Complaint for Slander per se and Intentional Infliction of Emotional Distress.* Only Stephanie was named, charged with spreading damaging and untrue rumors of incest to the *Register* and to the Mondavi organization. But page 1 held the possibility of expanding the suit to catch Isabella in the legal net: "Plaintiff is ignorant of the true names and capacities of defendants sued herein as Does 1 through 10 . . . Plaintiff will amend this complaint to allege their true names and capacities when ascertained." It was standard boilerplate for lawsuits, but it held the promise of more defendants.

The divorce, with the first of its three trials on property, support, and custody beginning in six days, was now overlaid with Holly's lawsuit against her father and Gary's against his wife. Gary's ferocious energies and frustrations finally had a focus. His life had purpose again; he had a job to do. He called Pope at McLean, urging him to be an expert witness in his own as well as Holly's lawsuit.

The skeptical scientist was nearly ready to commit. Pope and Hudson had swiftly completed an evaluation of the literature on bulimia, driven by the question: Is bulimia caused by sexual abuse? Their findings would skewer one of the sacred cows of survivor therapy and eating disorders. "I was surprised to find that . . . the few data there were fell apart very quickly under my critical analysis. And that there was no acceptable scientific evidence that childhood sexual abuse could cause bulimia." A sizable number of bulimic patients reported a history of sexual abuse; but nonbulimic women in the general population reported *at least as much* sexual abuse. The two psychiatrists wrote up their findings in a paper, "Is Childhood Sexual Abuse a Risk Factor for Bulimia Nervosa?" and sent it off to the *American Journal of Psychiatry;* it was published the following January. "I would never have written the paper had Gary Ramona not started this thought," Pope said. Like Terr's and Loftus's experience, his involvement with the recovered memory phenomenon was leading him to new directions in his thinking, research, and writing.

His global search on bulimia took Pope another step toward believing that Holly had been mistreated in therapy. He and Gary discussed the notion of suing the therapists "with terrible reluctance" because of the effect it might have on Holly. Caught in an illness she could probably not have avoided, led into fantasies she was too needy and naive to resist, "Holly was the helpless figure in this whole drama," Pope felt. Could they somehow force a family meeting or get Pope to speak to Holly? "Many thoughts were floated; all came to naught" because of "a devastating Humpty Dumpty–like effect where things could not be pieced back together," Pope realized. By March of 1991, one year after the confrontation, "it became obvious to both Gary and to me that there was simply no choice but to launch a malpractice suit." Pope would play the role of strategist, Gary's éminence grise, while Hudson acted as expert witness. Harrington began preparing the First Amended Complaint, a revision of the initial lawsuit that would name the therapists and hospital as defendants as well.

Gary was fired from the Mondavi winery at the end of April. On June 12 he broadened his slander suit against his wife to include the people he held responsible: Marche Isabella, Richard Rose, and Western Medical Center, suing them for malpractice. His lawyers still warned, "The chances are remote that you'll get a jury to hear your case." But he had thrown down the gauntlet.

Gary Ramona hurled his lawsuit against the most formidable concentration of therapists and mental health practitioners in the world. Gross numbers told the story: half of all the master's-level family therapists in the United States were based in California — *23,000* of the nation's 46,000. Those numbers were swelled by roughly 13,000 interns and trainee MFCCs in the field, 21,000 clinical social workers and other mental health specialists, plus an uncounted number of ministers, rabbis, and priests who practiced counseling and therapy free of any regulation or oversight. Many Ph.D. psychologists had joined the ranks, getting an MFCC license as well. Their sheer weight threatened to tip the West Coast into the Pacific.

Why was California so top-heavy with therapists? Critics of California's culture leaped to an answer: it was the crazies who have always been drawn to the continent's edge. Or perhaps it was the state's huge, prosperous urban population, which could afford to indulge its angst. But several other factors played a part. A state whose laws have always favored family counseling, California became the first to license family counselors, in 1945 licensing clinical social workers, the core from which the family therapy specialty grew. MFCCs were licensed next, in 1963. Combining the practical family-fixing tradition of social work with the inward-looking psychotherapies being embraced by Californians as the human potential movement spread from Big Sur and San Francisco in the 1960s, MFCCs were put under the umbrella of the Department of Consumer Affairs, which oversaw the state's mental health regulatory boards. With marriage and family therapy now a formal, licensed, accredited profession, an infrastructure grew up around it — schools, training, supervision, exams, standards, and conferences — attracting more to the field.

The numbers grew after 1974, when mandatory child abuse reporting laws offering therapists immunity from liability for making the report created a growth opportunity for family therapy. A boom was caused in the 1980s when California's new Freedom of Choice law required insurance companies to pay for psychotherapy services by MFCCs. Much of the credit for that law and for the growth in California is given, by those who fight and fear him in Sacramento, to Dick Leslie, the legal counsel for California's MFCC professional organization since 1979. Playing a role like that of a union lobbyist, from the first Leslie fought "for laws that allow the profession to compete on an equal basis with the other mental health professions." He fought for insurance reimbursement, for expanding the scope of services therapists could provide, for the right of therapists moving to California to practice there, for shrinking the large list of college degrees the board would accept for licensing, an "arguably irrelevant" laundry list that hurt the MFCC image, Leslie feared. When Leslie started in 1979, there were fewer than two thousand members; when Gary Ramona sued in 1991, that number had grown more than tenfold. Family therapy's turf had expanded dramatically.

But Leslie's lobbying was "not a quality argument; it's a numbers argument. It's access," worried Kathleen Callanan, who took over the Board of Behavioral Science Examiners, MFCC's regulatory and licensing board, in 1985. She was appalled to find a profession run amok. As a group, most agreed, these were good, sensitive people who wanted only to heal. "From my heart, this is the most altruisic group of people in the world," confirms Eric Marine of American Professional Agency, which is insurance agent to more of the nation's therapists than any other — and was Isabella's insurer. But Callanan found family therapists with barely a year of graduate school gamely treating mental illness that might have daunted psychiatrists with eight years of graduate training, fledgling therapists armed with a master's degree in *dance*. At hearings before a state Consumer Protection Committee in 1992, she would say, "I doubt seriously that when the legislature started the marriage counseling license" in 1963 "that they really had any idea that they would be out treating serious mental disorders." With recovered memory, MFCCs were handling clinical depression, bulimia, multiple personalities, and suicide.

"I think Dick Leslie's played a big part in that," Callanan told a journalist. "He *is* the association. He makes all the decisions. He's had a master plan: by little bootstrapping pieces of legislation here and there, he's extended the scope of practice. He's a master at putting political pressure on everyone — at exercising bully-boy politics."

"Disturbing, insulting, and arrogant," said Leslie, dismissing the testimony of his archenemy. But, he admitted, "it is all about turf and it's all about money." With psychologists battling for the right to invade physicians' turf and prescribe psychotropic drugs, he said, half laughing, to the psychologists' lobbyist in the hallway, "if you get prescription privileges, we'll be right there."

"It's out of control," summed up Jeffrey Younggren, a psychologist and ethics consultant to the state's regulatory boards. "Quote me on that — the master's-level system, the MFCC license, is *out of control*."

Gary Ramona had found the right candidate for reform. The problems were deep and systemic.

Educational requirements were alarmingly low and inappropriate. When Callanan took over, you could sit for your MFCC exam with any one of eighteen "equivalent" degrees — including art, theology, and dance, subjects that had nothing to do with the complex psychodynamics of families. The list had been reduced to six relevant degrees in 1986, but with the old list grandfathered in for years, it had so far had little impact on the quality of training. Therapists still hung up their shingles "not well trained in diagnosis, with very limited basic science training — and very, *very* limited scientific underpinnings of memory," confirmed Martha Rogers, a forensic psychologist in Orange County who, in twenty-five recovered memory cases in the early nineties, had seen the full range of therapists' capabilities. One therapist had called Dick Leslie, saying, "I'm surrendering my license"; she revealed that her therapy involved placing crystals on her naked patients' private parts. Often with nothing more than a weekend course and a pop-psych paperback, MFCCs were treating profound eating and memory disorders. Rogers was disturbed by the "conservative, evangelical subculture" flourishing around her.

"Orange County is the hotbed of this stuff. It produces more recovered memory cases and satanic ritual abuse claims per square inch than anyplace in the country," Rogers observed. She had seen the fads sweep through — primal scream, age regression, now women who claimed memories of rape by the feet of a Barbie doll. In this rich county, she proposed, economics was a fundamental motive for recovered memory. With too many therapists competing for the shrinking managed care market, they had to create niches for themselves. Recovered memory was, financially, the perfect niche. "If their insurance runs out, these young women can afford to pay for their therapy." Or their fathers could.

A huge moneymaker, according to Callanan, yet little known by the public was the system of state "approved schools," nonaccredited schools that served as degree mills for a fast master's or Ph.D. in clinical psychology and were accepted for MFCC licensing. An incestuous system in which the owners of the schools also sat on the council that regulated them, some of these schools granted master's degrees in four to six months — without a bachelor's degree as prerequisite — Ph.D.'s in a year, without a student's ever attending a class. Some were legitimate; others were flaky, fly-by-night "schools without walls" in which you could trade your "life experience" for credit; Callanan had seen an engineer qualify. These people "who get Ph.D.'s out of a Cracker Jack box" were a threat, feared Rogers. "They call themselves 'doctor,' get an MFCC license, and the general public doesn't know the difference — they think they're licensed psychologists."

Inadequately supervised interns concerned Younggren: "People pursuing this license will do anything they can to get their hours" — at least two years and three thousand hours of supervised therapy experience were required before taking the exam; half the hours could be gained before earning a master's. This supervisory process was what really trained a good therapist; it was where good habits were learned and where therapists learned the limits of their powers. Yet it required spending only one hour with a supervisor each week. "There's no way on God's earth you can train an adequate therapist of any kind on an hour a week of supervision," Rogers felt. A supervisor need not even be where the therapist was working. Younggren strongly believed that supervisors should be onsite at least 50 percent of the time. "Bad habits often only surface at the cost of licensing and disciplinary actions — and through human pain. There's a victim."

And the system had no effective way of screening wounded healers. "Impaired providers are a big concern to me," said Younggren. Rogers was starting to see "a second and third generation of MFCC or social work therapists who themselves have recovered memories and . . . become therapists . . . involved in cases of alleged recovered memories." She had seen a young woman who had taken her grandmother to trial on baseless charges of satanic ritual abuse go on to become an MFCC and to practice, currently, in Orange County.

Today they are called "impaired providers." Yet the tradition of the wounded healer has remained strong from the time of the legendary Philoctetes, who was rescued from abandonment on an island for his incapacitating snakebite to grow through his suffering to become a great leader. Holly was in her third year at Irvine, studying psychology and planning to become a therapist — an MFCC like Marche Isabella. It worried Gary. "Holly's my daughter and I love her very much. There isn't anything in the world I wouldn't do to help her to be successful, or support her. But . . . what concerns me is to have another Marche Isabella running around. In my opinion, as long as Holly is brainwashed to believe this hocus-pocus, then I have real concern whether she would be capable of separating that from reality."

Harrison Pope said of young women with recovered memories, "One cannot escape the feeling that this has become the psychological center of their life — the thing around which their whole self-image comes to be built — and therefore it would be unthinkable to relinquish it, unthinkable to even question the truth of it." Sudden loss could be devastating. The only way, Pope speculated, was with the sympathetic support of a therapist who gave the patient the space, the freedom, and the safety to slowly relinquish the false memories.

Instead, they had lawsuits.

10

The Gathering of Evidence

n a two-day psychiatric exam her father had forced Holly to take in late November 1991 as part of discovery in her lawsuit, she was asked, "What would you hope would happen to your father?"

"I would hope that he would end up going into therapy and getting help . . . I hope that he will stay away from children."

"What are your hopes and expectations about your mother?"

"I hope that she'll get on with her life and put this behind her, get married again, and be happy."

With the series of family lawsuits now moving forward like a juggernaut, it was a naive hope. The legal war machine took on a shape and life of its own, an engine that could not be stopped, dragging the traumatized Ramonas along with it. But to the attorneys being called to defend the two therapists and the hospital, the lawsuits were not about the Ramona family; they were about insurance.

In the bottom-line world of managed health care, the subjective art of psychotherapy was being forced, for the first time, to show measurable positive results. It had to be cost-effective. Gary Ramona was suing for $8.5 million. Nothing would stop recovered memory therapy faster than expensive lawsuits. If Gary were to win his malpractice suit, it would be far more than vindication. A multimillion-dollar award to a third party would be a surgical strike at the most vital and vulnerable part of the profession. For it was the insurance companies, not Marche Isabella or Richard Rose, who would pay. Insurance was psychotherapy's fuel. It paid most patients' bills as well as the costs of lawsuits. Even if the companies started getting badly hurt by recovered memory lawsuits, they would have to be cautious about refusing insurance or raising rates beyond reach — therapists were their livelihood. But they could certainly put powerful "educational" pressure on the therapy profession.

On a clear day Ed Leonard could see, if not forever from his Orange, California, law office, at least as far as Disneyland, a few miles away. The case that Western Medical Center–Anaheim had just handed him beat them all. A guy who was not even a patient was suing his daughter's therapists and the hospital — and the daughter, Holly, happy as a clam with the care she got. It was hard enough to satisfy your patients. When you've got to start satisfying their parents, God help you. In the hundred malpractice cases he'd defended for the hospital, he had never seen a third-party lawsuit, much less a recovered memory. This was a case that should go no further than the first complaint.

First, Leonard filed a motion to move the case from Napa back down to Orange County, where it belonged. The whole thing — Holly's flashbacks, therapy, sodium amytal, hospital stay, the confrontation — had happened in Orange County. All the defendants but Stephanie were based here. Suing Mrs. Ramona for slander, then adding on the hospital and therapists, was clearly a scam to get the case tried in Napa, where they'd have the hometown advantage. It was also Mondavi country, where there might be some sympathy for the guy. The climate for the defense of a malpractice case would be better in Orange County, where most of the lawyers and judges were conservatives who disliked "progressive" law.

Then Leonard filed an old-fashioned demurrer — as he explained, it was a "legal shrug of the shoulders which says, So what?" — that there was no cause of action, no case. He sent a young lawyer who had just joined the firm, Jeff Schroer, up to Napa to argue both motions at hearings before Judge Donald R. Fretz. Jeff would get only a little courtroom experience from the assignment. It should be over swiftly.

Marche Isabella had already been subpoenaed by Gary to be deposed in Holly's case against him. When she received notice that Gary intended to sue her, she called her insurance carrier. "It's just a nuisance suit," they advised. "He's not your patient. Notify us when you're actually sued, and we'll provide legal counsel." She called Dick

Leslie, the counsel for California's MFCCs, for advice on how to conduct herself in the first deposition of her life. But she went off to give it alone, without a lawyer.

Gary watched on a monitor from an adjoining room as Isabella spilled her theories on repression and sodium amytal, her orchestration of the confrontation and her lack of specific training in eating disorders and memory. She admitted she would believe a patient's reports of witchcraft under sodium amytal if confirmed by other personality aspects. Showing a familiarity with the recovery of memories, she claimed "the process of recovering is gradual . . . It took many, many months." She admitted that she'd recommended the sodium amytal and that she told Holly afterward, "You did not lie." That was gold for Gary Ramona.

Leonard and Western Medical Center were already involved in Holly's lawsuit as well. A nurse from the hospital was being deposed in Holly's case against her father. Charged with defending any matter that could involve the hospital in liability, Leonard had had to rush off to a law office in Irvine for the depositions. When an attorney started questioning the nurse about Holly's care, Leonard interrupted. Whoa! Where are the hospital records? How do we defend the hospital unless we know what went on? "This witness is not going to talk about *anything*," he snapped out, "unless I have some kind of written stipulation or authorization from Holly Ramona that I can get into her medical records." Technically, Holly had waived therapist-patient privilege when she sued her father, but Leonard wanted access guaranteed, here and now. All eyes turned to a girl with long dark hair sitting silently at the table. Leonard had not known Holly was in the room. On the spot, he drafted a simple document and had her sign it. "That was the basis for disclosing all the information in this case . . . If Holly Ramona had never bothered to sue her father, there is no way her father could have mounted an effective suit against us," Leonard would later reflect ruefully and often.

In a malpractice suit like Gary's, the hospital would be most vulnerable, Leonard knew, because it carried the most insurance. Rose and Isabella were covered for up to $1 million each; the hospital's coverage went up to $35 million. With California's liability laws based on "comparative fault," even if his client, the hospital, was found only 1 percent responsible and Rose and Isabella 99 percent guilty, the jury could order the hospital's insurers to pay 100 percent of Gary's loss of earnings claim of $8.5 million. But Leonard didn't dream that Gary's third-party lawsuit would be given the time of day.

"We were slaughtered," Leonard was stunned to hear from Jeff after the first hearing in Napa in July. Jeff had argued that the case should be moved to Orange County, but for now, they were stuck in Napa. The second hearing, on whether the case should proceed or be dismissed, was scheduled for August. "We were slaughtered again," Jeff reported when he returned. Judge Fretz had said the case could go ahead. In arguing Gary Ramona's right to sue, Harrington had raised the contentious word *Molien,* a 1980 landmark case in which a Northern California doctor at Kaiser had misdiagnosed a woman for syphilis; he told her to go home and tell her husband to get tested, too. The shock, anger, and distrust that erupted from the specter of syphilis destroyed their marriage. The couple sued the doctor for malpractice and won.

Upheld on appeal, *Molien* became a binding precedent for all future cases in California courts that tested the reach of a doctor's responsibility to nonpatients — to third parties. That decision said that the doctor should have *foreseen* the damage his order to tell the husband might cause; liability lay in that order, involving the husband. Harrington had argued a connection between *Molien* and *Ramona* — that Isabella and Holly's suggesting and then urging Gary to attend the confrontation created a duty to Ramona. When, therefore, Gary was invited and came to the confrontation on March 15, he entered the same sphere of protection from foreseeable damage a patient entered when seeing a doctor. The confrontation was Harrington's wedge into court.

Leonard decided he'd better get himself up to Napa the next time and get involved. But he didn't blame Jeff. Harrington had apparently found a sympathetic judge. Since 1980, *Molien* had been steadily undermined by subsequent cases and was now so discredited, as Leonard saw it, that he could not imagine its surviving as a cause of action beyond this preliminary skirmish. But it would be a more interesting challenge than he'd thought. How deep should duty go? There had to be reasonable limits. Once you opened the floodgates to a patient's relatives, it could end the practice of medicine. It could cost insurers an unfathomable bundle.

This murky issue of foreseeable risk to a third party had sent chills through the therapy profession in 1974 with *Tarasoff,* when a thera-

pist at UC Berkeley had failed to warn a young woman, Tatiana Tarasoff, that her psychotic boyfriend had threatened to kill her. When the
woman was stabbed to death, the therapist was found liable. But
Leonard did not think *Tarasoff* applied here; there had been no specific threat to kill in *Ramona*. The court also had to weigh a social
concern: the need to deter childhood sexual abuse. On appeal, they
would certainly reverse this maverick ruling from a county courtroom
in Napa.

As he filed his appeal, Leonard recalled the cynical joke lawyers
often cracked when these liberal decisions came down: *"On a clear
day in California, you can foresee forever."*

Through the spring of 1991, the property battle focused on Stephanie's right to buy a house for herself and Shawna. She had demanded all the remaining cash from the sale of the new house,
$305,000, to buy a tract house just a block from their old home on
Pinot Way. She was terrified of Gary's willful squandering, his deceit-
ful "squirreling away" of assets; his profligacy would leave nothing
for the girls' schooling, therapy, legal bills, security. The judge was
awarding her scraps — the '84 Mercedes, half the wine collection, ten
strands of pearls valued at $600 from Stephanie's Designs and Im-
ports, while permitting Gary to block her on the big issues, like buying
a smaller house. Gary had whipped the divorce into a costly frenzy in
a vindictive response to Holly's lawsuit, Sandra Musser accused on
Stephanie's behalf. And now he had petitioned the judge to suspend
spousal and child support.

Stephanie's fundamental motive was to destroy him, Gary claimed,
asking the judge to consider what she had said to him as they shared
an elevator at Barry Grundland's: "I want to be there when you fall
. . . I am going to screw you royally . . . You're never going to see your
family again . . . I want to be there when you're dead" — strong
words. Stephanie claims they were in response to Gary's threat that
he would destroy the family and join forces with Mondavi against
her. Stephanie could go ahead and say that "Gary has superior earning capacity and can generate cash for his needs." The reality was
that, thanks to Steph, "my savings account has a balance of $57," his
checking account was reduced to $6,000, and his "earning capacity is
in serious jeopardy." It had, in fact, abruptly died in April, when he
was fired from Mondavi. On July 12, Gary stated, "It is ridiculous for

Petitioner to buy a home and go into debt when she has no income and I have no income." He refused to give up any claim to the old house until Judge Fretz ordered him to sign the quitclaim deed and ordered Stephanie to settle for half, not all, of the cash from the new house. Stephanie signed escrow on July 17, closing the purchase, and prepared to move.

But first they had to break up the old house and divide the spoils of twenty-five years of marriage. They'd need to go through the records and papers in the garage. Gary turned up in his running shorts on a Saturday morning, a time arranged by Stephanie's attorney. "He showed up in those godawful shorts that reveal everything, those nylon shorts with the curves that go way up the side," said a disgusted Jean Sawday. "He thought he was Mr. Hot." She, Karen Maestas, and Renee Lawson were standing outside the garage like palace guards when Gary arrived. They did not speak to him. But when they couldn't get the door open to the big Dumpster in the driveway, Jean thought, "I'm going to ask Gary to open the damn door. It's his junk we've got to put in here." "Gary, can you open this?" she called out.

Gary came over and opened the door. That moment of interaction was, for Jean, the experience of looking into the face of the enemy, into the eyes of evil. For Gary, though, it was the only remotely friendly act from any of these women since they had turned him out of their lives. They had been neighbors, old friends. Now they were true believers with fire in their eyes. They went back to the job of riffling through and reading his papers — his personal papers, his business accounts!

"Hey, what are you doing?" he called out, shocked.

"You're not taking anything . . . I want to look at it first," Steph snapped.

"I got to tell you something, ladies. *This is my personal stuff.*" It was nuts. He grabbed the files and stacked them in his car.

"They're just a bunch of busybodies," Gary said. "They ought to get a life." And he was sure Steph encouraged them with her dithering: "Gee, I don't know. I mean, what if he takes this paper, how do I know . . ." She had listened to too many women who had had bad experiences with their divorces. But Gary knew that these women were good people driven by empathy and concern for Steph and the girls. Numbers were flying through the media that 60 to 70 percent of all women had been sexually molested in some way. The slogan Believe the Child was everywhere. And celebrities — the TV star

Roseanne Arnold, a former Miss America, Marilyn van Derbur — were coming out with recovered memories of incest. Mothers as protective as Steph would naturally feel revulsion and fear of a possible "baby raper" in their midst. But none of these women even questioned his guilt.

In shielding Stephanie, were they shielding themselves? If it could be Gary, it could be anyone — it could be their own husbands. Gary had to be demonized. He must be revealed as a monster among normal neighborhood fathers, or all their daughters and marriages were vulnerable.

In June, Dr. Richard Rose notified Holly by letter that he was leaving the practice of psychiatry and moving to Hawaii to enter a completely different line of work — a commercial printing business. Although the Ramona case and several other claims against him made the practice of psychiatry in Orange County less hospitable than it had been, he was leaving a successful practice for essentially personal reasons. Following a very painful divorce — and raised in a family that had been printers for generations in Philadelphia — the opportunity in Hawaii was very appealing. "Positive transference," Marche Isabella noted when Holly reported the grief she felt at losing him. Within a month, however, Holly was abandoned by Isabella as well.

In July, Isabella told Holly she would be moving to Fairfax Station, Virginia, near Washington, D.C. She and her husband had come to think of Orange County as an unsuitable place to raise their three children, who ranged from nine to fifteen. "I got sick of California, plastic Orange County . . . unscrupulous people, the instability and transience . . . The East is home," she said, defending the move. "We . . . decided before any lawsuit was filed." She did not tell Holly that Virginia was one of the few states that required no accreditation before a therapist set up a practice. Or that malpractice suits threatened to send insurance rates soaring and, had she stayed in California, "my insurance would have been raised 250 percent."

For Holly, "things started getting rough again. The bulimia started acting up." She made a brief, fitful stab at finding new therapists — she saw a psychologist and a psychiatrist a few times — but quit, took herself off Prozac, and then, "I was on my own." On September 10, 1991, she flew to San Francisco to attend Shawna's first deposition in her, Holly's, lawsuit.

Discovery permitted Gary to call anyone he wished for depositions, but he shouldn't have forced Shawna to do this, Stephanie fumed as she and Shawna drove to the attorney's office in Napa. He was harassing his daughters, her women friends, the Mondavis — even her mother — by forcing them to the deposition table. But Shawna was just fourteen. She had the look Stephanie's father must have had — fair skin and hair with hints of red, fresh and healthy. Gary was only doing this to get information for his own lawsuit, she had no doubt. "Shawna, do you want me to come in with you?" she asked. Shawna wasn't sure, so her mother decided to wait outside. But as she looked in, she held her breath. It was a big room. "Gary had all the backdrop. The video cameras. All these attorneys." She was frightened for Shawna. Everyone was silent as Stephanie came in and sat down, with attorneys between her and Gary. Holly was sitting in a corner. Bare deposition desks in attorneys' offices had become the family table, the only place they talked.

Harrington began, trying to set the teenager at ease. "It's not quite like what we see on television . . . I've never watched *L.A. Law,* but I'm told that's very dramatic. This is not very dramatic. We're just going to ask a few questions. Okeydoke, your name is Shawna Ramona . . . and your father is Gary Ramona? . . ." As Shawna listened, alert, Stephanie turned toward Holly. "Our eyes filled with tears and, it's funny, we both thought the same thing. *How sad that our family has come to this.*"

That sadness permeated Gary's final divorce deposition a week later, on September 19. Of course it was about money. But the human disaster drowned out even the loud acrimony over dollars and cents. As Gary tried to tell the story of his termination from the winery, he got as far as "They put me on a leave of absence. Two families had . . ." but couldn't go on. Stephanie started crying, too. "I wish the record to note that Magowan objects and that both principals are in tears," said Sandra Musser.

Gary was so out of touch with his children that he didn't even know that Holly was in her senior year at college or that Kelli was at school in Colorado. The fees for the year hadn't been paid. That was Stephanie's worry. With Gary's erratic withholding of support, she still kept her survival nest egg hidden in the baking soda box in the fridge. She and the girls were eating a lot of beans. She couldn't afford to get her hair colored. But forget hair — he had stopped paying for their education. "The agreement was that he *would* . . . He told me he

would always pay for their educations. And he stopped. Period. Kelli
had been accepted at Boulder when all this came up and thought she
couldn't go anymore. I said, 'No, you're *going!*' I paid for their educations," she said later.

She was struggling to draw water from a drying well, for Gary had
no income. He had been living off assets since his termination at Mondavi, liquidating everything — including his truck and trailer — and
had borrowed $17,000 from his mother. In August he had formed his
own wine marketing company, Advantage Wine Group. But the rumors were reaching out ahead of him, like fingers of fog, cooling the
climate as he tried to get his life going again. Bob and Margrit were
fantastic, and Margrit was designing a logo and label for Advantage.
They flew to Oregon to back him up when he negotiated with the
Montinore Winery to work out a deal: based on results as their marketing consultant, he'd gain some ownership in the company. Gary
and his oldest friend, Scott Evans, drove up to Oregon together and
talked about buying land and moving there. But Scott was worried.
You had to be stylish, had to spend money to market wines. "With
Mondavi he had the bankroll, the sky was the limit," Scott observed.
"Gary's got the strong fight to him — I guess you'd say stamina. I
wouldn't be the one to say, 'This'll never happen, Gary.' But he's going
to have a harder time this time." And could he ever get the old drive
back?

Gary did indeed strike a deal with Montinore, but the big introduction of their wines he had scheduled at the Century Plaza in Los
Angeles had to be canceled when the city was swept by the Rodney
King riots. It was a disaster, and the relationship with Montinore died
within a year.

He kept trying. He felt hopeful when he met with Eleanor Coppola, the wife of moviemaker Francis Ford Coppola, to explore an
opening at the family's Niebaum-Coppola winery, but he received a
sincere little note back that they had gone with another firm but might
be in touch. He had discussions with wineries in Mendocino County
as well as Napa. The few times salary was discussed, it was in the
range of $50,000-$100,000 year, a humiliating reduction from the
half million he'd earned at Mondavi. No one mentioned the allegations. "These people are certainly not going to say, 'Gary, we're not
going to put you on because of rumors or allegations being made in
the Napa Valley.'" But no one offered him a job. He clung to Advantage Wine Group as a corporate vehicle, but it had no income — not

even stationery or business cards. His only listing was in the Napa phone book; his office was in his mother's home. Instead of a Mercedes, he now drove an Acura Legend. The cloud had preceded him. "The questions had been put out there."

One day it all came home to him. Even if his lawsuit were to clear his name, his life had been stripped of its boundless potential. "There's no way I could ever run for public office, even if I had the desire. There was no way I could get a major corporation, who in the past were hungry to have me take a look. Do you think any of them are going to make me president or put me in a high position?" He could never do community work if it involved children, ever. His reputation was destroyed.

The growing team of lawyers flew to Hawaii in November 1991 to depose Richard Rose. At the first red arc of sunrise the morning before the depositions, Ed Leonard raced his linebacker's bulk across the sand in front of the hotel for a quick swim. "I'm without my contact lenses, swimming pretty deep, and all of a sudden I see something moving toward me in the water, moving kind of slow, and I thought, 'Jesus Christ!' and I look up and it was *Gary Ramona*. He never missed a deposition."

From the beginning, Leonard had made the dismissal of the case on the grounds of no duty his personal mission; he would force Gary's side to fight off eight challenges before the issue was finally decided on the eve of the trial in 1994. He needed a sympathetic judge on the case.

As the November sun rose over the eastern range of Napa Valley, Scott Snowden, a sandy-haired forty-five-year-old St. Helenan, checked out the vines on his daily run to the top of his family's mountain vineyard. In the Napa courthouse two hours later, he donned black judicial robes and took his place as ringmaster for the Ramona legal circus. Both Holly's and Gary's cases — and trials, if it came to that — had been assigned to him. Snowden was exhilarated by this country bench. It was not because of the big trials; he rarely got them. What he loved was "being there with people at the extreme moments of human contact and experience . . . trying to make sense out of what they're going through . . . and, to some extent, participate in and guide the situation." On this human level alone, *Ramona* promised to be incomparable.

The issue of duty to a third party would also prove fascinating. *Ramona* would test the powerful principles laid down in *Molien*. Snowden would walk where a Napa judge rarely trod: in potential landmark territory. The lawyers had already argued for and against applying *Molien* in the early rounds, before he took over. They would continue to argue it. It would be his to decide.

Even back in the fourth grade, Snowden knew he was meant to be a judge when, instead of getting picked for a team, he was asked to be the umpire. He grew up in Berkeley, but in the mid-fifties, his father bought a 160-acre mountain ranch in Napa Valley, where the family first summered and eventually moved. Snowden took his first degree at a small liberal arts college in Virginia, Washington and Lee, and his law degree at Berkeley's Boalt Hall. Practicing in Napa for several years, this Shakespeare-quoting fly-fisherman had developed a distinctive courtroom style, a blend of patrician grace and "rasty pioneer rebelliousness."

Appointed in 1979 to a seat on the Municipal Court bench, in 1984 he ran for and won retiring Judge Thomas Kongsgaard's seat in Superior Court. Judge Scott Snowden anticipated a very interesting time ahead as he entered Courtroom B on November 19 to assume *Ramona*.

Stephanie needed another lawyer, her fifth. Things weren't working out with Warren Green, the lawyer in Sausalito she'd hired to handle Gary's slander suit against her. "He was nice, but not aggressive enough," she felt. On November 8, 1991, Sandra Musser called Neil Shapiro in San Francisco to see if he would represent Stephanie. Handsome and fit at forty-five, Shapiro had, in a year at Brobeck, Phleger and Harrison, achieved a thirtieth-floor corner office with a panoramic view of San Francisco Bay. A lover of books, he had developed a niche doing copyright and First Amendment libel law for publishers and the media. Yet he was restless in a big law firm that valued billable hours above all else and lacked a soul. He agreed to meet with Stephanie.

Musser had prepared him. "She told Neil I'm ditzy," Stephanie said, "and I am ditzy sometimes." But when she walked in that Thursday, she looked to Shapiro more like a woman "in shock . . . tired, frightened, and just . . . stressed. She didn't speak much. When she did, it was in halting bits and pieces, not sentences." But she seemed credible. Within a week — the same day the Ramona cases were handed to Judge Snowden in Napa — Shapiro would be examining Gary Ramona in two days of depositions, laying the groundwork to get Stephanie dismissed from Gary's charge of slander.

Shapiro met Holly for the first time when Stephanie brought her to San Francisco for lunch; they had sandwiches at Tommy's Joint on Van Ness Avenue. "She was nice enough. A little pudgy. Wearing a big, baggy sweatshirt and some kind of pants. She was very quiet. Not anybody you'd even notice."

Continuing to drift without a therapist, Holly had found an incest survivors group at UC Irvine and attended every Monday from three to five. But her fear that her father might subpoena the group destroyed that refuge, and she was prepared to quit abruptly if necessary. The fear of her father's power to damage ate at her so ferociously that she drove out to see JoeAnna and Lloyd Jenkins, old family friends; she was suspicious that Lloyd, her father's accountant, was doing "creative accounting" that was hurting the Ramona women. "Stay out of what's going on in the family," she warned them, "and if you ever have grandchildren, *be careful*." Although she hadn't purged for a few months, she continued to binge. She was still living at her grandmother Nye's. She had just sold her piano — the piano her grandmother Garnet had given the girls and that her father had shipped south to her when she asked for it. Holly had no hobbies, no boyfriend. She went to the movies by herself.

She still had flashbacks. She could call up old flashbacks at will and see them with ever richer detail by concentrating. But she never knew when a new flashback would hit; she couldn't control them. She had had a new flashback just the week before: she was lying on a bed, he was on top of her, coming down, there was a sheet, her father's back and head.

The quiet girl was getting a rigorous training in public speaking, as speaking out — which "doesn't always go over very well . . . in my family" — intensified with an accelerating schedule of psychiatric examinations, lawyers' meetings, hearings, and depositions, with their array of video cameras and court reporters.

On Monday morning, December 16, and for two long days of depositions, she told her life story while her father listened. For the first time he heard her view of the family. Where Gary remembered warmth and happiness, Holly remembered distance and hostility. Prodded by attorneys' questions, she poured out her grievances, hurts, and fears. Confined to the time frame of her flashbacks, her retelling of the (to Gary) happy events "ages five to eight" took on sinister significance: ". . . from ages five to eight . . . I never initiated any type of hugging . . . with my father, that I can remember." Nor had her sisters. Holly's memories were of her father's violence, her parents' fights, of Stephanie's threats that "we'll be leaving soon."

Gary heard her describe the weight and image anxieties that had built to bulimia. If her sisters and parents knew something was wrong, they were "in their own world . . . didn't have time to sit down . . . and figure it out" or may not have cared, Holly recalled. He listened to the terrible story of a child wandering at the Concord Mall, binging and then vomiting it up. Whatever Harrington's strategy — establishing dysfunctional family patterns quite apart from any incest or the life-long basis of Holly's eating disorders — his dogged pursuit of the theme made food a powerful metaphor for the Ramona family's failure to communicate.

But "it's an exaggeration," Gary thought as Holly talked about never eating together. Her story of her childhood had shocked him into seeing some flaws in the family. He hadn't been the role model he thought he'd been for his daughters. He'd let them grow up without knowing his side of the family. But this eating business — "What's taken out of context is to say that we didn't have dinner at *home* a lot together. But we would take the girls out to dinner. We loved to get together and spend time together."

There was a moment when Holly halted her sad litany to confess, "I mean, I love my father. I think there are times when he, when he does love me." But at the end of the day, Holly had revealed a life ruined by her father's molesting her, over and over, "from ages five to eight." Gary felt fury toward the people who had distorted a wonderful childhood, who had transformed him in the eyes of his children into a monster — a man who, Holly claimed, demanded "an image presented for work and for the rest of the community that we were the perfect family."

Stephanie was usually too ready to blame herself. But when she heard what Holly had said about never eating with the girls, she rebelled inside: "No, you're *wrong,* Holly." She thought a lot about it, tried to remember. She could see herself standing at the kitchen counter stirring their spaghetti or whatever, serving the girls their dinner while they chatted about — about what? She racked her brain. They'd talked about light, practical stuff — schedules, mostly. Had they ever really talked? She checked with the girls, later, for their memories. They confirmed her fears. They hadn't talked. The most serious talk she could remember Gary having with Holly was in a restaurant, when they'd talked about a car he was going to buy her and some trip he wanted to take. Stephanie felt a terrible wave of guilt as she had to face Holly's charge: "I can't remember one time in our entire lives that we had what you'd call a real talk."

She'd been saying to the girls, "We're still a family." But now she wondered if they had ever been a family if they didn't talk to one another. This nightmare had forced them to talk. They couldn't avoid it. Starting from scratch, they were learning to open up. But where did you start when people have shut you up all your life? "I'd get a look from Gary and I'd shut up." After they separated, Stephanie realized that "I was still waiting for Gary to tell me I was okay." It was in a deposition that she finally thought about the years of being undermined and put down. "I realized I didn't need his approval. If I said the wrong thing, it didn't matter . . . But it was very weird. All of a sudden you have this voice and what do you do with it?" How could she start really talking to her daughters if she had nothing to say? She had to fill up the hollow spaces, learn things.

But not now. After the divorce. The divorce proceedings shut her down. "I just felt like a bad little girl in the courtroom. I wasn't allowed to defend myself." Gary "kept filing all these documents about me, things that weren't true. Like I went out telling Dorothy Mondavi. It was the women who pursued *me*. Gary could always say what he wanted." He knew he had a powerful person, Bob Mondavi, behind him. "And I couldn't respond. I wanted to fight back . . . but Sandra wouldn't listen to me . . . It's like I had no avenue to take."

Only rarely, no matter how pressing the trial or case, did Bruce Miroglio not make it home to dinner. There were now three children, and even the youngest loved to "do my day." "Is it my turn yet, Daddy? I want to do my day!" the kids would squeal as they went around the table and burst out the story of their day. When it was Daddy's turn to "do his day," Miroglio told the gang and his wife, Mary, pregnant with their fourth, that he'd been hired for a major case that December day. John Suesans, national vice-president for claims for a major insurer of physicians in Napa, the Doctors Company, had needed an attorney in Napa to represent their insured, a Dr. Richard Rose, since the case was in Snowden's court there.

Miroglio knew Tim Mondavi through their sons, who shared school and soccer teams. He'd lived in Napa Valley all his life — went to Justin Siena High, where Mary, the homecoming queen, had played Marian the Librarian to his Professor Hill in *The Music Man,* and they'd first kissed onstage. A veteran of the school musicals, the debating team, and sportscasting on the local radio station, he loved performing. A trial was theater. *Ramona* was a tempting stage as well as a chance to establish his credentials in his home valley — most of his best courtroom work had been in adjoining counties. The tall, ambling partner in Gaw, Van Male, Smith & Myers wanted to see his name painted on the door of the firm as a full partner.

Because he lived in Napa Valley, Miroglio informally became the point man for contact with the Ramona women. As he got to know Stephanie and the girls, he liked them all. He believed Holly. They were so scared of Gary Ramona, you'd think he was a serial killer. Actually, as far as he and Mary were concerned, a child molester was as bad. In the courthouse, Bruce often dealt with the violent results of family meltdown. And Mary's part-time job in the pathology lab at Queen of the Valley Hospital showed her the reality of child abuse in Napa Valley; she examined cultures of venereal diseases and semen taken from the mouths and genitals of children.

As boxes of documents were sent to him through December 1991, Miroglio got up to date on the case. In the office he studied videotapes of depositions, appalled when he saw his new client, Rose, wearing a gaudy Hawaiian shirt; when Harrington ordered Rose deposed in San Francisco, Miroglio would make sure he wore a suit. On Napa's bright winter days, he sat in his special chair on the back patio, reading documents. If he glanced up over the vineyards, high and deep in the trees he could see a bit of the pyramidal roof of Gary Ramona's dream house. That coincidence appealed to him.

Neil Shapiro and Bruce Miroglio met for the first time when Gary's depositions resumed on January 27, 1992. Miroglio had been officially named Rose's counsel of record in Gary's lawsuit just four days earlier. Shapiro's job today was to get the goods to get Stephanie dismissed from the slander case. While the other defense attorneys would take the cynical tack that Gary had sued Stephanie only to get the case tried in Napa, Shapiro suspected that "Gary initially sued her to shut her up, and he achieved that." She had been intimidated by the lawsuit and ordered by the judge not to talk. Also, Shapiro suspected, Harrington knew he had a weak case against Stephanie. "Even if I couldn't establish Gary's guilt, Stevie was not necessarily liable. What Gary had to prove, and I had to defeat, was a charge that she spread *false statements* . . . about his guilt which were damaging to his reputation." This was the key. If "she *believed* it to be true and had a reasonable basis for that belief, she could not be held liable." The "reasonable basis" was there, he felt: Stephanie believed her daughter. She had believed Marche Isabella when the therapist told her, basically, "I think Holly's telling the truth." The gullible "fluffball" image Gary had painted could even work in her favor, making it more likely that she would believe a therapist. But in order to force Harrington to dismiss Stephanie from the slander suit, Shapiro must get Gary *to concede that she believed it* — that she truly believed in Gary's guilt.

To Gary, Shapiro was as abrasive as Harrington had been when he interrogated Gary the first time. For fifteen minutes, he focused relentlessly on the one question: "You have no reason to doubt that Stephanie Ramona believes the truth of the allegations, do you?" Gary was an artful dodger, dancing around the question — "Stephanie has told me she believes it" — evading a direct answer. Tenaciously rephrasing, Shapiro finally asked, "I take it you're reasonably comfortable, sir, with the notion that Stephanie Ramona, rightly or wrongly, believes in the truth of the allegations?" As Gary responded, "Wrongly, she does believe in them," Shapiro had him cornered and closed for the kill. "But she *does believe*, whether she should or not, she *does*, as far as you can tell?" he hammered. "I believe so," Gary admitted, then he exploded with righteous anger: "Number one, they're totally false! . . . And I'd like her to show me one piece of evidence, one time in twenty-five years, that she has any reason to even begin to consider that bullshit!" Let him vent, thought Shapiro. He had what he needed. He had it on tape.

Miroglio whispered to him, "Beautiful, you've just set him up for summary judgment" — formal dismissal of the slander case by the judge. But instead of filing for dismissal, Shapiro decided to write Harrington several letters, threatening to file a lawsuit on Stephanie's behalf against Gary if he did not dismiss her from the case. Shapiro was finessing.

On April 27, 1992 — a week after her forty-seventh birthday — Stephanie was dismissed from the case, having spent $65,000 in attorney's fees to defend herself. The three remaining targets — Isabella, Rose, and Western Medical Center — now faced malpractice charges in Ramona's backyard.

Stephanie no longer needed Shapiro. But she had finally found an attorney she trusted. He told her he would be there for her *pro bono* — free — if she needed him. He identified with Stephanie. They were both just beginning to emerge from lives of pleasing other people. Gary had manipulated Stephanie's life since she was a teenager, he saw. Shapiro's life had been shaped to please his father, who had never been satisfied with his own, or his children's, achievements.

And both of them, he sensed, were just beginning to blossom. Soon Shapiro would leave his unhappy marriage, start therapy, and move to a small law firm in a restored brick Victorian coffee factory he had looked down at, enviously, from his lofty corner office. He would watch his best friend die of cancer, and, cautiously, he would learn to ride the big old Harley-Davidson motorcycle his friend left him, discovering adventure again.

Stephanie, too, was emerging. "She had been put in the position of being a Barbie corporate wife. She's a lot more than that. She has a sense of humor . . . She's got a quick mind. I think it's just been turned off . . . It's as if she's awakening from a coma of twenty-five years."

The Gathering of Witnesses

Holly was lying in bed in her mother's new house in Napa after her first deposition in December when she had a memory that was different from all the others — it took place not in Diamond Bar but at the house in St. Helena. "The memory is of me in bed . . . My father is on top of me, and he is putting his penis partway inside of me . . . and there is me watching from far away. And the time is at night." The memory reappeared several times as she lay there. She could see her orange and beige bedspread. She was between fourteen and sixteen years old. *Her memories of rape now extended from ages five to sixteen — twelve years.*

But just at the time this new memory came to her, Holly's lawsuit against him was unraveling. The problem was the sodium amytal. Holly had staked her entire case on memories emerging from a drug deemed so unreliable that the testimony produced under its soporific haze was largely forbidden in court. If you underwent hypnosis or sodium amytal, you would probably not be allowed to testify in your own case. Naive, Holly had let her first attorney state, back in the original filing of her lawsuit on New Year's Eve 1990, that sodium amytal was the sole source of her memories and of her charges of abuse; none of her earlier flashbacks was mentioned — a serious error. William Tyson, Holly's new lawyer in Northern California, where so much of the legal activity was taking place, made the same error in the complaint he filed. When Holly hired Pat Gray to try her case, Gray saw "this huge mistake." An attorney who had been trying recovered memory cases since 1985 and, with Mary Williams, fighting for abuse victims' access to the courts, Gray prepared for trial aggressively, deposing Park Dietz at the cost of $400 an hour — "an amazing performance." Holly faced a dazzling show by Harrington: "He had all the experts there for every deposition, costing him thousands an hour — he'd already spent a million on the case. His drama was very impressive, and very hard for Holly." But the real danger lay in going to trial with this complaint; they'd never let Holly testify, she feared. Gray made a motion to amend the complaint and waited. Then, just days before the trial, set for February 24, 1992, Judge Fretz denied the motion — a mistake the judge himself was heard to admit in Tyson's presence during a later court hearing. Frustrated, Gray had no choice but to dismiss the case. On the eve of the trial, Holly's lawsuit was dead.

A few months later, on May 4, Tyson refiled for Holly, seizing on the extended statute of limitations that permitted her to sue until age twenty-six. Sodium amytal was not mentioned: "In or about January of 1990, plaintiff discovered that she had been subjected to childhood sexual abuse by defendant Gary Ramona." The early flashbacks as well as the new were included in the complaint. "Lurid acts" were alleged to have occurred "also in Napa County from age eight to sixteen."

But her case had been hurt. Holly had changed her story, offering a vulnerable flank to the other side. Even if her attorney deleted all references to sodium amytal from the new suit and the defendants tried to present their involvement with the drug as merely a harmless favor to Holly, words were already embedded in the sealed affidavit that had driven Gary to sue — that the drug had been used "to ascertain the truth of the matter . . . to verify the truth of the memories" that would come back to haunt them. Holly's medical records, released to her father, could not be withdrawn. As her case lost momentum, Holly endured the added irony of watching her father attack with the weapons she had given him.

At the same time, Gary's case was gaining momentum. The legal costs for the divorce and lawsuits were high, but Gary still had a war chest. He and Stephanie would each receive more than $1 million in assets and income in the final disbursement of what had been Gary's fortune. Gary's half-million-dollar settlement with Mondavi did not have to be shared; it was not joint property, the judge decided. Gary would spend the money on being as prepared for trial as the Allies for D-Day. In complex cases like this one, requiring specialized knowledge beyond the ken of the average juror — DNA, fast-changing technologies, the science of memory — both sides hired experts to educate and argue their points. That was the next step for the attorneys.

Charging between $300 and $400 an hour, experts tended to be defensive about the charge that they were hired guns. It was only their time, not their opinions, that was for sale, they testily claimed. But when they said yes, the hiring attorney could confidently expect that the expert would argue on the side of the client — and that equally qualified experts would make diametrically opposing arguments for the other side with the same conviction and authority. Gary had found his bulimia expert in Harrison Pope. He now directed Harrington to hunt down the nation's best experts in memory and repression, hypnotic drugs, psychiatric testing, and medical and psychotherapeutic standards of care.

Harrington hired Dr. Robert H. Gerner, a psychiatrist in Los Angeles, to do the critical psychological examination of Holly. Her only evaluation by Gary's side, it would be used by all the other experts as the basis of their testimony. Seeing Holly twice in late November, Gerner issued his report in January 1992. He painted a devastating picture. A suggestible young woman who had difficulty separating reality from fantasy, Holly had "little appreciation for the enormous disruption in the lives of all her family members . . ." Insecure, socially withdrawn, and childish, she suffered from schizotypal tendencies and, very likely, mild brain dysfunction and learning disability. Her depression might well relapse, and the bulimia continue, without medication. Her flashbacks were consistent with "spontaneous panic attacks"; her memories were false. "During her treatment, while she was severely psychologically compromised, she developed fantasies of a sexual nature that were projected onto her father."

As for Marche Isabella, she had so overstepped her limits as a nonphysician, Gerner found, that it might constitute practicing medicine without a license — a professional lapse serious enough to strip a therapist of her license.

Miroglio had read Gerner's report on Holly, had met the doctor in depositions, and had found him one of the most arrogant and obnoxious witnesses he had ever met. Gerner's report had triggered the distaste. "I read this fairly pleasant interview he had with Holly. And then, in his report, he put out this psychological hit piece. He basically described her in terms that she needed to be strapped to a hospital bed. It simply didn't make sense." He heard reports about Gerner. "He was described as a haughty, know-it-all doctor and that we were mere dumb lawyers. His nickname was Rocky. He drove a Rolls-Royce in L.A. and had a reputation of flashing his M.D. to get a restaurant reservation." He affected black shades and shirts and wore his hair slicked back over the nape of his neck. Miroglio said to himself, "This guy is either the biggest whore in the world or he has an agenda." There was something about him. Miroglio would do a little sleuthing.

As Harrison Pope and Jim Hudson read the case on Holly Ramona — all the reports and depositions sent to them by Harrington — they agreed: "Well, this is the typical case of bulimia. We have patients like this: the bad depression and unhappiness, self-recrimination, the obsessional preoccupation with the body and sexuality, the obsessional intrusions mislabeled as 'flashbacks' and very different from a Vietnam vet's intrusive posttraumatic memories, anxiety symptoms, all manner of symptoms." Studies also showed considerable long-term success with both antidepressants and cognitive behavioral therapy — with and without drug treatment. Much research was still needed to know what combination worked best. But even now, "our patients come, they get better, they go home. Why did this happen? There's just no excuse." Holly, Pope proposed, had been extraordinarily suggestible when she was exposed to Isabella's influence and had grasped at the suggestion of childhood sexual abuse in her hunger to understand her symptoms — chalk it up to the compulsive human search for meaning.

Satisfied that childhood sexual abuse was not a cause of bulimia, Pope and Hudson now focused on the more central issue: Can you be sexually abused over a twelve-year period, from the age of five to sixteen, and simply forget the entire thing? In other words, did "robust repression," the massive burying of sexual abuse memories, exist? The evidence in Holly's case offered them no proof. The two decided to examine every serious study on repression in the literature. "It was a revelation to find how thin the actual literature was," says Pope. After a global search, they found only four — *four!* — studies. And these four were quoted so often as hard evidence by the recovered memory movement that their very names had become a shorthand for "See, here's proof": Herman & Schatzow, Briere & Conte, Linda

Meyer Williams, and Loftus et al. Having become one of repressed memory's most vocal skeptics, Elizabeth Loftus was a surprise in this company, although her paper, in fact, claimed no corroborated recovery of "robustly repressed" memories but straightforwardly reported the claims of women who had forgotten their abuse for a time and then remembered.

Pope and Hudson found that, upon "a critical scientific analysis, the literature fell apart." All four studies, they felt, suffered from flaws in methodology: they lacked proper corroboration of the alleged abuse or of the amnesia that followed it. "There was no acceptable evidence that you could have a series of terrible traumas and simply forget about them." They were particularly surprised by Herman & Schatzow, which claimed a high percentage of repressed memories, for in Herman's book, *Father-Daughter Incest,* just six years before the study, she had described forty female incest victims, every one of whom had clear and lasting memories of the abuse. She had written of the "incest secret." But "repression" did not even appear in her index. As Pope and Hudson wrote up their repression findings, words scarcely captured the excitement they felt: "Thus present clinical evidence is insufficient to permit the conclusion that individuals can repress memories of childhood sexual abuse."

Dr. Park Elliot Dietz, the nation's leading forensic psychiatrist, was very selective in the cases he handled. Usually a witness for the prosecution in homicide cases, Dietz was particularly effective in proving sanity against the insanity defense, which absolved killers of responsibility for their acts. Finding the evidence that John Hinckley, Jr., had acted under free will — the legal distinction between the sane and insane — he had helped prove the sanity of the man who shot President Reagan. He had recently put away one of America's most unspeakable monsters, the serial killer Jeffrey Dahmer. He was hired by movie stars to get inside the minds of celebrity-stalkers and consulted by the FBI and CIA. Solving crimes was his greatest fascination; the courtroom was his arena.

The Franklin case had led him to believe that repressed and recovered memories might exist. His skepticism would grow, but for now he could make an incisive case against the therapists without resolving the repression debate. As Gary Ramona read Dietz's declaration, his opinion of the Ramona case, he was dazzled. Dietz had stripped the chronological story of all the myth and emotion, broken it down, and rebuilt it, step by step, into a logical construction that led to his conclusion: Holly's memories were false, the therapy below the "standard of care" — the level accepted by the professional community. "The tragedy," Dietz would reiterate in court, "is that it's impossible for her to evaluate her own seeming recollections." His bill to Gary Ramona would reach $60,000.

A report arrived from Martin Orne, a leading expert on hypnosis. Orne had collapsed on the deposition stand and was forced to drop any active role in the case. While debate raged over the cause of his collapse, Miroglio was sure that Harrington had pulled him because Orne had admitted, in depositions, that he had conducted a sodium amytal interview for clarifying a family dispute and Harrington knew the defense would nail him with this in the trial. But, in place of Orne on the stand, his declaration would still add strength to Gary's case: "Holly's memory has been so distorted by the use of sodium amytal and the false facts proffered by her psychiatrist Dr. Rose and her therapist Marche Isabella that in my expert opinion, Holly no longer knows what the truth is and what it is not."

As the expert declarations arrived, Gary worried. Had they covered everything? They had not developed an expert response to the charges of bestiality or pedophilia. What about the hymen? From the beginning, Gary had nagged Harrington to get an expert opinion on it. How could Holly's hymen have a separation so slight that the gynecologist had said it could be caused by falling from a horse, a handlebar — or could have been that way when she was born — if she'd been continuously raped? "It doesn't make any sense that if you're going to have repetitive sex, this isn't completely destroyed." But what he already had, Gary hoped, would reveal Isabella's quackery and make his family see Holly's memories for what they were — fantasies.

On Memorial Day 1992, Gary sent a gift to his old friends Larry and Anna Graeber, a shiny blue three-inch-thick binder containing the Gerner, Pope, Dietz, and Orne declarations, with a note: "Larry and Anna — I hope this helps convince you that nothing really happened." Including a tape of an Oprah Winfrey show on recovered memory, he sent a similar binder to several other old friends. He sent the same package to Kelli and Shawna and one to Holly with a note:

"Love, Dad." Holly was so upset she called Marche Isabella in Virginia.

As Gary tells it, he drove over to Steph's one afternoon with the declarations locked in his little corrugated file box, and she let him read them to her. He was moved. It was like a miraculous little truce signed in the middle of war as they sat down together on the front lawn under the pine tree. "Look, you don't have to agree with it . . . but you ought to at least hear it," he said as he laid them out. Steph sat on the grass, and Gary leaned against her brick planter as he read to her for three hours. "I read them from cover to cover."

When he came to the part about repressed memory, Stephanie stopped him and asked, "Well, do you believe in repressed memory?"

"I don't know all the particulars, but I can tell you this, Steph, that in regard to Holly, nothing's been repressed. It's all been Marche Isabella . . . You think that a sixteen-year-old is not going to have any recall, any memory, any thoughts, any anything? If you believe that, I think you got problems . . . Steph, listen to what these people have to say. These are some of the world's best experts . . ."

"They're *your* experts."

"Wait a minute, they're just taking the facts . . ."

He continued reading until he'd delivered every word of what, to him, was an overwhelming body of opinion. Finished, he waited for Steph to fill the silence.

"Gary," she said, "I've been going to church lately . . . and I want you to know that I forgive you."

Gary exploded. "I don't need your goddamn forgiveness!" He grabbed the papers, threw them in his file box, and left. He couldn't believe it. She'd never gone to church with him. Now, out of nowhere, she's finding religion. "I forgive you." I've done nothing wrong. I don't know where the hell you're coming from. Blindly angry, he drove about a mile, past the Louis Martini Winery on Highway 29, pushed the brake to the floor, and headed back to the house. He had to try to say to Steph, "We don't need this. Our family can't take any more turmoil." But he was so livid, so mad at this righteousness suddenly being laid on him — this "I have religion now." "If God himself came down and told them this was not true, there's no way they'd believe him. From the beginning, they've all played God." He stopped the car, his head bursting. The salesman finally got the message. He had made his major presentation, and the door had been slammed in his face.

He still blamed Marche Isabella the most. But, finally, he held his family responsible, too. "Steph. Do I hold her responsible? Absolutely. Do I hold Holly responsible? Absolutely. Do I hold Kelli and Shawna responsible? Absolutely. And I hold Betty Nye responsible, without question. Am I angry? I'm angry in one sense. But I'm sorry for these people that have to live with themselves . . . Steph's nothing but a puppet. It's extremely difficult for them to realize they made the biggest mistake in their lives. And that doesn't mean being married to me. That's up to Steph. Steph was very unhappy with herself. No other man or other person can make her happy. I'm talking about allowing peripheral people to control her — her mother, Marche Isabella — about basing your actions on absolutely false accusations by a stranger."

Steph, he finally forced himself to see, would never open her mind and listen. And now she had this so-called T-graph, this list of clues to Gary's guilt she supposedly created from her memories of their life together. Like Martin Luther and his ninety-five theses nailed to the door of the church at Wittenberg, Steph had written down her twenty-eight reasons for condemning Gary and nailed his reputation. But she'd never produced the damn piece of paper, though Harrington had requested it. She just couldn't find it, the defense contended. But Gary believed that "the T-graph's a big joke," a legal contrivance created yesterday. But even though it wasn't proof, it could have a powerful emotional impact on the jury. At one of her depositions in the spring, Stephanie had described writing it: when Holly said that her father had raped her, "I sat down and I made a *T* on a piece of paper. I wrote all the reasons why Gary wouldn't do something like that and all the reasons — that caused me to believe Holly . . . I wrote down everything that I knew and observed in our family." On the side of Gary's guilt was a list so long it spilled up the side of the page; on the side of his innocence there were only two items. "One thing did not mean that he had raped his daughter. But I believe it put together a puzzle."

Holly's lawyers had started alluding to the list even before Stephanie said it existed. Gary had been alerted to it in January when Holly's new lawyer, Bill Tyson, had started probing him in depositions about incidences he'd never heard of. Had Gary encouraged Stephanie to go out and leave him with the kids? Did he find Stephanie sexually desirable during pregnancy? Did Gary remember discussing douching with his wife? Tyson pressed on. Had Gary cut her face when he struck her, hit her on the back of the head, held her by the neck against a wall, said he wanted to fuck a neighbor's wife? What was this! Again and again, Gary was accused of ignoring Steph's early reports of Holly's molestation. The "first time I had any understanding, whatsoever, of any allegation of anything in regard to any sexual activity with anyone was on March 15, 1990. That was it!" As the string of ugly anecdotes unfolded — and more would come — he seethed inside. "Bottom line, absolute lies."

Then the skewer: "Do you recall any particular type of lock on the front door of the house at Diamond Bar?" Gary heard, for the first time, about Steph's driving to the beach, forgetting her towel, coming back to a locked front door and ringing the doorbell — Gary in his underpants and no Holly in sight. He knew that there was no bolt on the inside that you couldn't open on the outside. Steph's keys opened every door in the house. "How the hell is this woman remembering if she had a yellow towel or a white towel?" Impatient with what he termed Gary's tendency "to ramble about things," Tyson cut him off. "I understand how you feel about wanting to make your points. This is not a sales meeting."

No, it was not. It was his life. Stephanie was not going to turn the years at Diamond Bar into a dirty horror story. He called some former neighbors on Holly Leaf Way and asked them to come share their memories of the Ramonas over wine and cheese. Twice, he and Harrington flew down to meet with his old neighbors and videotape their recollections of a hugging, happy family and a great father to use in court. Gary and Scott Evans drove over to the old house and photographed the front door lock that was Steph's premier piece of evidence against him on her T-graph; the deadbolt, they found, did unlock from the outside. Steph could have unlocked it at any time! Rummaging through old photos, Gary found a picture of one of Steph's relatives, standing by the front door. The lock on the door in the picture was the same lock he'd just photographed at the house.

For Gary, reality lay in the stack of pictures he'd retrieved from the house — to Stephanie's distress — and in the home movies he was editing to show the jury at the trial. "I've begun to understand why they don't want to look at the old home movies. They don't want to look back at who we really were."

At Holly's deposition in Southern California in early August 1992, when her new memories "to age sixteen" were explored, the defense team took Holly to lunch at a Chinese restaurant in Orange. In addition to Miroglio and Leonard, the defense had taken on a young San Francisco attorney, Jeffrey Kurtock, to represent Isabella. Tall and youthful, the three lawyers looked like a football team's defensive line. It was Miroglio's first meeting with Holly. "This girl has never kissed a man. She's had one real date in her life. She's been asked to dance twice in her life . . . We're squeezed in a booth so she can't get out." She was clearly "petrified," Miroglio saw. Ed Leonard, "eating like a horse," is urging her, "'Come on, Holly, *mange, mange,* this'll be good for you.'" Miroglio nudged him and whispered, "Ed, Ed, she's *bulimic!*" At the end of lunch, Miroglio's instinct was to give her a bear hug — but he didn't dare.

Leonard, too, was touched by Holly and believed her memories were real. One of the things that convinced him was Gary's response to hearing that Holly had been molested. How could a father say — as Stephanie said he did — "That's a shame" and turn over and go to sleep? "My response would be, 'Get my gun, I'm going to shoot me some perpetrator.'" Leonard, a new father himself, guessed that next he would have tried to help. "What really got me is that he never, ever, said to his daughter, '*Honey, somebody has hurt you. I'll work with you to help you through this.*'"

Instead of help for his daughter, Stephanie's women friends saw a ceaseless pattern of cruelty. To them, the wine and cheese parties Gary staged for the Diamond Bar neighbors were coercive and beneath contempt. But the last straw was Gary's sending the binder to Holly telling her she was a psychotic train wreck and signing it "Love, Dad." "If you're really the wonderful, loving father that Gary is trying to portray himself as . . . is this what a loving father would do?" Jean Sawday asked. Her rage rose every time she thought about his behavior. He'd asked Stephanie to betray Holly and turn on Marche Isabella, asked "me to join him in the lawsuit to sue them for $10 million . . . He was going to sue their asses," he'd reportedly called and told Stephanie.

It could have ended; it didn't have to come to this, they believed. All Gary had ever had to do was confess, apologize, and it would be over. Holly would drop her refiled lawsuit. Stephanie would drop spousal support — she wouldn't starve; she'd have some income from the divorce settlement. Judge Snowden had tried to resolve all the issues at once at a settlement conference on January 23, 1992 — the divorce, the family lawsuits — but it had failed. The Doctors Company, which insured Rose, had offered several times to settle his case for $100,000, but Harrington held out for the limits of his insurance coverage, $1 million. Holly had tried to settle with her father at an early conference, saying, as Miroglio heard it from an attorney who was there, "Look, Dad, you're not going to apologize. I'm not going to back down. I'll drop my lawsuit if you drop your lawsuit against my therapist." Gary, reportedly, looked across the table, put his face right in Holly's, and said, "You don't have any idea of reality, do you, little girl?" and got up and left the room.

Over and over, Steph had said to Gary, "Settle this, you're going to lose. You're going to lose." He had always said, "Steph, you don't get it. This has nothing to do with money. I'm not going to allow these people to get away with what they did to our family and my daughters. I will see them fry in hell before I'll settle." But his principles were costing money, his assets draining. Still tramping to divorce court, Gary argued on July 17, 1992, that he was broke and that lawsuit costs to date were nearly $360,000. The first year and a half, Ephraim Margolin's legal bill had been $120,000; at one point he simply stopped billing. Fighting to protect Stephanie's diminishing returns from the divorce, Musser went on the attack that fall, arguing that, through his lawsuit, Gary was bankrupting himself and his family "for a highly unlikely and probably impossible goal."

With the hiring of Elizabeth Loftus to testify on memory, Gary's goal became substantially less unlikely and improbable. With Loftus, *Franklin* and *Ramona* — the two most important recovered memory cases to date — intersected. She read Gerner's report and Holly's transcripts. She noted Prince, the family dog — ah, bestiality. The memories were stretching into the bizarre. "I love it when they start in with this satanic stuff; I say you're lucky," Loftus said, calling on the black humor that can keep defense witnesses sane.

She was struck that Holly's memories had extended to age sixteen. "Even if the dog hadn't entered the story, the fact that she knows nothing at age nineteen of rape from five to sixteen I think . . . was pretty suspicious." Holly's story not only followed the same suggestible chain of events that was the common pattern among patients whose memories were, to Loftus, suspicious, but her memories had also evolved in the usual way: from a few plausible scenes of abuse to a tangle of increasingly fantastic images. Eileen Franklin Lipsker came to mind; the prosecution had tried to keep it under wraps, but Eileen's flashbacks had expanded to seeing her father commit several more murders, none corroborated. "I've seen so many cases where they go right into the satanic" — ritual baby killings and cult torture. Loftus doubted that Holly's memories had fully bloomed.

Loftus had not been idle since *Franklin*. She had been called in on ten other recovered memory cases, and the title of the book she was just completing revealed her position on the controversy: *The Myth of Repressed Memory*. She had never seen proof for the kind of memory being claimed in *Ramona*. Yet legions of her colleagues across the continent believed in — and many worked with — recovered memories. It was more than loyalty to Freud's legacy. "We want to believe — in fact, we need to believe" in these memories because it "affirms that our own minds work in an orderly way . . . In a chaotic world, where so much is out of control, we need to believe that our minds, at least, are under our command." Her colleagues were not so tolerant when Loftus attacked the very basis of her own profession. "Calling repression 'the foundation on which psychoanalysis rests' is just a way of saying it is a widely held tenet," Loftus responded. *"So was witches!"*

A backlash against recovered memories had begun by the summer of 1992, when Harrington called her to join the *Ramona* team. Loftus was instrumental in the backlash. A quick tally of her Frequent Flyer miles attested to the vigor with which she spread — in trials, conferences, classrooms, speeches, papers, books, and on radio and TV — her message of skepticism about repression.

Loftus was invited to be on the advisory board of the False Memory Syndrome Foundation (FMSF), begun in the spring of 1992 as a voice for accused parents — the official birth of the backlash. Founded by Pamela Freyd, an educational psychologist accused with her husband of unspecified abuse by her estranged daughter, Jennifer, FMSF started with six hundred parents. Quickly becoming the base camp and lifeline for this new subculture of parents, it had been contacted by seven thousand people within a year — sixteen thousand by the time of *Ramona* in 1994. From the first, the FMSF was attacked as "a haven for pedophiles and perpetrators." Its numbers were inflated, Miroglio suspected, by counting his own call for information as an "accused parent." But by lashing its public posture to a mast of respected scientists and scholars, with Elizabeth Loftus cutting the waves on the prow, it gained almost immediate credibility with the media.

In time for the Ramona trial, Loftus had completed a study that excited her greatly. It would add to her daunting body of evidence that memory was a malleable, permeable reconstruction rather than a perfect playback of the past — that memory was suggestible. Called "Lost in the Mall," the new study was a dramatic demonstration of how suggestion can lead someone to create entirely false memories. Searching for a way to implant in the mind a whole, detailed memory of a mildly traumatic event, the mall scenario had struck her a year earlier, as she was driving by a shopping center in Atlanta. With the cooperation of relatives, subjects would be told a series of true family stories from their childhood; one would be false, a story about the time they were lost in the mall.

The idea for the study came from an earlier single study of a fourteen-year-old boy, Chris, who became a household name for anyone following recovered memories. His older brother, Jim, had planted the story in a note to his brother: "I remember that Chris was five. We had gone shopping at the . . . shopping mall in Spokane. After some panic, we found Chris . . . crying and holding the man's hand." Chris, like 20 percent of the twenty-four subjects in her larger study, integrated the story into his memory, embroidering it in the retelling, creating vivid detail from thin air. Chris believed in his memory so deeply that he would not relinquish it, even when he was told it was totally false. "Chris had become an honest liar." The study would be attacked as being too unlike the real experience of trauma to be relevant. But Loftus knew she had the kind of powerful story that would captivate a jury. It was also, she believed, a small step forward for the science of memory. Quoted almost mandatorily in the burgeoning literature denying repressed memory, "Lost in the Mall" became the single most influential piece of research countering the repression studies quoted just as ceaselessly by "the other side."

One of the most potent blows of the backlash was struck from the feminist ranks in 1992 by the social psychologist Carol Tavris in *The Mismeasure of Woman,* where, she charged, the victim culture had become so absorbed in its own personal "healing" that it had betrayed the political dimension of the feminist rallying cry: "The personal is political." "The effort to achieve social change has been co-opted into a focus on psychological solace . . . The horror of a child being beaten or raped is defused by the claims of some adults that they were beaten and raped as children too, in a previous life."

Yet false memories and accusations in all their richly varied forms continued to erupt. The vast majority of Americans, with little if any understanding of the phenomenon, saw sensational stories of trials and convictions and imprinted them in their memories. The backlash would take time.

But another cloud was falling over the recovered memory movement as the nation's largest insurer of psychologists and MFCCs grew impatient with its stridence. "*This* is where the backlash is coming from," Eric Marine said of the movement. Vice-president of claims for Isabella's insuring agent, New York's American Professional Agency, he found that, at meetings, your attitude to "the adult survivors movement became the litmus test of your political correctness." If he showed any ambiguity in his feelings about false memories, clinicians would confront him with: "What do you mean you don't know? This *happened!*" It had nothing to do with the right or wrong of child abuse. "We've set up a system in the United States where you're either a victim or a perpetrator," says Marine. "If you didn't believe them, you were sexist."

In early 1993 Miroglio hired the most obvious antidote to Loftus: he asked Lenore Terr, the superstar from *Franklin,* to be an expert witness. Hearing his description of *Ramona,* Terr was excited. "It was the first huge backlash case. It was a father suing a daughter for coming up with memories." Terr heard nothing that suggested Richard Rose or Marche Isabella had made any major mistakes. Challenging Loftus again was tempting, but she wouldn't say yes until she'd seen Holly. After spending six hours with her on March 10 and 12, 1993, Terr agreed to take on the case. Miroglio sent her a $2,000 retainer.

It was "a shy, frightened, and saddened little girl, not a young woman," who entered Terr's office on Sutter Street in San Francisco on March 10. Sharing offices with her husband, a physician, Terr had chosen the smaller, cozier room, covered the windows and sofa with an indigo blue and white print, and filled the space with objects of healing and pleasure — toys, "things," art, books. Looking like a cross between a Tolkien Hobbit house and a Victorian dollhouse, it was a place hundreds of traumatized children had already come, a place where wounded children could feel safe while they explored an antique Austrian tea set, checkers, a Zuni bear carved from turquoise, fossil shards, miniature Peter Rabbit cups, drawers full of crayons and

Magic Markers, dinosaurs, lions, and cats. An amiable, sandy-haired mother of two grown children, Terr guided her troubled clients gently through the shoals of their trauma.

"Holly was wearing loose clothes. She had a headband pulling back her hair, but it was so long that it would come over her face and she would look shrouded. She had made no effort to make herself glamorous for me. In fact, she would have liked to shrink into the woodwork and somehow not be seen." Terr got an immediate impression of Stephanie, who arrived with Holly: "She was beautiful. Not at all faded. And she was dressed for the occasion, the doctor's office in downtown San Francisco . . . It struck me that Stephanie was a great beauty and that Holly was plain . . . That would have had to play a part in who Holly was."

Terr was already satisfied, reading the case, that Holly had *external* corroboration for her memories — the long record of visits to the pediatrician, the feeling of glass in her bottom, the urethrogram, constipation, the damaged hymen. "I'm a detective of the mind," says Terr of her search, next, for *internal* corroboration, for rich detail in Holly's memories. For emotion accompanying the memories. She would look for behaviors that were the body's way of expressing the abuse. She would not administer tests or play games with Holly. They would talk.

Terr liked to hear the "whole hideous story" first, so she asked Holly to tell her all of her memories, in order. As she listened, she observed Holly as "very young, very hurt, very shy, unable to use certain words. In that generation that's usually saying 'fuck' and 'shit' every other word, here is this little girl saying 'down there' and 'his thing.' Twenty-year-olds don't talk to me like that — never. At the movies she couldn't watch the kissing scenes. Very quaint. Very naive." She saw a very sensitive, smart girl. Not just average — bright.

Terr looked for Holly's "cluster of symptoms and signs," the traces of past trauma that showed in behavior; without them, she would seriously doubt that trauma had occurred. Symptoms and signs were there in abundance, however. Holly's food fetishes were consistent with sex abuse: she couldn't stand mayonnaise, cream sauce, melted cheese; she had to cut up bananas and pickles — all foods that could remind her of a penis, oral sex, or semen. Terr saw a reenactment of the abuse in Holly's girlhood games of Wonder Woman and Charlie's Angels — women fighting evil men. Holly had no sense of a future and feared men. The memory about Prince, though, was troubling.

Terr made notes: "*Father undressed . . . Held the dog against front of him, put her on ground, and put his arms around bottom of dog, brought the dog to her and made her copulate the dog.*" She could not find symptoms and signs related to memories of Prince; Holly had no problem with animals. It was the only memory she found unconvincing. "I couldn't say that I could find internal evidence for every single detail." But, Terr claimed, she had no reason to disbelieve any of her memories simply because they might not be supported by symptoms and signs. "I believed in the *gist* of her memories." That Gary Ramona did not confess did not surprise her. They never do. She could confidently argue in court that from the dark well of repressed memories, Holly had brought up traces of true events.

"But a list of memories does not make a diagnosis." Holly's, she decided, was a classic Type II trauma, the repeated trauma that is repressed — her own, new theory. The larger diagnosis was PTSD — posttraumatic stress syndrome. It was a daring diagnosis because, although amnesia could be a symptom of PTSD in Vietnam vets, far more common were intrusive memories so real that sweating veterans relived in detail the terror of ambushes and the slaughter of best friends. They didn't forget repeated trauma, nor did survivors of Auschwitz. One of Terr's achievements had been to get *children's* symptoms of posttraumatic stress — different from those of Vietnam vets, she claimed — included in the diagnostic bible for the mental health professions, *DSM-IV* — the fourth edition of *Diagnostic and Statistical Manual of Mental Disorders,* coming out in 1994.

The *DSM* was a political game, for a formal diagnosis listed there guaranteed insurance coverage — and, therefore, a busy practice — as major mental disorders like schizophrenia and depression passed from psychotherapy to treatment by drugs. Childhood sex abuse trauma held the promise of new diagnoses — of a whole new industry, cynics would say. It was Terr's landmark Chowchilla study of the children kidnapped in a bus and buried alive that had virtually defined childhood trauma and put Terr on the trauma committee for *DSM-IV.* Terr's diagnosis would challenge the findings put forward by the psychiatrist for Gary Ramona, Robert Gerner. But Terr would stand by her diagnosis.

Terr red-charted Holly Ramona's file — most files were white; red meant trauma — and waited to be deposed.

*

Gary was flat on his back, having his wisdom teeth extracted at Dr. Bird's office in Napa, so he couldn't talk, but he noticed the blond surgical assistant. She seemed in command but friendly and warm, and was as trim as Steph. Her name was Barbara Stewart. He sent a few bottles of wine to the office to say thanks and she called him to ask about them — the best excuse she could find for making contact. She, too, was reentering single life after a failed marriage, and they began to date. It was months before he could bear to tell her the story, but nothing changed for Barbara. She believed in his innocence. Her friends and children accepted him openly, easily. Barbara was affectionate, would take Gary's hand under the table at a restaurant. Bob and Margrit invited them to dinner. Barbara, knowing it was the test, was nervous at first. At one point Margrit led Gary to the kitchen while Bob questioned Barbara rather directly at the table. She knew what it was about: Was she good enough for Gary? "I must have passed. They've been so sweet to me."

"He needed somebody so much, and now he had this lovely person who sticks with him," Margrit observed. "That is when he started taking Stevie down from the goddess level. I think he stopped loving her when the new woman came into his life."

Almost lost in the intense trial preparations was Gary and Stephanie's official divorce on October 23, 1992. Final trials and hearings would trudge on for another year, but Stephanie was too caught up in her troubles with Sandra Musser to notice. "She won . . . almost everything for me. But I've never been treated so poorly in my whole entire life." Responding to a letter from Stephanie accusing that she "wasn't representing my interests," Musser resigned at the end of the year and, in January, sued Stephanie for nonpayment of fees. This was not Neil Shapiro's field; she needed another lawyer. But no one would take her case. "We were at the end of the divorce, there wasn't any money left. Everything was going. I would bet $400,000 had gone to lawyers." She found George Luke, in Santa Rosa. "Thank God, he took my case. I was begging, begging." He helped her settle with Musser. It was therefore anticlimactic to hear that the divorce had gone through. Luke took her down to the Napa courthouse to prove it to her, to show her the piece of paper. "I thought, 'Great, at least that's one less thing.' But I felt nothing. I felt nothing."

Eva, one of her favorite aunts, died at the end of March. On a trip south, Stephanie took her mother to the beach at Balboa, and the two women mourned. Stephanie was still an elegant beach girl — slim, tanned, with a mane of streaked blond hair, Newport-chic slacks and shirts. Inside, she didn't know how she could contain the tumult, the worry, the sadness, without bursting. But at the beach she could still find the little girl who had tried to put salt on the pigeon's tail.

Stephanie had lost all trust in men, all ability to relate to them, Miroglio noted. On first meeting Mary, his wife, she had said to him, "You ought to be ashamed of yourself, with such a beautiful wife." When he asked why he should be ashamed, she said, "Because you probably fool around on her. All men do. It's just men." When he said, astounded, "Stevie, all men don't do that. I never have, I never would," she was shocked. She had lost her trust in people. She was paranoid with fear that, to defend the therapists, the attorneys might turn the blame on her. *Loss of trust, terror of Gary.* Like a dramatist structuring a play, Miroglio was beginning to shape his arguments for the trial, which was scheduled to start on June 7, 1993. What were the major themes and subthemes for each witness? What do I want to get from them? He'd scratch thoughts on pads of yellow paper, then sit down at his computer and write an outline.

His principal challenge was how to draw Gary's character for the jury in Courtroom B. Control began as the main theme, with manipulation as a subtheme. "This lawsuit is about Gary trying to control Holly. He tried to control her when she was a kid. He's still trying to control her," he ruminated. He would paint Gary as the patriarchal, self-obsessed father who controlled his child through rape and who would hound her wherever she went, trying to control her again. The theme that had been sounded first by Marche Isabella and played in several variations by Sandra Musser throughout the divorce would now be featured in the trial.

"Those who say it's all about power are following a political agenda. Abuse of patriarchal power doesn't explain all the erections!" believed Dr. Fred Berlin, director of the Johns Hopkins Institute of Sexual Disorders. "There's compulsion. Most of these men feel terrible about what they do." The feminists' profile — they're all giants of the community and could be anybody — was too simple to explain the thousands of perpetrators examined by Dr. Pierre Gagne. In his role as a researcher and director of the forensic clinic at the University of Sherbrooke in Quebec, the psychiatrist had quickly spotted that, although he might look like a paragon on the surface, the incestuous molester was too consumed by his uncontrollable attraction to children and his guilt to function well. He did not stop with one daughter but worked his way through the sisters, the neighborhood girls, nieces. Almost always, he had been molested himself, Gagne and Berlin agreed.

The defense attorneys had recently sent Gagne several accused fathers who staunchly denied their daughters' recovered memories. A different breed from perpetrators in his experience, they were almost unreal models of leadership, success, community service, and loving parenting. As Gagne examined them, he couldn't find the traits of the perpetrator familiar to him. His findings mattered, for in Canada child sex abuse — even abuse claimed after the age of majority — is a criminal offense. These men faced jail in a country being swept, like the United States, with sympathy for recovered memories, from Victoria, where *Michelle Remembers* had virtually triggered the movement, to Thunder Bay's satanic sex cult hysteria. He concluded, "We are in almost total darkness regarding who are the men falsely accused of sexual misconduct and what is their fate after the truth has come out."

Gagne had only a handful of accused fathers to work with, but he set up a study to compare eleven of them — all later proved innocent by reliable corroboration — to eleven who denied but were later found guilty. Between the two groups, there were clear and dramatic differences in such things as emotional reactions, the consistency of stories, and a refusal to plea-bargain; nine of the eleven innocent men scored zero on a scale of major indicators of pedophilia — a childhood history of abuse, strong sexual urges, immaturity, family influences, psychopathic tendencies, a large collection of child pornograpy, a child-oriented career choice, and so on.

His study might help identify innocent men and reduce the numbers of cases wrongly brought to court. But the sample was too small to have any real impact on the hundreds of court cases raging in both countries. To gain serious scientific attention, Gagne knew he'd have to compare at least a thousand of each category. In the meantime, innocent men, he feared, were being tried and convicted.

"I recognize that a trial is the world's worst way of resolving a conflict," Bruce Miroglio admitted, as he struggled with the profoundly troubling human issues that rose from the stacks of cardboard boxes and thick blue deposition books that held the legal record of *Ramona*.

Lenore Terr knew that her intimate office was a better place for fixing lives than a court of law, and she was frustrated by "the irreconcilable differences between the law and psychiatry. Science is always looking forward, saying what's the next thing we need to know, how do we build on this. Law looks backward. Always arguing from the past." Yet how were the terrible patterns of child abuse to be broken? Generations of permitting it to go unchecked in a family, the pattern of abuse broadening exponentially, explained today's epidemic, Terr suspected. Education was needed. It was one of the reasons she kept going to court. As she sent her evaluation of Holly Ramona off to Miroglio, Terr still believed, "A court of law is the best place our system has for educating the public . . . It gets people to think. After courtroom battles, laws are passed. Books are written." She was already writing a book on repressed memories.

The hope that something good might come from it all was one of the few things that gave any meaning to the hell Gary Ramona had lived through for three years. Although still shell-shocked and lacking purpose, preparing for the trial occupied his ferocious energies — it got him up each morning.

But while Gary acted, Stephanie reacted. She did not find the lawsuits a replacement for her former role of running a household. Dismissed from Gary's suit, through with the worst of the divorce, she continued to troop obediently to hearings and depositions. Neil Shapiro had seen the promise of a suppressed spirit coming alive when he got her dismissed from the slander suit. But the defense lawyers winced as she stumbled through depositions, paralyzed by competing pulls: trying to help Holly, trying to respond to the lawyers, trying to stay true to her own realities. She could be a catastrophe on the stand. But Miroglio's heart ached. He was so fond of Stephanie, and he feared he was hearing the voice of a battered woman.

Holly may have been a shy and sad little girl when she met Lenore Terr in May 1993, just a month before the trial of her father's lawsuit. But within her cocoon of baggy clothes, a metamorphosis was taking place: evolving was a more poised and articulate butterfly. Part of it was simply practice. Part of it was training; she had been schooled by the lawyers in the strategy of the upcoming trial. If she was to help her therapists contest the charge of having manipulated a sick and suggestible girl into false memories and a confrontation that destroyed her family and her father's life, Holly must be seen as the master of her fate; her assertiveness would be the most effective defense. It must be *my* decision, *my* sodium amytal, *my* confrontation, *my* memories — *my* rape. She was disciplined; until her bulimia came up, she had always done well whatever she set out to do.

Holly's emergence may have meant, also, that she was getting better: Prozac, though intermittent, seemed to help. And — an irony Harrington would drive home in court — her functioning did seem to improve after her therapy with Isabella and Rose ended in mid-1991. Part of her poise grew out of the supreme conviction characteristically displayed by young women who have recovered memories of sexual abuse, a clear and incandescent sense of their own truth. It grew out of her belief that going public was a social good. Her father must not win. If Holly had any doubts that he had raped her, she never showed them as the videotape rolled. And she was riding a train moving far too fast to jump off.

12

The Memory Lesson

A pril 22, 1993. Elizabeth Loftus had barely unpacked from a trip to
Philadelphia the previous week for the first conference of the False
Memory Syndrome Foundation (FMSF), which had attracted six
hundred accused parents. Now she, Park Dietz, and Harrison Pope
were arriving at San Francisco's airport, renting cars, and driving up
to Napa for the evidentiary hearings, the major test of strength before
the opening day of the jury trial on June 7.

Three vital issues would be argued at these hearings. First, could
Gary sue? Would the judge permit him to sue as a third party? His
right to sue had to date survived court skirmishes and appeals. Now
Molien would be definitively argued, and Judge Snowden would come
to a decision. Second, would Holly's sodium amytal interview be
allowed into court, given the legal restraints on the introduction of
any drug- or hypnosis-altered testimony? Holly had lost her first case
against her father over it. Now Harrington was fighting to keep her
from testifying about the amytal interview, a ploy to keep her from
testifying at all. He knew how sympathetic a jury would be to a sweet,
clearly honest young woman. Finally, would Stephanie be allowed to
testify about the early violence in their marriage? Any suggestion of
wife battering would be a sympathetic issue and could compromise
Gary with the jury.

Gary's team stayed at the Napa Sheraton, preparing there before
and during the two days of hearings. Pope was thrilled to be in a room
with these great minds, to be drinking good Cabernet provided by
Gary, discussing strategy with Dietz, Loftus, and Harrington. Gary
listened as they talked, captivated, too, by the intelligence, the ideas,

the accomplishments. With these experts, albeit strangers, he felt a kind of compensation for the two families he had lost. These people turned down most of the cases they were offered. They were here because they believed in him.

As they entered the courtroom and sat down at their table the next day, the lawyers for the defense said to one another, "Good luck. We're all counting on you." That line, from the comedy *Airplane,* had become their bond, their tag line for the lawsuit. It had started two years earlier when several attorneys gathered for a drink after depositions in Harrington's office in San Francisco. They decided the way to separate men from women was to ask them if they liked *The Three Stooges* or *Airplane* — women hated both, they agreed. They replayed the memorable lines in *Airplane* with total recall, but the one line the physician kept saying to the stewardess as she prepared to land the jet made them double over: "Good luck. We're all counting on you." From then on, whenever anything important was about to happen, they used that line to loosen things up.

The hearings were, most of the participants agreed, two days of memorable courtroom debate. As he listened to Dietz lay out Gary's case against the defendants — the argument that they owed him a duty because he had been called to the confrontation — Ed Leonard felt he had witnessed one of the great courtroom performances of his career. "The confrontation has always been the key to it," thought Judge Snowden. It was what tied the case to *Molien.*

Snowden's decision on *Molien* was eloquent and reasoned: ". . . there would not be a cause of action for negligent infliction of emotional distress under the circumstances of this case if there had been neither a direction to Holly to confront her father, nor a meeting at which her father was confronted." The makeup of the Supreme Court "has drastically changed since the *Molien* case was decided," Snowden admitted; it was much more conservative and might well continue to whittle away at *Molien,* as several cases already had. But today *Molien* lived. Gary could sue.

Gary also won on the issue of Stephanie testifying to the violence early in their marriage. To him, her claims were lies. To the judge, they were ancient and would be unfairly prejudicial. Stephanie was furious, sick of what she saw as judicial favoritism toward Gary.

But Holly could testify: her testimony about the amytal interview would be permitted. "It's what the case is about," said Snowden. Jeffrey Kurtock led Loftus into agreeing with him that the "trappings" of a hypnotic situation — "a special room . . . a special chair where they always told the truth . . . some mysterious way to record their statements, and some sort of authority figure to mediate the process" could create a suggestive atmosphere. Then he sprung his trap, reminding Loftus that, sitting under oath in a courtroom, she was in "a special chair, in a special room, with a special recorder and special authority figure." In defense of Marche Isabella, he made the point that the courtroom held all the elements of suggestion that an amytal interview held — that both could produce truth, lies, or honestly believed falsehoods. It was, in Leonard's opinion, Kurtock's finest hour.

Flying home to Washington after hearing her therapy condemned for two days, Marche Isabella broke into tears and wondered, "Did I really do all those things?"

Then, suddenly, the June 7 trial was canceled, knocked off the docket by a mass murder in Northern California's Gold Country. A man accused of murder had the right to a swift trial, and Snowden had been assigned to the case. *Ramona*'s momentum stopped dead.

As the Ramona trial was canceled in Napa, a handful of elite scientists and scholars gathered for a retreat on June 4 and 5 at the American Academy of Arts and Sciences in Cambridge, Massachusetts. All members of Harvard's interdisciplinary Mind, Brain and Behavior Program, they had come to plan a conference that would ultimately draw them directly into the memory wars. Professor of psychology Daniel Schacter was the prototype of the memory scientist being attracted — passively, at first, as he received a trickle of calls and letters from accused parents, then with growing interest — to issues he saw memory scientists increasingly asked to solve. He had remained ideologically neutral as he watched these controversial memories propelled into, as a therapists' magazine described it, "the maelstrom of politics as perhaps no other mental health issue ever has before." Yet he could not just stand by. His work had suddenly taken on social urgency. This was more than an interesting cognitive phenomenon. It had "significant applications for the day-to-day lives of many members of our society." Searching for a theme for the conference, to be held in the spring of 1994, Schacter came up with "the perfect issue" — memory distortion. The conference would not be an attempt to adjudicate the false memory debate. It would have no political agenda. Paper topics would range from the cellular memory of a sea slug to the cultural memory of the Holocaust. But he and his colleagues must at least try, he felt, to get the recovered memory issue cleared up, "not only to relieve the suffering of the unjustly accused . . . but to protect the legitimacy of the real memories." Invitations would go out to a crossdisciplinary group of several dozen scientists.

For years, Schacter had studied distortions of memory in brain-damaged patients. If these new memories of childhood sexual abuse were false, as the parents claimed, science had on its hands the phenomenon of massive memory distortion in apparently healthy brains.

If they were true, then what was going on? A vivid display of Freudian repression, a theory that had eluded scientific proof for a hundred years? Schacter could see why repression was an attractive explanation, for it permitted you, while still living a relatively normal life, to bury only a specific experience — incest, in these cases — and forget nothing else. Or might these memories, as the clinical psychiatrist Bessel van der Kolk at Harvard Medical School was claiming, be the product of *dissociation,* the theory championed by Freud's French rival, the psychiatrist Pierre Janet? If so, the fathers of Schacter's field were still fighting from the grave for intellectual dominance. By the dissociation theory, traumatic memories too terrible for the mind to face would detach, split off, from consciousness into fragments, be stored somewhere as sense memories and then resurface as multiple personalities or as flashbacks and full-blown stories of repeated sexual abuse. Schacter knew dissociative disorder as a very serious illness that could take the form of amnesias between a host of multiple personalities. Could it explain the memories of apparently otherwise normal, high-functioning young women? Of a Holly Ramona?

Amnesia had fascinated him since he saw his first amnesiac on a golf course in Toronto in the early 1980s. Hoping to be a professional golfer, and with a handicap of 3 and a lanky 6-foot-3 athlete's build, Schacter had, at seventeen, been the youngest country club champion in New York State. But he dropped serious golf when he discovered psychology, and as a fledgling memory scientist in Toronto, he turned the golf course into his laboratory when he took a brain-damaged amnesiac patient out for several rounds of golf. The man could talk glibly about the lore and technical details of golf, but he could not remember the game he had just played or the shot he had just made. The experience impressed on Schacter, very early, the "fragile power" of memory and the tragic hole in a human life created by the loss of a man's personal history.

Might these lost-and-found memories be some form of *functional amnesia,* the memory loss that, Schacter knew from his own research, occurred rarely in the normal brain in response to a severe traumatic event with, at times, a total loss of identity and personal past? The recovered memories being reported — usually of a series of repeated acts of rape and molestation, occurring over years — did not seem to fit the picture of functional amnesia in undamaged brains, which was normally triggered by a single event and caused amnesia for many things — not just for childhood sexual abuse.

Were these memories simply the rich tapestry of truth and fantasy the mind so capriciously wove in normal minds every day? Or the "directed forgetting" all of us do to keep unwanted memories out of mind? Memories left to languish, unrehearsed, tended to fade with time, Schacter knew. And if, in fact, they were repressed, by what mechanisms could they be retrieved? Scientists needed to know. Used to working quietly in their labs, far from the maelstrom, they were suddenly being seen as high priests who held the keys to vital secrets.

It was a heady time to be a memory scientist. The 1980s had launched the golden age of memory, a burgeoning of research that ballooned when the 1990s were declared the Decade of the Brain with a neuroscientific research budget of $2 billion that proved more a rallying cry than a reality — it was never funded. The disparate disciplines that had worked in isolation from one another — "separate tribes of cognitive psychologists, clinicians, and neuroscientists," as Schacter described them — had come together to forge a new field, cognitive neuroscience. This marriage of two alien cultures, psychology and biology, was so new that the Cognitive Neuroscience Society had not yet held its first annual meeting, but the cross-fertilization of research had already created a breathtaking revolution in the most fundamental concepts of memory. Schacter was one of a few dozen scientists who were dispelling what they called "the deep myths of memory," myths that had been absorbed into the psychoanalytic and cultural lore.

Two discoveries rode high above all the others, discoveries that left popular assumptions about memory behind with the flat earth theory. Memory was not based in a single site in the brain but was distributed through *multiple memory systems,* with roughly five or six different memory systems identified. Even the simplest memory of, say, a cup required interaction between many sites to learn, store, and then retrieve the memory. The discovery of memory systems had led to the recognition that memories were not retrieved whole and pristine but were constructions, assemblages of many elements from many sites converging to form a "memory" of a cup.

Schacter had been on the frontier of a second seminal discovery, that there are two fundamentally different kinds of memory. There is "explicit" or "declarative" memory — the conscious memory of facts and events that set you in time and place and give you your general knowledge of the world. And there is "implicit" or "nondeclarative" memory, the unconscious, intuitive "knowing how" to do things — to ride a bike or run from danger. With no access to language or a narrative story, implicit memory revealed itself in behavior and ran parallel to explicit memory, interacting with and reinforcing it. As a young doctoral candidate at the University of Toronto in 1980, Schacter, his mentor Endel Tulving, and Larry Squire were among the handful of scientists whose work converged into the discovery of what came to be called "implicit memory."

It was in his experiments in a research technique called "priming" that Schacter had moved into the mysterious realm of implicit memory. He discovered that when a group of subjects was asked to study a list of words and was shown fragments of the words later, they could easily fill in the blanks; their memories had been *primed* by the list to come up with the solutions to word fragments. Then something intriguing happened. A week later, the subjects had lost most of their conscious memory of the list of words. But the priming effect — their ability to fill in the word fragments — was just as strong. They were able to complete a word fragment *for words they had consciously forgotten seeing.* These words, then, had not just been consciously memorized; some other mechanism was at work. "The results pushed us toward a strong, seemingly unavoidable conclusion: priming occurs independent of conscious memory. These findings hit us with the force of an avalanche. We felt a bit like astronomers must feel when discovering a new star or an entire galaxy whose existence had been only suspected." As research into priming and implicit memory "exploded during the early 1980s," Schacter found himself drawn to the points of convergence between the two kinds of memory, the territory that would become the central battlefield of the memory wars.

But in 1993 the exciting work being done in labs in the United

States and Canada was, as yet, little known to the public. Lawyers viewed memory, at the neurological level, as too arcane, too inaccessible for juries. Many scientists, like Schacter, shied away from the courtroom witness stand, fearing that alignment with one side or the other could compromise their scientific neutrality. Scientists mostly talked to one another — at conferences, in journals. Because of this isolation, Schacter feared that clinical therapists with a master's degree in social work were using this powerful new recovered memory phenomenon with virtually no formal training in memory. When he had lectured to hospital staff in the past, Schacter would ask, "How many of you are involved in treating a memory-impaired patient?" and 90 percent of the hands would go up, but when he asked, "How many of you have graduate training in the study of memory?" he might get one hand. How much had things changed? he wondered.

For the memory distortion conference, Schacter would gather a powerful group of scientists whose research touched directly on the issues of recovered memory and distortion — experts on suggestibility, emotional memory, hypnosis, neurobiology, reality monitoring, computer modeling of memory, and explicit, implicit, and sociocultural memory.

Although Joseph LeDoux, a neuroscientist at NYU, would not be present at the conference — UC Irvine's James McGaugh would be covering LeDoux's specialty, emotional memory — his work would flow through the proceedings like an underground stream, for it was central to what was becoming the memory wars' "hottest" search — the keys to understanding traumatic and dissociated memory.

This club of scientists knew one another well. Schacter had met Larry Squire, known to some of his peers as "the king of declarative memory," and Loftus at a conference in 1979, when Schacter was, as Loftus laughingly recalled, "little Danny Schacter. Now he's *big* Dan Schacter." Schacter, Squire, and LeDoux worked in the realms of the memory wars most fraught with biological controversy. But they resisted commitment to either side. They went where science took them. But they did not testify in court, they did not join the FMSF advisory board, and their work had not yet crossed over from academia to the mainstream. Yet these three scientists — with Loftus and several others — would make memory science the stuff of prime-time TV, would move the special language of memory into the public vernacular and do for memory what Carl Sagan had done for astronomy.

Larry Squire had claimed explicit — conscious, declarative —

memory as his territory. Like Schacter, he knew the thrill of discovery. For him, it was his recognition of the existence of the brain's multiple memory systems. An upper-middle-class kid from Ohio who spent a year in graduate school at Stanford mostly playing poker before he found his way to an environment of Nobel laureates and a doctorate at MIT, Squire made his base at UC San Diego. In experiments with monkeys in the early 1980s, he had begun to explore the function of the hippocampus, a small seahorse–shaped structure in the brain behind the ear.

Another moment of discovery came during an experiment in which the monkeys had been trained to remember a hundred objects and had then had their hippocampus surgically removed. The monkeys suffered amnesia, notably, only for the recently learned objects; the more distantly learned, the better they were remembered. Most dramatic was that the objects that had been learned just days before surgery were completely forgotten. But the objects that had been learned several weeks earlier were well remembered — there was no impairment. This led to an extraordinary conclusion: some time — days, several weeks, perhaps — after memory was processed and formed by the hippocampus, it settled in its permanent storage site — the neocortex, the outer layer of the brain that is the seat of cognition, Squire was sure.

When events flooded into the brain, he saw, they were distributed throughout the neocortex. Most were short-term memories, never stored; they vanished. But the hippocampus seized events destined to be long-term memory and became the control center for the formation of memory that could be stored and used. Once the hippocampus had organized the raw information into memory, its importance gradually diminished as the burden of long-term permanent memory was assumed entirely by the neocortex, leaving the hippocampus available to process new information. With this insight, light had been shed on one of the deep myths of memory — that all memory resided in one place. The hippocampus was the central switching station and temporarily crucial for the initial formation of memory as it entered the brain.

Simultaneously, in his warren of small laboratories off Washington Square, Joe LeDoux was plumbing the secrets of the amygdala, a small almond-shaped organ nestled near the hippocampus. There he made his fundamental discovery: that one kind of implicit memory, emotional memory, took a separate track into the brain. Where the hippocampus was the seat of conscious memory, the amygdala was the base of unconscious, emotional memory. Emotional memory, he was discovering, was more deeply imprinted than ordinary memory. It was indelible, "forever."

A Cajun from Eunice, Louisiana, whose father was a butcher and cattle farmer, LeDoux had been raised with the music that, at the time, was a symbol of a "backward, illiterate culture everyone was trying to escape." He escaped to college to get a degree in marketing and wrote to the Harvard behaviorist B. F. Skinner to ask if he'd be willing to help him develop a model of consumer behavior. When Skinner "wished me luck but said that he objected on moral grounds to using his psychology for that purpose," LeDoux switched to psychology. To become a professor of neuroscience and psychology at NYU's Center for Neural Science, he had learned biology "on the job." Where Schacter's and Loftus's subjects were students sitting at computers, LeDoux's were rats in cages. Ethically, you couldn't invade the living human brain, "but with rats, you can do the next experiment, and the next, and the next."

LeDoux's search for memory was at the level of neurons, the tiny biological units that host the process of memory. Neuroscientific terms — synapses, neurotransmitters, receptors — did not begin to catch the drama of the process. For LeDoux, memory was a chase along microscopic freeways in the brain where incoming signals raced, passed from neuron to neuron by the firing of tiny electrical explosions that shot a trace of chemical hormone across the infinitesimal distance between neurons, the synapse, to bind with a friendly receptor in a neighboring neuron and forge a synaptic connection. That process, repeated over and over, created memory. An actual memory trace, an engram, was the change that occurred in the neuron at the point of synaptic connection. For these scientists memory was not the stuff of poetic metaphor. It was, to LeDoux's colleague Larry Squire, "an assembly of synapses and neurons that are connected together with different kinds of strengths."

The sites where these neurons assembled were where each memory's battle for survival was fought, neuron by neuron, for each site held intersecting and overlapping signals competing for the brain's finite billions of neurons. In this world of competition, weaker or stronger synaptic connections between the neurons created weaker or stronger memories. Old memories, weakened by lack of exercise, were subsumed by the new, their neurons cannibalized to forge new connections. It was a world of plasticity and flexibility where even behavior and the human cultural setting — the very act of therapy — appeared to trigger neuronal change, a world in which an emotional memory could be altered by a shot of adrenaline even after the memory had been formed. The emerging picture of memory was the opposite of a hermetically sealed vault in which everything ever experienced was "in there somewhere," neatly stored, as in the deepest, most stubborn myth of memory.

LeDoux's quiet thrill of discovery came as he tested the most primitive implicit emotion, fear, sending a weak shock to the rat's feet through the metal floor while simultaneously making a sound — a high-pitched tone. The rat exhibited the classic fear response: it froze; its heart rate and blood pressure went up, its hair stood on end. Repeating the test, the rat performed the fear response just on hearing the sound, without the shock. This was a conditioned response, like that of Pavlov's dogs, where, through training, memories become associated in the mind. With only this mild training, LeDoux had created powerful implicit memories; the rat's brain now intuitively remembered the shock with just the sound and activated the fear response.

The real breakthrough came when LeDoux damaged the brain's sound-processing cortex, then sent both the sound and the shock coursing into the rat's brain en route to the amygdala. He'd expected the sound conditioning to be blocked. But the rat — with no signals from the auditory cortex — learned about the sound and shock and had the full fear response to the sound alone. But how? With the discovery that the auditory cortex was not a necessary link to the amygdala, LeDoux began his detective work: he traced linkages and pathways until he found a memory path from the brainstem to the amygdala that bypassed both the sensory cortex system and the entire hippocampal memory system. This path had raced low-level sensory information to the amygdala before the "sound" cortex had access to it — before it fully knew what the stimulus was and before the hippocampus could encode it as a conscious memory of the event.

It was a giant step for understanding multiple memory systems. And it identified, for the first time, "emotional memory" as distinct and separate from conscious memory.

Now came the theory that would make LeDoux, unwittingly, the darling of the recovered memory forces. This emotional fear memory did not fade. Over time, the physical response to the triggering sound remained powerful. Why? The answer lay in the neural battlefield, he theorized. When the foot shock fired and intersected with the sound signal fired at the same time, a dramatically strengthened connection was forged at the place where the shock and sound collided, producing a strengthened output — a strong reactivation of the stress response. This extra-strong connection seemed, somehow, to smooth the way for future similar signals fired across the synapse, more easily triggering the fear response. These emotional memories appeared to be not only stronger but virtually inextinguishable. The conscious memory of the emotion fell prey to distortion and forgetting while, LeDoux saw, "the stuff the amygdala is doing may last a lifetime." His work explained the sweating, pulse-racing horror of a Vietnam veteran who could not escape memories of the butchering of a comrade or a child. "Posttraumatic stress syndrome leaves very strong memory . . . They won't go away, and what Joe LeDoux is concerned about is the *permanence* of these emotional memories," said Jim McGaugh; he knew, too, that the characteristic of emotional memories — good or bad, happy or sad — was not that they were forgotten but that they were enduring. In fact, in a 1991 study, LeDoux had said, "Emotional memory may be forever."

As Schacter planned the conference in 1993, LeDoux was publishing a paper that identified an "emotional memory system," which combined the powerful emotional significance in the amygdala's "memory" with the conscious memory of the event processed by the hippocampus. "Memories stored through both the amygdala and hippocampus, when retrieved, have a different flavor . . . a special quality," he said.

LeDoux's findings, combined with everything Schacter and Squire understood about memory, were not heartening to those invested in recovered memories. Not only were traumas generally well remembered, but the possibilities for distortion were so abundant and pervasive that, as Squire observed, "the remarkable thing about declarative memory is that it can so often be accurate." Survival required it, of course; a consistently distorted memory system would not be likely to be preserved by natural selection. But as Squire scratched some arrows, boxes, and circles on a piece of paper, he illustrated a dramatic scenario for distortion in just one site in the brain, the medial temporal lobe — the hippocampus and its related structures, the site of much visual memory. There, three different kinds of visual functions coexisted, superimposed and intermingled: long-term memories, new memories, and conjured-up images. In this one area, you could be simultaneously imagining a dog, seeing a real dog on the street, and superimposing both images on top of a long-term memory of a dog you had as a child. "Elements of one could show up in another. It's a wonder we ever keep it straight," said Squire.

In his view, "we're very good at generalizing . . . at inferring, at forming concepts" — not at remembering details. "It is more important to understand what a dog or a cup *is* than to remember a specific example." This power of human memory to form concepts gave us "flexible use of knowledge" unique to complex human survival, but it played havoc with accurate recall.

Early on, Schacter had been fascinated by the distortions created in one of the most important sites for long-term memory, the frontal lobe, that spongy serpentine of brain tissue in the forehead — his paper in 1984 was the first of the current burst of research into the loss of source memory as a major cause of memory distortion. He, and others, observed that when people lost the source of their memory, they often fabricated — confabulated — a memory to explain what they could not remember. It appeared that if a memory lost its anchor in reality, it could more easily become distorted and mixed with fantasy and other memory traces. Since the frontal lobe developed late in children and deteriorated with age, source amnesia occurred most often in children and in the old, which made it a potential path for understanding, and perhaps correcting, Alzheimer's and other kinds of memory loss in the aging population.

But could the loss of source memory also be a cause of false memories of sexual abuse? Could a young woman construct a fantasy tableau of incest in her mind from fragments of images — from childhood, from anywhere — which had been cut loose from their source?

LeDoux, too, feared that this human hunger for explanations could lead to confabulated stories by someone who was experiencing disturbing emotional arousal from a persisting emotional memory that was not available, for whatever reasons, in conscious memory. "When you're emotionally aroused for reasons you don't understand . . . you seek — you almost *demand* an explanation. So you create a narrative. But there's no way to know whether it's true or not, in the absence of corroborating evidence."

As a scientist, Schacter continued to let his thoughts evolve; as a psychologist, he was not immune to the trends of his profession. He had innocently given ammunition to recovered memory advocates

when he wrote, in 1992, "What Breuer and Freud meant as unconscious (or repressed) memories, we can substitute implicit ones." He
had folded the notion of multiple personalities into his work during
the reported epidemic of them in the 1980s. But by 1993 he had become more skeptical and "would not get involved in a study of multiple personality today." Given the potential for memory distortion,
Schacter's tentative conclusions for recovered memories were that
they "come closer to the rubric of ordinary forgetting and remembering." So little was definitely known. But as Schacter and others tried to
make sense of the phenomenon, "I ask the following question of myself: 'Could you find a respectable memory researcher who would go
in and make the case for the other side?'" — the recovered memory
side, with its intense mobilizing of theory, passion, and politics.

Bessel van der Kolk was doing just that within a few miles of
Schacter. A clinician and researcher, and chief of the trauma unit of
Massachusetts General Hospital, van der Kolk had a passionate
agenda: to resurrect and elevate to a position high in the pantheon of
psychiatric theories Pierre Janet's theory of traumatic memories —
that they were more durable and accurate than ordinary memories,
and that they could be banished by dissociation but, indestructible,
could resurface much later as reliable conscious memory of childhood
sexual abuse. Dissociation sat at the theory's heart. On the surface —
in courtrooms, in the media — the memory wars would continue to
be about Freudian repression. But, as proof of the massive repression
claimed by these memories continued to elude researchers, a groundswell of enthusiasm for dissociation and posttraumatic stress was
building as a rationale for recovered memories. One of its most powerful, perhaps principal, attractions was that PTSD was an official
diagnosis in the diagnostic manual *DSM,* and therefore covered by
insurance; memory loss was one of PTSD's many recognized symptoms. Over the next few years, it would become, to the "true believers," the principal symptom.

With a cascade of shocking statistics, van der Kolk also proposed
childhood sexual abuse as the most rampant cause of adult emotional
illness; according to his numbers, at least half of all emotionally disturbed patients, whatever their formal diagnoses, were in fact survivors of childhood abuse — and 100 percent of patients who tested
high on dissociation tests reported sex abuse as children. Van der Kolk
had waged a campaign to have the new *DSM-IV* recognize the package of adult symptoms he believed were caused by sex abuse as a

discrete new syndrome. Though defeated, he was treated, in the *Family Therapy Networker*, as a prophet ignored. "How can we accept the possibility that hundreds of thousands, perhaps millions of children, have been and are being abused, tortured, even killed by the people most obligated to love and protect them?" asked Mary Sykes Wylie, the senior editor. "What does it mean to acknowledge that this is happening in virtually every American neighborhood by people who look and sound and dress exactly like us?"

From this inflamed ideology was emerging the complex theory for recovered memories that would overtake repression and establish itself as the basis of the argument for the memories by mid-decade — a theory linking dissociation, new speculation on the linkages between unconscious and conscious memory, and memory retrieval. It would create an impassioned legal and scientific struggle that would drive the memory wars to new intensity.

In a 1991 paper, van der Kolk had revealed the workings of the theory. "The current revival of interest in the role of overwhelming experiences on the development of psychopathology has stimulated a fresh look at how memories are stored." For seventy-five years, he argued, Freud's repression of sexual fantasies had "virtually ignored the fact that actual memories may form the nucleus of psychopathology and continue to exert their influence on current experience by means of the process of dissociation" — and that fragments of these traumatic memories continued to show themselves through symptoms, behavior, and perceptions. Dissociation occurred, he claimed, at the moment the trauma was occurring and moved the memory of it into "an alternate stream of consciousness." While most memory was malleable and prone to inaccuracy, traumatic memory was "fixed in the mind . . . not altered by the passage of time . . . Traumatic memories are the unassimilated scraps of overwhelming experience, which need to . . . be transformed into narrative language." But how could you convert these "unassimilated scraps" into a conscious story of rape, as he claimed? In that same paper, van der Kolk revealed his answer: exciting new studies in animals were showing that, under extreme stress, the hippocampus could be impaired — shut down, in effect — by overloads of adrenaline. Then, somehow, those slumbering memories could be reawakened when triggered by the "forever" emotional memories in the amygdala. By some marvelous mechanism, the unconscious was transformed into the conscious.

The *Family Therapy Networker*'s September-October 1993 issue, going to press as Schacter planned the conference, gave van der Kolk and his theories a huge boost with its cover story on the false memory debate. The players were there, the stars of the survivor movement, all of them clinicians: van der Kolk, David Calof, Colin Ross, John Briere, Judith Lewis Herman, Christine Courtois.

Attempting balance, the magazine gave the FMSF and credible skeptics their due. But its sympathies and agenda were not in doubt. Wylie revealed the passion driving the child sex abuse survivor movement as she quoted a survivor in the last lines of her article — it could have been Holly Ramona speaking: "Victims challenge everything we believe about ourselves and our world. People do not want to face the fact that their peers do horrendous things, but they're going to have to take reality as it is. I will be free, and I will do whatever is necessary to become free. Don't get in my way. People are shackled by lies, by silence, and I will not live in silence anymore."

Mixing *The Courage to Heal* with Elizabeth Loftus, creating a blurred collage of science and pseudoscience, the magazine went out to tens of thousands of therapists.

Within months of the *Networker*'s paean to van der Kolk's theory, recovered memories were given the tentative imprimatur of one of the most distinguished figures in memory science, the Columbia University neurobiologist Eric Kandel, who had built his towering reputation studying the memory of a simple sea slug, *Aplysia*. His colleagues would be shocked as they leafed through the May 1994 issue of *Discover* to find an article coauthored by Kandel and his daughter, a feminist attorney in California active in the movement to free battered women jailed for violence against their husbands. It argued that, "viewed from a biological perspective, there's reason to believe that both sides of the repressed memory debate can be valid." The article was a cautious and fascinating speculation on how leading-edge biological science might eventually explain the repression and retrieval of abuse memories, but it lacked the spirit of rigorous testing and the critical edge expected of Kandel. Balanced to the point of softness, it uncritically reported Lenore Terr's "clues" to the credibility of Eileen Franklin's memories at a time when convincing challenges to Franklin's veracity had already been published.

And while the article did not misrepresent LeDoux's work, it used a benign comment about his studies of emotional memory as a point of departure for a tantalizing scenario of the conversion of emotional memory of childhood sexual abuse into a conscious narrative — a scenario that went far beyond LeDoux's findings. It was laced with studies on hormonal inhibiting and heightening of memory and on the stirring of weak explicit memories by implicit sense cues. By association with the theory in this single influential article, LeDoux's work and prestige were coopted by the advocates of recovered memory.

The piece closed with rhetorical questions that were unabashedly political: "Do the questions of the critics reflect a genuine effort to get to the truth, to defend the innocence of the accused? Or are we sometimes witnessing a backlash against the struggle to bring child abuse out of the family closet?"

When several of his colleagues expressed surprise at the article, Kandel said, "I'll do anything for my daughter." Any father understood his sentiment, and it might have gone unnoticed in a less volatile climate. His colleagues guessed that it was an exercise in possibilities never meant to be measured against his other work. But in this emotionally charged atmosphere, even the perception of sympathy for an ideology that shaped science to its purposes was dangerous ground for a scientist. Kandel's name on the article made it eminently quotable by the survivor side.

Schacter was having difficulty with van der Kolk's and the survivor movement's reading of PTSD symptoms as reliable clues to childhood sex abuse. Working back from a shopping list of symptoms to a diagnosis of abuse was "unacceptable" to a scientist. He was having difficulty, too, with a theory that had at its heart the loss of conscious memory by hippocampal shutdown and its later emergence, full-blown and accurate, triggered by the amygdala's emotional memory. "There is no evidence for the hippocampal system somehow partially shutting down, shunting these memories off somewhere, and somehow you reconnect with it," said Schacter. "It is speculation, pure speculation — it's a guessing game." Squire was blunt: "You can't turn a sow's ear into a silk purse." If, at the time of learning, the hippocampus only records, for example, 3 percent of an event, you'll never remember more than 3 percent of it. "All you're going to have is a 3 percent memory in there. And maybe because it's weak, you'll do more interpretation." People did not grasp, he feared, that "in true biological forgetting, like the melting of an ice cube or the losing of the branches of a tree, it actually is gone.

"But it is also true that there are lots of things that are only partially available," Squire added, opening the door to LeDoux's view of the hippocampal shutdown. "On the more subtle level, there's evidence that temporary stress *can* shut down the hippocampus. Glucocorticoids are nature's healthy response to stress; they mobilize the body to react. But when the levels of these hormones get too high, when the hippocampus is awash in them, the hippocampus malfunctions." LeDoux speculated that "it might be possible . . . that the hippocampus might shut down . . . because steroids are released from the adrenal gland, go back to the brain" and "the memory that's being formed is shut down before it's completely consolidated," creating an abnormal memory. But nowhere had LeDoux said that emotional memories could flip over and become conscious. "Nowhere is there a statement that says, 'Oh, by the way, emotional memories also lead to their blocking so they are unavailable until a psychotherapist can pull them out later,'" said McGaugh "You will not find that stated by people who work on the psychology of emotional memory." Schacter expressed the consensus: "That which was never encoded by the hippocampal system is never going to be recoverable in an explicit, conscious form."

In Schacter's view, dissociation also carried some baggage. There were such things as dissociative disorders, he believed, but in his experience they were associated with profound pathologies. You'd expect to see a trail of psychiatric problems, of problems with memory and time. But to evoke them in cases "where people seem to have led what, by all accounts, is a relatively normal life with its share of ordinary problems doesn't make any sense to me." In sum, the myriad forms of ordinary forgetting and remembering seemed the most likely explanation. "We don't need this fancy neuroscience to explain them."

McGaugh spoke very straight for the neuroscientists: the only basis on which you could conclude that the memory had been recovered was if there was documented evidence. But like his colleagues, he was open to new proof. "All it takes is a half a dozen really good, well-substantiated clinical cases. Then people like me would begin to buckle and say, 'Okay, you're making your case. I can see it' . . . These therapists say, 'Trust us. We know.' Trust doesn't mean anything in science." Nor did a middle ground that offered sops of legitimacy to both sides.

The future held promise. Powerful new neuroimaging techniques like PET (positron emission topography) scans permitted, for the first time, "a direct window on memory," Schacter marveled. They let us "see the brain in action while people remember." Recording surging blood flows, PET scans lit up the brain sites where memory activity was occurring. Scientists could not yet always tell whether they were viewing the struggle to recall or the real act of remembering. But tools like PET were helping them map the many scattered sites of the memory network, each playing its role, each contributing its fragment to the reassembling of parts into a whole memory. The memory distortion conference would help carry the latest findings from the laboratory to the larger world; it would encourage more rigorous scientific scrutiny of the memory feats being claimed as the wars grew more intense.

But, for now, the child memory expert Stephen Ceci summed up the stance of his colleagues: "I don't walk down the middle of the road . . . Science is not in the middle of the road. It's not a tribute to a scientist to walk where the data are not."

Loftus flew to Toronto during the lull in the Ramona trial. There, the deep divisions over recovered memory between clinicians and laboratory scientists erupted publicly on the podium of the American Psychological Association's annual convention on August 26, 1993, during a debate between Loftus and John Briere, a childhood trauma specialist and clinician at UCLA as well as an advocate of recovered memories. Briere began attacking Loftus in his opening speech. When Loftus warned the audience that if he talked about studies supporting total, or "robust," repression, they should "view this research with some skepticism . . ." he retorted, "We are not talking about repression. We're talking about posttraumatic dissociation . . . Flashbacks are a sign of PTSD — brief, intrusive memories of previous trauma that are now emerging into awareness."

"How do you know they're memories?" asked Loftus.

Confident that he spoke to a largely sympathetic audience of clinicians, Briere replied, "I'm not being snide, but if you actually read more of the trauma literature, you'd have a better grasp of what flashbacks are . . . If I brought up ten people here who report repressed memory, Dr. Loftus would . . . tell you they are either pathological, highly credulous, or evil or twisted." Loftus's isolation in the laboratory made her a danger in the courtroom, Briere suggested. "You're very smart," he said. "People take you very seriously. So if you testify in a case of a kid that you did not evaluate — and are not qualified to evaluate . . . unfortunately people will listen to you."

Loftus replied, alluding to the Ramona case, "The threat of these lawsuits might prompt some therapists to reconsider whether sufficient support exists for them to join in confrontations, accusations, and lawsuits that can have such devastating results."

"Now she's threatening us," jeered Briere. But even this partisan audience had had enough and started booing. The following year, with Loftus absent — and a press and public increasingly skeptical about recovered memory — a chastened Briere would deliver a speech that was a model of appeasement and conciliation.

For Loftus, it was just another bruising day. She had become the principal lightning rod in the memory wars, drawing attacks against the FMSF and the growing number of skeptical scientists. On a plane, she had been struck on the head with a rolled magazine by a seatmate who discovered she was sitting with "that woman." Loftus was increasingly booed on hostile podiums as the wars became more heated. A lively divorcée, her private life had shrunk to late hamburgers with graduate students and wine with colleagues in hotel bars at the end of a conference day, moments of respite that turned into intense debates. She felt increasingly alienated in the APA, where clinicians sympathetic to Terr, Briere, Herman, and the rest now predominated. Her distress over the hostility between clinical and research psychologists was deepening as she worked on the APA's task force on recovered memory; created in 1993, this group would suffer the embarrassment of seeing both the American Medical Association and American Psychiatric Association issue their cautionary statements about recovered memory before it. The three clinicians and three scientists assigned to write the position statement instantly drew battle lines: between repression and dissociation, between scientific and clinical "truth." The struggle went on for three years before a statement could be struck, and they never did agree.

Ed Leonard was like a caged lion. He had cleared his calendar for the June 7 trial and now he had nothing to do all summer. The next trial date was January 24, 1994, but he'd believe it when he saw it. Then the decision on the Burgess case, the third decision that chipped away at *Molien,* came down from the court of appeals; suddenly he was very busy. If these cases had come down before the arguments in April, Gary would never have sustained his cause of action, Leonard believed. He prepared a motion for summary judgment — to dismiss the entire case based on these new precedents — and filed it with Snowden's court.

But in January, when the defense and prosecution lawyers all flew in for another round of argument on the duty issue, Snowden ruled once again that the case would go forward. Leonard immediately appealed the decision to the state Court of Appeals. "Snowden's ambitious . . . He wants to get this to trial so that he has a shot at a landmark case," Leonard thought. "He's never going to let it die." The appeals court upheld Snowden. But again the trial date was canceled. The players waited, once more, for a new date.

Holly had gone to Ed Leonard's office in Santa Ana for a briefing on a trial issue, and it was dark when she and Miroglio left the office. Miroglio said to Holly, carefully, "I'd like to walk you to your car if that seems appropriate to you," and she said, "Fine." She was doing better, Miroglio observed. She was definitely more poised and forceful than the girl he'd first met. But as they walked to the car, he felt her nervous tension about men. "She's emotionally thirteen or fourteen years old." In depositions, she'd confessed that "making out" was something she knew only from movies; she'd never had sex with a boy — didn't know what petting was!

As she reached out to shake hands, he felt enormous big-brotherly affection for this kid. Maybe Marche Isabella had given patriarchal Italian men a bad name in Holly's eyes, but he said, "Holly, I'm sorry, but I'm Italian, and I don't shake hands with pretty women." He gave her a hug, just a light hug, and she hugged back. "Is that okay?" "Yeah," said Holly. "That's okay." "I think I'm the first guy that ever hugged her," he thought.

Gary, Barbara, and the Jenkinses were in Boston for a wine conference at the end of October 1993. Salem was just half an hour north, so Gary had to go. They arrived there on Halloween, the climax — unknown to them — of a three-week celebration when America's "witch city" became "the Halloween capital of the world." He hadn't expected the streets to be jammed or shops cluttered with tourist mementos. Despite the pouring rain they walked down a few of the streets, past the Chamber of Horrors and Haunted Witch Village. Hiding its history for nearly three centuries, the Chamber of Commerce had only in recent decades discovered the tourist gold in Salem's grim history. But the old village was gone — the courthouse, the dungeon, the houses. No one knew for sure where Gallows Hill was. Gary wanted to come back when it was quiet, to get in touch with the ghosts, to search for clues to how the human destruction by false accusations could have happened, to them, to him. "The embarrassment of Salem isn't going to be anything even close to the embarrassment of the psychological profession over repressed memory," he predicted and hoped.

After more than three years, three trials, and seven thick volumes of court documents, the Ramona divorce finally sputtered out a week later in a final wrangle over life insurance policies. It had cost nearly $1 million in lawyers' fees. Now the emotional cost would soar even higher; Gary's twice-delayed trial was scheduled for March 21, 1994.

Gary and Stephanie ran into each other outside Safeway a couple of months before the trial began. Steph stood by the new white Mercedes sedan she had bought with money Gary had released earlier than required by the court agreement.

"I feel guilty about getting this car," Steph had said.

"Why would you feel bad?"

"Because I'm spending your money."

But what a car. Gary whistled. "Beautiful car, Steph. Let me have the keys for a minute. I want to sit in it."

For a moment it was the old Plymouth, and they were piling in to go to the beach or just tool around, maybe drive south on I-5 or go to In-N-Out, where she would have him all to herself. The curly-haired beach girl and the boy who could always make her laugh. They could climb in and drive away. She handed him the keys, and he was getting in behind the wheel when she looked around, suddenly nervous, agitated, furtive. "Do you have anybody watching us?" she asked.

Oh, Christ! he thought. Of course she'd see this as a plot. He'd hired a detective to watch them talk in the Safeway parking lot so that he could get her and control her in some evil conspiracy with Bob Mondavi to destroy his whole family. She believed it! It was more than a total loss of trust — it was trust transformed into a sick, ugly paranoia, a suspiciousness that poisoned her whole life. "The hysteria ends up turning so much in her mind that if a beautiful white dove were to fly by, I'm sure Steph would see a vulture." He gave her back the keys, shook his head, and turned away.

"This Mercedes was going to make me happy," she called out, her words scattering across the parking lot like a broken string of pearls.

They would next see each other in Courtroom B.

THE TRIAL

13

Courtroom B

For four years, the Ramonas' tragedy had cast its pall over an expanding universe of friends, lawyers, and experts. But as jury selection began on Monday morning, March 21, 1994, the case had not yet caught the public's eye. Even the *Napa Valley Register* had not yet picked up the story, although the lawyers had noticed a young woman from the paper at all the hearings. Their interview with Holly a year earlier seemed to have vanished without a trace. "I'd been under the impression that Robert Mondavi had put the squelch on any writing by the local press up here," said Ed Leonard, echoing Stephanie's fear. But with microphones shoved in his face as he arrived for the first round of jury selection, he mused, "Apparently the squelch is off." He had flown up the night before, joined Mary and Bruce Miroglio for a pleasant dinner at Terra, and turned up that morning in a sport coat, not expecting to be met by ABC, NBC, AP, the *Register,* and the San Francisco dailies. As Leonard and Miroglio were pursued by reporters, Miroglio quipped, "What I want to know is, where can I get a toupee by tomorrow?" Leonard responded, "Yeah, and how do I lose a hundred pounds?"

That morning, San Francisco's major paper, the *Chronicle,* had run a teaser to the trial. The *Register* followed, that afternoon, with a front-page story, the first of almost daily front-page, color-photo coverage. As the story spread nationwide — and *People* magazine and ABC's *Inside Edition* sent reporters to cover the trial — people lined up at the courtroom door, vying for the fifty available seats.

What lured them to the Ramonas? The sensation, of course — incest, hate, money; the prospect of lurid sex and a peek at the Ramonas' marriage bed; the glamour and fame of the Mondavis and the promise of a father and his sons battling in public. Some came seeking a touchstone to their own experience. For some, the magnet was the controversy growing, nationally, around the issues or the chance to witness a landmark case — the first court challenge to recovered memory by a third party against therapists. Some came to learn from what promised to be an extraordinary seminar on memory and psychology. Some came as pilgrims paying homage to their own beliefs and biases.

All came hungry for clarity and answers to the gut questions: Did Gary do it? Are Holly's memories real? Does repression exist?

Driving down from her gray stone mansion that dominated a hilltop north of Napa, Nell Sweeney passed by the vineyard and winery she hoped would get her excused from jury duty. While her husband was away, running the international hotel business that had built the wine enterprise, she was in charge of the vineyard at the most critical time of year — that week or two when the bloom on the breaking shoots could be killed by frost before the grapes had set.

A vineyard had not been part of Nell's plan for her life. She had raised four children and lived out of suitcases during the building of the hotels. "My husband's the kind who said that we should plant grapes. I planted grapes. Then he said, 'No, we're not selling them. We're making wine.' So now I make wine." Built with a hotelier's sense of scale and theater, their home was reputed to have the largest square footage of any in the valley. It was a monument, in the eyes of many, to the ostentation of a rural valley increasingly become a valley of the rich. But the droll and common-sense manner Nell brought to the courthouse was anything but pretentious.

Yolanda Nash helped get her seven kids — all under thirteen, including triplets — off to school, then drove north to Napa from her small tract house in American Canyon. Her husband had left at a quarter to five to drive nearly two hours south to San Jose, where he was an analyst for Pacific Bell. The house was too small for them, and American Canyon was an undistinguished bedroom community recently sprawled to cityhood astride the commercial strips on Highway

37. But its location just inside the southern border of Napa County made it a symbol of escape from the crime-filled neighborhood Yolanda had left in Vallejo, just to the south. There, she had come home one day to find her fence torn down and her yard and the girls' dollhouse trashed; she said, "We're movin'." She felt the same fears of many black mothers. "Vallejo's gangs are just totally outrageous right now. My son is thirteen, okay? . . . I have to protect my child." The older kids would soon be at Silverado, a good junior high school in Napa where they'd see alternatives to gangs, drugs, and violence.

Yolanda had finally married Othell, the kids' father, two years earlier; a collage of their wedding photos was the centerpiece of the living room wall, Yolanda in a classic white off-the-shoulder wedding gown and Othell in white tails. She'd had parents; her kids were going to have parents. Othell often changed his schedule to be at baseball practice with the boys, and she'd traded a two-hour commute to San Francisco for a twenty-minute drive to her new job as a receptionist at the Napa Valley Country Club, which got her home before five every day. There was no library yet in American Canyon, so Yolanda took the kids to the Vallejo library for their science projects and book reports. Sunday was a family day, when they all went to the nondenominational Vineyard Christian Fellowship church, a converted supermarket just three blocks away, then to a park for a picnic or to visit relatives. The kids got an object lesson on crime when Yolanda's church choir sang in a youth guidance center, where they watched a line of youngsters come out with their arms and ankles chained. Yolanda had read books about child abuse to the kids and told them, "If anybody, even your father, does this, even if he says he's going to kill you, you tell me right then and there. I'm here to protect you and I'll be damned if I'll let anybody hurt you."

A trial would be hard, very hard. The hours didn't work as well as her job at the country club. Her mother-in-law would have to take care of the kids and her sister-in-law come up from Vallejo to help them with their homework. Yolanda would try to get off.

On his way to the courthouse for his first call to jury duty, Tim Holewinske, a young cook at the Veterans Home in Yountville, drove by some of the best restaurants in the valley. Piatti's. Bistro Don Giovanni. The Veterans Home was next to one of the finest of them all,

Domaine Chandon. But Tim didn't envy the chefs who worked in their kitchens. He didn't aspire to train at the Culinary Institute in St. Helena. It would be too high pressure and competitive for his temperament, he guessed. His goal was to get his college degree as a dietician and "go as high as I can go in the food service department."

Institutional food was his calling. Since he'd started cooking, at thirteen, for his six younger siblings after his mother walked out, it had been his way of comforting himself and those who needed it, especially in human crises. Employed by the state since he joined the California Conservation Corps out of high school, he'd fed National Guardsmen during the L.A. riots and exhausted firefighters in several big blazes; he'd fed the rescue squads at the Landers earthquake and at the Los Angeles floods. He knew their needs: good steaks to keep their energy up, fresh fruit to put in their pocket.

Now twenty-six, he was feeding an army of old soldiers. He cooked spaghetti sauce in steel vats the size of cement mixers. He set up eighteen regular and six diabetic baking trays of bread pudding for twelve hundred desserts. "But I try to spice it up a little." And when someone on the food line said, "That bread pudding was real good," it made his day. A soft-voiced, slim young man with pleasant features, he put on his white jacket, pants, and cap with pride as he went in to cook for these shuffling old boys. "If they've risked their lives to give me the freedoms I have, it makes me feel good to be giving something back to them."

"Uh-oh, this is more than a car theft," thought Kenneth Keri, a United Airlines mechanic, as he watched a television camera panning the crowd of people reporting to jury duty in the basement of the county criminal building. None of the potential jurors knew what trial they had been called to. Beth Clark, a mother of five who worked for a JCPenney catalogue store at Bel Air Plaza, grasped the size of this trial when, around the corner in the basement, came the same man she'd caught a glimpse of on television as she'd gone out the door that morning, "the guy with the eggbeater hair," as Ken described him — the dapper attorney Richard Harrington.

On Wednesday, the panel of thirty who had survived two days of winnowing were marched out of the criminal building and over to Courtroom B. When they saw a row of reporters taking notes as

Judge Snowden, six lawyers, and a court reporter walked in, the import of the case hit home. *"Pick me, Pick me,"* Ken Keri prayed. He'd watched several jurors eliminated by the question "Do you have any issues of abuse in your family that might bias you?" At least half were affected, Ken observed, amazed that so many Napans had abuse issues. Rebecca Strunk couldn't believe she'd survived the question. She was barely eighteen, and in high school she'd done peer counseling on sex abuse and eating disorders; she'd read the books, taken psychology classes. Expecting to be dismissed, "I had my car keys ready." But she was still here. No one had been disqualified for reading the article on the trial in Monday's *Chronicle*. Tim had started to read it, said to himself, "This may be the one I'll be called on," and "my sense of civic duty made me put it down." Marcellous Cook, a bank manager in Berkeley, read the story as he was sitting there in the jury pool. "It's okay," said the judge. "We hadn't admonished you about not reading yet."

Now the final choices were being made in the courtroom that would hold fourteen of them, twelve jurors and two alternates. As eighteen chairs were filled for the final rounds of questioning, the opportunity for the lawyers to shape the jury to their wishes narrowed. Both sides had twelve challenges, and with each they used up, they had fewer choices to fine-tune at the very end. Michele Maynard still thought she'd be "blown away" when the lawyers learned that, as a pharmacy and former psychiatric technician at Napa State Hospital, she had used sodium amytal to calm aggressive patients.

Beth, Tim, and Shelley Maynard still held their seats. Becky Strunk had survived, no one knew why. Nell was still there, resigned that they were not going to buy her hardship appeal. A final few were seated to fill the gaps. Tom Dudum, a textiles executive. Marty Cook, the bank manager. Gisella Fort, retired and living in Yountville. Keith Himmelman, the catering director at Silverado Country Club. Martha Piccolo, a partner in a painting and paper hanging business. Yolanda, who was sure she'd been chosen as the token black woman, was in. The last two to be called were Christina Rivera, an administrator at Napa College, and Ken Keri, as alternates. Harrington had exhausted his challenges. Both sides were now going on their instincts. Miroglio had bad vibes about Yolanda and Shelley, the psych tech. But Leonard loved them. "I just feel rapport with them," he assured Miroglio. Sharon Chandler, one of the attorneys for Marche Isabella, told Miroglio she "just related" with Yolanda. Miroglio had "horrible vibes" about Ken Keri. But it was too late. It was the end of the day, and the Ramona jury was set. The trial would begin the next day.

From the first day, and for seven subsequent weeks, Courtroom B played out in microcosm the recovered memory wars. Spontaneously sensing allies as they claimed their places, the observers formed territorial camps. Unaligned, the media tended to sit in the front rows on the left, where they could get the best view of the action and be near the door so that they could bolt for the telephones. But the rest split informally down the middle, pro-Holly on the right, pro-Gary on the left.

Marian Dodds arrived in old jeans and a baggy gray sweatshirt, the combat clothes she wore in defense of Holly Ramona. But she was there, too, to defend her own fragile world of just-emerging memories of sexual abuse and the pantheon of multiple personalities her Marin County therapist had helped her draw out. She wanted to understand, to be rid of the rage and get on with her life. An intelligent woman, she wanted a good debate on both sides of the issues. She wanted affirmation, allies. Marian quickly identified her side of the courtroom, seating herself behind the little cluster of Holly's supporters, drawing strength from them.

For John Carver, a retired Napa physician and accused parent, Courtroom B held hope for, someday, reconciliation with his two daughters, who had accused him of abuse in 1987. In his uniform of turtleneck sweater and tweed jacket, his face showing the scars of seven years of deep sadness, and carrying a briefcase heavy with material against recovered memory, he took a seat in the front row on the left, establishing himself as the headquarters for dozens of accused parents who would be drawn to the trial over the coming weeks. An active member of the False Memory Syndrome Foundation, he'd set up the first meeting of lost parents like himself in Yountville the previous August, expecting only a handful; sixty-four people came.

Settling into his seat that first day, John turned to scan the room. There, sitting two or three rows back, was his daughter Connie! He had last seen her two years earlier at her wedding. She had been "hugely angry" when he put her on the False Memory mailing list, "but they've got to be reading about all this. They can't avoid it anymore." She was so bright, a journalist in San Francisco. How could she not read it? His hopes flared when he saw her; she had voluntarily come to listen and learn. At the first break he went over and talked to her. "This is *wonderful,* Connie. It means so much to see you." She was cool, but he sat down and chatted with her for a bit. When he came back from getting a drink of water and took his seat, she had gone. The person behind him handed him a piece of paper, a brief note from Connie. The substance of it was: Do not ever, ever talk to me about this subject again. She never came back to the trial.

John Carver would take heart as a retractor, Deborah David, became a regular, always surrounded by a special aura of celebrity. A pretty blonde in her mid-thirties, she was a breed few had ever seen — a woman who had renounced as false the memories of childhood sexual and satanic ritual abuse with which she had flayed her parents and, for a time, destroyed her marriage and alienated her children. Now she and her entire family were suing two MFCC therapists, her minister-counselor, and the authors of *The Courage to Heal* for $14 million; she was hoping to learn how to handle herself in court. Deborah was always surrounded by accused parents, for whom she was a surrogate for the daughters they had lost.

The ghost of Freud had lured Dr. Leo Stoer to Courtroom B. An octogenerian psychologist from Vienna, Stoer had been part of the Jewish flight from Europe in the late 1930s. He had traveled, intellectually, from the excitement of Vienna to the crenellated turrets of Napa State Asylum for the Insane (now a new facility, Napa State Hospital). America was the temple now, the most fertile place, for the study of psychotherapy. A small and dignified man, Stoer brought to Courtroom B the hope of seeing revived the spirit of the early psychoanalysts, who believed they had broken the code of the unconscious and unlocked the secrets to mental illness. An expert witness many times himself, Stoer was the most senior of a floating group of staff from the state hospital, retired and active, who set up camp.

Carolyn Thompson, too, had been in Courtroom B before. On Valentine's Day 1989, she had discovered that her toddler, Aaron, had a bleeding and abraded rectum, with red cracks and what looked like small burst blood vessels. Her husband, Tom, had finally confessed to raping and sodomizing his son and, just three months before the Ramona trial, Judge Snowden had sentenced Tom to ten years in prison for sexually molesting Aaron. For years, Tom's denials and Caroline's battered state had left her uncertain about her own reality, even after confession — might she have convinced Tom and Aaron that some-

thing had happened that had not? But she believed the story told by
Aaron's behavior — behavior so inappropriately sexual and out of
control it verged on sociopathy.

As Carolyn found her place in Courtroom B, her two children beside her, her life was still a tangled nightmare of never-forgotten abuse
of all kinds — from her siblings, family friends, her husband — mixed
with the emerging images of her parents molesting her. Carolyn had
come to the trial "to be talked out of my memories, my flashbacks" —
flashbacks that had started about a year and a half after she started
therapy. "I have this doubting part of myself that's saying 'I want
another explanation.' No one would choose this reality, you know."
Perhaps from this courtroom, also, she and her children could draw
strength to break the terrible cycle of abuse. Her own God-fearing
Seventh-day Adventist family — like Tom's family — was rife with
abusers. She had been attracted to abusers, tolerated Tom's dehuman-
izing treatment, the callousness, the cold-blooded rapes. She feared
that Aaron would also abuse unless his transformation to a functioning child that seemed to have begun when Tom started treatment,
confessed, and showed remorse continued. The three would be here
often in Courtroom B, her ten-year-old daughter, Alison, serenely
reading *The Secret of Nimh* and, like her mother, disguising the horrors that had nearly consumed them under an aura of calm. They had
so far to go.

"Where's Mrs. Ramona? Which one's Stephanie?" the press and
audience whispered to each other. But Stephanie was conspicuously
absent. As with the winery parties the last few years of her marriage,
she was determined to do the trial on her own terms, not Gary's. On
the eve of the trial, she had gone into hiding somewhere outside Napa.
She told Bruce Miroglio, "I'm not going to let him subpoena me. I'm
not going to let him use me to help his case." She could not stand to sit
through it and watch the whole thing — to hear Gary's version of the
story of their life. But she had her surrogates, the women from the
neighborhood — Jean Sawday, Karen Maestas, Leann Knickerbocker,
Lois Swanson, and a few others. They would spell one another, making sure there was always a little circle of support.

Scanning the courtroom, Jean was like a circling beacon that
caught enemies in its hostile glare. She would tell the true story to
counteract the lies she feared were being whispered to the press by
Gary's side and by the False Memory people. She'd challenge the me-

dia: "Do you believe in repression?" — the litmus test of loyalty to Holly. Jean expected the worst. She had heard rumors that the Mondavi winery had poured money into Snowden's campaigns. And she knew that Kelli had driven with her dad to deliver wine to Snowden's home long before Holly's memories surfaced. Jean appeared on the second day of the trial, direct from the golf course. "At the break, Gary got up and walked over to me and says, 'Hi, Jean,' like we're buddies — in front of the jury! I mean a total show, I thought, to mislead the jury, like I'm there to support him. I had trouble sitting there."

Gary's team did not have a presence like Jean Sawday, nothing like the critical mass usually gathered on Stephanie's side. "Who's supporting Gary?" Jean scoffed. "This weird guy, Lloyd Jenkins, who seems like Gary's gofer at the trial. He's from down south, and he's handled their money. So what Gary has paid him or hasn't paid him to do this I don't know. Gary buys everybody." It was true that JoeAnna and Lloyd Jenkins had a business relationship with Gary. But it was their twenty-three years of friendship that had brought them to Napa for the duration of the trial. They had suffered with Gary as the scandal spread through the industry. They had watched him live and feel like an outcast. He had warned them of the risks they took standing by him. "If this becomes public, if it goes to trial, it's really going to hit the fan," he had said all along. JoeAnna couldn't visualize it. But when she saw the reporters and TV cameras, she said, "I had no idea!" Lloyd dutifully rolled the dolly in and out of court each day, delivering the boxes and displays Harrington needed. JoeAnna guided Gary's mother, Garnet, to a front-row seat and sat with her. Garnet sat, impassive and silent, from the first days of the trial, her white hair as stiffly coiffed as Betty Nye's across the aisle, grandmothers who had shared the girls' childhoods and hadn't spoken in four years.

Stephanie's mother was a regular presence, a positive image for the defense. Dressed in a tailored blazer over a silk shirt and skirt, she was always carefully made up. Though tense and full of hate for Gary, Betty Nye was a lady, and she mustered good manners for the press.

For three hours on the morning of Thursday, March 24, the jurors waited in the jury room, stiff and guarded on their first full day together, with no idea why they were waiting. The first of many dramas

they would never see was being played out at Judge Snowden's bench
and in his chambers as the lawyers tussled over the evidence the jury
would be allowed to hear. There was a final round of posturing by
Harrington, to keep out Stephanie's reports of violence early in the
marriage, and by the defense, to exclude Holly's memories after the
March 15, 1990, confrontation — the memories that went up to age
sixteen and included sex with the dog, Prince, memories a jury might
find difficult to believe.

Snowden ruled against admitting the reports of early violence into
court, evoking an outburst from Jean Sawday to reporters afterward.
To her, the violence was the story — violence that could be found in
the divorce documents right here in the courthouse — and the judge
had wrongly slammed the door on it. But he did permit Holly's later
memories, explaining, "Things that happened after the meeting may
be relevant to the charge that Marche Isabella planted false memories
in Holly Ramona. *This case is about false memory.*"

"Bailiff, please bring in the jury," Snowden ordered.

The jurors knew the cameras would be there, but most of them felt a
rush of exhilaration as they entered the courtroom. Propelled by "a
citizen's duty" but fearful that he'd fall short when it came time to
make a decision, Tim felt overwhelmed. He planned to face the task
ahead by "tentatively believing that everybody was credible" and letting them prove themselves otherwise. The jurors entered in no particular order, searching for their numbered seats. "But we soon knew
our pecking order," says Ken, the single alternate left when Christina
became a juror after a last-minute dismissal. "Keith first, Becky second, and me last."

As they filed in, Gary Ramona stood before them in a gray suit and
crisp white shirt, hands clasped in front, chin up and looking into
their eyes. Too nervous to turn their heads, they snatched first impressions. Thinning black hair neatly brushed, a face full-lipped and pleas-
ant-looking, he seemed serious, presentable, even attractive. But he
stood so close to their path that they almost brushed his suit as they
went by. While the defendants, Rose and Isabella, sat inconspicuously
behind the defense attorneys' table, Gary had placed his chair at the
left end of the plaintiffs' table, as physically close to the jury as he
could get. His body language — "I stand before you with nothing
to hide" — was a risk; sitting close to the jury, making eye contact

each time they filed in or out, was seen by some jurors as intrusive, "in your face."

The jury listened with fierce attention, made notes, and did not smile or interact as Judge Snowden gave them their charge. Cautioned not to speak among themselves about the case, weighted with the duties being outlined to them, they sat in awkward isolation. As they broke for lunch before Harrington's opening statement, they filed out and sat silently in the jury room: Nell with her winery and mansion on the hill. Yolanda with seven kids under thirteen. Becky barely out of high school, a checkout girl at Safeway. Shelley, a nurse who had witnessed psychiatric horrors the rest could never imagine. Tom worrying about how his associates were running the wholesale textile business. Ken, eager to get outside for a cigarette.

At one-thirty, the jury went to work as Richard Harrington rose to make his opening statement. As classically Irish as Ramona was Italian, Harrington's fair skin blended with his tousled dun gray hair into a vague paleness. The slim, graceful body of a man who had studied ballet was crisply defined by an elegantly cut double-vent navy blue suit and navy rep tie with a thin yellow stripe. While Gary sat with his jacket open, his right shoe up on his knee, Harrington stood looking out over glasses pushed forward on his nose, giving the impression of a preoccupied classical scholar. His voice was light and at times seemed to fade, as if a wind had caught his words, making his bold statements and preemptive strikes, when he chose to make them, all the more effective. To the several academics in the audience, he held the promise of elegant debate.

"Let me start with Holly Ramona," Harrington began, laying out the story they would hear over the coming weeks of the extraordinary events that had unfolded from the day Holly Ramona's bulimia entered her family's life. He presented the impressive credentials of each expert witness who would come to testify to malpractice on the part of Rose and Isabella and gave a summary of the testimony that would, he promised, tell a compelling story of sexual fantasies implanted by two therapists and a hospital whose behavior had fallen catastrophically below the acceptable standard of care. Provoking the defense, often, to leap to their feet to object, he gained a psychological advantage: the slight, middle-age gentleman facing three broad-shouldered young attorneys evoked comparisons with David and Goliath. "The linebackers and the leprechaun," quipped a reporter.

"Let me then proceed to a life history of Holly Ramona," said

Harrington as the jury sat forward in their seats, ". . . to give you some understanding of how a lovely young woman could come to this condition where she could be overinfluenced by suggestion into making these bizarre and false charges." For the next two and a half hours, he described the drama that sat, feet deep, in deposition books, court documents, and videotapes. The childhood infections. Bulimia. Sodium amytal. The confrontation. The termination from Mondavi. With the distracting click of Judge Snowden's computer the only other sound in the courtroom, Harrington left two words ringing in the jury's ears: "false charges."

Leonard "didn't want this case tried twice — in the courtroom and, then, in the hallways," where he feared "Gary was going to put on that puppy dog look, hang his eyes low, and say, 'I've been falsely accused.'" But as the defense heard that Harrington had called press conferences with several of his witnesses — and with two or three weeks of strong plaintiff witnesses scheduled before the defense could mount its case — Miroglio and Kurtock began to let their clients, Rose and Isabella, speak to the press in the hall. Isabella had just arrived, wearing one of the feminine, floral print garden party dresses she would wear throughout the trial — gathered at the shoulder, their short sleeves and belted waist revealed dimpled elbows and a full-busted, round-hipped figure. For someone who stood accused of incompetence and irresponsible technique, the look, some observers commented, was too soft for the professional appearance she needed. Yet when asked by the press, "Do you believe Holly?" a well-rehearsed Isabella stated with an edge that belied her look: "I believe *Holly* believed her father raped her." Rose, too, avoided committing to whether Holly's memories were false or true, admitting only that "*Holly* believed." From day one, they were distancing themselves from the charge that they had reinforced the fantasies of a suggestible girl by saying, "I believe you." To the media, Rose sounded another defense theme: "The case could have a very chilling effect on the whole concept of therapy."

Jeffrey Kurtock, Isabella's attorney, began his opening statement by launching into the defense's control theme: "Her father is trying to *control* her, cutting her off, showing her that he can still make her do what *he* wants her to do." In his low-key, pedantic style, he laid the trail of evidence that, like the separated hymen, "was not proof but corroborated her memories." He returned to his theme as he closed half an hour later. His deep voice quietly fierce, Kurtock ended on an ominous note: "Gary is saying to his daughter, 'You can run, but you can't *hide*. I'll *get* you!'"

Bruce Miroglio, defending Rose, picked up the theme of control the next morning in his opening statement. Acknowledging that the jury had heard from Harrington "a very impassioned telling of a shocking story," he proceeded to present an even more impassioned one, feeling "extraordinarily emotional" as he evoked the all-powerful father who still stalked his daughter's life, a man whose evidence would be a shameless distortion and manipulation of the truth. Miroglio's intensity grew as he repeated Holly's frightened plea to Dr. Rose that he stay loyal to her as her doctor despite any attempt by her father to undermine the relationship: "You don't know my dad. He's the most controlling guy I've ever met in my life. He's going to try to find out everything I've told you. Please, Doctor, will you be my doctor!" JoeAnna Jenkins rebelled inside. "Holly picked her college. She picked her car. If Gary was really controlling, these are two decisions he'd make for his child!"

Miroglio's voice rose as he promised, "Stephanie will testify how, to her horror . . . she came to the conclusion that these events took place — what I believe will be one of the most significant parts of the trial." Inside, though, he was concerned about Stephanie. She could be one of his strongest witnesses — or one of the weakest. He would work with her more as her day on the stand approached. Finally, Miroglio hammered home his plea to the jury to withhold judgment: "You're going to have to wait until *our* end of the trial to hear from Holly . . . You'll have to *wait* until Holly tells you the true story of the terrible trauma that was inflicted on her as certain frightening mental images began to invade her . . . vivid and detailed . . . acts of specific and graphic sexual abuse . . . Do they constitute proof that Gary Ramona did these things that Holly believes he did? Of course not," he told the jury. Gary's guilt was not the issue. They were here to test a therapist's freedom to deal with incest and recovered memory issues when they came up — to test the right of one retributive father to paralyze an entire profession from helping its patients. But for the courtroom and for the nation, Gary's guilt was, in fact, the only issue.

"I waive my opening statement until later, Your Honor," said Leonard, setting his strategy in motion. His goal: "to make sure the hospital receives some separation from the other defendants, and to keep as low a profile as possible." Every one of his moves — words, body language — was designed to persuade the jury that his client, Western Medical Center–Anaheim, shouldn't be there. Leonard would melt into the woodwork — difficult, admittedly, when you're the size of a small sumo wrestler.

As Nell Sweeney listened to the opening statements — and heard two totally different versions of a family's story — she learned her first lesson as a juror: "The first thing you sacrifice in litigation is the truth." "A lot of lying," thought Becky, already disillusioned by the process on the second day of the trial. "Each side makes their version very colorful, and they leave out the things that are going to make them look bad."

Leonard had scarcely taken his seat when Harrington stood and said simply, "I call Gary Ramona." The jury was jolted. They hadn't expected Ramona right out of the box, just like that. But for Gary this moment — his day in court — was four years overdue. "I didn't know whether I'd win or not. I knew from my experience of being told I was guilty on March 15 of 1990 that I was going to be already guilty when I walked in. But I never doubted, I never doubted once, that if I could ever get these people into court, I'd be able to show the truth. I believed that. I prayed a lot."

Gary was serious and prepared. The laugh that had so charmed Stephanie was nowhere to be heard. Harrington led him methodically through his childhood, his early career, his marriage. Through the birth of his children and Diamond Bar and the cul-de-sac on Holly Leaf Way. Through the trips to the beach, Indian Princesses, the birthday parties, the trip to Europe. Tim Holewinske blanched when he heard "Diamond Bar." He had lived there for a while when he was with the Conservation Corps, and he didn't know it well. But might it bias him one way or the other? Should he tell the judge? He did not, but he suffered over it for days.

Gary smiled when he said, "Holly was born on the sixteenth of August . . . I interviewed with the Robert Mondavi Winery in October of 1970." He spoke of a solid family life in St. Helena, on the cul-de-sac on Pinot Way. "I attended almost all of their school events . . . my family took priority. The only time I couldn't change a schedule, unless somebody was ill, was for board meetings . . . only four times a year." He choked up as he talked about his father's death but otherwise kept his emotions in check until Harrington handed him Exhibit 115 and asked, "Can you tell the court what that is?" They were Holly's notes and cards — he'd saved them all. Harrington read one to the jury. "'Have a Happy Father's Day,' it says. 'Love, Holly. You're the best.'" Gary read the next. "'See you in . . . two . . . weeks, Dad.'" His face flushed, he paused between words, trying to compose himself. "What do the Xs and Os mean on there?" asked Harrington. "Love and kisses, hugs," said Gary, unable to take any more. He put his hand over his eyes, wiping tears, and sobbed as the judge called a brief recess. Cynical about Gary's tears, Miroglio suspected the emotional moment had been carefully timed. Harrington continued as Garnet watched quietly from the front row, gripping a Kleenex. "Do you recognize the handwriting?" Gary responded through tears he could no longer stop. "That's my daughter Holly." He read the note she'd left on his office memo pad the summer she worked for Mondavi. The note she'd sent him when he was on a trip to Europe. Several in the audience were visibly moved as he described the little pencil holder Holly had made from an orange juice cylinder, a treasure he kept with the notes "because they're letters and cards from my children. They mean something to me."

Jean Sawday could scarcely contain herself. Trapped by loyalty to Stephanie in a room where she was forced to listen to a man she despised, she kept her sounds reduced to a frustrated expulsion of breath. But her body responded instead, twisting with impatience. She shook her head, rolled her eyes, nerves and muscles responding with disgust. At the break, she stood and talked forthrightly to reporters, warning them not to be taken in, that Gary was painting a picture of lies. After lunch, the jury would be shown — and she had to endure — the home movies edited from the boxes Gary took from Pinot Way. They would see more fun and hugs and happiness than she could stand. What a charade!

As the jury watched the movies — the trips, the BMWs, the yearly cascade of Christmas gifts under the tree — John Carver kept shaking his head and whispering to his seatmate, "Overindulged kids . . . overindulged kids." It was the pattern they were seeing in false memories. A successful doctor who had raised his children with all the trappings of prosperity — the ski houses, Europe — he felt guilty of overindulging. Had he and Gary and fathers like him, who thought they had given their daughters everything they could need or want, failed them?

Then Harrington marched Gary through the events leading up to the confrontation, to the moment Holly said, "You raped me." Step by step, Gary described the collapse of his life, the loss of his family, sobbing as he relived the terrible scene when "Shawna ducked down. She went and hid in the bushes" as he honked his horn.

But there was another aspect to this trial: the Mondavis. To win the $8 million damages Gary was claiming, Harrington must prove that the malpractice had cost him his job, that he was fired because of the allegations, not, as Kurtock claimed in his opening statement, because "Gary wasn't doing a good job." Now that the winery's stock had gone public, the Mondavis would have given anything to be able to strike this phase from the trial. Every headline embarrassed them and could hurt their stock. They couldn't stop it, but Tim and Michael would testify in defense of the winery's decision to terminate Gary.

Harrington led Gary into the Mondavi years: the growth of sales, his phenomenal success, gross revenues of more than $110 million and a net income of $7 million in 1990 — the highest in the winery's history. "I was considered a family member of Robert Mondavi in the winery as well as in the marketplace, on a national and international basis." Gary described the paper trail that had begun with the leave-of-absence letter, the trail he believed had been laid to divert him from the real reason he was fired, the rumors spread by Stephanie. Gary sipped some water as Harrington led into it: "What was the next board of directors meeting . . . after May 31, 1990?" "June 18, 1990." Gary had attended it, and the Mondavis had asked to meet with him outside afterward. "They had a document, a letter . . . prepared . . ." Harrington pressed gently, "What did the letter do?" Gary Ramona was more undone by his next sentence than by reading Holly's Father's Day cards: "Put me on a leave of absence."

On that tortured note, the judge dismissed the court until Monday. The jury and audience filed out, deeply stirred by the moment, emotionally drained. Miroglio knew good theater when he saw it and believed it had been just that — an act. He couldn't help recalling the times they'd deposed Gary. "The questions we asked that man! And he had no problem answering them without tears."

That weekend, Gary Ramona's team settled into its trial routine. Gary had bought a double duplex just north of town, and during the trial, he says, "I was running a boardinghouse." The Jenkinses, the attorneys, the experts — everyone stayed there — in three bedrooms on "the boys' side," two on "the girls'." "I mean, it was full. There were times we would have ten people for dinner." They went out to eat roughly twice a week. JoeAnna, Garnet, and Barbara cooked the rest of the time. For the daily working lunches at the duplex, they'd order sandwiches or pizza, or JoeAnna would fix leftover roast or Harrington's favorite, steamed vegetables. Garnet did the thing she took pride in, the laundry, and did it "her way — each bed had its own wash, the towels done just so."

The main living room was set up as a warroom, with computers, a fax machine, and a printer. Every deposition was on the computer and could be called up in court on Harrington's portable notebook. His bad back kept him standing at the computer as Harrington punched in the research he needed; he was connected by a modem twenty-four hours a day to his office in San Francisco and to his research service. Gail Saliterman, the lawyer who sat silently with Harrington in court, riffling through files and handing him papers, came into her own in the preparation of the case. "We worked seven days a week," says Gary, "from six in the morning to eleven, twelve, one o'clock at night. Saturday and Sunday was a little less." But he was as close to happy as he'd been since March 15, 1990. He was part of a family again.

"A family he paid for," Miroglio scoffed, convinced that it was the defense that bonded despite challenges Gary's side never had. Because they were sharing the case, the defense attorneys were forced to accommodate, as Leonard recalls, "the needs and egos and desires" of one another. They'd learned to compromise in choosing the jury. They informally divided up the preparation each day, deciding who would examine whom, but there was an underlying tension that could never go away. The highest obligation of each of the attorneys — Miroglio, Leonard, and Kurtock — was to his own client, to the insurer who paid him. They felt the pressure of being the visiting team on Gary's turf. Had they known then what Miroglio learned from Harrington after the trial, they would have felt even more pressure: Gary had staged two mock trials before the trial itself and had never got less from the mock juries than a $9 million award. There were also inherent power struggles. Kurtock, with the most vulnerable defendant, Marche Isabella, claimed the right to do the first cross-examination of each witness and to shape the strategy more than Leonard and Miroglio might have liked. "I told Doctors Company from day one, 'We can't win on Did Gary do it?'" says Miroglio. But Kurtock carried that as an issue to levels that damaged the defense, in Miroglio's view.

They also weren't sharing living quarters. Rich Rose and Marche Isabella stayed at the large Inn at Napa Valley, a pink and flowery former Embassy Suites hotel built by Nell Sweeney's husband. Jeff Kurtock and his colleague Sharon Chandler stayed there, too, but they also commuted from San Francisco. While Gail Saliterman would remain a stranger to the jury after seven weeks of trial, Sharon Chandler would be given considerable courtroom time to examine witnesses. The two self-admitted "huggers," Miroglio and Leonard, had a hard time getting close to Chandler, whose appearance was as hard-edged as Isabella's was soft. She was brisk in and out of the courtroom. Although resisting any questions about her private life, she admitted to several marriages. That was about it. Reminiscent of Joan Crawford, with brilliant red lipstick and large clear-framed glasses, her hair chic, short, and dark, she was given to wearing power suits and dresses and scarves in bold colors.

Nor did the defense eat communally. For lunch, Chandler and Rose made a beeline for the little low-fat yogurt shop beside Mervyn's department store. Kurtock and Leonard favored the deli sandwiches a block away. After court each day, they met back at Miroglio's office, worked for an hour or two, then dispersed to do more individual preparation. Leonard lived at the Harvest Inn, upvalley in St. Helena and just across the street from Miroglio's. The equivalent of their warroom was a conference room they'd booked at the inn mostly to prepare witnesses. Leonard and Miroglio had become friends; they often drove home together, stopping not infrequently for margaritas at Compadres and an occasional dinner at Piatti's. It would be "a many-margarita trial."

The jurors were taking time to learn to live together. "At first, when we'd go into the jury room, everybody sort of stuck their noses in their own books, walked outside, and never talked to anybody," Nell observed. They felt silenced by the judge's warnings: "You may not base a verdict on factors like sympathy, prejudice, public opinions, speculation . . ." There must be no TV or newspapers. "This is a case everyone's going to want to know about . . . but there's only one proper answer: 'I have very strict instructions not to discuss this case at all until it's over.' And when it's over, you can talk to *anyone* about the case." Snowden was impressed by the extraordinary focus they were bringing to the job. "They know they're in the 'big time,' and they're paying attention as if it were a capital case . . . The jury is taking it very, very seriously."

With the resumption of Gary's testimony on Monday, the emotion became more intense. As cross-examination began, the three defense attorneys came at him in successive waves, each attacking the picture he had painted. The jury heard the Ramonas' sex life dumped into court: their problems with intercourse; Gary's emotional defense of his happy marriage as Miroglio tried to knock holes in the story.

Gary had said, "There were difficulties she had, in terms of sexuality . . . from the beginning of our marriage, but Stephanie and I had a very, very good marriage."

"You had no problem. It was her problem," Miroglio jabbed.

"I would not want to say it was her problem . . . She had very difficult times the first six months of marriage to have intercourse."

"In fact, you didn't consummate your marriage for the first six months you were married."

The defense had suggested he'd married Steph just to avoid Vietnam, insinuated he was fired for incompetence, accused him and Grundland of lying, and was now coming into his bedroom!

"I loved my wife. We got married. The marriage *was* consummated!"

"This is murder, trying to say nothing," thought Marty Cook at the end of the day. It had to loosen up. On Tuesday morning, the jury's fourth day of the trial, one of them arrived at the jury room with some food and a game. It broke the ice. Other people started bringing snacks. Crackers. Doughnuts, cookies, pretzels. Keith brought bags of doughnut holes from Butter Cream Bakery. From then on, there was always something to eat on the table. At breaks they started playing board games, Twenty Questions. Rummy became the favorite. "We got to know each other by playing games," says Marty. Nell and Ken were the only two who went out for a cigarette, but everyone treated them respectfully. They began to look forward to the breaks. "After a while, we didn't want to be interrupted to go to court," Marty laughs. Sometimes the bailiff would peek in, waiting for the stragglers to return, and find them with cards in their hands.

Ed Leonard had pushed Gary on the issue that had disturbed him: denying that Holly had ever been sexually abused. "It is a fact, in my opinion, that my daughter has never been sexually abused by anyone," Gary had asserted. Leonard knew that strategy was involved in that response — to admit that Holly *might* have been abused opened the door to the possibility that her memories were real, even if Gary was not the perpetrator. To win, he must prove that the memories were fantasies, false memories implanted by the defendants. But it still upset Leonard as a father. Marty Cook, the juror and bank manager, was bothered, too. "When he said that nobody had ever done it, I thought, 'Well, how could he know that? Somebody could have done something to her. He was away from home a lot. I'm a father. You just don't see a father react that way.'"

Miroglio ended the cross-examination by returning to Chandler's aggressive charge that Barry Grundland had told Gary about the confrontation. If the jury could be convinced that Gary was armed with knowledge before he went willingly to the confrontation, it would strip Isabella and Rose, his client, of responsibility for the meeting Judge Snowden had made the crux of the case. "Again, you don't recall whether or not you spoke with Dr. Grundland on March 9? . . . And, sir, isn't it true that the reason you scheduled that is you knew what . . . that meeting was going to be about with your daughter?" "That is absolutely incorrect," said Gary, and he left the stand.

By midmorning on Tuesday, after more than two days on the stand, Gary finished telling his story. He had survived the humiliation of cross-examination. He had survived the hurtful questions like, "The American Institute of Food and Wine is having a dinner tomorrow night for Robert Mondavi down in San Francisco. Are you going down for that?" They knew he was not. He had been forced to violate his deep sense of loyalty to Bob and the family by revealing the intimate workings of the winery — the family's power shifts, the rivalries, the wives, the gossip, the financial details. When Miroglio asked him if Bob had lost power to his sons, Gary had responded impatiently, "He had enough [of a] say, but he was also striving to turn over the reins to Michael and Tim . . . and this was a major embarrassment. We're talking about a winery of . . . 160 million gross revenues that needed to go public. It could not have me out there [with] the public knowing just exactly what's happening here in this courtroom today."

And now his mother had to endure it: Harrington called Garnet to the stand. The wisp of a woman, now eighty-two and wearing a diamond-patterned black, white, and red sweater, was barely visible behind the high witness stand. Ears strained to hear a voice as thin and fragile as a china teacup. Harrington wanted just one answer from her brief appearance: "Were you ever raped by your two brothers?" "No, where the heck do they get that stuff from?" Leonard asked on crossexam, "Is there anybody in this world who loves Gary more than you? You'd do anything to help him, wouldn't you?" "If it's the right way, yes," she answered, stepping neatly out of the trap. Leonard would win no points by further attacking this little old lady, so he closed with a vague and futile question: "Is that a lie you just told us?" to which Garnet, of course, said no. JoeAnna helped her on with her gray quilted raincoat, which wrapped her like a cocoon, and she left the courtroom.

The jury had not been won over. Most were far from deciding Gary's guilt one way or the other. Becky had been surprised that Gary had been put on the stand first, but now she saw the strategy: "I had a lot of problems with his testimony, and it's better to do it at the beginning, where we forget." Several saw Gary as arrogant. No one's life was that perfect. Nell thought Gary's tears were disingenuous and kept track in her notebook of the times he cried. Putting Gary on first was just fine, Yolanda thought. "Gary had to lay his foundation. Maybe he is arrogant and egotistical. Maybe he has an attitude. But that's the way he is. So what? It doesn't make him guilty." The juror Leonard and Chandler "just loved" was feeling some early sympathy for Gary, but she was a mother of seven, and she hadn't heard Stephanie or Holly yet.

Harrington's direct examination of Gary had been brilliant, Leonard conceded. "A good sense of humor, self-effacing enough to enjoy a good spoof on himself. Very smart — no one ever said Harrington was a dummy." Leonard also knew, from three years of bruises, that "he projects such an urbane, genteel individual. But he's a banty Irishman — a street fighter!" Crediting Gary with the power over his tears that Mondavi had over the valley, Miroglio had to admire Harrington's "direct" as his "best work. Carefully scripted." For now, the defense could only build a case in the hallways.

"We're not saying this is the house from hell. We're saying that it's not Ward and June Cleaver," Miroglio said of the marriage Gary had painted as so perfect. "Here's a man who looks through rose-colored glasses," Leonard added. A few feet away, Gary struck his own blow with the press: "I lost my marriage of twenty-five years. I haven't seen any of my children since March 15, 1990. Somebody has to put a stop to this quackery." But what about Holly's allegations, the memories? His voice shook: *"It's absolutely not true."* *Newsweek* and the *New York Times* were listening, but his family hadn't been there to hear a word.

The next day, the experts were coming to tell their truths.

14

The Great Recovered Memory Debate

The great recovered memory debate began in earnest when the forensic psychiatrist Dr. Park Elliot Dietz took the stand. Neat and polished almost to the point of slickness in a navy blue suit, Dietz proceeded in a cool, cerebral manner to present his daunting credentials to the jury: a Ph.D. sociologist, too, he was president of the American Academy of Psychiatry and the Law, on the editorial board of a dozen peer journals, author of a hundred papers, consultant to the police department of almost every state in the Union, a witness in hundreds of trials, and wreathed with awards from Phi Beta Kappa to the American Academy of Sciences for his work on sex offenders. He had served on the Attorney General's Commission on Pornography and been given, through the FBI, a privileged view of sex abuse "most people never see in a career — the most atrocious kinds of crimes against children . . . and bizarre kinds of sex offenses." He knew the terrible reality of child abuse. He later sobered the jury and the courtroom, when torn hymens were discussed, by explaining that his knowledge came largely from pathology labs, when sex abuse was the cause of death.

Where Gary had told the human story, Dietz's was a forensic tale. The events of Holly's life were systematically examined to show, in sum, a young woman whose flashbacks were far more likely to have been rooted in traumatizing events of childhood — enemas, a snakelike catheter stuck up her urethra without anesthesia, a babysitter simulating intercourse. There would be no tears as Dietz unfolded a tale of suggestive "mischief" played by inept therapists that had led, not to true memories, but to sad fantasies woven into the "obsessional intrusions" — of a depressed and bulimic girl.

When Harrington brought up the sodium amytal interview, Ken Keri, the alternate juror, heard Dietz say that not to have video- or audiotaped it was below the national standard of care. Keri was thinking, "I don't care about videotape or audiotape. She didn't even take *notes* . . . They think there's child abuse . . . Gary may be in *jail* if this is proven — and she didn't even take one note? Come on!"

Late that afternoon, Kurtock began his cross-examination of Dietz with the theme of repressed memories. Yes, there were "concealed" memories, forgetting, Dietz admitted. But the *reality* of memories had never been an issue when psychoanalysis reigned, he said, because of confidentiality. "Now there has been a major change. With modern . . . therapies, they don't have that rule of confidentiality." Rushed confrontations and family catastrophes like the Ramonas' were the result. Now it mattered very much whether these memories were, in fact, real or even possible. The long-term repression of memories and the recovery of memories must not only be questioned, they must also be vigorously tested. He cited the soon-to-be-published study by Pope and Hudson that disarmed the claims of repression made by the four touted studies of Herman, Briere, Williams, and Loftus. Finding "no credible evidence that repressed memory exists," Dietz closed for the day with a strong statement: he believed there was "*no* suppression . . . No long-term suppression of serious events."

That night, the level of intensity in the boardinghouse soared. Dr. Robert Gerner, the only expert witness in Gary's entire retinue who had seen and examined Holly, had flown in from L.A. to testify the next day. Skip Pope had flown in as the orchestrating strategist and Jim Hudson as a witness for the vital eating disorder dimension. Pope, Dietz, Gerner, Hudson, and Harrington were planning, preparing. Ephraim Margolin would drop by. Gary listened and watched in awe. He had never expected to be running an intellectual salon.

More than that, these brilliant minds were helping him "in being able to pull myself together." It was their encouragement, "this expectation that somehow I'm going to be able to pull all this out and move on and be successful," that inspired him. Their decision to take him on in the first place had helped most of all — that they "believed in me

— not just in the case, in me as a person. The way Bob and Margrit believe that I can make this happen again." How could he be getting through this without the Jenkinses or Scott Evans flying up? Or the "100 percent supportive" call from a cousin in Oklahoma. But the experts had given him "a whole new standard."

That night, Miroglio tucked his notes into the four-inch-thick trial book he carried to court each morning in the battered lawyer's brief-case that had become his lucky talisman. Gerner would be on the stand the next day, Thursday. Miroglio had been waiting for this mo-ment for more than a year, ever since — smelling something about Gerner's past — he had searched the files of the L.A. Superior Court and discovered the lawsuit in which Gerner admitted having sex with a patient. It was clearly the most serious ethical transgression a physi-cian could commit, especially a psychiatrist, who deals with the emo-tionally vulnerable. The patient and her husband had both sued Gerner. The case had been settled for a rumored $875,000.

Harrington was staking so much on this man's credibility. Dis-credit Gerner, and he would discredit the testimony on which every other witness based his or her opinion.

This information had to be kept secret, or Gary's side would pull Gerner as a witness. Miroglio told only Leonard and Kurtock, swear-ing them to secrecy, and John Suesans at the Doctors Company, who said, "Gerner — I think he's one of ours."

Now he would "nail this creep and blow Ramona's case out of the water." In the shower, in the car, over and over, Miroglio had prac-ticed the subtle order and timing of the questions that would deliver Gerner's head to the jury, just at the end of the day. His greatest fear was that Snowden would stop him halfway and say, "Irrelevant." He must convince the judge that Gerner's case had a relevant connection to Ramona or Snowden would never let it in.

The day had taken its toll — sparring with a brilliant forensic mind, being "sandbagged" by Snowden as he battled at the bench to contain Dietz's damage, preparing for the moment of truth with Gerner the next day. Miroglio felt frustrated, exhausted, and couldn't sleep. In his "heart of hearts," he believed Gary did it. "But I went through incredible doubts. I thought, as I would a hundred times, 'What if I was Gary and I didn't do it?' My daughters share a bed-room. I sat at the end of Celia's bed and I cried. I thought, 'How would it feel to have a daughter accuse you if you didn't do it?' How would it feel, *the loss of daughters!*" Mary would get furious if he woke the baby. "But I picked Celia up, slid her into my arms, held her. 'What if someday I lose her because she accuses me of doing something I didn't do?' Yeah, I was feeling empathy for Gary."

The cross-exam of Dietz went on until midafternoon the next day. Kurtock, Leonard, and Miroglio continued to try to catch him in inconsistencies. Kurtock came close, reminding Dietz that, in 1992, he had stated that he thought repressed memories of sexual abuse were possible. "I've learned more, changed my mind," Dietz responded. "Two years ago, I believed repression might exist because of the Franklin case, but didn't know enough . . . Since then, I've learned that everything the daughter remembered had already appeared in newspapers and is invalid."

Dietz reminded the jury that Holly's memories of rape by her father were always ambiguous and unclear — even under sodium amytal she was unsure — and that it was the interpretation by Isabella and Rose that had given them flesh and reality. Among his last words to the jury were: "I believe it's only after sodium amytal that Holly becomes persuaded that she was raped by her father."

Yet Dietz did not charm the jury. His cool, methodical style had informed but not involved them on a human level. Nell's opinion was: "They're paying him over eighty grand! He could have stayed home." "A lot of wasted money," Tom Dudum silently agreed. "Dietz was good," Yolanda was thinking. Throughout his testimony, she'd been going, "'*Really,* huh!' There were a lot of things I didn't know. He laid a foundation for me." But she had a feeling that it didn't matter what the experts said. The testimony that was going to matter to her was Gary's, Stephanie's, and Holly's.

At two-thirty, Gerner was called to the stand. The picture he painted in his testimony was of a desperately sick and dysfunctional girl — of paranoia, schizophrenia, sociopathic abnormalities, reality distortion, and sexual fantasies projected onto her father. She had "a marked difficulty in seeing the world the way . . . most people see the world." This was the normal-looking little girl the jury had seen in the home movies? "Extreme, very extreme," thought Becky. "You can tell they're exaggerated." She could see that the eyes of some of her fellow jurors had glazed over, and she stopped taking notes when he got to characterizing Holly as a schizotypal sociopath. She hadn't seen Holly yet, but from the evidence already there — from the picture her own father painted, a girl who's okay enough to be getting her master's degree in psychology — "nothing else is supporting that she's a sociopathic paranoid schizo."

Leonard began a brief cross-examination of Gerner. To him, personally, Gerner was "that smarmy little guy with the green shirt and black tie and suit coat thrown over his shoulder in some kind of an Italian gigolo look." As a lawyer, "the problem I had was he called a twenty-three-year-old girl psychotic, schizotypal, sociopathic . . . based upon tests that were invalid." When he was done, he passed the cross-exam to Miroglio with a whispered "Good luck. We're all counting on you."

Miroglio stood as far away from the witness stand as he could, to keep the jury focused on Gerner. He led the doctor into a meandering discussion of how one gets the best information from the patient in a psychological exam — keeping patients comfortable with air conditioning, and so on. As Miroglio carefully crept toward his ambush, Judge Snowden jumped in with precisely the kind of distraction he had dreaded. The unseasonal heat had led to a running joke about the courtroom's malfunctioning air conditioning, and, like a solicitous hotelier trying to please his guests, Snowden said, "What caused you to bring up the subject of air conditioning? . . . It's working? Oh, great. It's working! I beg your pardon, Mr. Miroglio. Please go ahead."

Wanting to at least look calm, Miroglio kept his line of questioning moving. With the goal of discrediting the validity of the psychological tests Gerner had given Holly, he tried to get Gerner to admit that the quality of the information he drew from her could have been compromised by, for example, Holly's fear that her father had ordered the exam and would use it against her and her therapists. Yes, Gerner reluctantly admitted. Then Miroglio deftly shifted the question: "Could the bias of the individual interviewer impact the . . . ultimate conclusions . . . from that interview?" Gerner, a little impatient, responded, ". . . one would hope that a good clinician would have worked through those types of issues." One would hope.

"Beautiful," Leonard exulted silently, knowing that, with even this indirect admission that the interviewer's bias could affect the results, Miroglio had established the relevance of Gerner's scandal to the case.

Miroglio moved in for the kill. "So it would be permissible to take advantage of your therapeutic relationship to fit your own agenda . . . to fit your own needs?"

"Well, you're there to help them, not them to help you."

Miroglio dropped the bomb. "Doctor, the truth is, when you first heard about this case you felt an empathy with Gary Ramona . . . the man who's accused of sexual abuse in this case. Isn't that true?"

"No."

"Sir, wasn't it true that you yourself were under allegations of inappropriate sexual behavior at the same time?" After twenty minutes of boredom, the entire courtroom suddenly snapped to attention. Miroglio saw Gerner's jaw go slack. He glanced at Snowden, saw him smiling, as if to say, "Ah, you've brought it all home." Miroglio knew he had Gerner trapped.

"Yes, there were charges of that, now resolved," Gerner said with a voice suddenly gone dead.

"Just charges?"

"Resolved . . . It was settled."

"And that was in the case of [name deleted] . . . and her husband . . . You were seeing both these patients in therapy, weren't you? . . . And isn't it true, sir, that . . . the complaint alleged that you encouraged the husband to disassociate himself from his wife because the relationship was dysfunctional . . . that at your deposition you acknowledged that you had advised the husband to move on with his life?"

Harrington leaped to his feet as Miroglio's formless questions suddenly took on a dangerous shape.

Leonard couldn't stand the tension. *"Stick the fork in this guy! Stick in the fork!"* he hissed at Miroglio as the clock ticked to the end of the court day.

Returning to Gerner, Miroglio demanded, "And isn't it true at the same time that these events were going on, you were involved in a sexual relationship with the wife . . . ?"

"Well, it depends on what you call a sexual relationship."

At 4:20 P.M., Miroglio stuck in the fork. *"You allowed her to orally copulate you in your office. Isn't that what you admitted?"*

The courtroom was stunned, paralyzed.

"No, that's not what I admitted."

"You didn't say that in your deposition?"

"I didn't say I *allowed* it."

"*It took place?*"

"Yeah."

A shock wave coursed through the room, leaving in its wake, for a microsecond, absolute silence. Then, as attorneys rushed to huddle at the bench, a wave of whispers and nervous laughter rose up. The jury had, as one, stopped taking notes. Ken Keri whistled to himself, "They've just blown his testimony right down the tubes." Journalists rushed to the phones.

Gamely trying to resurrect Gerner from the devastation, Harrington limped on for a few painful minutes with technical questions about the half life of sodium amytal. But it was impossible to refocus attention, and he'd run out the clock.

Miroglio had one more small job. He asked Leonard to do it for him in his fleeting cross-exam. The California Medical Board was examining Gerner's "incident," was it not? Has it made a decision, taken any disciplinary action?

"No," said Gerner.

Has the National Data Bank been advised yet of this lawsuit and settlement?

"It will be. It always is."

"And that is something that will follow you around forever, correct?"

"I imagine it will," said Gerner.

Miroglio had it on record and in the jury's mind: a malpractice finding against a physician sat in the National Data Bank, a ghost that would haunt him for the rest of his life. Be very, very careful, jury, before you doom Richard Rose to this fate.

The day ended in uproar and disarray. As dazed as the audience, the jurors tried to contain themselves as they paraded out. The press seized Miroglio and Harrington in the hall. "Mr. Harrington, did you know about this?" "No," he said, then added, "Not all of my witnesses are equipped with halos, but that has nothing to do with this case."

Elizabeth Loftus, who had created a stir when she arrived at the courthouse to observe earlier that day, put her hand on Gerner's shoulder and asked, "Are you okay?" as he slunk away. He'd been a jerk, perhaps, but Loftus couldn't help finding a crumb of compassion for a wounded colleague. His transgression was intolerable — he had exploited the vulnerable, broken the most basic code. But humans, like memory, were fallible. Her testimony rescheduled because of a conflict in the timing of witnesses, Loftus flew home to Seattle, but she would be back in Courtroom B.

Marian Dodds left court that day angry. When she heard Gerner call Holly a schizoid sociopath, she lost all hope of hearing the open debate she had come for. Moving in and out of the room now with the group of women defending Holly's side, sharing their anger and support, the rage she had brought to the courtroom began to assert itself. Over the days to follow she gradually shed her camouflage. She replaced her gray sweatshirt with tailored shirts and sweaters, put on a bit of makeup, and began talking to the press in the hallways. Marian Dodds was emerging as a survivor activist.

The day ended for Gary with a letter to the editor from his daughter Kelli to the *Register*'s op-ed page. Attacking her father for bringing "all of this heartache to the public," she wrote, "Silence is where the truth lies. I am angry that my privacy, that of my sister Holly, mother and younger sister was invaded. We walked away from a horrible reality . . . It is devastatingly painful and sad that my father has made a mockery of what happened to my sister." It was her "feelings, dead instinct," she said, that had led to her "100 percent belief" in Holly's story.

That night Miroglio invited the defense team over to his house and rented a videotape of *Airplane*. They ordered in pizzas, uncorked some good Napa wine, and watched the movie, roaring over every slapstick scene. When it got to the line at the end, "Good luck, we're counting on you," they fell apart.

It was April 4, Easter Monday. Gary began the day by giving a bear hug to an elderly man with a warm, friendly face — Dr. Lon Klink, Holly's pediatrician from the Diamond Bar years. Klink had been called to testify about Holly's medical records. Referring to his years of record-keeping, Klink cast doubt on Marche Isabella's assumptions that rape had caused Holly's urinary tract infections or that he might have missed a damaged hymen or genital abrasions through improper examination. From the time Holly was five and a half — a dozen times, specifically at the time of the urinary infections, too, he confirmed — he examined her genitalia as part of his "complete physical

examination," laying back the fleshy lips of the labia and looking in at
the hymen with his otoscope and flashlight. Had he ever found any
signs of sexual abuse, he would have reported it to the police and child
protective agency. But he never did.

Klink cast doubt on childhood sexual abuse as the cause of Holly's
urinary tract infections when he stated that "the most common cause
is . . . wiping in the wrong direction." Harrington drew from Klink
responses that could suggest to the jury that Holly's physical ailments
and procedures might well be at the root of her "memories." The
"snake in her vagina" could have been the snakelike catheter inserted
in her urethra without anesthesia when she was seven, a procedure
called a voiding cystourethrogram. Harrington had Klink describe the
sheets, the frog position — the child on her back with the soles of her
feet touching and the knees spread apart — the pressure and need to
urinate when the tube was pulled out, giving the jury images that
would fit Holly's memories when they later heard them from Holly.
Harrington's penchant for theatrical tricks was revealed when he had
Klink pull out a twisting black catheter and display it to the jury.
There it was, the snake of Holly's dreams and flashbacks.

Stephanie would never forgive Klink for what she saw as betrayal,
if not outright perjury. He never put Holly in that frog position. Not
once, ever. She had been there for every exam, she told Miroglio,
distressed, when she heard what Klink had said. She didn't remember
his ever examining Holly's internal genitalia, her hymen. But to attack
the integrity of this seasoned pediatrician too aggressively could be as
dangerous as arguing that Dr. Spock was a charlatan. Dr. Klink had
won the jurors. His citing of medical procedures as possible causes of
the memories had made a strong impression.

Holly's hymen. With Klink, it had come up again. That's what
bugged Ken Keri. "Holly's was ripped . . . But how could a woman be
raped repeatedly — they kept saying 'repeatedly' — from age five to
sixteen and still have a hymen left at all?" Yolanda, too, had her
doubts. "They say that hymen's just slightly moved. And yet they said
she was 'penetrated,' penetrated vaginally and anally. And she still has
a hymen? Oh, *please*. Over a period of time, he's doing it over and
over and over, from five to sixteen — eleven years — you don't *have* a
hymen, honey. You don't have *anything*."

As if anticipating the interest, Harrington had showed the jury, just
before Klink's appearance, a short videotape of the deposition of Dr.
Stephanie McClellan, the Orange County obstetrician who had exam-

ined Holly's hymen. The defense planned to put her on the stand as their witness and Harrington would have a chance to cross-examine her then. Now, however, he wanted to get into evidence and before the jury portions of McClellan's deposition that undermined Isabella's use of the hymen as one of her "proofs" of Gary's rape. The jury heard the defense's own witness state that, in an examination which had been "quite an unremarkable office visit," she had found a minor posterior separation that could have been caused, she said, by any number of things ranging from intercourse "as one extreme" to a straddle injury, say, from a bicycle. It didn't address Ken's doubts about any hymen's surviving years of penetration by a grown man's penis, but Klink and McClellan had very neatly put to rest Holly's hymen as *proof* of sexual abuse.

No subject in the entire trial touched the interest of the women in the courtroom more than eating disorders. As Dr. James Hudson, Pope's research partner at McLean, took the stand, they searched his words for an understanding of their own personal issues. Who didn't have a daughter with weight or self-esteem problems or an anorexic friend? Who had not absorbed from the air the assumption that sexual abuse and weight problems were somehow connected? Could Hudson really show that Holly's memories were caused not by rape but by bulimia and depression?

Like a nervous stage mother trying not to coach from the sidelines, Pope, as strategist, tried to contain himself at the plaintiff's table. The defense would have preferred to see him on the stand instead of having him, as Miroglio said, "pogo-sticking around the courtroom." Miroglio was eager to use a statement from Pope's deposition, to the effect that "life's events have no impact on depression," to try to nail him as an excessively Prozac-happy scientist. Instead they had put on Hudson, "the ultimate boy scout."

Hudson laid out his credentials. Isabella's claimed knowledge of eating disorders withered before his leadership in the field. He had founded the Academy for Eating Disorders, was named one of the "Best Doctors in America" for his expertise in eating disorders and psychiatry, and had, quite literally, written the book on the subject. Coauthor with Pope of *New Hope for Binge Eaters,* Hudson had helped write the official diagnosis for patients with eating disorders, in *DSM-III-R.* His research on Prozac cast him as a scientist, yet he was "a *clinical* researcher," having seen from one to two thousand patients in his office at McLean since the early 1980s.

Now if, as Hudson had said, major depression and bulimia are caused by chemical imbalances, "Is there any proof," Harrington asked him, "that childhood sexual abuse causes a biochemical disturbance in patients?" "None that I'm aware of." On the other hand, said Hudson, drugs like Prozac and other antidepressants that correct a serotonin imbalance in the brain "can cause complete remission of the symptoms of both bulimia nervosa and depression." Hudson presented his proof of a familial and probably a genetic link between bulimia and major depression. That they, rather than sexual abuse and bulimia, were causally related. To combat Isabella's claim that "70 to 80 percent of bulimia patients have been sexually abused," Hudson had his own statistic — "70 percent of people with bulimia have either depression concurrently or at some point in the course of their lives." And that the serotonin reuptake inhibiting drugs had a 70 percent chance of working for both depression and bulimia the first time one was tried, an 85 to 90 percent chance "of actually getting your symptoms better" if two or three were tried.

Harrington was planting seeds of skepticism about the barrage of "symptoms and signs" he knew Lenore Terr would offer as proof of sexual abuse when she appeared for the defense in a week or two. Hudson must show Holly's behavior, her weight obsession, her food fetishes, as symptoms of bulimia and depression rather than sexual abuse. Bulimics have a "preoccupation with food and rituals, superstitions or other eccentric habits surrounding food" — eating some foods and not others, aversions to mayonnaise or unsliced bananas, cutting and placing foods in certain ways, eating in a certain order. But none was "evidence of childhood sex abuse," Hudson said with building intensity. "Low self-esteem, preoccupation with body shape, poor self-image . . . *They're symptoms in the 'diagnostic criteria' for bulimia.*" He reeled off a list of the symptoms that the jury, by now, knew Holly had. Citing his own and others' research, Hudson explained away everything Terr might offer as a symptom of sexual abuse as *more likely* to be a symptom of depression and bulimia — and, perhaps, of obsessive-compulsive disorder.

Hudson now tied it all together to explain Holly's memories of abuse, her "images." Bulimia and obsessive-compulsive disorder were part of a linked family of disorders and shared some symptoms, for example, "obsessional rituals . . . and *intrusive mental images*," he said. These "recurrent thoughts" were fairly brief, did not record real events. They were fantasies, not repressed memories. "Dr. Hudson, is there any evidence at all that a person who has been sexually abused from age five to age sixteen could have repressed it and forgotten the whole thing?" Harrington asked. "No," Hudson responded. "People who have been forcibly raped over an eleven-year period from age five to age sixteen just don't forget." Harrington summed up with the sweeping question: "Are there any other symptoms that Holly Ramona exhibited that would lead you to suspect sexual abuse?" "No," said Hudson.

Kurtock's cross-examination of Hudson was proving frustrating to him, as evidenced by his increasingly abrasive voice. As Kurtock tried to pin him down to numbers, Hudson explained, again and again, that statistics and studies on sexual abuse were skewed by the wild variation in definition. How could you study sexual abuse when it was described in terms that ranged "from a *request to do something sexual*" to forcible "rape by your father" and gave equal value to "an uncle rubbing his beard on your cheek" as to violent incestual rape, events that might leave *no* trauma or *severe* trauma — that might have symptoms of *high* or *low* self-esteem? "So . . . you don't *care* whether they were sexually abused or not?" Kurtock demanded, becoming hostile. "I care a lot . . . But I don't think an experience of sexual abuse is in a privileged position relative to other bad things that happen in life — watching a parent murdered, for instance."

When he picked up on Tuesday morning after Easter, Kurtock tried to rehabilitate Isabella's casual use of statistics. One study, he led Hudson to admit, the Oppenheimer study, showed a 69 percent connection between bulimia and sexual abuse — again, using the broadest of definitions. "That could be very misleading, but technically could be construed as true," Hudson admitted, attacking the vagueness of definitions that made findings meaningless. "On the dance floor a kiss, if you find it unpleasant, is *sex abuse!*"

To a jury and observers hungry to know the truth about the connection between bulimia and sexual abuse, Hudson did concede that there was an emerging consensus, within the broad definitions, that "20 to 50 percent of patients with bulimia . . . and with major depression . . . would have had that kind of [sexual abuse] experience." But, he cautioned, in his and Pope's study on the causal connections, the very same percentage — 25 to 50 percent — of the general population *without* bulimia report sexual abuse — numbers that made any causal connection very dubious.

Kurtock tried to discredit Hudson as an overzealous pill pusher who never tried therapy. One of the defense's arguments was Holly's admitted resistance to taking Prozac or any other medication. "Do you think Holly was . . . a danger to herself or others for failure to take medication?" Kurtock asked. Hudson deftly turned the question to an attack on Isabella's and Rose's standard of care: "I think that she was severely ill . . . and that vigorous attempts should have been made to have her *take* medication treatment."

Kurtock had touched on some of the doubt and confusion among experienced eating disorder therapists about whether drugs really were a magic cure for bulimia. A cultural anthropologist, Margaret Mackenzie, citing her own studies on bulimia, believed that "too much bulimia gets cured by therapy, not drugs, to believe in genes and biology as the sole cause. Eating disorders are usually a metaphor for other disorders in a patient's life." Following the trial from her office in St. Helena, Sarah Boggs, the valley's best known eating disorders therapist, also saw metaphor in bulimia: "Purging is a violent act, a violent outlet for something suppressed. You have to stop the violence with antidepressants first — with Zoloft or Paxil, I get 60 to 70 percent response — then treat the cause." Like Hudson, she found no clear causal link between sexual abuse and bulimia. In her bulimic patients, there was a high incidence of sexual abuse, but not in all.

Addressing the controversy in answer to Kurtock's drugs-versus-therapy question — "And what do these studies show as to the effectiveness of cognitive behavioral treatments alone versus from use of medication alone?" — Hudson said, "People on medication treatment . . . or people with cognitive behavior . . . do better than people with no treatment." He denied that cognitive therapy was proving more effective than medication "to any statistically significant degree." Well after the trial, the FDA would approve Prozac to treat bulimia, citing research Hudson had helped conduct, which indicated that Prozac reduced bingeing episodes by two thirds and vomiting sessions by one half. Recent studies, though, were claiming that drugs can have a good short-term effect on bingeing and purging and depressive symptoms, but that better long-range results are being achieved by cognitive behavioral therapy, which replaces classical psychotherapy's prolonged dredging of the past with real-world modifications of attitude and behavior that often underlie the vicious eating patterns. Hudson personally believed that "family therapy can be an important component for an adolescent or young adult who's still very connected with their family."

Kurtock finished his cross-exam at 3:05 P.M. Tuesday. At one point, he had become so heated that he bared his teeth in apparent anger and frustration with the witness. His last question was a final aggressive demand for a yes or no answer: "Was Holly Ramona lying?" "I don't think she's consciously lying but saying things that I think are untrue," said Hudson, a scientist unwilling to give the black or white answers lawyers wanted. Hudson left the jury with the strong impression that it was Marche Isabella's suggestive therapy that had helped create Holly's false images of abuse, and that lack of medication had been a serious failure in the treatment of Holly's illnesses.

15

The Power of Suggestion

"**M**y name is Robert Mondavi. M-O-N-D-A-V-I. I'm in the wine business," said the seventy-nine-year-old man in the tan jacket, limping slightly as he took the stand on behalf of Gary Ramona. This craggy, still-handsome witness needed no credentials. The courtroom was full, expectant. Word was out that father and sons stood opposed in this trial; Tim and Michael would take the stand the following week. Nearly thirty years earlier, another Mondavi family feud had spilled into public view. Then it was the struggle of two brothers for the loyalty of their mother and the control of the family's winery, Krug. Robert had lost that struggle. His mother had died before they could reconcile, and he had been forced out of the family winery to start his own.

Now another deep and emotional division within the family was on view, this time over the fate of the man Michael Mondavi feared his father loved more than he loved his own sons. Again Robert Mondavi had lost, for he had seen his protégé banished, a tragedy he would tell the jury was "one of the worst things that ever happened in the winery." To his wife, Margrit Biever, sitting in the front row in court, it was worse than the death of a loved one, because a man had been condemned to a living death without trial or proof.

Mondavi would try to redeem some of the loss here in court. His answers forthright, blunt, and strong, he told the jury the intimate story of Gary's and the winery's interwoven rise to success. The Gary Ramona he knew was not the omniscient manipulator the defense had painted in its opening statements; he was a man who displayed "a lot of affection," who "was always open to suggestion, and would always do what was asked of him." This was the man, he said, whose share in Mondavi's success could be seen, by one measure, in case sales moving from "about twenty-eight, twenty-four thousand cases" in 1970 to, in 1990, "around two million cases." He told of the moment in 1986 when he pulled back to chairman and gave the reins of power to his sons, which led to an erratic tandem gallop for several years.

"Shocked" is how he felt when his sons came to him with the rumors of incest that had so distressed their wives. "My daughters-in-law were tremendously upset . . . They didn't want to have anyone who would molest a child be working for the company. And I agree with them. But I did not agree that he had molested a child. I know it more so now than ever before!" But his pleas had not been able to stop the spread of the poisonous rumor of the power of sodium amytal as a "truth serum," which they had all seized on as proof. "The rumor was like wildfire. Not only in the winery, but everywhere."

During the break he told the press, "I don't believe it *is* a truth serum. I didn't know that then. *But I know the man!* He works with his heart and soul. A man of great character. I think that more than ever. I feel he's an adopted son." With her hand on her husband's arm, Margrit added, "I just stood with Bob and said, 'This is not so.' All I had ever seen was caring, concern for his children, his wife . . . But he lost everything, much more than we can ever imagine."

The jury and the audience were again transfixed as Mondavi told how his and Margrit's cries for proof and justice had gone unheard. Gary's shoulders heaved with emotion as Bob read to the jury the leave-of-absence letter. The courtroom heard Mondavi confess, his strong voice close to breaking, that his sons "just outvoted me."

Harrington ended his direct examination with one carefully phrased question: "If these rumors of the sodium [amytal] had not happened, would any of this loss of employment have happened to Gary Ramona?"

"In my opinion, no," Mondavi replied.

For a moment in Sharon Chandler's cross-exam of Mondavi, she seemed to be getting what the defense wanted: Mondavi's admission that the Price Waterhouse report had not been a paper trail to set up Gary Ramona for termination. "Absolutely not!" Mondavi declared. There had been no hidden agenda. But Chandler's cool, brittle style could not stop or contain his impact as he spoke from the heart about his disagreement with his sons over whether Gary should go. Michael and Tim "thought they did it on business, but I also feel their subconscious mind . . . with this sodium [amytal] idea, and the wives being so concerned, I feel it had an effect on their judgment . . . They had reasons of their own I didn't agree with." Mondavi had revealed the subtle motives and emotions the Ramona affair had evoked in the valley's most famous family.

Leonard wanted to work Mondavi over before they released him from the stand, but Miroglio wouldn't let him. "You don't attack Bob Mondavi in Napa Valley." But Leonard asked two quick questions. "Did you raise your sons to always tell the truth?" "And do they always tell the truth?" Mondavi said yes to both as Miroglio whispered to Leonard, "Nicely done." At 11:04 A.M., Harrington said, "Thank you, Mr. Mondavi." "Is that it?" He laughed and gave Gary a hug.

As the Mondavis left the courthouse, they faced another loss. The *Register*'s Kevin Courtney caught them on the steps, where Bob managed a formal statement on the death of one of his mentors, the legendary winemaker André Tchelistcheff, the previous night.

Knowing the fireworks that would come in the train of Elizabeth Loftus's appearance the next day, Harrington turned down the emotional heat with two meat-and-potato witnesses from Southern California. Dr. Sherry Skidmore, a clinical MFCC and Ph.D. psychologist, and Dr. Richard Rada, a physician and hospital administrator, were there to do the job that — other than reconciliation with his family — Gary Ramona wanted most from his $2 million and four years' of pain and effort: reform of the therapy industry; reform of inadequate training, accrediting, and clinical practices; and a curbing of the greed of at least some of California's twenty-three thousand licensed MFCCs. Gary wanted "to prevent more Marche Isabellas." While Skidmore and Rada hammered in, again, that Isabella, Rose, and Western Medical Center had "fallen below the standard of care," the courtroom waited for Loftus, who brought to the stand, this time, four years of seasoning since *Franklin*.

Loftus had tied her hair back with a black ribbon, leaving tousled bangs curling around her face, framing fine-boned classic features. Wearing dark-rimmed glasses and a discreet but stylish double-breasted pearl gray jacket, she first helped Harrington lay down the requisite red carpet of credentials — math and psychology degrees, Phi Beta Kappa, summa cum laude, Stanford Ph.D., sabbaticals spent at Harvard, fellowships, prestigious associations, author of two hundred and fifty papers and eighteen books, the majority on memory. Then Harrington said, "Have you formed an opinion whether Holly Ramona's statements after March 15, 1990, can be taken as reliable evidence . . . ?"

"First of all, without corroboration," Loftus replied, "there is absolutely no way to know whether somebody's memory is a real memory or is a product of suggestion . . . I base the opinion . . . on several decades of work on how suggestion . . . and suggestive technique can and do lead to the creation of false memories and false beliefs." Then, turning directly to the jury, she said, "Memory does not work like a videotape recorder . . . we play back at a later time. The process is much more complex" and is divided "into three major stages." She left the witness box and walked over to an easel to illustrate her point with a series of boxes and lines. "Acquisition. Retention. Retrieval." She was lively, emotional, intelligent. A professor for twenty-one years, fully tenured at the University of Washington for ten, she knew how to hold a classroom's attention.

She drew lines to illustrate how, once a real event has been acquired and stored in memory, it was subject to contamination. As time passed, the old memory got weaker, like a fading battery, and became more and more vulnerable to invasion and contamination by new events and information flooding into the memory storage areas — images, fantasies, snippets and scenes of books, films, conversation. "That is really what memory *is* . . . a *reconstruction* . . . bits and pieces of our experiences, combining them with, perhaps, a few memory traces."

She moved on to her principal theme, suggestibility: how easy it was, in her own and others' studies, to implant false suggestions that were taken up as factual memory. She described her friend Dr. Stephen Ceci's studies on the distortions of children's memory, work that was bringing some healthy caution to the interviewing of child witnesses and helping to reverse the wrongful prison convictions of teachers jailed for life terms during the preschool sexual abuse hysteria. California's McMartin case came quickly to mind.

Her current work was showing that "you . . . can actually create an *entire memory*." Holding the jury's interest with her anecdotal style, she delivered "Lost in the Mall," the study that was swiftly becoming her signature, in which the false story was suggested, and *believed,* by 25 percent of the subjects.

Figures of authority — a medical doctor, a therapist, and hospital trappings — too, could be suggestive. "Is a therapist an authority figure?" Harrington asked her. That was, Loftus said, "a situation with an awful lot of suggestion." Loftus built a daunting list of suggestive events that, she believed, could have strengthened Holly's false memories: Marche Isabella's "verbal contagion" in the use of provocative but unproven terms like "emotional incest," "truth serum," and "generational rape"; in the trappings of authority, in the repetition of false information, in pushing the *sexual* explanation. As a whole, what happened "can only be characterized as a fairly outrageous degree of suggestion."

Loftus was demolishing the idea of memory as a neat, perfect tablet of truth to be retrieved intact, like artifacts in a sealed tomb. The defense wanted to close her down, and they wanted the plaintiff's charming expert to take her seat. She was, Leonard said like a pious preacher, "standing up lecturing down to the jury. And I don't think she has . . . a way of getting back to her chair gracefully."

But her boldest theater was yet to come. She was looking for an opening for a reference to the dog. She assumed that Prince had been brought up earlier because it was so potentially damaging to the defense, but she wanted to get it into her testimony, too. Holly's flashbacks of Prince should stretch the credibility of her memories in the jury's mind beyond what common sense could accept. She saw her opening when Harrington asked, "As the flashbacks get increasingly *lurid* . . . is there any scientific study . . . anywhere that shows that a person who has been continually abused sexually from ages five through sixteen has no memory of it?" She rolled it out: "There is no scientific support that you can be raped, molested, anally raped — and *bestiality,* spanning an eleven-year period, and totally forget about it, block it into your subconscious, and then reliably recover it later. *No* scientific support for this anywhere." The defense team leaped up to object. The jury was excused.

The defense would fight to the wall to keep the compromising memories out of the evidence — even though the judge had permitted them just days earlier. Evoking the old control theme, Kurtock growled that "the principal benefit of it is to allow Gary Ramona to slap his daughter." To punish, punish. Oh, no, said Harrington, Marche Isabella planted false memories, which followed a classic pattern and became implausible. That pattern must be shown. Knowing that any mention of Prince would be explosive, Miroglio, too, challenged the plantiff's motives. Were they saying that the defendants had "made up a bunch of stuff and put a time bomb in her that later exploded?" Loftus heard "time bomb" and squirmed, trying to catch Harrington's eye. Did he get it — that Isabella had planted a "time bomb" that was ticking toward an explosion of God-knows-what memories? As Harrington noticed her, she nodded and silently mouthed "Time bomb!" The "banty Irishman" moved fast on his feet. Raising his voice to a ringing pitch, he declared, "I think, Your Honor, that Mr. Miroglio got it just right! These defendants planted a *time bomb!*" By implanting false memory, they caused continuing damage because the elaborations reinforced Holly's false belief.

How dare Harrington blame the therapist for Holly's getting "sicker and sicker" after her memories? Carolyn Thompson fumed as she sat in the courtroom with her two children. Of course you got worse. "You can't let this information in without being devastated," as Carolyn knew from her own agony. "Everybody was saying, 'Quit . . . You were a thousand times better . . . it's destroying you, destroying the children.' It took years, years . . . to crawl out of it." The books warned you clearly. "Do not confuse healing with the absence of pain, for healing wounds, whether physical or emotional, always hurt," *Repressed Memories* had said; *The Courage to Heal* had warned that this "emergency stage" could lead to suicide attempts, self-mutilation, total incapacitation to carry on normal life.

But Harrington had made a strong point: you could not ignore Holly's later memories, for they were the direct and inevitable product of the first. They were continuing detonations of the same time bomb. His voice cracked as he went on: "Number one they planted a false memory . . . and Holly is still suffering from it because she's now producing these increasingly bizarre mental productions."

"I don't like the idea of bringing in evidence that's viewed as lurid," said Snowden as he ruled that Holly's postamytal flashbacks could be admitted into testimony. "I'm sorry to say, however, this case is about lurid recollections . . . This is a lurid case." "Prince" would become one of the trial's bywords, like "Gerner," full of meaning for those who were there.

Back on the stand before the jury, Loftus sought her opportunity to talk about Prince. She found her moment as Harrington reminded her of "confabulation," a word she had already added to the jury's vocabulary — "the filling of gaps in your memory" that could "come from suggestion, from inferences, from implausibilities" . . . Confabulation results "when we plant seeds of false memory . . . and exert some pressure on the individual to produce more memories. They will produce more memories . . . more detail, more examples, more sensory information."

Were Holly's memories "a process of increasing elaboration?" asked Harrington.

"Yes," Loftus confirmed. In her review of the case, Holly's flashes were preceded "by sexual abuse expectations followed by sexualized interpretation . . . and more flashes which are . . . more unusual, let's say . . . over many, many more years . . . many more activities . . . and finally bestiality and sex with a dog. I'm not sure it's ended yet, but that's where it ended in my last review." Attorneys knew that "once a bell has been rung, you can't unring it." Twice Loftus had rung "bestiality" in the jury's ears.

The bailiff, Larry Fontana, was disturbed, with Loftus's mention of bestiality, to see a young woman with two children sitting on "Holly's side." Why would you bring kids here? This wasn't Disneyland.

In cross-exam, Loftus handled Holly's memories far more gently than Hudson had when he declared with "a medical certainty" that they were false. When Kurtock asked her, "Can you testify that Holly's memories of sexual abuse are inaccurate?" she responded, "I can't say they're false . . . I don't think they're trustworthy." "Do you think there is any evidence that Holly was lying?" he asked. "No, I don't . . . I see no evidence that she was deliberately lying. False beliefs, false memories, false constructions — we're talking about people who are trying to tell the truth."

Both Leonard and Kurtock attacked Loftus for her lack of clinical experience. As an academic researcher, they implied, she was out of touch with the clinical reality of repressed memories and was ill equipped to judge the truth of Holly's memories. Leonard came close to scoffing as he demanded, "Just for the sake of clarity, you've never conducted a clinical practice in your entire career, am I correct?" "Correct," she admitted, musing to herself that she was constantly asked the question and yet "the little darlings on the other side don't have to be clinicians. Linda Meyer Williams, who has done the study most widely cited now, is *not* a clinician — she's a sociologist!"

Now Miroglio and Leonard tried to poke holes in the validity of her research — her subjects were healthy students, not traumatized children; her success in false memory implants was only "20 percent" ("sometimes 80 percent," she corrected), and the false memories she did plant didn't seem to last very long. True, there hadn't been time yet for long-term followup. But Loftus offered a compelling defense of her research. In over twenty-five years of doing several hundred studies involving perhaps twenty thousand people, she had not distorted all, but certainly a portion, of her subjects' memories. "And I believe that the *mechanism* by which we can convince people that they were lost, frightened, and crying in a mall is *the same kind of process* of influence." She couldn't resist voicing her concern that "our uncritical acceptance of every dubious claim" increases the suffering of genuine victims. To Miroglio's final question, "As you sit here today, you cannot rule out that, in fact, Holly Ramona is one of those innocent sufferers of sex abuse?" Loftus responded, "I can't rule it out." She swept out of the courtroom and was gone.

As Leonard feared, Loftus's stand-and-deliver memory lecture had been effective. Her candor had disarmed the jury. She had said "some things that maybe favored the other side, but she answered it honestly. Open and honest," thought Marty Cook.

The march of witnesses went on. Rada returned, as did the economist who justified Gary's claim of $8 million damages. Dr. Leon Epstein, the towering, square-jawed psychiatrist from the prestigious Langley Porter Institute at UC San Francisco, had seen Gary twice in June 1992 and gave the defense a gift. When asked in cross-exam whether Gary Ramona could have suffered the *same* symptoms Epstein diagnosed as adjustment disorder if he had done what his daughter alleged, Epstein answered, "Yes." But the courtroom observers quickly grew impatient with the bit players on this epic stage, and they stirred with excitement when word spread during lunch that Marche Isabella and Richard Rose — then Stephanie Ramona, if they could find her — would appear next. Isabella and Rose had become familiar fixtures in their seats behind the defense attorneys' table throughout the trial. Rose, neat, serious, wearing glasses, had never smiled. Isabella sat with her chin up, attentive. The aquiline nose and weak chin of her profile, her porcelain skin, rouged cheeks, and thick, wavy blond hair had become indelibly familiar to the regulars. But after nearly four weeks of testimony, the jury had not yet heard a word from either one.

"We're seeking to subpoena Mrs. Ramona, but we've been unsuccessful so far," Harrington reported as a big television set was hooked up in court. On this hot day, the jurors were not happy to learn that they would be watching three hours of clips from Marche Isabella's depositions before hearing from the lady herself. But it proved to be an interesting afternoon at the movies.

Isabella had struck Miroglio as the defense's most vulnerable client. Her depositions had not been strong; now they were coming back to haunt her in court. The first clip was from her first deposition, for Holly's lawsuit, when she'd faced Harrington with no attorney at her side. In a prim black and white print dress with a white Pilgrim collar, she was every inch the righteous young woman who had studied Christian education in college. Her statements expressing uncritical belief in Holly's memories would later help Gary's case.

"I believe everything that Holly told me . . . Holly second-guesses everything . . . The reality was too painful . . . This is what Holly reported to me. I take it as *true.*" Of Holly's statement while she was under the sodium amytal that her father had said her grandmother had been raped by her brothers, Isabella said on the tape, "Holly stated it. I have no reason not to believe it." She had defined repression as "a memory that has occurred on a subconscious level you have chosen not to remember because the emotional pain is too great for you to deal with." While soon both she and Holly would claim that the sodium amytal interview was all Holly's idea, Isabella said in her depositions, "The sodium amytal interview was my idea . . . I informed Stephanie Ramona that this is what we're going to do." Isabella had told Rose that she wanted "to verify" that Holly's memories were "completely accurate."

Some jurors heard a flip edge to her voice when she was asked why they hadn't taped the interview: "We didn't decide not to. We never considered it." To Holly's question of whether she had told the truth in the interview, Isabella and Rose had said, "We all assured her" she had. Rose had told Isabella that you would have to be trained to lie under the drug. She had later told Gary Ramona that sodium amytal is "kind of like a truth serum . . . like in the movies."

Isabella was led into an easy, jargony discussion of what she had said to Holly about her father's sexual look being "emotional incest" — that giving a sexual look, or even being seen in his underwear or a tight bathing suit, could be a perpetration of emotional incest that could cause trauma later in life. While Isabella was finding incest even in a tight bathing suit, Harrington pointed out in the video that the hospital nurse had reported, before the amytal, that Holly was very vague and "feels that maybe nothing really happened . . . Holly vacillated back and forth on what she would remember at that time." Holly "does not get a major memory of everything that occurred all at once. It's a gradual process." Isabella recalled, too, that Holly had remembered almost nothing from the sodium amytal interview, words she would later change.

In the second deposition, wearing a mauve floral dress, Isabella was a little more guarded as she read from her notes of Holly's reported flashbacks: the snake in her vagina; Kathy the babysitter having surrogate sex with Holly. Explaining why Gary had never been asked about the charges before the March 15 confrontation, Isabella stated that "you don't typically report to a perpetrator what is going on" — clear evidence that Gary was already guilty in her mind.

One of the most memorable moments for the jury came with Isabella's admission that, since starting her practice two years earlier, she had seen "maybe two thousand different people, possibly — in- and outpatients." She also revealed that she kept fewer and fewer notes — "I hate notes," she said — and that she had taken no notes of the sodium amytal interview. Nell Sweeney was disturbed by this. "She said she could remember her patients week to week without a lot of notes, but she also said she was seeing two thousand patients. I'm sorry, no one's memory is so good." To Gary, the two-thousand-patient load sounded like "a money machine. She was not in business to help people. Just to make money." The mass production numbers would look even worse when a defense witness, a distinguished psychiatrist, claimed that he routinely had perhaps forty patients in his clinical practice.

In the third deposition, the video showed a listless, unhappy woman deep in a malpractice lawsuit. She was far less forthcoming. The busy print of her dress almost camouflaged her against the patterned wallpaper of a Washington hotel room. Now the jury saw Harrington expose her as inadequate to treating a young woman seriously ill with depression and bulimia: Isabella had only a vague memory of classes and texts she had studied; she had had loose supervision as a trainee therapist and few specific courses in eating disorders.

It was a long day at the movies. The therapist's ordeal showed in the color picture on the *Register*'s front page the next day — Isabella stood alone, her arms crossed over her chest in a gesture of resignation, her eyes lifeless and unfocused, her face drained of expression.

The next morning, Isabella herself took the stand in a flower-sprigged black dress with a white lace collar. Her light, lilting voice was carefully modulated to keep the tone sweet with a biting edge to the words — like smiling through gritted teeth. The change in her from the first deposition was breathtaking. Presenting a scrupulously professional air, she lectured fluidly on Freud, the Oedipal complex, and adolescent sexuality. She assured the court that she had, at the outset, urged Holly to see a psychiatrist, to think about Prozac. "Holly refused . . . Holly said, 'I don't like medication. I don't want anything to control me.' . . . Holly is as stubborn as her father." She smiled.

She had planted the seed of her central theme: Holly as a powerful, stubborn, independent person immune to suggestion or persuasion — traits that had scarcely been part of her personality profile. She described the moment when Holly emerged from the sodium amytal, confident at last that she wasn't crazy, the doubting little bird now strong as an eagle, ready to fly off secure in her truth. "No, we didn't tell her she was telling the truth," Isabella affirmed, casting herself as a benign facilitator of truths Holly had known all along. Sodium amytal had only reinforced her memories, giving Holly "a sense of continuity . . . that, Okay, I can believe me now . . . She now had confidence in her *own* memories."

Laying the foundation of her own innocence of planting sexual fantasies, Isabella confirmed that the first months of therapy with Holly had been empty of sexual content — that, in fact, in her very first meeting with Stephanie she had suggested possible *medical* causes of abuse images — and that the first breath of sexual content, the "sexual look," had not appeared until January 1990. It was Stephanie, not Isabella, who had first brought up molestation, she recalled. And "I believe the first report of anything that we could construe as possible physical touching was February 13, '90." After a day and a half of testimony, Isabella had transformed herself from a chatty and unguarded woman who had not yet been sued to a well-rehearsed witness backed by a line of insurance lawyers in an $8 million lawsuit; her New York insurers had their man there, sitting quietly in the courtroom. She had become a conservative therapist to whom, one imagined, the very term "sex abuse" would be alien and distasteful.

For the jury, however, the more mainstream and professional Isabella appeared on the stand, the more her depositions screamed out in

Attorneys escort Holly into court for her testimony on behalf of her therapists. FROM LEFT: Ed Leonard, Holly, Bruce Miroglio, and Neil Shapiro, Stephanie Ramona's lawyer. *(Al Francis)*

Richard Harrington, Gary's attorney, argues for a
malpractice verdict against the therapists charged
with implanting false memories in Holly's mind.
(T. J. Salsman, Napa Valley Register)

Holly is comforted by her
mother after an emotional
moment in her testimony.
*(T. J. Salsman, Napa Valley
Register)*

The Ramona women stand by Holly as she testifies.
FROM LEFT: Kelli, Shawna, Stephanie, and Stephanie's
mother, Betty Nye. *(T. J. Salsman, Napa Valley Register)*

Under the watchful eyes of past judges, Superior Court Judge Scott Snowden orchestrates Napa's first internationally publicized landmark trial, *Ramona* v. *Isabella*. *(Christie Johnston)*

The defendants. ABOVE: a grim Marche Isabella. BELOW, a reflective Richard Rose, the psychiatrist who conducted Holly's controversial sodium amytal interview, flanked by Isabella and her attorney, Jeffrey Kurtock. *(T. J. Salsman, Napa Valley Register)*

A reunion of jurors at the courthouse.
FROM LEFT, BACK ROW: Tim Holewinske,
Ken Keri, Marcellous Cook;
FRONT ROW: Beth Clark, Yolanda Nash,
Rebecca Strunk, Keith Himmelman.
(Christie Johnston)

Tom Dudum, the foreman,
kept the jury focused
on evidence, not emotion,
during deliberations.
(Christie Johnston)

the Napa Valley
Register

Home Delivery 28 Cents a Day

131st Year No. 232   Friday, April 1, 1994   35 Cents

Evening of Honor
Fourteen public safety officers will be recognized tonight at the annual Napa Chamber of Commerce Evening of Honor. Several were cited for heroism. Each was selected by his or her public safety department as officer of the year.
See Page 1C

RON BELL/REGISTER

Dr. Robert Gerner, the director of the Center for Mood Disorders in Los Angeles, responds to questioning in court Thursday.

Recovered memory trial
Attorney attacks witness's credibility with sex revelation

By EMELYN CRUZ LAT
Register Staff Writer

NAPA — The participants in the "recovered memory" trial playing out in Napa were in recess today, giving them time to consider a startling revelation from the plaintiff's expert witness Thursday.

Former Robert Mondavi Winery executive Gary Ramona is suing marriage, family and child counselor Marche Isabella and psychiatrist Richard Rose for allegedly planting false memories of childhood sexual abuse in the mind of his 23-year-old daughter

Holly, who emerged from therapy convinced she was raped by him.

Dr. Robert Gerner, the director of the Center for Mood Disorders in Los Angeles, testified Thursday morning against the therapists, citing unprofessional conduct. But cross-examination of Gerner revealed Thursday afternoon that he himself had agreed to a confidential out-of-court settlement with a patient with whom he had a sexual relationship.

Defense attorneys repeatedly attacked Gerner's credibility as an objective witness in the case.

"Isn't it true you felt empathy for Gary Ramona who was accused of sexually molesting his daughter?" questioned Napa attorney Bruce Miroglio.

"I didn't even know him then," replied psychiatrist Gerner, who conducted psychological tests on Holly in 1991.

"You were accused of doing the very thing we're talking about — taking advantage of a therapeutic relationship. You allowed (a patient) to orally copulate you in your office?" fired back Miroglio.

"Not allowed," Gerner responded.

"It took place?" the attorney asked.

"Yeah" said Gerner.

During testimony Gerner denied any misconduct in the incident, but the revelations came as a surprise to Ramona's attorney, Richard Harrington, who objected to the questions.

The California Medical Board is in the process of reviewing the case and has not taken any action at this time, Gerner said.

The testimony brought a surprise ending to the ninth day of

See RAMONA, Page 2A

The psychiatrist Robert Gerner became the most sensational witness at the trial as his own sexual ethics violations were revealed. *(Ron Bell, Napa Valley Register)*

A famed child trauma expert, psychiatrist Lenore Terr argued for the authenticity of Holly's memories. *(Al Francis)*

The psychologist Elizabeth Loftus, a leading researcher and court witness on the suggestibility of memory, argued that Holly's flashbacks were unreliable. *(Courtesy Elizabeth Loftus)*

As eating disorder experts for Gary Ramona, the research psychiatrists Harrison Pope (LEFT) and James Hudson proposed that Holly's bulimia and depression were possible sources of her flashbacks of sexual abuse. *(Christie Johnston)*

If the mysteries of recovered memories are ever solved, it will be through the work of leading scientists like Harvard psychologist Daniel Schacter, here examining PET scans, which for the first time show the living brain in the act of remembering. *(Christie Johnston)*

Vindicated by the jury but stripped of his former life and family, Gary Ramona tries to rebuild with his partner, Barbara Stewart. *(Christie Johnston)*

Stephanie Ramona, saddened by the verdict, leaves the courthouse still loyal to her daughter's memories. *(Al Francis)*

contrast. In Harrington's hands, she was being revealed as the worst thing a witness can be — inconsistent.

"And you told them that it was a truth serum?"

"That's a misstatement, Mr. Harrington!" Isabella declared, emotion breaking her modulation. "I did not tell them it was a truth serum. I never believed it was a truth serum."

"Well, you told them they couldn't lie under it unless they were trained, isn't that true?"

"That was my understanding at the time."

"It's totally false, isn't it?"

"I would imagine, depending on the person," Isabella answered limply. Harrington led her into Holly's deteriorating condition in January 1990. In a sweet, controlled voice she described the horrors of bulimia and major depression left unattended for five months — and untreated by drugs until summer.

"Her depression was getting worse on the twenty-third of January, isn't that true?"

"Yes, the symptoms of depression increased."

"How often was she binging and purging . . . ?"

"It was probably getting up to about four times a week . . . may have been more than once in one day."

"Bulimia can be fatal, isn't that true?"

"Absolutely."

Cheerleading in the hall at lunchtime, Miroglio told the media, "Harrington is getting *waxed* by Marche Isabella. Now you're getting a chance to see what she's really like. Isn't she *terrific!*" Miroglio, who suffered inside as he said it, claimed she was proving to be "one of the major stars." By late afternoon, her star was falling.

On Monday, April 18, after a five-day break, Harrington the showman was ready for a climactic finale. Isabella had flared with indignation on one of the deposition tapes when she had been forced to confess that she subscribed to only one professional magazine and a bimonthly newsletter and that she couldn't remember the "big book" where she read that "80 percent of individuals with eating disorders have been sexually abused at some point in their life." As he pushed her again for the name of the "big book" — a book by Garfinckel, she thought — Harrington picked up a huge armload of textbooks, slammed them down before her, and said, "I've brought all the books

Professor Garfinckel ever wrote . . . *Show* me where . . . sex abuse [as cause] for eating disorders appears in any of those books." The moment summed up her lack of scholarship and the flimsy basis of her "proofs" of Ramona's guilt.

In closing, Harrington stood next to one of the huge blowups of her depositions that he used for emphasis and asked, "Suppose a patient presented reports to you . . . under sodium amytal . . . of numerous incidents of witchcraft that they had been subjected to. Would you take those as true . . . ?"

"I would have to look at the whole clinical picture as well as . . . the interview," said Isabella.

Harrington moved inexorably to the blowup and read: "Page 172, line 20. Question: 'Well, now, suppose the patient presented reports of numerous incidents of witchcraft that they had been subjected to. You would take those as true if the patient reliably reported that under sodium amytal; is that right?' Answer: 'My own personal opinion, I would probably accept that as true if the patient reported that under a sodium amytal interview . . .'" No equivocation could erase the words. Harrington read on: "'. . . in conjunction with all of the other aspects of the personality that I had observed. My medical background proves that a lab test is only good in conjunction with all the other aspects of the examination.'" Taking his glasses off, Harrington, reminding Isabella that she was a licensed vocational nurse, asked her bluntly, "Do you have any other medical background?"

"Not specifically . . ."

"I have nothing further, Your Honor," he said, as Isabella stepped from the stand.

The retractor, Deborah David, was welcomed like everyone's child as she and her husband joined a False Memory summit meeting at a lunch orchestrated by Jack Carver at the Chinese restaurant on First Street. Still alienated from their daughters, several Northern Californians had come to Napa to hear the two major "culprits" of the case, Rose and Isabella. There was Rudy Laubscher down from Sacramento. Charles Caviness up from Marin County. Jack and Pat Collier from Santa Cruz.

"The Mondale Act. That's what really let this thing get out of hand," said Jack Collier, referring to the 1974 Child Abuse Prevention and Treatment Act, which made the reporting of child abuse mandatory and set up a bureaucracy of child protective services dependent for its funding, this group felt, on the number of reports of abuse. It had made child abuse a growth industry that had spawned false accusations. Until the matching federal funds that made it so profitable was halted, the epidemic would continue, they feared. The New Age magazines that bred like flies in Marin County were still loaded with recovered memory therapists' ads, Caviness reported. But there was good news. Some of the horrendous prison terms assigned at the height of the preschool sex abuse hysteria were being reversed. There was a buzz about Kelly Michaels, recently freed after serving five years of her forty-seven-year jail sentence for more than a hundred incidents of abuse in the notorious Wee Care case — the verdict overturned, her case dismissed. Articles by Dorothy Rabinowitz in *Harper's* and the *Wall Street Journal* and by Debbie Nathan in the *Village Voice* were proving instrumental in exposing these travesties. They hoped Lawrence Wright's *New Yorker* series a year earlier and Richard Ofshe's new book, *Making Monsters,* would free Paul Ingram in Olympia, Washington. The tide was turning. But the parents at this table had no idea if their own daughters would ever come home. Tears filled his eyes as Jack Collier read his fortune cookie: "There is no grief which time does not lessen and soften."

Just after the lunch break, as Rose was about to take the stand, Judge Snowden lowered the boom on the audience. He was fed up with all the partisan gestures and facial expressions. He had been patient. But the jury could be affected by this display. Through the cross-exams of the last few witnesses, Jean Sawday had chuckled and silently but visibly cheered at every point struck against Gary Ramona. They didn't know her name, but the jurors had been noticing her. "Every time something would come up, she would go 'Uh-huh' and start talking to someone next to her," Tim observed. Yolanda had also been distracted by "the lady with the shoulder-length brown hair" — Katy Butler, a consulting editor for *Family Therapy Networker* — "who was always talking to her, taking notes, and had a guy come in with a computer." "Talk about body language," Ken Keri thought, watching Ed Leonard. "Oh, boy, did he make facial expressions," thought Tom. Leonard redeemed himself by being "very funny," Yolanda felt. Snowden was not amused. In the sternest voice he had yet used, he warned the room: "I get complaints from the attorneys . . .

appropriately raised, about members of the audience making gestures, facial expressions, and sounds to indicate either support or disapproval. That's going to have to stop. So if anybody does do anything like that anymore, I'm going to have them removed."

It was time for Harrington to call Richard Rose to the stand. Miroglio was relieved that he'd caught Rose's Maui deposition in the Hawaiian shirts and kept the video away from the jury. He also kept out the fact that Rose had left the practice of medicine and moved to Hawaii; the judge had agreed it was "not relevant." But before Harrington started his questions, Miroglio heard him slip out the comment, "Well, when Dr. Rose's deposition was taken in Maui, Hawaii . . ." Miroglio "flipped out," just as he had when he first saw the video; he strode to the bench and said, "Judge, what the hell is going on here?" Harrington apologized, promising not to do it again. "The man has no moral compass," Miroglio railed inside as Rose's testimony began.

The picture Rose painted on the stand was of two well-meaning professionals who had lost control to the formidable will of a distraught and determined young woman, a lifelong mouse whose roar, suddenly awakened, could not be denied. As he increasingly disclaimed support of using sodium amytal with Holly, the ethical question grew: Why, then, had he and Isabella done it? Why had they, as a team, done several of these interviews if they were, as they now claimed, of no help in learning the truth? Why had Rose, Holly's physician, not prescribed Prozac instead? The $14,000 hospital bill plus their own bills posed a possible answer: an incestuous marriage of convenience between therapist, psychiatrist, and hospital to generate cash flow and fill hospital beds in a belt-tightening health care economy in which Western Medical Center was losing $3 million a year. It was an easy target for Harrington.

Meeting and evaluating Holly, Rose had faced a number of symptoms — of depression, bulimia, and terrifying flashbacks. "I strongly recommended Prozac to her, but she refused to take it." Her mood had been one of desperation, he confirmed. She needed to know if her memories were true. "She thought she was going crazy." Relenting, Rose had given Holly 600 milligrams of sodium amytal, and, unrecorded, Holly talked from the dreamy half-sleep of the drug of sexual images, of "a shadowy image, but . . . the quality of her thoughts . . . was that this is my father, I feel it's my father," Rose had observed. As Holly emerged from the twilight world of the hypnotic drug, Rose and

Isabella told her what she had said. Rose calmed her doubts by reassuring, "as I did many times in the hospital, 'No, I don't think you're lying,'" and released her to confront her father.

"Were you concerned at any time that the procedure might result in false memories?" was Harrington's final question.

"Yes," said Rose, very soberly.

The jury was picking up discrepancies from both Isabella and Rose. "Uh-oh," thought Tim. "Dr. Rose *telling* us about his purpose for the sodium amytal interview is different from when he wrote down on the hospital record that the purpose was to *verify*." After what Tim had heard, "I probably wouldn't be giving it to her at all." The tactic to shift responsibility to Holly was having some effect on Marty Cook, though. "I don't think the therapists were just manipulating her, I think she manipulated the therapists." But the strategy was backfiring. "It seems like they were letting Holly guide. *They're* the professionals. He's the doctor," Marty was thinking. "Rose should have given her more medication. He shouldn't have let Holly convince him to give [her] sodium amytal . . . He should have gone in and said, 'No, I won't do this.'"

Miroglio was fond of Rose. "But he didn't come across as well as he does in person . . . It's my analysis that he didn't do a particularly good job on the stand." The jury wanted more emotion from Rose, he felt.

When at last, six weeks into the trial, Rose decided "to break my silence" and issue a press release revealing his and his wife's decision to make major career changes — "to move to the most wonderful place on the face of the earth" and to buy a commercial printing business on Maui — the news raised not a stir in the corridors. Win or lose, Rose and Isabella were making legal history as the first therapists to be tried for recovered memory malpractice by a nonpatient; if they lost, *Ramona v. Isabella* would be remembered as a defeat for their profession. But as Carolyn Thompson, in the audience, said — as most in the courtroom felt — "I always thought it was Gary versus Holly, not Gary versus the therapists." The two major defendants had become footnotes in their own lawsuit.

Harrington had been ordered by the judge to finish by the following morning. Gary's partisans were tense as the last moments of the plaintiff's case ticked away. Since they hadn't found Stephanie, Harrington told the judge he planned, instead, to read briefly from her deposition. Snowden cut in: "Then you'll say 'I rest'?" "Yes," said

Harrington. After weeks of painstaking, often tedious, repetitious work through every point and witness, he would be done in ten minutes.

First, however, he would give the jury a glimpse of Stephanie to hold in mind during the days the defense held the floor. Playing a videotape of her deposition, he read his question to her: "Did Marche Isabella tell you '80 percent of bulimics had been sexually abused?'" and then her response: "She said, after I kept at her about it — yes. I think she did."

"Did she give you any other causes of bulimia?"

"I think she may have said to me something about a, uh, a pattern . . . a pattern. I don't know. She gave me a number of reasons, I believe."

As he heard Stephanie's words stumble and drift off into uncertainty, Miroglio felt a pang in his gut. Holly was in town. He'd work with her again that evening. She'd be on the stand the next day. She'd knock them dead. But Stephanie still held the risk of being an awesome hazard — or one of their best witnesses.

At 10:38 A.M. it was over. Snowden directed himself to Harrington, a scarcely containable grin playing at the corners of his mouth: "Does that conclude the plaintiff's case?"

"Yes, Your Honor, the plaintiff rests."

The defense was coming, and an air of agitated excitement spread through the courtroom. But Judge Snowden seized the half-hour hiatus between attack and defense to issue his final ruling on the "cause of action" issue that had run as a leitmotif throughout *Ramona v. Isabella*. The defense lawyers made one last energetic attempt to convince him that he should accept their motion for "nonsuit," halt the trial, and send them all home. Then Snowden turned to the courtroom.

"It has a salient emotionalism to it," he said of the trial he saw as really two trials, "the trial in the hallway wherein . . . the soap opera of the case is played out . . . and that which occurs here in the courtroom . . ." Ejected again and sensing drama, the jury fumed. "It's unfair," thought Tim, "I feel totally cheated, totally manipulated." They felt they were being denied important information. Several jurors pressed close to the door, trying unsuccessfully to listen, while Snowden delivered his ruling on the defense motion for nonsuit. This was the motion, he explained, "made at the end of the plaintiff's case asking that the plaintiff be denied the opportunity to have the jury even decide the case." The lawyers had raised three issues. It was the third, the old "cause of action" issue, already "argued before me twice," that was "the most interesting and compelling and difficult one in this case . . . It brings into conflict . . . several really important policies in the law. This is the question of whether a father may maintain a lawsuit against the therapists or other health care providers of his daughter alleging that he was damaged by their negligent treatment of her.

"On the one hand, the defendants argue, if you allow nonpatients to sue health care providers, it will have a terrible, chilling effect" on the delivery of the health care the patient needs to receive. "Of equal significance, however . . . is the question of what is somebody . . . to do if confronted with the unfounded and incorrect accusation of having molested [his daughter] which results in his loss of everything? . . . For those of you that are interested in the emotionalism . . . it certainly is a compelling and interesting case. But for those of you that are interested in the law . . . *this* is the great and interesting issue of *Ramona v. Isabella*."

It was in the fluid and fast-changing tort actions of the courtroom — not in the legislature's statutes — that these conflicts in social policy were being resolved and new law forged, law that in turn became part of the dynamic body of concepts "handed down through cases and through traditions, through precedents, according to which we regulate ourselves as a society." This neighborhood courtroom was, for Snowden, the nerve center of the civil society.

Returning to Gary Ramona, he said, "I have found that a duty did exist to him by reason of the circumstances of the case under Supreme Court law . . . which I have found still exists": *Molien v. Kaiser Hospital*. "The defense lawyers have argued that I should view the *Molien* case as being history; that the Supreme Court has whittled away at it so far that it no longer exists. And I'd be arguing the same thing in their place . . . But it's quite clear, I think, that the *Molien* case is still the law, because the Supreme Court has had numerous opportunities . . . to simply say it is no longer the law." Yet, just recently, the Supreme Court had "stressed that the reason Mr. Molien had a cause of action was because of the instruction to his wife to go home and tell him about the diagnosis of her" — the misdiagnosis of syphilis that had destroyed conjugal trust and, ultimately, their marriage.

Think, he said, how similar that is to the Ramona case. "Not only did somebody tell the patient, go home and tell your father, but, in fact, the father was summoned to the meeting and the confrontation and presentation of the charge occurred. There is no question in my mind . . . doing the job I'm supposed to do . . . that that cause of action exists in California today." He denied the motion for nonsuit.

Snowden finished up. "I am not expressing an opinion as to how I think the jury will or how the jury ought to resolve this case. We're only halfway through . . . I am simply now . . . ordering the case to go forward." He nodded to Fontana. "Would you bring the jury in . . ."

The defense began. Ed Leonard stood to deliver his opening statement at last. Designed as a strategy to separate the hospital from the other two defendants, it now became an opportunity to prepare the jury for Holly, who would appear, center stage, in less than twenty-four hours. He delivered a taut chronology of the events in Holly's life that had led to this moment in court, weaving in a submotif that had not been raised before this trial — that Holly had known, even when she denied to her mother that her father had molested her, that it was her father, that "she had always known." In his final minutes, Leonard deftly led from the stubborn young woman who had insisted on sodium amytal and the confrontation to the little girl in need of help. As he closed, he called on the compassion of this group of twelve mothers, fathers, brothers, and sisters and placed Holly's care — her future — in their hands. When it came time to deliberate, "as you sit there in that room and look around at those eleven other faces . . . you're going to determine, Who can Holly turn to? Who can Holly trust? Who's going to believe Holly?" He paused and scanned each face in the jury. "Why, it's *you.*"

The judge's gift to the jury, restless after four weeks of intensity and emotion, was the afternoon off. Miroglio was restless for his chance to stage his side of the case. To rehabilitate Isabella and Rose on the stand. To fire *their* big guns. He was feeling that Gary had done a much better job of public relations and influencing minds than the defense had. He felt that most of the court — the bailiff, clerks, court reporters, the judge — came in believing Gary was innocent. "That's all we heard." He felt the press only played Gary's side of it. "And the people in this town were absolutely hostile to us . . . I was getting people contacting me through my parents and my neighbors, saying, 'Well, you know, I don't want anything bad for Bruce. But I sure hope that the guy gets those sons of bitches.'" His mom and dad were fiercely loyal; they'd tell people they ought to wait and hear the whole story, but it hurt them, he knew. Miroglio had snuck away a couple of times to go to his sons' Little League games. "And I'd sit at the Little League park in St. Helena in my suit after court all day so I could see my son bat, and have people come up and say, 'How could they do that to that poor guy?' It's my job, but I'm not immune to it."

The defense was clearing land mines before their offensive. They had been unhappy over Gary's positioning himself so close to the jury since the beginning of the trial. "The judge never lets a client sit and get in the jury's face like that. I can't believe that Scott's letting him get away with it," Miroglio had fumed. He'd noticed, too, that Gary had gradually turned his chair so that it more directly faced the jury. Wanting no manipulative grandstanding from Gary to distract the jury from Holly, he finally fussed to the judge: "Your Honor . . . Mr. Ramona is sitting right here in the jury's lap and . . . I would once again request that he sit back with the rest of the clients." Kurtock chimed in, "Next time . . . he's going to stick his hand out and shake everybody's hand." "I haven't noticed a problem . . . but, Mr. Harrington, he should remain with you when the jury comes in," Snowden urged, a futile request.

Gary was angry, thinking, "Cheap shots. Complaining about I'm looking them in the eye. I'm the closest to the jury box. Well, *of course!* I've had nothing to hide from day one. And I'm the one who was accused. I'm the plaintiff that's saying this is not true. I'm the one who was totally humiliated — not one of the jurors. Certainly not any of the attorneys. Who's the person who has everything to lose? Me. Nobody else. Even Richard will be all done at the end. Everybody will be done. God bless them, but they pack up and go. They walk!" Gary would not budge.

Snowden had some final housekeeping on the eve of the major counteroffensive: assigning the principals seats for their families the next day, assigning twenty seats for the media. He warned everyone: "Be here early!"

16

Holly's Day in Court

Just before 9:30 A.M. on Wednesday, April 20, 1994, Holly Ramona and her entourage slipped quietly into the Napa courthouse and up the exit staircase, out of sight of the crowd that awaited them. The press and the spectators had been lining up behind barriers since seven o'clock, the regulars joined by onlookers drawn by the previous night's *Ramona* segment on the NBC tabloid *Hard Copy*. That evening a competing tabloid on ABC, *Inside Edition,* would be airing its report on the trial being touted as a major showdown for recovered memories and the therapy profession, rushing to beat out NBC's *Dateline,* which had elbowed in and won more interviews than anybody. Now the European press was here, joining *Time, People,* Reuters, and the rest of the media mob. Photographers in the hall rushed to catch Holly through the wall of women who surrounded her, following the buzz as she approached. Running interference, Ed Leonard led her swiftly through the crowd into the courtroom, leaving only fleeting impressions of the girl everyone had waited weeks to see.

Holly, Kelli, and Shawna filed into the courtroom. They did not turn their heads to acknowledge their grandmother Garnet as they walked past her and joined their mother in the front row on the right. The entire courtroom stirred, trying to get a better look. Stephanie seemed more glamorous than she'd looked in the deposition clip, wearing a pale gray silk blazer and a long, slim white linen skirt, her signature slash of pale lipstick giving a sensual pout to her lower lip. The perfect blond mane of hair framed a beautiful, impassive face masked by fastidious makeup. Kelli, who had flown in from Colorado, looked sporty and attractive. Shawna, the tall, fair seventeen-year-old with the lilting carriage, bloomed with a fresh, natural beauty. Betty Nye, sitting with them, was the conservative matriarch in her classic blazer.

"She looks just like her dad" was what most people thought when seeing Holly for the first time. She was short, as they'd heard, but surprisingly trim after all the talk of weight. Her hair spilled over her shoulders and to the middle of her back, a fall of tawny red-blond hair pulled back from her forehead with a headband comb whose tines separated the hair into a halo of dark streaks and scallops where the roots were exposed. Her outfit was smart, authoritative: the short red blazer with black braid trim, longish black skirt, stockings, and shirt had the classic look of a Spanish riding costume. Holly kept her mouth half open, as she would throughout her testimony, exposing her teeth, shifting nervously from a tentative smile to seriousness. She was no beauty, but she looked bright, appealing, well dressed — a girl parents would be happy to have their daughter or son bring home as a friend.

Neil Shapiro, Stephanie's lawyer, had driven up from San Francisco to act as Holly's attorney; he sat in the front row with the Ramona women. "I hadn't seen Holly in about two years," since the sandwich at Tommy's Joint in San Francisco, "and I was stunned at how much she had grown . . . She looked older. But she was much more confident, outgoing, and poised." In some ways, she seemed more poised at twenty-three than his own daughter at twenty-six. But he would tell her these things after the testimony. His job was to try to keep her calm, to ask her, "Are you comfortable?" To protect her from Harrington's rapier cross-examination.

Stephanie had become very nervous as the trial got closer, and Shapiro had offered to come up as a friend to give her support. "You're not serious," she said. He was. As the trial got under way, Bruce Miroglio had called, concerned that Holly would not have counsel when she testified. Could he be there for that as well? Shapiro was leaving the stuffy big law firm anyway. What the hell! "I'll make a deal with you, Bruce. I will do this for Holly and Stevie, and my fee will be a bottle of red wine, *decent* red wine, for each day of testimony I have to endure." He would spend six days in Courtroom B.

In an interesting convergence of legal issues in the recovered memory wars, Shapiro, a specialist in First Amendment law, had just been hired to represent Laura Davis in Deborah David's lawsuit against her and Ellen Bass and their book, *The Courage to Heal*. John Carver was quietly circulating a secretly acquired draft of a new chapter, written as a retort to the False Memory folks, in the new edition of *Courage*. Davis and Bass had called Lenore Terr months earlier, asking her advice on changes. She'd told them, "For God's sake, eliminate the sex abuse symptom list." In the new book, the authors would also delete the most inflammatory of all their maxims: "If you think you were abused and your life shows the symptoms, then you were." Its replacement: "If you're not sure whether you were sexually abused, don't feel pressured to say that you were — or that you weren't . . . People who pressure you either way — and this may include your therapist, your incest support group, or the people in your family — are not helping you." The bible of the survivor movement was being subtly reconstructed, a sign of the way the winds were blowing.

Judge Snowden emerged, his black robe bringing a tone of sobriety to the buzzing courtroom. This was the second time he had presided before his old Boalt Hall classmate Neil Shapiro. A year earlier, Shapiro had appeared with Stephanie for the settlement conference Snowden had staged, "a marvelous global scene with ten lawyers and Snowden dreaming that he could settle everything" — all the lawsuits — "at once," Shapiro recalled. It failed, of course.

The level of excitement in the courtroom on this day was so high that the judge lectured again about "shows of partisanship." He ordered the women to remove the shiny sprigs of holly they had pinned to their lapels as a sign of support for Holly. "Okay, I understand that," thought Stephanie. "But why is it still okay for the False Memory people to pass their stuff out? That upsets me."

As Holly took the stand, the jury watched father and daughter face each other, like mirror images: the same olive skin, broad face, toothy mouth. Holly had the Italian genes. Gary, wearing a restrained gray plaid suit, his hair curling a little down the nape of his neck as if he hadn't had time to get a haircut, showed no emotion as he faced his daughter for her swearing-in. Gary's old pal Scott Evans had flown up for moral support on this difficult day.

Miroglio's wife, Mary, was there for the first time to watch him work after five weeks in Harrington's shadow. This was the defense's chance to catch up. "We started behind the eight ball because we were tried and convicted in the press before this case got started," Miroglio claimed. "For five weeks, the press has only been playing one side of it." He was infuriated that some of the national press — *People* magazine, the *New York Times* — had come and gone before the defense started its case. Miroglio's strategy for examining Holly was to stay invisible. He would follow the general rule of trial: If you've got a strong witness, you want to disappear.

He'd been practicing with Holly at their conference room at the Harvest Inn. "I deliberately didn't want her to come down to my law office to get ready for testimony. It's too sterile and lawyerly." On breaks, they would walk over to Miroglio's house, next door. "She'd play 'fetch' with my dog and play with my kids. She got to see me interact with my kids, and I got to know her real well. She's a terrific young lady." His home had been the site, the Saturday before Holly's testimony, of a gathering of all five Ramona women — the first time in months they had been together. Stephanie, who was still avoiding Harrington's subpoena, turned up. Kelli had just flown in, as had Betty Nye, whom he was meeting for the first time.

For both Stephanie and Holly, Miroglio had done something he had vowed he would never do. "I wrote out all the questions first and prepared them: This is what I intend to ask you, what would your answer be?" He'd write down the answers, transfer them to the computer, and refer to them each time he questioned either one, watching for changes. The danger was that you got a scripted witness. As Holly was about to take the stand, he went up to her and whispered one of the defense team's two stock laugh-getters for courtroom jitters: "Oh, by the way, a horse is a horse, of course, of course" — from the TV show *Mr. Ed.*

More than her father, Holly held the case in her hands. The tendency to "believe the child" was still strong. If she could convince the jury that her memories were real, that they had not been suggested by the therapists — if the jury believed Gary had raped his child — the case against the three defendants was over. How, though, would her flashbacks play to twelve random Napans in a conservative agricultural valley? And to the media, whose attitude had evolved from uncritical awe of Eileen Franklin's memories of murder toward increasing skepticism?

As Miroglio stood to begin, he had before him his list of questions to Holly with a short outline of her answers. "In case she didn't come up with the right answer, I could then lead her back to where I wanted to go." But as she boldly delivered her first simple response, "I was born on August 16, 1970, in Pasadena," with poise and a smile as big as her father's, Miroglio knew that all he would have to do was structure a question and she would roll with it. She usually ended her statements with a question mark, an affectation of her generation, but any tentativeness was overcome by a high, lilting voice full of enthusiasm. This was not the child Stephanie had watched turn shy and inward at the age of two, who had presented herself to Lenore Terr just two years earlier with her body shrouded in baggy clothes, her face masked by hair, the girl "who would have liked to shrink into the woodwork." Holly the cheerleader had come to Courtroom B, her apparent health and energy a seeming testament to good treatment by the defendants. "Holly's flowing pretty easily. She's bright and articulate," Miroglio was thinking, relieved, as her testimony began.

In the audience, Carolyn Thompson was also relieved. "The prosecution had painted Holly as this overweight, paranoid sociopath. When I saw her, it's like, *No.* I'm really pleased that Holly is the spokesperson for us."

Together, Holly and Miroglio built up the picture they had planned to paint: the two sides of the Ramona family. A life divided into two opposing parts: the side the world saw — the fun, travel, holidays, the perfect family. "We were supposed to look perfect, and act perfect, and be perfect" — and the other part — "a lot of fighting — it was scary . . . a lot of chaos . . . my dad always yelling . . . all afraid of him. My parents . . . always on the verge of getting a divorce or separation." A family of no affection, few hugs, that did not even share the dinner table. Forthrightly, Holly described a father who, from her earliest memories, ruled and manipulated his family's actions, minds, appearance. She had spent a lifetime feeling uncomfortable around this tyrant, for whom, Holly said, "his work appeared to me to be the most important thing. Nothing else mattered" — a man who was mean to her mother, a "nurturing, regular, great mom" who urged education "so that you're not stuck in the same position that I'm stuck in." A mom who constantly threatened, "We're leaving."

"She was a fairy-tale princess," JoeAnna Jenkins fumed about Stephanie as she heard Holly condemn the life Gary had given her and the girls. "She had no responsibilities, a $30,000-a-year clothes allowance, everything she wanted, and yet she's telling her daughter 'You don't want to *live* like this!' Most people would think that you couldn't *have* a better life." It was not dissatisfaction with Gary that had made her complain, JoeAnna suspected, but "Stephanie's dissatisfaction with herself." JoeAnna had heard similar complaints from Stephanie for twenty years: "I want to do something. I want to be something besides a wife and mother. I want to go to school. I want . . ." Time and again JoeAnna had said to her, "Stephanie, it's feasible. Why don't you *do* it?" It just never happened.

Ken Keri didn't buy the "two parts" of the Ramona family. "Holly herself admitted in one of the depositions, 'I had a happy childhood until this came up.' Either you did or you didn't. How can it change all of a sudden?"

It was painful for Stephanie to hear her family dissected. But she was amazed as she watched Holly begin her testimony. As a mother, she sat back and thought, "Wow, when did this happen? She's not the same person she was. There's been a big change. A completely different Holly. She grew up. She can handle herself . . . She's very, very brave." Flanked now by her daughters, hearing her confident child on the stand, she felt, "They've outdone any dreams I could have had for them . . . They're harder. They have some cynicism. I hate to see that, but I think they're going to be better equipped to live in this world."

Holly stayed poised and animated as she told the story of her childhood. She described the health problems — the bladder infections, the cystourethrogram, the constipation. There had been no pain, no trauma. She remembered the tubular catheter clearly. "Did it look like a snake? Did it look like a worm?" Holly responded emphatically, almost laughing, "No, *no!*" "Was it painful?" "There weren't any painful parts." Her memory of the procedure, even without anesthesia, had not been traumatic, she said. Constipation took on a certain charm, of Stephanie teaching Holly her ABCs while she sat on a toilet seat shaped like a little duck. Enemas had been "no big deal." There had been no childhood of enemas; she could remember only one. "No big deal?" thought Nell Sweeney, a mother of four. "You can't tell me that having enemas when you're a tiny child would not be traumatic." Tim, too, went on alert: "The defense is trying to downplay the enemas. They *were* traumatic." But Holly persisted with her description of a childhood free of trauma. She had been a "chubby child and had brown hair — and that's about it." Had she been unhappy? "I don't think I thought about it a whole lot."

"Holly's doing better than well — she's doing wonderfully," Miroglio thought. He would walk up and hand her an exhibit, then drift back and disappear. His voice swelled with dramatic intensity in certain statements, but, increasingly, he let his voice drop softer, softer.

He made sure he didn't move, didn't gesture. He wanted the jury riveted on Holly.

As he led her to talk about her teens, the story took a sad and desperate turn: her sense of failure to meet her family's expectations; her growing unhappiness with herself, which took the form of, first, an obsession with weight and, then, of deepening depression and bulimia. "It was about in junior high" that she felt her family putting importance on appearance. "We were supposed to be thin and look a certain way . . . expected to not really be like kids . . . The message was that it wasn't okay to be overweight. You needed to keep your weight down and to look good. I got a lot of the message from my father, and from my mom . . . I was afraid to be me. I was ashamed of my body. I was not comfortable with it." Swimming, "I'd wear clothes." Both parents applied pressure; both dieted; her father bribed her with tennis rackets. Her mom didn't mean to, but "she was trying to help me in something that was important to her." As bulimia took hold in her first year at college, "I'd go on large binges . . . just eat everything in sight, then go in the bathroom and vomit the food up or take a laxative."

Miroglio narrowed the focus to her father's domination of the family when she went off to college. She had chosen UC Irvine because "I wanted to be free, and to be away from my father, and to maybe figure out who I was." But she felt his power follow her. Caught in the desperate bulimic cycle, she found professional help in her second year but feared her therapist and doctors would run to him. "He's always been very controlling . . . my food, the comments, the clothes I wear, what school I went to, what major I was going to have." Nothing led her to believe he would behave any differently with her doctor.

Gary Ramona was incensed that the defense lawyers — "the three stooges out there for the insurance companies," as he called them — were still pushing the control issue. "I didn't pick her clothes, I didn't pick her schools, I didn't pick her music, I didn't pick her sports. I mean, *where am I controlling?*" It was Stephanie who had chosen the therapist who was on trial.

The defense was building not only on the control theme but also on the theme of Holly's stubbornness as the cornerstones of their case. Holly's defiance of any physician who suggested she take medication — the psychiatrist Dr. Barry Grundland, the endocrinologist Dr. Rhie — had been an early sign of her stubbornness. The message had come from her family. "I inferred from the way my family worked that you don't go to therapy, you don't get help for your problems. I felt I would be weak if I did that." In the Ramona family, you didn't take anything unless "absolutely necessary." "I think Marche Isabella mentioned Prozac. I wasn't going to go on it," Holly declared.

As the issue of sex abuse was introduced, her story departed from every deposition. Leonard had said it in his opening statement: "She always knew it was her father." Miroglio, too, had already suggested that Holly's first flashbacks did not emerge from a vacuum — that Holly, on some intuitive level, had always known. If convincing to the jury, the argument would help absolve the defendants of the charge of implanting her memories.

Holly told the jury that when her mother came back from her first meeting with Isabella and asked if she'd ever been sexually abused, "I said, 'Well, I'm not sure. I don't want to talk about it' . . . The first thought that came to mind was 'my father.'" But, fearing her mother wouldn't believe her, "I kept quiet." When her mother again brought up the possibility of Holly's abuse and demanded, "Who was it?" naming several people in the neighborhood, "she did ask if it was my father. Verbally, I told her no, but inside was something else. I was ashamed, afraid she wouldn't believe me." "You didn't know at that time whether or not he'd ever abused you. But you had a *suspicion?*" asked Miroglio. "I had a suspicion," she said, bright as a cheerleader. She had screened this suspicion from Isabella, too, Holly said. "She asked me if I had ever been sexually abused. I said I wasn't sure and then ended up telling her about the incident with the babysitter. I wanted to talk about my father. I didn't know if I could trust her. Would she report it to my father?" Isabella had asked "that one question, then let it go." Sex abuse never came up again that fall.

By the morning break, Holly had painted her first months of therapy as benign sessions devoted to chatting about family dynamics, with no mention of sex abuse. A strong new Holly had also been established. "Did you do everything Marche Isabella wanted you to do?" Miroglio asked.

"*No!* Number one, I was not going on an antidepressant. Number two, in the hospital they asked me to stay longer and I said, 'That's it,' and left. From the beginning, I asked for sodium amytal."

"Were you using your own mind, Holly?"

"My *own* mind, for *my* decisions."

But Holly had not been able to control the horrors of incest once they started stumbling into her mind. Her father's "sexual look" at Christmas as they sat on the floor near the tree, the "very strong, steady gaze" that reminded her of the look he sometimes gave her mother, had frozen her "and reminded me of things . . . but there weren't any real concrete memories." She described the first flashback at Palm Springs of her father's hand on her stomach. "I knew . . . the hand was my father's. It was my father's hand." In another, "He was on top of me . . . heavy . . . and I could feel his skin and smell him . . ." She revealed to the jury the confusion and anxiety she had felt as the images began to appear. The flashbacks "caught me off guard. I thought maybe if I didn't think about it it would go away." She hid them from Isabella for several weeks. "I was confused. I was afraid. What would she think of me if I told her . . . ?"

Miroglio moved back, away from Holly, leaving the room's attention fully on her as he led her to the explosive flashbacks. "Did she tell you it would be *good* if you had some more to tell her?"

"*No.* But very just kind of blah, just kind of even."

Now out of the jury's sight, Miroglio dropped his voice to a whisper and asked gently, "Did you have other memories that disturbed you . . . ?"

"I had memories of my father doing other things . . . raping me . . ." The courtroom fell silent as Holly described her first flashback of forced intercourse with her father. "I was on a bed and there was a lot of white . . . a white sheet . . . and my father was on top of me and his penis was inside me, and I remember seeing that look again, that kind of glazed-over look . . ."

"Where inside you, Holly?" Miroglio whispered.

"His penis was inside my vagina."

She delivered these horrors in a bright and innocent voice without a pause or break. Tim Holewinske was aching to believe her, but he was thinking, "She's a professional witness." With her practical nurse's mind, Shelley Maynard, too, was thinking, "This has been repeated, repeated; there've been so many depositions it becomes pat answers. I worry about her."

Holly spoke of a period of conflict, of her fear that she would not be believed, of her own disbelief that "a father, who was supposed to love me, could at the same time do this to me," of finally — crying, upset, wanting to get off the phone — telling her mother "my father had raped me . . . I told her it *happened.* I knew inside it had happened . . . I wanted to confront him right in the very beginning," she said, describing Isabella's urging her to hold off, her mother's wanting to confront her father and telling Holly she was divorcing him. Holly described her internal tumult over being the cause of breaking up the family, then hearing about sodium amytal from a member of her eating disorders group. It was maybe "a way where I could check what was happening . . ." Isabella had resisted, saying, "You don't need sodium amytal." But "I was determined that I was going to have it. I wanted to check all the avenues. Hoping that it would do the opposite. That I was just crazy. I didn't want to feel physical pain anymore." It was not a truth serum, Rose had told her; "it was no more accurate than if somebody was intoxicated." She laughed. "I *wanted* the sodium amytal."

Pursuing his job of absolving Rose and Isabella from responsibility, Miroglio moved to the trial's central event, the confrontation. If the link to *Molien* and to liability was the confrontation, as the judge had said, Holly's biggest job was to lift the responsibility for that meeting from the shoulders of the three defendants.

"Whose idea was . . . this meeting?"

"It was *my* idea," said a perky Holly.

"Whose agenda was presented . . . ?"

"*My* agenda was presented. I ran the meeting. I did much of the talking . . . I *started* the meeting. I *finished* the meeting." Marche "was there for support." The meeting she remembered was the very opposite of the one her father had described, a meeting run by Isabella. One of them had to be lying. Or their honest perceptions of events were wildly different.

Holly risked sounding self-absorbed as she spoke of learning under the sodium amytal that her grandmother had been raped by her brothers. When Miroglio asked, "Did that mean anything to you?" she replied, "Not really . . . That wasn't what I was real concerned about." Several in the audience winced.

"Were you pleased with the treatment from Western Medical Center, Marche Isabella, and Richard Rose?" asked Miroglio, summing up.

"Yes," said Holly.

Winding up his direct exam, Miroglio deftly brought it back to what had happened to Holly. His voice dropped again to a whisper and all eyes focused on Holly. "Who *did* molest you, Holly?"

She looked straight at her father, hard and emotionless. "My father molested me."

"And that's Gary Ramona, sitting here in the courtroom?"
"Yes."
"That's all, Your Honor."

It was a powerful start for the defense. Holly was spirited out of the courtroom before the press could catch up with her. Gary, who had not twitched a muscle all morning, hurried out, too, but he gave the reporters a few cordial words: "We need to spend lunch looking at where we are. I'll talk to you at the end of the day." As Marche Isabella left the courthouse with her attorneys, she was asked how she felt. "Great. I'm pleased to hear Holly be able to tell what really happened. Today, you heard the *true* story . . . Does Holly look like someone I could plant memories with?" She laughed, flushed and triumphant. Kurtock reiterated that all Gary had ever had to do was say, "Holly, I care about you. How can I help you? How can we get past this and be father and daughter again?" — even if he *had* raped her. Instead, he had petulantly sued the therapists, "destroyed his family and irreversibly given up any chance of any reconciliation." During a later break, Holly would tell a TV reporter, "If he's not willing to say he's sorry for what he did, then there's absolutely no possibility of reconciliation."

"But what if the father were correct and the daughter were wrong about this?" a reporter asked Kurtock. "What recourse does he have if he can't sue the therapist?" "His recourse would be . . . to talk to his daughter and try to persuade her that she was wrong . . . and establish a new relationship with her." Kurtock did not mention that that was precisely what Gary Ramona had tried to do from the day of the confrontation, both with his daughters and with Stephanie.

During lunch, Harrington pulled his own "Gerner," slipping to the press a thick document containing five lawsuits against Richard Rose, several of them not reported in depositions — possible grounds for impeachment. Scanning them, a journalist spotted the explosive one. On the same day Rose had given Holly sodium amytal, he had injected a depressed patient with testosterone to "kick-start" him out of his impotence — acceptable treatment only if the patient was free of prostate cancer, which testosterone caused to spread and flourish. Two years later, the man was castrated as treatment for prostate cancer.

On the steps of the courthouse after lunch, the media cornered Miroglio and Rose and, waving the packet, asked, "What's your comment?" Shocked, Miroglio tried to keep his composure. "Could I take a look at that?" Swiftly skimming it, he recalled asking Rose during his depositions if there were any skeletons in his closet. There were clearly some Rose had forgotten. He broke away and asked Rose urgently, "Rich, what are these about?" Three of the cases he had revealed, Rose told him; one he didn't know about — it had been filed but not served. The other, Miroglio was ready to believe as he listened, had just slipped his mind. Miroglio glanced over it and shuddered. The words "testosterone," "prostate cancer . . . patient castrated" leaped out. Rich said, "I just didn't think about it as a psychiatric case. I erased it from my mind."

Later, Rose told him the details. Even if he had done a rectal exam, as Miroglio understood it, he wouldn't have found anything. No cancer cells had been found until a year and a half later, absolutely none. But it was a nightmare. Harrington would try to get it before the jury. "Harrington's trying to smear Rich . . . I call it a slimeball tactic in retaliation for what had happened to Gerner," Miroglio said angrily. Castration! If Harrington got it admitted, the jury would not forget. As they all said, "You can't get the toothpaste back in the tube again."

Harrington launched his cross-examination by using gentle ridicule to let Holly herself undermine the charge of a "manipulative, controlling" father. Did your father buy your clothes? No. Holly and her mother had. And was it not your mother who dressed you and your sister alike until fourth or fifth grade? Yes. Did you know he deposited his entire paycheck in your mother's account? Who decided that you would stop riding? Who chose your other activities — ski club, cross-country? Holly had. Inviting her to reconsider, Harrington asked, "You say he made the final decision on everything?" "It's not overt . . . It's underneath . . . more manipulative." Harrington seized the opening to ask Holly about chores, about the girls' taking the garbage cans out — and how her dad got mad when they didn't. When he had made them take them out one night in a thunderstorm, Holly had balked, scared "we could be electrocuted." Asking her to take out the garbage — was her father being "overbearing in making that demand . . . was that his authoritarian Italian background . . . ?" "No, that was pretty regular," she admitted weakly.

Harrington moved on to Holly's issues with food, eating, and weight — the part of her life that had started this unstoppable ball rolling, the part, Pope and Hudson had argued, that could account for her memories of abuse. Stephanie again had to endure the story of her tacking up a picture of a model on Holly's bathroom mirror. "I didn't want to disappoint her or my father. Mom knew that I looked at models and thought . . . that it would be an incentive for me to lose weight . . . I'm not built like that . . . It was a little bit discouraging." Reinforcing, Harrington asked, "Your mom who put that up?" "Right." Her voice was peppy, but the words saddened the courtroom. This girl had spent her childhood trying to force her body into a mold it would not fit. Suggestions of abuse other than sexual were emerging from her testimony — abuse that Stephanie, too, might have thoughtlessly committed.

Guilt washed over her mother as Holly repeated the heartbreaking admission, made first in her depositions, that she walked through shopping malls feeling insecure and fearful that "I'm so ugly that nobody's going to want to look at me." Stephanie agonized over it. But she was finding the courage to look hard at herself; she knew in her heart that she purposely hadn't told the girls they were beautiful because she feared that they, like her, might be perceived as nothing more than pretty. They mustn't be stereotyped as she had been. She wanted her girls to look beyond surfaces, to look into themselves. "I wanted other people to see *more* in Holly."

New guilt was ahead as Harrington brought up the family eating patterns, the theme that kept recurring: ". . . the Ramona family didn't eat together as a family?"

"Usually on holidays."

"Your mom would refuse to join you and Kelli in eating dinner . . . ?"

". . . She would usually have eaten before, or she would kind of eat as she was cooking dinner for us . . . snacking along the way . . . My father ate alone sometimes in the evening."

"Well, tell me the first time you can recall how your parents ate?" In his computer were the depositions that quoted Holly as saying that she had never seen her parents sit down to share a meal together.

"Did that make you believe that the family was an unhappy one because you were not eating together?" Harrington asked, suggesting the empty family table as a metaphor for other hungers that could have found their expression in the obsessive hunger of bulimia and in fantasies of sexual abuse. He pursued the theme a little later, asking Holly about the times she fasted in ninth and tenth grades. "When you ate by yourself, did you eat at the dining room table? . . . And did you ever eat by yourself at the kitchen counter?"

Holly's image of a family that never ate together shook Miroglio. In the heat of the trial, with his most important witnesses coming on, he had been missing dinner with his family. He was only getting home for "do my day" two or three times each week. He would be billing three hundred hours in April! Mary told him that Cara had said, "I liked it better like it used to be, when Daddy ate with us." Hearing Holly, he suddenly realized, "I'm becoming Gary Ramona. I'm so focused on this trial that I've forgotten what's important."

Holly was stirring the valley beyond the courtroom. As she saw the *Register*'s front-page story on Holly, Maggie Kelly, the Ramonas' old neighbor, read hungrily about the "sweet, smiley, easygoing little girl" who had given no sign, as she babysat for the Kellys' girls, that she was being repeatedly raped by her father. For nine years Maggie had been teaching the last-chance kids in the Napa public schools' Opportunity class. All were kids of divorce. The dinner table was dead among her kids. "They never, zero, *never* eat together." These kids fed themselves. Their parents sent them down to the Table at the Methodist Church to eat, free, with the indigents. "I think divorce has done a lot to the dinner table . . . You sit down as a family but, with stepparents, you can't talk about the other parent. You can't talk about 'Mom and Dad's house,' about grandparents. Virtually half the children's life can't be brought up. You can't sit around and tell stories about Grandpa coming over on the boat from Ireland."

"We've abandoned our children," mused Richard Mullins, a psychologist in Napa. "Children can't forgive abandonment and abuse as an adult can, so they strike back however they can. An unhappy child could look for some external validation of the internal unhappiness — in incest, abuse."

Harrington moved on from the dinner table to Holly's digestive tract, dragging her through a discussion of her constipation, the enemas, the cystourethrogram. It was important that he establish a pattern of childhood enemas, with their potential for having been one of the traumatic bases of Holly's flashbacks. Always probing for inconsistencies, he challenged her when she claimed, "In my mind, I remember *one* enema." Directing her to the depositions, he read from "page 20, line 8: 'Do you recall receiving enemas for constipation?' Plural, was it not?" He read on: "'And how frequently did she give you enemas?'" and Holly's answer, "'Whenever I was constipated . . . I can't give you frequency. I know that I was constipated often.'" The "one enema" she now remembered sounded convenient, dissembling.

Harrington asked, "What position were you when you got the enema?" Lying on her back.

" . . . on a bath mat in the bathroom?"

"Right."

"You held your legs up to get the enema?"

"I believe so," Holly admitted.

He also directed her to describe the childhood cystourethrogram procedure, which, several times now, he had raised as the source of her images of snakes and penises in her vagina. It was a scene she had never forgotten. As if he had written the script, Holly responded to his question, "Who is in the room?": "A doctor. They're in white coats. I'm on the bed. Draped in a sheet. The nurses hold my arms and legs while inserting whatever it was. I felt my legs apart."

"Was the doctor a man?"

"Yes."

In making the argument that the invasive procedures of Holly's childhood could be the source of her traumatic images, Harrington was seizing on theories increasingly supported by distinguished skeptics like Cornell's Stephen Ceci, a leading expert on child memory. During the Ramona trial, Ceci and Maggie Bruck, a psychologist at McGill, were completing a book that would have been gold in Harrington's hands. Holly's lighthearted memory of the cystourethrogram as "no big deal" contrasted greatly with Ceci's description of preschoolers subjected to the same procedure, "involving the insertion of a probe into the child's genitalia, following inflation of the bladder with fluid . . . It is not only painful, but embarrassing, because after the child's bladder is filled to the point of extreme discomfort, she is encouraged to urinate on the examining table in front of strange medical personnel . . . Indeed, one might well imagine that the young child feels betrayed by a loved one who delivers him to a medical team and leaves the room while the team engages in painful genital procedures." That had been precisely Stephanie's guilty fear after finding Holly huddled and alone after the test.

Holly's childhood of catheters, suppositories, enemas, constipation, and infections raised another concern for Ceci: Why should memories of sexual events only, and not of a whole range of other assaultive events, be given special status? "Why should sexual events such as genital touching, anal insertions, and vaginal penetrations, but not nonsexual events such as vaginal catheterizations, be uncovered in therapy?" Despicable and unforgivable as any form of child abuse was, Ceci and his colleagues knew that not all sexual abuse of the young child was necessarily interpreted as assaultive. Sexual abuse had been given a special status that, if revealed as spurious, could hurt the larger need for prevention of all forms of real child abuse.

Harrington then set out to reconstruct the father-daughter relationship Holly had painted as cold and uncomfortable. "In point of reality, you had an affectionate relationship with your dad."

"That's not the reality . . ." For the first time in four hours there was a hint of a crack in her polished delivery. "There were times when I loved my father . . . He'd say, 'Come here and give me a hug' . . ."

"And you said, 'There are times when he does love me,' is that right?"

"I hope so," said Holly, her voice dropping its sparkle and sinking to sadness. Her mouth was still half open, unsure whether to smile, and her chin quivered.

"You'd leave notes for him at the Robert Mondavi Winery?" he asked as he handed her the notes and cards that had brought her father to tears weeks earlier. "Would you please read them, Ms. Ramona?" The spectators were suddenly witness to a scene almost too intimate to watch. Silent, hardly daring to breathe, they sensed something delicate unfolding as Holly struggled to read "Happy Father's Day . . . to . . . the dad who's got it all . . ." and tried valiantly to control her tears and return to the strategy she had rehearsed. Gary tried to suppress his sobs, but his shoulders heaved as Holly choked out, "There were parts of him I loved. And when I'm giving him a card, it's the good part." Prodded by Harrington, she read on: "You're great. Love, Holly."

But the feelings overwhelmed her and she looked up at her father and cried out, openly weeping, "There are times now that I'd give anything to have a regular hug from my father, just a regular father-daughter hug . . . But I was afraid he'd take it the wrong way." Tears streaked down Holly's cheeks as Gary looked at his daughter and sobbed uncontrollably. A spark seemed to leap between them. The jury and the spectators fell away. For that instant, it seemed possible that they would run to each other across the twelve feet that separated them and hug.

Judge Snowden broke the spell, saying, "This is probably a good time for the afternoon recess." Gary rushed from the courtroom.

Holly stood by the witness stand, alone, wet-faced, dazed. She walked to her mother and collapsed into tears on her shoulder as the women gathered round to comfort her.

In that moment of electric contact between father and daughter, the full dimensions of this human tragedy were revealed. The physical distance between them was a symbol, suddenly glaringly clear, of a great gulf that might never be closed. Holly's first show of spontaneous emotion touched the crowd's collective heart and forced them to face their feelings.

"This was the defining moment for Holly's cross-exam. It was wonderful," thought Shapiro, deeply touched as he watched. "This poise just crumbled because this was the little girl crying."

The jury was profoundly moved. For Tom Dudum, the heartrending scene had shown that you "can't repair your family in a court of law. They should have stayed in therapy." To see a child's desperation exposed in this forum was heartbreaking for Shelley. "It broke my heart for this to happen to *anybody's* child. My husband would die before he would see that happen to his children. This should have stayed in their family to begin with."

Yolanda was undone. "When Holly started crying, I just saw seven kids. That really did something to me. If I would have stayed in the mode that I was in, Gary would have been guilty right then, because I'm a mother and because the child said he did it . . . But I kept reminding myself: 'This is not your family. You're here to find out the facts. You're a juror.'" She echoed the silent consensus: "This should have stayed in therapy, period." Rape or no rape. "But the *father* should have been involved in Holly's therapy," thought Marty Cook, disturbed that "the mother was brought down to resolve the issues. How come the father wasn't? I think if the therapist had brought the father in for a confrontation on the control issues and all that, maybe it would have stopped there."

For the rest of the day, Harrington forced Holly through every flashback. Many had been two- or three-second black-and-white freeze frames, which Harrington refused even to dignify with the word "memories." "Now, in Palm Springs, you had your first flashback. Is that right? And do they feel a little bit different than *memories* to you?" Holly insisted, "No, they *are* memories!" Persisting in calling them "mental productions" or "alleged images," he asked her repeatedly, "What happened before . . . ? What happened after?" while Holly answered, again and again, "No . . . I don't know . . . Nothing!"

Harrington was revealing Holly's images to be impoverished, largely naked of context, exposing the lack of detail that surrounded them, laying down his rebuttal to Lenore Terr's upcoming testimony that the test of a *real* memory was its rich detail. "Why wouldn't you know what happened before, what happened after?" Yolanda pondered. "So what are you saying: repressed memory is only limited memory? I don't understand this."

Harrington challenged Holly's perfect clarity about her age in the images when so much else was vague. "Well, let's go back to the first flashback. How old are you?"

"Between ages five and eight," Holly would repeat like a mantra for each memory. The time frame began to sound contrived, for it fit conveniently between an age when a child would be safely beyond the age of the earliest reliable memories — three — and the age when Holly left Diamond Bar — eight — still a small girl too helpless to resist, too scared to report what was happening to her.

"And is there anything in the flashbacks that told you that?"

"The size of me told me that."

Again, he challenged the length of the flashbacks. She had said "two to three seconds," then "two to five, somewhere in there." Which was it? Holly insisted, again and again, "No, two to *five* seconds . . . The same as the others, two to *five*." While some saw Holly's peppy ripostes and her surety about something as fleeting as a flashback as overrehearsed, Shapiro was impressed. "She's doing something very few witnesses do," he observed. "*She's not going to let him create her testimony.* Holly is poised because she knows what she knows and she's going to tell it. You can't train a witness to have that kind of poise."

Harrington seized every opportunity to emphasize the similarity between details of her flashbacks and her childhood experiences. When he brought up "the fourth flashback?" Holly described, ". . . I was at the bathroom sink, and the memory of my father, he was holding my arms . . . a sheet was flying, and we were struggling. And I was about five to eight again." Harrington made the sexual inference seem ridiculous by asking, "Did your father ever take your shirt off when you were a child?" He had diluted her image to the innocence of a father's helping his child take off a T-shirt. He scored again when she described the flashback of "my father's hand over my mouth . . . my hair, the white sheet, my father's hand . . . I'm on a bed . . ." Knowing the jury had just heard her description, a few hours earlier, of the cystourethrogram experience, he asked, "Did anyone put a hand over your mouth during the procedure you described earlier today, where something was put in your vagina? . . . Did the doctor put his hand on your stomach? . . . Do you know if the physician had to put his head between your legs to look into the instrument that went into your vagina?" he asked when Holly described a flashback of her father's head between her legs. Pursuing that image, he asked, "Now, is your father orally copulating you during that flashback?" "I'm not sure exactly what that is . . ." responded Holly.

Holly's extraordinary naiveté about her body startled Tim. "Here she is, a graduate student in psychology at Pepperdine, and she still comes up on the stand sort of childlike. I can't understand how she could still be that sheltered. There has to be some trauma there." "Yes, it's a defense," Beth was thinking. The same thought crossed alternate Ken Keri's mind. "Here's a twenty-three-year-old woman that used the terms 'front' and 'bottom.' She's had biology classes, and she does not know the term 'rectum'? Is it because she was sexually abused that she doesn't like this area down there?" Coming from a medical background, Shelley was amazed at Holly's ignorance. "She doesn't know that her voiding cystourethrogram happened not in her *vagina!*"

Near the end of that day's testimony, Harrington got to Prince. Once again he shook Holly's poise when he asked her to describe the flashback. ". . . There's movement in this one . . . It looks like I have some type of blue dress on . . . I think it had little white polka dots on it . . . My father's bringing the dog over to me and I can see the front of the dog, and he wants me to put my mouth on the dog — that area . . . the bottom area." Holly was crying, running her hand through her hair, obviously distressed by this scene. ". . . on the penis of the dog?" "I think so." As Holly wiped her eyes, trying to regain her composure, Harrington took her back to the image of her father bringing the dog's penis toward her mouth.

"In your flashback, do you put your mouth on the penis of the dog?"

"I usually do what my father tells me to do, so I did."

The jury hid its shock and discomfort in ferocious note-taking.

Bestiality. The word Loftus had introduced so carefully had now been vividly dramatized as the trial became every bit as lurid as Snowden had predicted. Except for Prince, Holly had described without emotion terrible violations of her body and soul by her father; she had shown, as therapists called it, "a flat affect."

Harrington had one more inconsistency between the depositions and the trial testimony to draw out of Holly before the end of the day. As he asked the question he asked after every flashback, "Can you tell the jury what happened before this memory . . . or thereafter?" Holly responded, "No, I can't."

Relentlessly, Harrington established the inconsistencies. "When you described this memory before . . . it was a freeze frame . . . And so now you're testifying today it's no longer a freeze frame?"

"Right."

"You're trying to establish major inconsistencies?" a TV reporter asked Harrington in the courthouse hall the next morning. "Well, yes," he responded, seizing on a glaring one, "that Dr. Rose's record after the sodium amytal interview showed that Holly had no memory at all of anything she said during the interview . . . Holly now says that she *did* have a memory."

"You also seem to be trying to show that she had doubts after the sodium amytal which were cleared away by her therapist?"

"Absolutely accurate! The records show that, before the amytal, she was never convinced. After the amytal she became convinced. Marche Isabella, who had no way of knowing whether anything was true, said, 'Oh, you were telling the truth.' Dr. Rose said, 'We know you weren't lying.' The psychiatric nurse employed by Western Medical said, 'We know you weren't lying.' They all told her it was true."

"Why is that crucial to your case?"

"Because this poor woman's had a false memory implanted by the defendants of what they heard during sodium amytal. It was never taped. Dr. Rose's account was all totally vague. Yet they assured her they were all true."

"So how do you account for the flashbacks?"

"Flashbacks are what Dr. James Hudson at Harvard Medical School calls obsessive intrusions, which are senseless, short flashes that occur very commonly to people with bulimia."

As he slipped into his chambers, Snowden saw the lights and cameras and was distressed. "I'm a First Amendment kind of guy," said the judge as court opened that morning to an even bigger crowd than on Holly's first day of testimony. The role of the media was critical, he said, in transmitting "the very important social issues to large numbers of people." But he was forbidding any more interviews in the hall, he announced, while qualifying his decision. "I don't, by analogizing to a circus, mean to suggest there is anything wrong with the publicity this trial is getting. This is as real as it gets. This is what the court process is for." This case would affect "the relationships between health care providers and the public . . . We, as a society, define ourselves by the way in which we resolve . . . the kind of conflicts this case presents. And so it's very important to me that this process be kept as solemn as the duty we are carrying out . . . in this trial . . . I'd like to have interviews far enough away from the courtroom that it will maintain the solemnity here."

It was April 21, Stephanie's forty-ninth birthday. In her worst nightmare, she would not have imagined spending it in a courtroom fighting Gary in a sensational incest trial. The wide red belt of her blue denim dress cinched the waistline of an eighteen-year-old as she watched a smiling Holly again take the stand. Except for the color of her short jacket, cream rather than red, her outfit was identical to that of the previous day — one of the few consistencies revealed that morning. Harrington caught her in so many statements that differed from those in her depositions that she began to respond with the same flip impatience Marche Isabella had shown. "I don't remember," she snapped over and over. "I don't remember . . . I'm telling you what I remember right now . . . I would say that I remember it differently . . ." As he caught her in changed statements about the "You have to be trained to lie under sodium amytal" issue, he asked, "But is your memory changed since December 15, 17, 1991 . . . ?" "I would have to say it has. That's not what I was focusing on." Harrington was so relentless that Sharon Chandler objected that he was "purporting to impeach the witness . . ."

But Holly kept her poise, doggedly refusing even to try to reconcile her old with her new statements, and in doing so somehow established her own kind of perverse consistency. Harrington drove on, trying to tear apart her new claim that she now remembered what she'd said under the sodium amytal.

"Did Dr. Rose tell you that you revealed . . . during the interview . . . that your father's mother had been raped by her brothers?"

"I believe . . . Marche Isabella told me that."

"Did you have a recollection of saying . . . that . . . under sodium amytal . . . ?"

With a grin that was disconcertingly out of sync with the subject at hand, Holly declared, ". . . It's not important to me . . . what I did or didn't say under sodium amytal. The fact is I had the memories before . . . The interview wasn't really going to change anything . . ." When Harrington asked about Isabella's not taking notes, Holly summed up the supreme unimportance of the sodium amytal interview with her response: "I didn't *need* to look at the notes. I *knew* what had happened."

"Are you lying?"

"I *know* I'm not lying. I *knew* I was abused."

Harrington moved on to the confrontation, the focal event of the trial. He triggered another rare display of emotion in Holly when he asked, "The first thing you said to your father was . . . 'You were never there when I needed you' . . . Did you tell your father what you meant by that statement?" But Holly had shed her last tear and this time exploded with hurt and resentment. Where her first outburst had been a heartbroken little girl's cry for a fatherly hug, this was an attack delivered with rage. She hurled her fury directly at her father, ending each sentence with her characteristic question mark.

". . . He wasn't there in the way that I needed him to be there? He wasn't somebody I could trust, that I would feel comfortable coming to if I had a problem? . . . He was there sometimes physically at different events, but he just wasn't there in the way I needed a father . . . In the way I would like to have a father?"

"Then you said to him, 'You're self-centered.'"

"I remember telling my father that he's self-centered and that the only person he cares about is himself," she said, telling him again.

"Was he self-centered when he gave you the car?"

". . . I'm not speaking in terms of physical things . . . Financially, my family was secured. My father bought nice things. I had . . . probably more than most kids had. But what I didn't have is something that maybe he's not capable of giving me. By self-centered I mean I want love. I wanted a father. I wanted something that's not — that's not material."

While Harrington pursued his search for inconsistencies, Holly kept steering her testimony back to things she wanted to say — about the lack of communication between her and her father, about her frustration over his inability to hear her, and about his blaming others. She glared directly at Gary as she poured out her anger:

"My father doesn't seem to get the point . . . that I'm the one telling him he abused me. He insists that it's everybody else talking . . . And I'm telling you now, I'm telling you it happened." He understood only "what he had been through, and how I had destroyed his life . . . that I had taken everything away from him. But he took everything away from me when he did this . . . I wanted to pretend that . . . I had a regular father who loved me . . . I didn't have that type of a child-hood."

The spark that, the day before, had seemed to leap the chasm between them, a bridge to reconciliation, was dead. The moment of hope was gone.

The women reporters rushed to American Bistro to compare notes over lunch. Huddled over three tape recorders, trying to fill the gaps in Holly's quotes for their afternoon deadlines, they ached for Holly as they heard the young voice played back: *I wanted love. I wanted a father. I wanted something that was not material.* Bonded by weeks of emotion, freed from the jury's job of reaching judgment, these four women used lunch not only as a reality check for quotes but also as a vital moment of catharsis before going back to work.

"That's *me* the first year at college," said one reporter, Kristina Flaherty, identifying with Holly. "Overweight, wearing baggy T-shirts, socially insecure, not finding her place — it was the story of so many freshmen."

Holly's testimony was winding down to its last few minutes, but Harrington had one more surprise for the defense — the two lawsuits Holly had filed against her father. The defense attorneys leaped up to object. The two documents were easy targets. The first lawsuit had not even mentioned the existence of flashbacks before Holly's sodium amytal interview, basing her complaint solely on the memories of rape revealed in the interview. Leonard stormed, "The lawyer made a mistake! Maybe that's why he's no longer her lawyer." Miroglio chimed in, "It's an attempt to smear. It's prejudicial. This witness had not *read* the complaint before it was filed." Holly's refiled complaint, her second lawsuit, was another gift to Harrington. Contradicting the first one, it claimed her memories went up to age sixteen. That complaint asserted that Holly had endured rape by her father up to the age of sixteen but remembered nothing until the flashbacks three years later.

"Overruled," said Snowden, dismissing the objection and allowing the two lawsuits to come before the jury. It was a triumph for Harrington, another of the infuriating decisions that played, the defense felt, in Gary's favor. Harrington would now be able to leave the jury with these latest memories lingering in their minds. He prodded Holly to describe the sordid events "between fourteen and sixteen," all of which had, apparently, vanished from her consciousness the moment they occurred. These later memories ranged from a penis in her vagina to her father's penis in her "bottom," and in her mouth — to anal and oral rape. An image of him forcing her to eat her own vomit capped the series of disgusting events that would have to have been, to many who heard them, unforgettable to someone in high school.

"At the time you saw Dr. Stiles . . . at the time you saw Dr. Grundland in August or September of 1989, you had no recollection . . . no memory . . . of any of these flashbacks, right? . . . As of January 1990, you had no memory of any of these flashbacks?"

"Right," Holly snapped back, still perky.

"Five to sixteen — you believe that?" the elder psychologist Leo Stoer stage-whispered into the courtroom air, shrugging his shoulders. "You'd never forget. She *could* forget, but only if she's mentally ill. And she may well be." These late memories did not sit well, either, with Yolanda Nash. "If she was five or six, I can understand you forgetting and going off into space and all this. But ten, eleven . . . to sixteen?"

In its final opportunity to rebut and correct some of the potentially damaging embarrassments, the defense attempted a feisty but confused explanation of why Holly had changed and corrected her December 17, 1991, depositions. "Do you know where the doctor put the tube?" asked Sharon Chandler. "It was in my *urethra*," said Holly, correcting her previous "vagina," relinquishing what she now admitted were "cute names" she'd used for her anatomy. Chandler tried to distance Prince from the defendants, asking Holly for the time frame of the image of her mouth on the dog's penis. "That part of the memory took place *after* sodium amytal — *after* I had stopped seeing Marche Isabella . . . and Dr. Rose."

As an attorney, Shapiro saw Holly's day in court as a triumph.

"Every time Harrington gave her an opening, she was shooting him. He went on too long. She just nailed him." After she testified, Shapiro told her, "Holly, you did a terrific job. I wish you could be a witness in all my cases."

Holly Ramona left the stand a celebrity in the recovered memory controversy — more famous, perhaps, than any of her classmates at St. Helena High would be in their lifetime. Her voice and conviction had held strong through two days of fishbowl interrogation by a consummately shrewd attorney. She had moved the jury and the audience to feel and to think. Facing a skeptical press, she had carried her shiny bright belief in her memories confidently to the jury and the TV cameras. While her parents sat on opposite sides of the courtroom, their lives still shattered, Holly's illnesses were being controlled by Prozac; she was slim, getting her master's in psychology from Pepperdine that summer. As Richard Rose observed with a physician's satisfaction, "Holly's better."

Among the jury, Holly had become everyone's child. But, as with their own children, they could love her without believing everything she said. "*Something* happened to the poor girl," thought Tim, who, just three years older, identified with her as a brother. Everybody had expected eighteen-year-old Becky to be pro-Holly, and she was. She believed in her memories and in her abuse. Beth, too, "had a strong perception that something terrible happened. I watched the two of them . . . It's possible it's someone else. It might have happened once, maybe not even the penetration, but in her mind . . . there's a problem between them." Nell was no fan of Gary Ramona, but the medical procedures, the constipation . . . She wondered. "Sexual abuse I don't think happened to her" was Yolanda's silent summing up. "I just think it was a combination of her life. Period."

Before Holly had begun to testify, Ed Leonard had made his dramatic plea to the jury in his opening statement for the defense. When you finally sit in the jury room to reach a verdict, scan the eleven faces around you and ask, "Who can Holly turn to? . . . Why, it's *you*."

Had Holly done the job she had come to do? Would the jury defend her, as Leonard had asked them to? The first burst of tears — the little girl wanting a hug — stayed in people's minds as a touchstone to a Holly who had become harder and harder to find over the two days of testimony. She had delivered her flashbacks with radiant conviction. She believed her memories; no one who had read her depositions or met her, plaintiff or defense, ever doubted it. She had seen the images. She was not lying. The courtroom wanted to be on her side, to believe her, to protect her. Her childlike freshness was endearing, her naiveté touching. Many among the jury and the spectators longed to hug her and take her home. But something disconcerting had happened. The doubts that had haunted and somehow humanized her early memories had gone. Details had changed, always conforming better to the legal strategy. There was a disturbing mismatch between her strong, smiling delivery and the terrible content of her words. She could describe without emotion her father — her father! — suppressing the screams of a struggling five-year-old with his hand as he raped her. The sweetness that had been her lifelong hallmark was being displaced by a new assertiveness, a Holly who used "me" and "my" constantly and with emphasis. Could it be that the assertive Holly was really the same obedient and compliant Holly, doing her best, as she always did, for new masters, the attorneys?

In the course of her testimony, a reluctant disillusionment had settled over the courtroom. It wasn't the memories. The mix of true believers, skeptics, and fence-sitters held a full range of opinions on their truth. If Loftus hadn't known for sure whether they were real or not, how could anyone? The disillusionment was over the loss of an innocence quite apart from anything sexual. This twenty-three-year-old who talked about "the bottom part" and "his you-know-what" was playing the litigation game. Shapiro and Miroglio may have admired it as a "terrific" performance, but the testimony recalled the words Holly and her mother had said silently to each other at Shawna's deposition: "How sad that our family has come to this."

Shapiro had helped Holly prepare a brief statement for the press. "I want to work to help these children to be able to speak out against child abuse," she said, speaking of her own goals as a therapist, "because the fact is that child abuse is occurring every day, and we need to stop listening to the perpetrators as much and start listening more to the children that are trying to tell us what's happening." Did she see in herself the growth in poise and confidence others had seen? "I'm happy I've done this . . . I've worked hard to get where I am today. I'm still in therapy, and I think I'm doing very well." Suddenly she was the little girl who needed a hug. "I'm very tired," she said, her chin quivering, and she was ushered down the back stairs.

Birthday cake, champagne, and balloons were waiting at Bruce

Miroglio's office two blocks away — a surprise party for Stephanie. She was shocked and touched, but balloons could not lift the heaviness. It was hard, as Betty Nye would say, to feel "shiny." The rain that was gathering in roiling black clouds — so heavy that it would wash out Napa's Earth Day celebration the next day — could not wash away the sad reality of how Stephanie had spent her forty-ninth birthday.

17

The T-graph

D r. Barry Grundland had been forced from the shadows by subpoena. As a psychiatrist to all the Ramona family, he had been
at the center of their explosion and collapse. As Miroglio said,
"He knew where the skeletons were buried." His power and success
as a therapist lay in confidentiality, anonymity, and trust, so testifying
was the deepest violation of his way of working. The defense created
mysteries around his professional life. Why did a physician with such
strong credentials — a residency at UC's Langley Porter Institute,
Napa State Hospital, further training in child psychiatry — have no
hospital privileges? If board-qualified, as he'd said, why not board-
certified? The mystery deepened when Grundland displayed two
pieces of paper — his bills — as his sole record of care for the Ramona family. "I do not keep records," he said.

Those pages held the dates of all his meetings with the Ramonas. It
included the March 9 meeting with Gary Ramona — the session before the confrontation that Gary claimed not to remember and that
Grundland had to be prompted to notice, the meeting the defense believed was central to winning the trial. For if Gary had been warned,
as the defense charged, and came knowing what to expect, he was not
a hapless victim lured into a destructive encounter by Isabella — an
important part of his charge against her. Gary was still adamant that
"I had no conversations whatsoever . . . I had no idea, no idea. I went
down based on a phone call." The Ramona women believed that
Grundland's soft voice belied betrayal and collusion with Gary and
Mondavi, a suspicion that deepened as Grundland affirmed that he
had never heard complaints at the winery about Gary's job perform-

ance, no hint of violent behavior, nor any indication from Gary of a shaky marriage.

Jean Sawday seethed. All along she had believed it was a conflict of interest for Grundland to see both parents and all the kids as well as the people at the winery. Now, she feared, he "lied through his teeth about everything."

Grundland did give the defense some useful ammunition. Even before Holly's amytal interview, he admitted, he had discussed with Marche Isabella Gary's potential for violence if confronted. And, yes, bestiality was sufficiently common that it need not be a fantasy, even though he had no reason to believe that Gary had ever had sex with a dog. He delighted the defense by admitting that he, not Isabella, might have been the first to refer to sodium amytal as a "truth serum." He confessed that Gary's belief that his marriage was happy was a delusion — that the Ramona marriage was troubled before the confrontation, that Stephanie wanted intercourse but Gary didn't. He confirmed that Stephanie had told him that Gary would "get on top of her but refused to put his penis in her vagina." He *had* seen Gary for two hours a few days before the confrontation. But when, to Chandler's question, "You didn't forewarn him?" Grundland said an emphatic *"No!"*, he denied the defense the admission they wanted most. He handed Harrington some useful weapons, too. Holly's memories, he posited, *could* be Oedipal projections or fantasies. He diluted the strength of the central theme of control by stating that neither Shawna nor Kelli ever mentioned Gary's being a "domineering Italian father." And the possibility of Holly's having been sexually abused before March 1, 1990, "never had entered my thinking."

But his middleman role in the Ramona family was unsettling to the jury. Holly's testimony had left most of them convinced that the family tragedy could have been avoided, rape or not, if it had never gone beyond therapy. Grundland knew everything. Might his office have been the place where it could have been mediated? As he finished his testimony, the mystery remained: What did he and Gary talk about for two hours on March 9, just days before the confrontation? He kept no clinical notes, and he didn't say. His testimony over, Grundland strode out, clearly eager to escape the forensic glare.

As an expert witness for Rose, Dr. Thomas G. Gutheil was in his element. A bearded, bespectacled Harvard forensic psychiatrist and

professor with a rumpled academic air, he had been hired by Miroglio
to defend Rose's standard of care. The phrase "standard of care" had
been repeated so often that it was becoming background noise. But he
infused his testimony with such brio, wit, and candor that he breathed
meaning into the phrase.

Tom Gutheil seemed an odd choice for expert witness — risky
even. Since his deposition in 1992, he had defended a father accused,
like Gary Ramona, of incest against a daughter whose ritual abuse
memories he did not believe. In his current writings, he quoted
Loftus's work on the easy contamination and implantation of memories. He criticized "the tendency of numbers of poorly trained counselors to seize upon childhood sexual abuse as a single cause for all adult
psychopathology." He had declared his skepticism of recovered
memories in an article in *Psychiatric Annals,* saying, "Like most human phenomena, memories may range from utterly true to utterly
false and everything in between . . . What galls us in the forensic community is the therapist testifying in court to reasonable medical certainty that *something really happened,* a conclusion based solely on
what the patient said. This confounds the true with the real. It does
not matter that the patient is convincing." He was galled, too, by "the
low credibility threshold" of *The Courage to Heal.*

In the "areas of interaction between psychiatry and the law" that
were his realm, Gutheil had come to believe that the courtroom was
alien to the goals of the psychotherapist. "In psychotherapy, you have
to immerse yourself in your patient's belief," he told the jury. "If he
told you a spaceship came down, you didn't tell him you believed it
really happened. You asked, 'What is a spaceship trying to tell us
about your inner life?'" Gutheil's research at the Psychiatry and the
Law program he directed at Harvard had led him to believe that,
rather than heal, litigation caused what he termed "developmental
arrest." "When you start bringing suit . . . It arrests people at the
victim stage, and you get stuck there . . . You sit and wallow in it, and
cannot go on with your life . . ." — the trouble with incest survivor
groups, in his view. Victimhood was a "developmental dead end."

He could, however, defend Rose with enthusiasm and full ethical
conviction. His primary goal was to redeem Rose's role in the sodium
amytal interview. It was clear to him when he first read the orange
crate of documents that the sodium amytal interview was successful
"in that it did exactly what he said it would, which is not much . . ."
The argument had emerged in Gutheil's mind that Rose's job had been

"to try to help someone who was really torn between the memories and the wish that they not be true. Holly was a torn suffering lady and he was trying to help." He told the jury, "He was faced with a very clearly suffering patient . . . looking for internal peace of mind." By administering sodium amytal, Rose had "responded to this, helping the patient clarify or sort out some of her inner experiences." Gutheil could conclude with confidence: "Dr. Rose's treatment was consistent with the standard of care."

Gutheil's job was also to establish that informed consent existed between Holly and Rose, although Holly's reported signed consent form had never been found. Informed consent — the patient's signed agreement that she understands the purposes, limitations, and expected outcome of any treatment or procedure she is to receive — was a huge issue in the memory wars. With the number of lawsuits increasing, insurers encouraged — some required — therapists to get informed consent as a way to avoid litigation. To Gutheil, informed consent was "a statement about the moral atmosphere of the relationship, if you will . . . It is not what you say, but what the patient hears." Real consent had occurred between Rose and Holly, he was convinced. "She understood quite well what she was going to get and what she would not get from the amytal procedure . . . which is the test . . . Informed consent had been obtained," he said very firmly.

Gutheil also held firm as Harrington, during his final moments of questioning, tried to get him to admit that Rose was below the standard of care in using sodium amytal as a truth serum. "Holly was suffering, and Dr. Rose tried to alleviate that suffering." Gutheil tried valiantly to cast the same cloak of professionalism over Isabella, but with less success. Harrington asked, "Do you think an MFCC just out of college with one year of postgraduate training is qualified to treat patients with major depression, in your opinion?" He tried gamely. "A number of new people are in the position of treating just such individuals in just such places. They usually do it in a dense supervisory network." Where had that dense network been while Isabella was treating Holly?

Gutheil captivated the jury. He was a deep, refreshing draft of erudition and open-mindedness. Nell Sweeney said, "He was the best. Oh, he was wonderful . . . He was completely honest." Tom Dudum agreed. "He was honest, the most honest person up there, without a doubt." So far, he and Loftus were the only two experts who impressed him as worth the money. Both had been willing to concede

points to the other side, which made them more believable. As Miroglio said, "No further questions," Gutheil exited with a bravura flourish. He had told Miroglio, "Don't expect me to hang around in court
. . . You lose the magic if you stay and join the audience."

"I call Stephanie Ramona."

Few acts other than Stephanie could follow Gutheil. But would she
let the jury peek beneath the glamorous surface? As she gave her age
under oath, there were few women looking on who did not squirm
with envy at the sight of this chic woman in a blue-and-white-striped
seersucker blazer, cuffs rolled back à la Newport Beach, a skinny
white linen skirt, and high heels instead of her usual flats. Showing the
understatement she had learned from her mother, her only jewelry
was a pair of small pearl earrings, tiny spots of luster in the cave of
shadow created by the sculptured head of streaked blond hair, forever
windswept. Her lips glistened with the palest pink lipstick as she prepared to break the silence forced upon her since Holly's flashbacks if
not for a lifetime.

Stereotypes had already been planted: here was the classic trophy
wife, a clotheshorse constricted by sexual neuroses, a helpless incompetent bypassed by a quarter century of female empowerment. Gary
Ramona might be the accused perpetrator of incest and Holly's therapists the defendants. But Stephanie Ramona was on trial, too, a suspect in at least *some* of her daughter's desperation, *some* of the family's dysfunction, *some* of its tragedy.

Neil Shapiro ushered Stephanie in for her day in court. She was, he
felt, a shy and private woman forced, in this fishbowl, to bare her
failure at the only job that gave her pride, mothering. The witness
stand was unforgiving, rules of law and evidence black and white. Her
weaknesses would be ruthlessly revealed. Miroglio knew it, too.

Miroglio had started working with Stephanie several weeks before
the trial. Stephanie worried that "through all the stress, my mind's
chopped up into little pieces." "I probably went through her testimony six, seven times, including the night before her testimony at her
house . . . It was a frustrating experience because things she would tell
me with absolute certainty on one occasion, she'd say she never heard
of on others." She, like Holly, had reviewed the script he had given
her. But he knew he would not dare to step back and become invisible
with Stephanie on the stand.

"My father's plane was — I think it went down over French Indo-china, which is now Vietnam." Feeding the practiced questions, Miroglio asked, "Did Walter Nye represent your only father figure?" "Yes, he did." That marriage, she thought, "started off happy, but he had . . . an alcohol problem." Her answers were correct. But Miroglio knew that "the worst possible thing had happened. She had memorized it . . . She started to focus on that rather than on what I was saying." At the first break he urged her, "Throw it out. Listen to me and answer my questions."

As Miroglio led her through the rehearsed story of her Las Vegas elopement, of Gary's urging marriage to escape the Vietnam draft and her resistance, Stephanie was smoldering. She was being stifled again, forbidden to say in court that she believed Gary did it or to describe her children's suspicious dreams. Her women friends could not testify to Gary's control and manipulation. Inadmissible hearsay, the judge would order if she tried. The early acts of violence had been silenced, as if they didn't exist. Exploring Gary's pushing her into marriage as a draft dodge, Stephanie found her opening, her voice. Miroglio asked, "Was he insistent about the urgency of this marriage?"

"Very! Um, I recall two incidences in his car," she blurted out before Miroglio knew what was coming. "He was nervous, he kept hitting his hand against the window. I think the first time he shattered the window and said that he fractured his hand. Then the next time he did the same thing . . . *again*. He didn't break a window, but his hand was taped."

Miroglio was aghast. He had ordered her not to say it. He had been frustrated by the judge's ruling, a year earlier, that no violence more ancient than ten years would be permitted. This was an extremely serious violation of that order.

Before Harrington could leap to his feet, Miroglio moved toward the witness box and snapped out, "So you agreed . . . to get married? . . . You were a virgin at that time? . . . On your wedding day, did you attempt to consummate . . . ?" desperately trying to divert her, waiting for Harrington to holler "Objection." Shocked, too, Harrington was hurriedly gathering his facts from his assistant, Gail, listening as Gary, explosively angry, whispered, "It never happened. I never heard it before! I've never broken my wrist, my hands, my finger. I'm going to get my hand X-rayed!"

Miroglio rushed Stephanie through a burst of questions about the secrecy of their marriage, their living apart for the first months. "Did anybody find out? . . . Did you have any intimate sexual relations? . . . Did it trouble you?"

"No, I was going to file for an annulment . . . I saw another side to Gary. Gary had hit — he was just violent." She had done it again.

The jury went on alert. "I suspected it all along, so it's no surprise," thought Becky.

Harrington leaped up. "Object!"

"Right. The jury will disregard the last comment of . . ." But Stephanie would not be stopped.

". . . the other side to him, it scared me. Gary became very angry, violent . . ."

Harrington cut her down. "Your Honor, may we approach the bench?"

The jury was ejected. They could sense the courtroom exploding as the bailiff closed the door behind them. Frustrated, they'd been given a vivid swatch of wife abuse, then had it snatched away. It was the problem with all the evidence. "It was too sugar-coated. It was so pretty when we got it. Too pretty," Yolanda fussed inside.

In the courtroom Harrington demanded: Why, twice, within two minutes, had the judge's order *in limine* — an order defining the admissible evidence — been violated? As Miroglio tried to explain — "I . . . discussed that with this witness" — Snowden directed his harsh words to Neil Shapiro. "Mr. Shapiro, do you wish to be heard on this matter? What I've just heard was obviously an attempt by either Mr. Miroglio or your client to do exactly what I ordered not be done . . ."

"I don't think . . . *either*," Shapiro snapped back. "My client is extremely nervous, trying her very best to follow the court's rulings . . . It's very hard in this circumstance to be absolutely perfect."

Stephanie sat in the witness box, silent, as the battle she had launched went back and forth.

"If it happened *once* . . . But it happened twice in a short period of time, and that gives rise to concern that nervousness may be only a partial explanation," snapped an impatient Snowden. "You'll think about it over lunch."

Gary's team raced back to the warroom at his condo. Harrington was more upset by this crisis than any other. Should they request a mistrial? With an hour to address it, he was back and forth on the phone to his office, standing at the computer accessing data bases on the modem. Checking the law, checking the civil code about dismissing the trial, checking the options.

After lunch, the jury was held back while the battle continued. In a courtroom limited to standing room because Stephanie was on the stand, Harrington argued, ". . . We've been placed in an impossible position . . . It's not feasible for Mr. Ramona to move for mistrial. He is simply out of funds, while the defendants . . . are represented by three very large insurance companies."

Snowden came down hard on the offenders, his anger barely screened by his eloquence: "I'm sorry we've gotten to the point where counsel, in a completely respectful and decorous fashion, come to each other's throats . . . There have been a number of occasions in which many if not all counsel have done things that I had to gently reguide or admonish . . . I view this situation as more serious . . . this is *serious stuff!*" Snowden announced that he would admonish the jury that all mentions of violence "are stricken from the record . . . You are to totally and completely disregard them . . . *They are simply not part of this trial.*" But another bell had been rung. Nell Sweeney thought, "A couple of times now when abuse was going to come out, they told us to strike it. But once it's in my mind, I can't exactly strike it."

When testimony resumed at two o'clock, Stephanie took the jury behind closed doors at Holly Leaf Way. ". . . Inside the house it was different . . . than it appeared to be outside." The view she gave the jury of their troubled early sex life was different, too, from Gary's story four weeks earlier. ". . . The way I remember it is, Gary would start to enter me, and he would say, 'It's not time. You're not ready. You're nervous' . . . I *was* nervous. But, yes." She wanted to proceed. She brought up douching. "He told me it was important that I douche every three or four days. He told me his mother did this . . . I should do this. We went down together" to get supplies.

Gary was livid. He whispered fiercely to Harrington that he never told Stephanie to douche, didn't know anything about douching. He phoned Garnet at the break to see whether she'd ever talked to Stephanie about douching. No. Where had it come from? It made him look sexually weird.

Miroglio stayed close to the witness stand to lend support to Stephanie through the afternoon's discussions of bad sex, douching, the unhealthy emphasis on appearances. "Images were very important to Gary, but I also — I played my part in it, too," she said, crying softly. "I tried exercising . . . That wasn't good enough." She could never measure up. He had undermined her, criticized her behavior at wine events, her body — cellulite on the legs, bottom too big, breasts too small.

Miroglio asked her, "Did you have family dinners together?" She started, "We didn't have many . . . We were doing wine tastings, and I'd feed the kids early . . ." but then stopped, her words hanging in space, as if she had drifted back somewhere and got lost in some sad memory. "I . . . I'm sorry." But as Stephanie went on to speak of telling Gary her suspicions that Holly had been molested, she did serious damage to Gary. "The TV was going, he was sitting on the bed. He looked at me, didn't say anything, and looked back at the TV. More of a 'shut up' look, you know."

"What did you interpret the look to mean?"

"Maybe he just couldn't talk about it." She brought it up again a little later. "I got into bed and I told him that I thought it was . . . Kathy. I remember him saying, 'That's a shame,' very flat . . . and he said, 'Steph, just leave it alone.'" She had brought it up again when Gary was going to work. He said, *"Goddamn it, Steph, just leave it alone."*

It made Gary look terrible. But, as he consistently claimed, he had been ordered to stay out of Holly's issues, and he had. He was "never asked *once!*" to get involved.

Stephanie's words had an impact on Tom Dudum, the wholesale textile executive who would become the jury's foreman. "My own daughter is only six months old, but if something happened to my daughter, I think that I would take an active role and I wouldn't give a damn if my daughter told me to stay out of her therapy or not . . . Gary Ramona didn't get involved." Tom was already finding Gary "his own worst enemy" in the courtroom, crowding the jury as he did, getting in their face. Now he wondered, "Could there be some shared negligence on Gary's part for not taking more of an active role?"

Stephanie's most damaging testimony came in the form of a sheet of paper, the legendary T-graph — her lists, pro and con, of why Gary would and would not have raped Holly, a mystery document mentioned in her depositions but not produced until now. It stood before the jury in a huge blowup Miroglio had had made. When asked her reason for writing it, Stephanie said, "I had to decide . . . if Gary would have done something like that and Holly was telling the truth." It was the only record that any of the Ramona women, ever, considered that he might be innocent. But the T-graph convinced Stephanie of his guilt. The jury read along from the blowup as she put on black-rimmed glasses; Miroglio asked her to read it aloud.

"Gary always pushed me to get out. He watched kids . . . but I thought a good father.

"Holly's bottom hurting — couldn't figure out why.

"Holly nightmares . . . Gary . . . lying beside her.

"Doesn't like Gary hugging her, stands back.

"Never knew Gary. I never knew his background.

"Locked door. Diamond Bar."

Down the entire left page and up half of the right, the list went on. Gary's planning to take Holly back East and leave Stephanie at home. His lack of reaction to Holly's molestation. His lies. The urinary tract infections. On Gary's side were two short items: "Wouldn't rape own daughter — wouldn't do something like that. Father."

"Did any of the twenty-eight items prove that Gary molested Holly?" Miroglio asked.

"No, not at all." But together they were a mass of evidence. She had still more vignettes, things that occurred to her at other times. Gary washing their sheets. Finding a pair of Holly's underpants in the dryer with them. The *Playboy* magazine in the bathroom, with pictures of the girls that fell out. It all fueled her statement, said with the same conviction that Holly brought to her memories, "My opinion is that I believe — my daughter and I do believe — Gary raped his daughter."

When Miroglio finished his questions about the T-graph, Kurtock dramatically held up the blowup of the document and asked Stephanie to read the three words scrawled at the bottom. "God help me," she read.

Lloyd Jenkins knew that he and Gary had photographic evidence that proved she could have unlocked the deadbolt. But many of her charges could not be answered so easily. How could Gary disprove some memory she just made up? The T-graph was dangerous.

For Becky, the towel didn't ring true. "Stephanie not only remembered that she had grabbed it from the wrought iron railing at the conversation pit, but that it was yellow? Would you remember the color?" And the date on the T-graph was disturbing. Who ever dated something "Feb 1990"? several jurors asked themselves. If you dated something, you put down the day. But the T-graph had hit home. Several items on the list were disturbing. Images she'd never forgotten. You didn't want to be suspicious, but . . . The lock. The sheets in the washer. The underpants.

Miroglio next asked Stephanie about the end of the marriage. "Gary . . . wouldn't enter me. I think I was around forty-five. So I would say probably five years" since they had completed an act of sexual intercourse. "Maybe I thought I was becoming unattractive to him. I did ask him 'Why?' I remember him saying, 'I loved you.' I asked him why again. He said, 'I don't know. I don't know.'" Later, she said, she had learned that he'd had encounters with two prostitutes.

As the jury heard about the years of no intercourse, there was some skepticism. Gary had made their sex life sound okay until the end. Yolanda thought, "I have to admit, that's strange." But the two prostitutes came as no surprise to her or her fellow jurors. "He wasn't getting it from her."

Gary surprised the press after the T-graph testimony by chatting about the Chilean wine business in the hall as if he were at the Mondavi booth at the Wine Experience. They grew quickly impatient. What about Holly's underwear in the sheets? "I have no specific recall . . . But it was not unusual for me to wash floors and dishes and windows . . ." What about being in Holly's bed, saying she had nightmares? "That is blatantly not true," he declared, pointing out that Kelli and Shawna slept in the same room. "I'm sure there's fathers in this group here who have, from time to time, gone in and assisted their children. It's easy to throw out allegations." He tossed back the accusations about trying to take Holly, without Steph, back East and skiing at Tahoe. "I gotta tell you. Stephanie, who I love dearly, traveled with me extensively, nationally and internationally. Now it's twisted, turned, blown up, as though somehow I didn't want my wife to be with me." With her suspicions heightened by her own insecurity, she saw monsters where there were none, he believed.

Gary remembered an example of how different their realities were — the business trip years earlier when he'd called her from the Roman opulence and mirrored beds of the Frank Sinatra suite at Caesars Palace in Las Vegas, eager to share his boyish excitement, and Stephanie had been so paranoid with suspicion and envy that he had stopped talking to her about these things. Her T-graph list might be twenty-eight Caesars Palaces. Misperceptions. But she believed them. Did the jury?

"What's cooking?" Judge Snowden asked the next morning. Hymens, it turned out. Stephanie's testimony would be delayed so that Dr. Stephanie McClellan could take the stand about her examination of Holly's hymen on March 1, 1990. Her thin, leggy body dressed in a black miniskirted suit, McClellan was one of Orange County's busiest ob-gyns. Kurtock asked the questions, and the defense was pleased to hear that "even if there had been injuries in the past that resulted in tearing and cutting, it is remarkable how well that area heals . . . It would be very difficult to detect." Holly, then, could have been raped, yet bear no trace of it. But McClellan gave Harrington what he needed, too. She cast doubt on the likelihood that Gary could have raped Holly, vaginally and anally, without detection or memory. Kurtock asked her, "If a five- or eight-year-old child had the type of traumatic injury that might cause separation of the hymen, it would be a very painful accident, wouldn't it? . . . Medically apparent to the doctor?" She replied, "It would be very painful" and would leave bruising in its acute phase that "should be apparent to the doctor."

"If there was anal intercourse, that would also be traumatic to a five-to-eight-year-old child?" Harrington asked. "I believe it would be very traumatic," said McClellan. Although "the most common cause of penetration that women experience is sexual activity," she said, McClellan's final answer was her most telling: Holly's "small separation of the posterior hymen . . . could be due to a number of factors . . ." A straddle injury, say, from a bike or a fall. It was not proof of rape.

Suddenly Miroglio felt it was crucial for him to know how big Gary's erect penis was. If it was very large, it would have inflicted damage, pain, and trauma that would have been difficult to miss or forget. If it was small, it was more likely that he could have raped Holly undetected. In spite of occasional ribald jokes, Miroglio considered himself "a pretty big square," but at the next break he took Stephanie aside and, mortified, said to her, "Look, I have to ask you . . . I don't know any other way to ask you this, Stevie . . . so I'm just going to ask you: How big was Gary?" It was horrible for them both as Stephanie held up her hands, gesturing, and said, "Well, I've only seen one man. So I guess he was about normal." So little dignity was left.

Stephanie McClellan was finished by ten twenty-five but stayed on to hear Stephanie Ramona's testimony until lunch. Perhaps the mother would shed light on Holly. Many women in the courtroom felt that Stephanie was the most sympathetic witness yet. They cared about Holly but regretted her polish. Stephanie wasn't polished at all. They suffered with her.

With Stephanie back on the stand, Harrington hit her hard about the T-graph. Why hadn't she produced it earlier? Stephanie answered wanly, "I found it going through my boxes in the garage and then gave it to Mr. Miroglio . . . That isn't something I particularly like to look at." He interrogated her on the lock and towel scene. She came back with intensity: "It was a combination of things . . . that I wake up in the middle of the night, that I remember to this day." But she stumbled badly when reading Dr. Lisbon's notes about enemas. "No, I just know that . . . I — I don't remember this," she said, sounding like an actress trying to remember her lines as she struggled with numbers of enemas and the ages and dates when Holly "complained of her bottom hurting." To Harrington's question, ". . . the cul-de-sac . . . was safe for your girls?" she came back with a fast, ironic quip: "I *thought* so." But the cross-examination was destroying her.

To McClellan, Stephanie was an abused woman, a woman "so fearful that she can't even get an answer out on the stand."

McClellan had lunch with the defense attorneys.

"What do you think of the trial?" Miroglio asked her.

"Why are you letting him do that to her? You're making me crazy. I want to stand up and say to the plaintiff, 'Do you remember what *you* were doing ten years ago? How *you* reacted at each doctor visit? Details of your children's febrile episodes ten, twenty years ago?'"

"Stephanie, if *you're* so offended by Harrington, what do you think the jury is?"

"I think you're taking a big risk, because I think she is working herself into a corner where she looks neurotic, incompetent, feeble — all the things that are going to work to her husband's advantage because he looks poised, consistent, articulate . . . I think you should get her off the stand."

*

Stephanie hated Gary so much she shook. Yet there was a moment in the trial when she almost seemed to be reaching out to him to say, "I would have stayed. We could have worked it out in the dream house." It was in the last moments of Harrington's questioning that he asked her, "*Now,* as of January 9, 1990 . . . you had no intention of leaving Gary, isn't that true?" Forcefully, she answered, "No, I wasn't going to leave." Throughout the trial, the defense had been rewriting the story of her marriage for her, hammering repeatedly at its having always been bad, that she'd always planned to divorce Gary. It served their purposes and disassociated Marche Isabella from the divorce. No intercourse equaled imminent divorce. But it wasn't that simple. Stephanie was sick of their writing her life for her. A year after the trial, she would stick to her story, telling a journalist, "I don't understand why Marche Isabella keeps saying that I was going to leave Gary before. I wasn't. The only thing that needed fixing was sex. And I figured we could fix that in therapy." When, in closing, Harrington brought up the dream house, Stephanie admitted, "I had mixed feelings, but I was excited about the home." After all the defense's efforts to paint a sick marriage long before the incest crisis, Stephanie left hints that there had still been something salvageable — a marriage that had not died until the day Isabella called and said, "It's rape."

Harrington's cross-examination had been a nervous nine hours for Miroglio, standing close to the witness stand as Stephanie struggled through it. He ached for her when her guilt over Holly's "weight issues" and her eating disorders came out. "I recall being worried that the way I dressed . . . would have caused Holly to be bulimic." Miroglio also suffered as, on several occasions, he heard her response as: "Well, no, of course not. I, no, I don't think so . . . Well, well, maybe. I can see . . . Well, yes, I guess, probably, yes, probably . . ." But all would be redeemed in the closing moments of her testimony as Miroglio wound it up. He salivated at the thought of the home run she would hit. Stephanie was going to describe to the jury Gary's modus operandi for raping his child. As they had been working the night before, she had told him a compelling story. She remembered one occasion when she woke up and Gary wasn't in bed. He was in the kids' room without any clothes on, although he always slept in his undershorts. That was unusual, but she didn't think anything of it at that time. Often Shawna or Kelli would cry in the middle of the night, and he would get up and take them back to the parents' bed. But when

Stephanie woke up a little later, he was gone, sleeping in Holly's room. He said that Holly was crying and he was comforting her. Miroglio was excited. He believed that he had just heard Stephanie describe, explicitly and for the first time, Gary's M.O. If she could just tell it to the jury with the same simple conviction.

Now, on Friday, April 29, it was up to Miroglio, in his redirect to Stephanie, to "bring it all home," as Snowden had ordered both sides. "Stevie, when the children were in the Diamond Bar bunk beds, now you've told us that, on occasions, Gary would get up in the middle of the night and bring Shawna back to bed with you, isn't that right?"

"Yes, or Kelli."

Miroglio was dying to ask her, "On those occasions, would he then get up and go . . . ?" but it would be leading the witness. He cautiously asked, "And then do you recall whether Gary would spend the rest of the entire night in your room?" *There's your opening — now, Stevie!* He waited for her to say, "No, when I'd wake up a little later, he'd be gone."

"I believe on one occasion . . . I — you mean the rest of the night?" she said, her voice clouded with confusion.

"The *rest* of that night?" *Come on, Stevie.*

"Yes."

He made one last desperate effort. "When Kelli was brought back into your room?"

"And then he stayed there, yes."

"*Did* he?"

"Yes."

It was over. She had gone into "vapor lock, more focused on 'What answer does he want me to give?' than listening to my words and telling the truth. So terrified of blowing the case that she couldn't see the big picture." The game was over. There would be no home run.

Stephanie burst into tears as she left the stand, realizing immediately what she'd done. "You've got to put me back on to clear that up. I blew it," she pleaded with Miroglio, and continued to plead for the rest of the trial. "I can't put you back on, Stevie," he said, trying to comfort her. "All I'd be doing is impeaching you." Harrington would nail her with "Were you lying then, or are you lying now?" There was nothing Miroglio could do.

In polling the jurors after the trial, he would learn that he should have played up the battering more and fought harder to get evidence in of Gary's violence. "It was almost as if she was a battered woman on the stand," a juror would tell him. "But we knew that couldn't be true because if she had been, you would have put on evidence of it."

In the hall, Shapiro tried to protect her from aggressive media questions, but Stephanie went weepy with the weight of "the last four years. I've kind of lived and breathed not just this trial but the suit he had against me. And my divorce. It was a horrible divorce. And then this trial . . ." Her voice trailed off. "I'd like to get on with our lives and see that our kids get on with their lives . . . I feel stronger, yeah. I don't feel it now, but I feel stronger . . ." Your goals, Stevie? a reporter asked. "Oh, uh, maybe I probably will consider doing some kind of training or studies to further my goal to work with abused children . . . but not now." Like a prayer, she added, "Just let me get through the litigation."

18

The Debate Continues

As Tim and Michael Mondavi took their oaths on May 2 and 3, the court settled in to watch them try to convince the jury that Gary Ramona's firing had had nothing to do with rumors of rape. At stake for the Mondavis was their reputation for fairness and family loyalty, the risk of another family schism — and publicity they did not want. At stake for the insurers was the $8 million Gary had demanded as recompense for the damage done to his career by the defendants.

The sons would tell a story as poignant as Willy Loman's in *Death of a Salesman;* they painted Gary Ramona as a salesman who had sunk in a swamp of unsophisticated and outdated thinking — a death of his own making. Harrington had already argued persuasively that the characteristics his accusers most criticized in Gary — his confidence, decisiveness, devotion to work, and so on — were the very hallmarks of a good businessman. But, to the brothers, Gary was a retail animal who had been in his element winning ends and sides in supermarkets but unable to evolve as the market grew more competitive. A man "limited by his weaknesses," as Tim said.

"I have always had great regard . . . great affection for Gary. I have admired Gary for his dedication, for his charisma, for his energy. But over time it became evident that his organizational abilities were not as strong as his charisma and dedication," said Tim, looking more counterculture than corporate with his full head and beard of sandy-red hair topping his double-breasted gray suit. His gentle look proved deceptive as Miroglio asked him, "Were you one of the people responsible for granting Mr. Ramona leave of absence on or about June 18, 1990?"

"Yes, I was."

"Were you also one of the people responsible for Mr. Ramona's termination from the winery?"

"Yes, I was."

Taking the stand the next morning, Michael looked as hard-edged and sophisticated as his brother had looked sensitive. His gray-flecked black hair, thinning at the forehead, was slicked back to outline the same strong craggy features of his father; a thick black mustache couldn't conceal the powerful similarity between father and son. His testimony did not reveal the "big heart" Gary had always seen in Michael. "A great salesman does not make a great sales manager," said Michael, fleshing out the picture of an old-time salesman "beyond his skills" in a consolidating marketplace. Instead of being one of "six or seven major brands . . . that a distributor carried . . . today we're one of three hundred brands. So we've had to change the way we've done business in the last four or five years." Under Gary, Mondavi was getting behind the wave in market positioning in 1990. It came crashing down in 1991. "I had tremendous faith and confidence in his sales ability. I didn't have that degree of confidence in his marketing. Marketing is your planning and your strategy. Sales is the execution." Yes, sales were $2 million over projection his last year. "And the costs were *$1.6 million over*," Michael reminded the jury.

Michael, like Tim, denied that the allegations of incest had had anything to do with their terminating Gary. There had been no paper trail, they claimed. "Because of the allegations, we probably were more scrupulous in making sure that we bent over backward to not have that influence," Michael said. But as both brothers invoked spousal privilege when asked about their wives' role, questions were planted in the minds of some jurors. What were they hiding? Isabel and Dorothy Mondavi were already on several jurors' mental lists of people guilty of spreading rumors at the winery.

Sharon Chandler was blunt in her final questions to Michael. "Was Gary fired because of his emotional reaction to his divorce?"

"No. Not at all."

"Was he fired because he was spending a lot of time building a house?"

"No."

"Was he fired because he refused to change his role at the winery at a time when the winery needed him to change?"

"Absolutely."

"Did your father agree with you and your brother that Gary Ramona's role . . . needed to change?"

"Yes, he did."

In cross-examination, however, Harrington effectively planted personal and business conflicts as motive. Tim blamed Gary for the failure of his baby, Vichon Winery, to meet its targets. "I think that Gary wanted to discount it more aggressively. I wanted to continue to position it . . . to maintain its reputation in the marketplace for high quality, and I am right in that." But wasn't it true that Vichon was now sold in Costco, the mother of all discount stores? asked Harrington. "Yes," said Tim, forced to admit not only that he had finally been defeated on the issue but by his brother. And the motive of jealousy was seeded: "Gary and my father had a wonderful relationship; essentially the adopted son that he was closer to than his blood children," Michael confessed to an amazed courtroom. "That was fine, but Gary felt that he could do what he wanted" whether the sons were supportive or not. "We were a nuisance to him at times . . . I felt that my father was being taken advantage of . . ."

Both brothers built on the impression given by such credible witnesses as Gary's psychiatrist Wolfgang Lederer that Gary's blinding desire to see only perfection did not let him see the flaws in his life. Even the fair-minded juror Tim Holewinske felt that Gary never saw reality. "He was incapable of it," Beth feared. Yet, despite the litany of flaws Tim and Michael had spent hours listing, there clearly remained powerful feeling for Gary in a winery that was still run, said Michael, "as a family business, with heart and soul." When Gary came into his office and told him Stephanie had filed for divorce, "he acted like he'd been hit by a ten-ton truck . . . He cried — we were both crying and we hugged . . . and I asked, 'Is there anything we could do?'"

The Mondavi brothers had revealed the personal anguish and conflicts beneath their smooth performances. Yet, as they finished their testimony, it was clear that they would not, this time, spill family blood. Within months Michael would be named sole CEO as Tim gracefully stepped down.

The jury, however, was left with the suspicion that the brothers' jealousy of Gary had played a role in his leaving his job. Most felt that he would never have run the company, even if he thought he would. Becky saw it in fundamental terms: "Gary's not blood." Yolanda felt that Gary's fate had been cast when the power went to the sons. "When Bob Mondavi gave Mike and Tim the company, Gary was out. There was too much jealousy." "Jealousy has nothing to do with reality," mused Tom Dudum, an executive in an old family business. "The reality is that business is tough. Money is tough. Retailers and distributors don't want to pay his $400,000-plus salary. The era of the Gary Ramona salesperson is not there anymore."

A few nights later, Gary and his party ran into Michael and Isabel Mondavi at Bistro Don Giovanni. As Gary got up to leave he had to pass by the Mondavis; he stopped and shook Michael's hand.

JoeAnna Jenkins couldn't believe it. "How can you do that after what that man said in court?" she whispered when they'd passed.

"Michael couldn't help it. He had to say what he thought. He's got his view of it, and I've got mine. I've known him for twenty-five years." It was that optimism, JoeAnna marveled, "that eternal optimism that keeps him going up that hill again."

While Mondavi's chief financial officer, Greg Evans, monitored the trial, his wife, Anne, was writing her own story between the English literature classes she taught at Napa College. Hers was a very different tale of incest, one she had kept a shameful secret. *Ramona*, however, had stirred her to write it down. Molestation by her stepfather had begun when she was eleven and continued for seven years. Anne remembered every detail vividly.

"The repeated visits to my room, the low, choked tone of his voice, its modulation from phony paternal to salacious . . . the asking to see, the fondling of small triangular breasts, the removal of cotton underwear, the unzipping of trousers." She'd learned tricks to get away by giving him only part of what he wanted. But she had submitted, polite, compliant, without protest. "Worst of all, why did I do nothing the day I came home unexpectedly to find him fondling my sister on the couch, her petticoats tumbled over her head?" Her stepfather was now dead. The incest was too late to undo. Why had he done it? She examined the story, the dynamics of his life. If Anne could understand just one perpetrator, it might give a voice to other women.

Within a few months of the trial, Anne published her story in the weekend magazine of the *San Francisco Examiner & Chronicle*. Her experience of incest — all of it had been dreaded, hated, repeated, *remembered*.

*

Harrington was proving every bit the sly fighter Leonard had predicted as he stripped the defense of one of the most potentially convincing pieces of evidence that Holly had been sexually abused.
Stephanie had claimed that Dr. Thomas Stiles, the respected family
physician who'd tried and failed to do a pelvic exam of seventeen-
year-old Holly, had asked her, "Has Holly ever been molested?" Stiles,
Stephanie said, was the first to raise the red flag of sexual abuse. But
even footwork by Miroglio so deft that he himself expected charges of
"Disingenuous!" from the judge had not been able to dislodge Stiles
from his failure to "specifically recall" having asked Stephanie the key
question. Harrington first got from Stiles a critical modification of the
statement. Yes, Stiles admitted, Holly had held her legs together so
tightly that he could not examine her. Then, seizing Stiles's doubt,
Harrington swiftly extracted the statement: "I did not have any discussion with" Holly about sex abuse. "I had a conversation with Mrs.
Ramona. I do not remember talking specifically about sexual abuse."
No, he had no conversation with Mrs. Ramona about sexual abuse,
he confirmed.

Harrington's cross-examination had also swiftly demolished the
credibility of a Santa Rosa psychologist, Dr. Albert J. Kastl. Hired
to examine Gary, Stephanie, and Holly as an antidote to Gerner's sociopathic, schizotypal, and paranoid findings for Holly, Kastl lobbed
therapists' jargon against Gary — he found "a significant personality
disorder" with narcissism, "obsessive-compulsive and aggressive features," and PTSD. But Kastl admitted he had not read Pope and Hudson's important new article on bulimia and sexual abuse, the study
inspired by this case. He was caught dead wrong when he claimed that
a report critical of Gary's performance at Mondavi had been published before the March 1990 confrontation. He admitted that the
healthier Holly he had seen had been free of Rose's and Isabella's
therapy for a year and was taking Prozac. Perhaps most damaging
was his admission, over hollered objections from the defense, that
Holly had still had doubts, even after the sodium amytal, about
whether her father had sexually abused her.

To the attorneys, arguing in an almost empty courtroom on the eve of
her testimony, Lenore Terr stood as the test of a pivotal issue: Would
her theories of the diagnosis of child trauma and sexual abuse be
admitted into testimony as scientific evidence? At stake was the right,

for this and future cases, to bring recovered memories before a jury. Harrington was evoking *Kelly-Frye,* a combination of U.S. Supreme Court and California cases, which said that, in lawsuits where "novel scientific evidence" — such as recovered memories — was involved, expert testimony was admissible only for science that was "generally accepted by the relevant scientific community." Four years earlier, Eileen Franklin's recovered memories had easily been permitted before the jury without the stringent tests of their right to be there. No longer.

In the Salem witch trials, excluding from testimony the "spectral evidence" of crazed young girls — Satan's presence, intangible, invisible to all but them, yet driving them to their fits and contortions — had finally stripped the hysteria of its fuel and let it swiftly burn out. Courts in the late twentieth century were beginning to treat recovered memories as spectral evidence as, increasingly, trial judges like Snowden were forced to be gatekeepers for controversial scientific theory. For judges it would only get harder. The trend was to test these memories in pretrial hearings before permitting them to be heard by a jury, leaving judges as the sole arbiters of the worth of theories on which scientists disagreed. Memory scientists were focusing research on the issue, responding to social urgency. But none had yet given judges clear answers. Snowden listened to the attorneys rail — Harrington that Terr's theories were purely her own invention and met no scientific standards, Miroglio responding that Terr was not only world-respected but would, definitively, explain repression — then posed the conundrum judges faced: "How do we know the difference between somebody who is a credible person . . . and a witch doctor?"

Snowden feared that the issues were "at a level of sophism that may be well beyond anything of significance from the jurors' point of view." And his. But he had to bring closure, so he put the memories to California's Kelly-Frye test, which required that a new scientific technique could be introduced into court only if a consensus of the relevant scientific community relied on it. If this had been a state that applied the new, more permissive Daubert rule, the courts would have required only that a reasonable expert relied on the new science. But this was California, and there was clearly no consensus in its scientific community on Holly's memories, so Snowden would not permit them to be argued as proof that Gary had raped his daughter. It was a quiet but important moment in the recovered memory wars, for other courts were watching.

But there was also the issue of fairness. Since Loftus had been permitted to testify that the alleged repressed memories were the result of suggestion, Terr should be permitted to contradict her — to try to prove that Holly's memories were based on fact. Snowden would permit Terr to try to prove the authenticity of the memories but with a strict limitation: she could not testify "to her opinion that Holly Ramona was the victim of childhood sexual abuse and to her opinion that Gary Ramona is most likely the perpetrator." There was a little sophistry in the solution, Snowden knew, but it was inescapable in this ambiguous climate.

Terr's appearance on Wednesday, May 4, created almost as much excitement as Holly's. The women in the courtroom who had endured weeks of attack on their recovered memories had anxiously awaited her. If anyone could give credibility to them — to repression, to the authenticity of Holly's memories — it was Terr. Where the plaintiffs had presented a string of distinguished experts — Loftus, Pope, Dietz — to address the issues of memory and repression, the defense was presenting only one. It felt confident.

As Terr entered the courtroom, a man grinned at her. "I thought he was going to stick out his hand to shake mine. I thought, 'Who is this man? Oh, my God, this is Gary Ramona.'" He was intrusive, committing boundary violations.

Sitting with the Ramona women in the right front row, waiting to be called, Terr was eager, as always. "I'm a mystery reader and I love courtroom drama . . . It has that wonderful mystery and that wonderful unraveling." A relaxed and amiable woman, Terr was smartly dressed but fell short of chic in a red blazer and white blouse, her short red-blond hair framing a pleasant, animated face. She had driven up from San Francisco the night before, had a good dinner with her husband and the Miroglios at Terra, then worked over Bruce's script for about an hour at the motel. He had studied her testimony in *Franklin* and in the Akiki trial in Southern California and had "organized a very carefully worked out pattern of presenting me. He knew what my answers would be to his questions."

She had never seen Harrison Pope before, although they had talked by phone and worked out a patient's medication together. Pope sat behind Harrington, leaning forward, his angular face as fiercely alert as an eagle's, ready to hand Harrington weapons against Terr. Pope would feed him information about eating disorders and food fetishes that the depositions told them would be a large part of Terr's argument in support of Holly's memories. The psychiatrist Richard

Rada, who'd testified earlier, had flown in from Orange County to observe Terr and to prepare a possible rebuttal to her for Gary's side.

Terr felt secure. She had written an enthusiastic chapter about her role in the Franklin case in her book *Unchained Memories,* which had just been published. A front-page review of it in the *New York Times* just after the trial distressed her, panning her for seductive writing and too-quick conclusions about memory.

Marian Dodds held the book in her hands on Terr's first day of testimony. Sitting in the front row with Betty Nye and Jean Sawday, she wore a cream-colored silk shirt and tailored black slacks — hardly the drab woman who had sat, sullen and anonymous, in her gray sweatshirt during the first weeks of the trial. With makeup and styled hair, she had joined the world. After court that afternoon, she planned to drive to her therapist in Marin County for a sodium amytal interview, hoping it would strengthen the credibility of Holly's amytal interview. Carolyn Thompson and her children sat nearby.

Terr had heard all about the debate the day before, with "Harrington tearing at my credentials . . . saying that I was a fringe doctor with fringe ideas," and made sure that Miroglio started by letting her recite her entire nine-page CV — the prizes, the groundbreaking studies, the peer review papers — a life of ascending achievement, from her Phi Beta Kappa award in college to this week's lecture at the Menninger Clinic.

A master storyteller, Terr turned toward the jury box and began the tale of Chowchilla. "Twenty-six ordinary California kids on a school bus were held for twenty-seven hours by three masked men toting huge guns." They were given no drink or food, driven for eleven hours, and then "buried alive for sixteen hours" in a moving van at a rock quarry. The horror of mass suffocation gripped the courtroom as she described the roof's beginning to collapse in on them. She told of their escape when they were finally freed by two boys who crawled out. Sharing the same terrible, traumatic event yet miraculously not injured, maimed, or killed, the children of Chowchilla were "the perfect study." Basically, that single trauma was remembered well. They might get the details wrong after a time, but the gist of it would be true.

Terr moved from "the single-blow trauma I described to you in Chowchilla," Type I trauma, to the "multiple-blow, or Type II trauma, some horrible childhood abuse," which she would argue was the explanation for Holly's loss and recovery of memory. But first she would talk about trauma. "Trauma is a psychological blow; it's a psychological karate chop; *not like getting lost in a mall,*" Terr declared, taking her first swipe at Elizabeth Loftus. How could one compare the horror of Chowchilla to an imaginary minor event in a shopping mall?

Terr began her memory lesson by describing the six different kinds of memory, but the jury wasn't with her. She couldn't make eye contact; this jury would not connect. She didn't get nervous, but it was a bad start to the day. Miroglio had held her as the last defense witness of the trial. "He wanted to end the case with a big splash," she says.

Perhaps Miroglio's next question would engage the jury, as it had engaged America: "Are some traumatic memories different from the normal memory process . . . ?" "Yes," Terr responded confidently. "The effect is so traumatic . . . so shocking, so unexpected and undetected that they're in the memory in a more striking way." As they're stored, "you get tremendous recall . . . very detailed stories . . . pieces out of order because kids are very bad at chronology . . . but a tremendously detailed event." Just as confidently, she dismissed the claims of top memory scientists that the earliest possible childhood memories were from age three and a half to four and claimed that, with psychic trauma, "you can get shards, just like pieces of broken glass — some tiny little fragment of the trauma that's earlier than that." As young as twenty months, or earlier. It was just this kind of colorful theory, which Harrington considered unverified, that he had tried to block from the jury.

Terr moved to the heart of her theory. "Types I and II are generally accepted . . . being taught in medical schools . . ." You couldn't prove them organically. Ethically, "I can't get into the brain with needles and stuff . . . But in my very strong opinion . . . children who had gone through many traumatic events remembered the events less well than people who had gone through just one event." The key, she said, was "anticipation . . . you *know* it's going to happen . . . you can suppress." You can put up defenses. Miroglio led her to the key question: "You believe in the existence of repressed memory?" She told the jury with ringing conviction, "Yes, I do. I see them and I've studied them . . . in depth . . . there's something like eighty-five years of single case reports of repression where patients' repression lifts . . ." She even had a time line for repression. It could occur immediately after traumatic events but more frequently within twelve hours.

Holly's was repeated trauma, "like water hitting a rock, trauma that is repeated so much that you anticipate it, you set up defenses against it — repression, dissociation, splitting, displacement, identification with the aggressor, denial in fantasy — all ward off the memory." Can the memories be retrieved? "I *know* they are . . . Do you know about the Franklin murder case?" she asked the jury, describing that case. She knew Park Dietz had told them he'd changed his mind about repression when he learned that Eileen Franklin's remembered details had all been in the newspaper. Dietz was wrong, Terr claimed, defending Eileen's memories.

Terr's initial five hours on the stand were all preparation for the payoff: Terr's six-hour examination of Holly, the raw material for her proof of Holly's credibility. If the jury was going to believe that Holly's memories were a reliable guide to veridical truth — that years of horrible rape by Gary Ramona had really happened — it would be in the next hour. The women jurors were with her. Terr had been hard for Yolanda at first. "But when everybody else had been saying *this* and suddenly she was saying *that,* she made the other side of my brain say, 'Hmmm?' She had us." Not the male jurors, though. At the lunchtime break, Terr's son-in-law asked, "Why aren't the men with you?" He'd seen one actually dozing off. "Now that's not me. I'm a really interesting speaker," thought Terr. "Had the men already made up their minds?" she wondered.

Why now? Miroglio asked after lunch. Why a sudden epidemic of "de-repressed" memories when the massive repression of incest trauma seemed not to exist until it burst into the work of Herman and Russell in the mid-1980s? The pervasive use of therapy was the answer. "Psychotherapy can be that secure ground, a comfortable and safe ground, for return of memories," Terr explained. "You get a cue — sounds, sights, smells" — all could be cues. And when the memories return, "Do they come playing out like a tape recorder?" asked Miroglio. "No, like a bolus, a large chunk." And they came out essentially accurate. Where "plain old memory" might be modified in storage, these extraordinary "traumatic memories are so burned into the mentality that it's hard to modify them much." Repression of childhood trauma, she summed up with Holly in mind, was "a response to an overwhelming event — not just a *thought,* but a traumatic event that can force a life to revolve around it, that can create the whole tone and theme in a life."

Then she introduced the jury to the rest of her theory, to that whole group of "symptoms and signs" that, as a package, were her evidence of authentic trauma. With no witnesses, no semen traces, no medical corroboration, no report of abuse from Holly's sisters, no apparent pattern of deviance in Gary Ramona, Terr's "cluster" theory — her clinical observations of symptoms and signs — was the best evidence of abuse the defense could get. "People can go see a Stephen King movie and get a run of repeated dreams," she explained, "but they don't have a whole disorder." They did not get the clusters of symptoms and signs that, her thirty years of research had taught her, could not be faked.

Terr began the afternoon by playing detective, looking for symptoms and signs in Holly. She had looked for anger or its opposite, passivity, she told the jury. She looked for helplessness and a whole array of fears — for repeated bodily problems and posttraumatic play and reenactment. In Holly she had found not just clusters but veritable galaxies of symptoms and signs. "It is my opinion that the images Holly had are actualities — memories of actualities," said Terr, seizing the ambiguous opening the judge had given her to counter Loftus's claims that the source of the memories was suggestion by her own claim that their source was fact — without naming Gary as the perpetrator. Holly had in abundance the four traits "that appear to last in abused children as adults." There was her tendency to reperceive the trauma — to "refeel" the rapes in the snakes that crawled in her bed and into her vagina. There was her series of fears — fear of her body, of young men, of sex. Of her father — "she can't stand Tom Cruise" because he has big canine teeth like her father's. Her fear of foods — avoiding anything that reminded her of penises, semen, oral sex. Holly "had to cut bananas and slice pickles," Terr said. "She avoids melted cheese, can't stand mayonnaise, and can't abide any kind of white or cream sauce — they're like male ejaculate." Third, there were Holly's behavioral repetitions of the trauma, the physical reenactments — so many pains in her bottom, the horrible constipation, vaginismus, which was the muscular tightness around the vagina she'd had throughout her life — she couldn't even use tampons. There were the games she played — Charlie's Angels, Bionic Woman, Wonder Woman — always with the same theme: "villainous men that had to be destroyed" — although that sign seemed a reach for many in the courtroom. What child hadn't played those games? Finally, Holly "has always had a sense of no future." She couldn't see marriage, a family. "She believed that she'd die young."

Concluding with a crescendo of affirmation for Holly's memories and for her diagnosis of posttraumatic stress syndrome, Terr subsided, at the end, with a perfunctory statement of support for the defendants, who had not been mentioned throughout her testimony. Addressing Rose's, Isabella's, and the hospital's standard of care, she got on record: "I don't see that any major mistakes were made." While she confirmed their innocence of malpractice, she still privately thought of the two therapists as "these two poor pawns." She had always felt Gary was really suing Holly, not the therapists.

After two hours of cross-examination, Harrington was about to put Lenore Terr's feet to the coals.

With her confident testimony about mayonnaise and pickles in mind, Harrington shifted to her credentials in eating disorders and extracted that Terr once almost did a study in the 1970s. For the first time, a crackle of impatience appeared in her voice: "So we started a study, but we didn't complete a study." Harrington next forced her to tediously count, study by study, the numbers of subjects in her research, trying to discredit them as too few and too focused on children to be significant or relevant. As he attempted to undermine the authority of her publications, Terr's tone got testy defending article number fifteen on her long list: "The *Journal of Pediatrics* is very, *very* peer-reviewed . . . *the* prestigious journal in pediatrics." Turning to her fascination with analyzing literary figures through their writing, Harrington made light of her diagnoses of repressed childhood trauma in one of her studies. "That's the one where you found that Edgar Allan Poe had been taken into his mother's bed when he was two . . . ?" he asked. "You never examined Virginia Woolf?" No, but she had sat next to Stephen King once in a restaurant and overheard him say things that had given her insight into the source of the violence in his writing, she said. Harrington drew discreet smiles from the spectators as he asked, "Do you feel you were able to make a differential diagnosis during his conversation?"

Terr tried to divert Harrington from the literary Never Land back to the here and now. "Well, I heard *today* about a demonstration of repression . . . a black man who —" He cut her off with: "I'm getting another anecdote . . . but I'd like to have my question answered first." After the judge ordered her to respond to the question, her voice rose as she snapped, "I'm trying to talk about something scientific. But you're not *letting* me!" She'd have to wait until Miroglio's redirect to tell the dramatic story of a young black man kidnapped as a child who had just been reunited with his parents through DNA testing, the Kevin Portis case. "She's trying to defend rather than just answer the questions honestly, like Loftus," Marty Cook observed.

Terr was still trying to capture the men. At the afternoon break, her son-in-law reported, "You've got them for a few seconds and then you're losing them." She could get their attention, she found, if she made a sports analogy or delivered a one-liner. She finally got a good laugh from the courtroom when Harrington, picking away systematically at the research so favored by repressionists, introduced a study from the Netherlands. As Terr scanned it, she cracked, "It's all Dutch to me." "But then they'd be gone again," Terr saw. She did not know that for the spectators, the most entertaining half hour of the trial was about to begin.

"Are you aware of the fact Holly testified she also wouldn't drink orange juice? Do you regard this . . . as evidence that memories are true? And hot dogs, they had been sliced, too?" asked Harrington, provoking Terr to defend Holly's food fetishes as proof of abuse. "You took one piece out of a cluster . . . You can only get trauma from a whole cluster of symptoms . . . the banana does not qualify sex abuse, the pickle does not . . . the mayonnaise does not . . . but when you start adding them on top of each other, they start to qualify sex abuse," she responded with a hint of disdain.

"Were you aware that she . . . binged on frozen yogurt?"

"No . . . She could not stand the idea of snails."

"Do you know that she worked in a yogurt shop in Southern California from one to two years?" Holly's food fetishes were beginning to sound just plain silly. "Do you regard yourself as an expert on bulimia?"

"I'm more of a clinical expert . . . and one thing . . . I do *well* is treat people with eating disorders. I know, inside myself, I'm as much an expert as anybody."

Then she told the story that would wake up not only the men but the entire courtroom. It had to do with the children's game Ring Around a Rosy. Harrington, who had done his homework, began by asking her if trauma was contagious. Yes, there was a "spreadability" because trauma was "so traumatic and it's so powerful," she said. ". . . Trauma can be carried over from generation to generation . . .

Ring Around a Rosy means the rosy from the Black Plague . . . Kids
are still dancing it . . . It doesn't traumatize them, but they make up
the anxiety connected with it and won't play it."

"The person who won't play Ring Around a Rosy was your own
daughter, isn't that right? . . . That was . . . four hundred years after
the Black Plague? But she felt the anxiety . . . ?"

"She felt a *whiff* of the anxiety."

"Did I hear right?" many in the courtroom wondered. Terr's
daughter had inherited a "whiff of anxiety" from the Black Plague?
Nell Sweeney caught the silent consensus of the jury: "She lost me."
"She's lost half of everybody right here," Yolanda mused. "Ring
Around a Rosy" would become, like "Gerner," another of those verbal markers the jury would carry away from the trial, a moment that
would bond them. Terr had slipped into a twilight zone from which
her credibility would never recover in this trial. Even teenage Becky,
who found Terr's psychology fascinating and was not the least upset
by her food fetish theories, thought, "Her daughter is not going to feel
the plague four hundred years ago. That's ridiculous." Shifting the
theme to Holly's depression, Harrington said, "Nobody ever diagnosed Holly was suffering from posttraumatic stress disorder except
you . . ." Terr snapped back with what she later claimed was one of
her attempts at a one-liner, but it came out as arrogant: "Well, *I've*
diagnosed her suffering from PTSD, and I'm not *nobody!*"

The courtroom seemed to recoil. "She's just lost the jury," thought
Betty Nye. "Why would she make a mistake like that?" Yolanda expressed what most on the jury were feeling: "She's getting an *attitude.*" As Tim heard it, "It seemed like when she was raising her voice
to him, putting him down, that she had to prove her theories from
sheer force of will — that they couldn't stand on their own." With
Loftus, he recalled, "they tried to ridicule her, but they couldn't. They
couldn't shake her."

At the end of the day, Terr had been observing Gary. "He was
such a salesman. So aggressive. Sitting in the lap of the jury. He was
smiling at them, often inappropriately. Somebody would be talking
about some painful thing that he was involved in, and he would be
grinning at the jury." Maybe it was his salesman's training; she didn't
know. "But he was actually intruding on the jury." For Gary, the
greatest test of the poise Terr found offensive was when they talked
about Prince. When Harrington asked her if Holly had had a "sexual

encounter with the family dog," Terr said she did believe it was possible. She had seen "one or two children who had had animal kinds of relations." Bestiality was out there. But to Harrington's question she admitted, "I don't know about that one. It's the least convincing of Holly's memories." It didn't have a whole group of symptoms. Holly could feed and handle dogs. She had had other dogs. But, ignoring Harrington to address the jury directly, Terr hastened to add, "I have no reason not to believe any of her memories because they're not borne out by her symptoms and signs."

She, like Gutheil, knew that "an expert witness concedes points." She had conceded Prince. But in expressing doubt about the reliability of one memory, she had raised the question in the jury's mind: Could the rest be trusted? It was the doubt Loftus had so deftly planted weeks earlier by introducing Prince into testimony. As Harrington had Terr read from her notes, the jury squirmed: "Father was undressed . . . held the dog against the front of him, and then put the dog on the ground, and folded his arm around the body form of the dog, brought the dog toward her and told her that she must orally copulate the dog."

Besieged by the young women who had made a pilgrimage to hear her, Terr could scarcely make her way to her chair when she arrived in court the next morning. "Could I call you? I need to ask your advice," asked a fortyish nurse suffering through her first flashbacks. She reached out to shake Terr's hand, as if she might be healed by contact, like contagious magic. "Thank you for what you're doing for us." "Would you sign your new book for me?"

Back on the stand, Terr reminded the jury that "I'm a psychiatrist who is acknowledged as a general psychiatrist of some rank and reknown . . . My writing has been acknowledged as pacesetting and as groundbreaking." Harrington meanwhile brought up her writings about the Franklin case, in which she claimed that the sign of a true memory was the detail that surrounded it: another thing you look for is "rich details, not really vague . . . strong perceptions connected with real memory." He was comparing, for the jurors, the lack of detail or context in Holly's flashbacks — their vagueness.

And, finally, what would you look for, other than symptoms and details, as corroboration of true memories? Harrington asked.

"I said, 'Accompanying emotion.'"

"Do you know if Holly Ramona displayed any emotion in this courtroom when she testified regarding these alleged acts of rape?"

If Holly had not shown emotion, Terr said, it could be "shame connected with having to confess it to all these strangers . . . Some kids . . . after a terrible experience, will talk about it like little robots."

". . . You said, for memory, you'd expect corroborative details, richness of details . . ." Harrington said, reveling in the inescapable conflict of Terr's words in 1990 with her findings for Holly three years later.

"I can't stand on that statement," Terr conceded. She would tell the jury why. "I testified that in 1990 . . . But medicine just keeps moving on." Sick of Harrington's "trying to keep me looking fringey," she had decided to seize and address the larger issue: the incompatibility of the scientific method with the courtroom — "the almost irreconcilable difference between the law and psychiatry." Holly's lack of emotion in court was a prime example. Correct, a true memory shouldn't be bland in the setting of a therapist's office. But it was different in the courtroom, where there were so many reasons for a "flat affect." The very nature of science — a constant challenge to prevailing ideas — made it a helpless target in cross-examination. It wasn't a matter of whether her theories were right or wrong. She continued to modify them. All scientists did. Yet she was trapped, in 1994, with her four-year-old opinions carved in stone. "*Franklin* was the first returned memory I had a chance to see . . . I'm being asked about things I thought *four years* ago. I've been learning since '90 . . . Information is growing rapidly."

Harrington's point was that her arguments weren't science. He reminded Terr of her own story that she had claimed a cohesive memory from the age of eleven months — an age much too young for full narrative memories, scientists said. Yes, she told the jury, "I have a memory of my grandmother holding me . . . and her placing a hot teaspoon in my mouth," filling in the rest of the narrative with what her mother had told her.

"So you would agree with me that if a trusted adult gave you a *false* story of what happened around that little fragment, you would adopt that as a memory also," he said.

Suddenly Terr exploded. ". . . I do not relish your insinuations that my mother is a false person!"

Nell took note. "She's getting rude." ". . . a little too defensive," thought Shelley Maynard. "Now she's just lost everybody," thought Yolanda. "But, hey, it's entertaining." She was getting bored. These were not one-liners. Terr was committing the cardinal sin, Marty Cook was thinking. "She's taking it personally."

Harrington continued his barrage, managing to insinuate that Terr believed in satanic ritual abuse and medieval cult practices. Then, out of nowhere, in the last minutes of his cross-exam, he repeated the term Terr had used to describe Holly's extraordinary muscular tightness in the vaginal area: "Did you know that Stephanie Ramona suffers from vaginismus? That Stephanie Ramona can't insert tampons in her vagina?" There were bellows of "Objection!" from the defense. But Harrington had planted the seed that perhaps Stephanie's sexual uptightness, not rape, might have inspired Holly's own vaginismus.

As the judge overruled the objections, Harrington said, "Nothing further, Your Honor." Then, the way the TV detective Columbo reopened the door in his disheveled raincoat, he turned back to Terr. "Oh, one other question. Do you know that Holly eats fettuccine Alfredo?" To the suppressed smiles and giggles of the courtroom, he said, "Thank you," and sat down. With that line, he discredited all the slimy semenlike foods — the mayonnaise, the escargots. On the other hand, there were still the sliced bananas . . .

In its brief redirect, the defense tried to rehabilitate Terr. Miroglio invited her to tell the jury the story of the Portis case she'd tried earlier to introduce as potential proof of repressed memory, to explain why Holly might have been emotionally flat in court, and to justify her diagnosis of PTSD. In the trial, she was using the draft of "a new diagnosis which is called 'childhood sexual abuse.' [It] was not available to those doctors in 1990," she told the court. It would be published just a few weeks later in the *DSM-IV* — not as one of the major mental disorders, an Axis One diagnosis, but you could use it for making a diagnosis, and insurance would pay.

"Do you consider it possible . . . that a person could experience a traumatic experience like childhood sexual abuse as late as the age of fifteen or sixteen and still repress it for three or four years?" Miroglio asked pointedly.

". . . Anybody can repress . . . You don't have to be a small child to repress." The former Miss America Marilyn Van Derbur, she reminded him, had been abused until eighteen with no knowledge of it until twenty-four. Though not subjected to the rigorous scrutiny that would satisfy Pope or Loftus, Van Derbur's claims were that, for survival, she had dissociated into a nighttime child and a daytime child, each innocent of the other's existence.

As Harrington closed in for the last minute of testimony from the last expert witness in the long trial, he returned to his persistent efforts, as Terr saw it, "to make me look like a . . . not very well accepted theorist who based everything on people like Stephen King and Virginia Woolf."

"You've told us about, I believe . . . Miss America, Stephen King, Edith Wharton, Marilyn Van Derbur, Virginia Woolf, Edgar Allan Poe . . ." he said with a smile of amused tolerance. "Is this what we call good theater, bad science? I have nothing more, Your Honor."

The prosecution's rebuttal began with an antidote to Lenore Terr. Dr. Robert Rada was very plain fare, but many in the courtroom were starved for just his kind of common sense. He had come to show them that for every symptom and sign that screamed sex abuse to Terr, "there are very logical options." Without corroboration, "she cannot take the symptoms and signs of an alleged victim and work back and say 'This is sexual abuse.'" Convincing the jury as Terr had been unable to, he quietly dismissed the professional acceptance of Terr's Type II trauma by saying that he, a psychiatrist experienced in child sex abuse, had first heard of it "reading Dr. Terr's articles." He held the balanced middle ground, avoiding the sound of advocacy that had hurt Terr.

"Dr. Rada is the most damaging witness for the defense," Dr. Leo Stoer whispered to his seatmate as Rada encapsulated his critique of Terr: "We don't have to look for deep-seated reasons for common things."

"As Freud said," Harrington quipped, "sometimes a cigar is just a cigar."

19

Verdict

It was like a testimonial dinner. From Diamond Bar, from Pinot Way, from the Mondavi winery, they had come to take the stand for Gary Ramona. Rebuttal was Gary's last chance to challenge and correct the arguments made against him. There was his St. Helena neighbor Charlie Piazza, sobbing as he said, "All I can say is they're great people . . . To me, Gary Ramona is *tops*." There was his former secretary Teresa Speck, talking of the boss who "was our leader, always available, always encouraged . . . who made me feel like an equal" — the boss whose daughter Holly was "a very relaxed, happy kid, a normal teenager" who'd "pop her head in and say hi to her dad." Two Mondavi executives risked reprimand to appear and reject Tim and Michael's "dictatorial" as an adjective for Gary and replace it with "collegial . . . communicative . . . A-plus at marketing." Eleven witnesses testified to the hugs and warmth and normalcy of the Ramona family they had known.

In Jean Sawday's opinion, Gary had influenced the neighbors' testimony with two wine and cheese parties he and Harrington had staged down south. "Ask the neighbors in Diamond Bar," Gary said later. "Go through the neighborhood. *Ask* them how they saw us as a family. They owe me *nothing*."

Why wouldn't Miroglio listen? Jean worried. She kept trying to tell him, "This is not a case of whether the jury is going to believe these doctors did anything wrong. This is a case of, Do you believe Holly or do you believe Gary? . . . If you don't bring forward the people who *knew* this family" — Holly's friends in St. Helena, the children of Stephanie's friends — "the jury won't get it at all." In fact,

Miroglio feared that if they put children on the stand who hadn't seen or heard a word at the very time Holly's father was allegedly molesting her, "Harrington would chew us up." The lawyers kept telling her, "It's hearsay. It's hearsay." Then why, Jean asked, aren't these *neighbors* hearsay? They were rebuttal witnesses, Harrington had convinced the judge, called to testify "that there was affection and hugging . . . to *rebut* that Holly never touched her father."

The word was out that Gary was going to put on one of Holly's good friends from middle school, Robin Whitney, now a law student at the University of Oregon in Eugene. Jean hated it that the only young person to appear would be this girl who "was not a good friend, ever."

Miroglio had allowed Jean and Karen to testify for two minutes each, just after Terr. But, warning them that they'd be held in contempt if they blurted anything out, he had shut them down, permitted them only to parrot each other like the Bobbsey twins. "Yes, Stevie told me, 'Gary told me to leave it alone.'" That was about it. If you'd gone for a drink of water, you'd have missed them.

Now they must endure Gary's rebuttal. Harrington had called him back to the stand, basically, to tell the jury that Stephanie's T-graph was a list of lies. As Harrington went over the issue of the locked door again, Gary again denied it. Privately, however, he honestly didn't know — given what he now knew about the fallibility of memory and the power of three years of repetition — whether Stephanie's story held any fragments of truth; for some forgotten reason — but *not* to sexually abuse his child — might he have locked the door? Sensibilities in the courtroom had been largely numbed by weeks of competing truths and lurid sex talk. But now Harrington led Gary through intimacies of the marriage bed so detailed that Stephanie's mother, sickened, was thankful her daughter wasn't there. Returning to the vaginismus theme — that Stephanie's vaginal constriction and "uptight" attitudes, not rape, were the root of the constriction and fears Holly's doctors had noted — Harrington began with a question about the Ramonas' early sexual difficulties. "Vaginismus, as I understand it, is tightness of the muscles in the vaginal area . . . When you first married Stephanie, was she tight?" Gary then described his chronic difficulty with penetration, his efforts to relax her with lubricating gels and with "fondling and masturbating," which worked fine as long as his finger did not penetrate her. He recalled buying Kotex for

Stephanie at the St. Helena Safeway — "she never used tampons." Because she couldn't get them in, Gary was suggesting.

"All lies!" Jean Sawday stormed to the media. "Stevie stopped using tampons because of toxic shock." She and Betty Nye were livid, trying to straighten things out during the break in Gary's rebuttal. After seven weeks of ladylike self-control, of trying to contain her frustration and hate, Betty Nye finally cracked. "He beat her, tried to strangle her! Why don't they let the *violence* in?" she snapped. "I've never lost my cool before," she confessed as she unleashed her feelings in a disjointed flood, crying, shaking, standing there in her red Ultra-suede jacket, wiping her eyes. "How could you have sex with some-one who's violent? *That's* why Stevie couldn't come today. She'd have screamed. *I* want to scream. Gary's *evil!*" "Do you fear his violence?" a journalist asked. "Yes, but he wouldn't do it himself. He'd have his lawyers do it . . . He'll sue us all." She had endured the judge's squelching defense objections again and again, denying their evidence. "I thought we'd get justice. I'll never trust the justice system again. I don't trust anybody anymore. I don't trust you. You're all being ma-nipulated. He's a master manipulator."

Miroglio had to decide if he was going to recall Stephanie to the stand as well. There were four things he wanted her to rebut and clarify: The tampons. Gary's modus operandi for rape, which she had blown in her direct exam. Her annual clothing bill of $30,000 — it wasn't, she'd say. And her claim that she never saw Dr. Klink put Holly in the frog position to do a proper vaginal exam. But he felt he couldn't risk the damage Harrington could do. Stephanie would not be called again, he decided. After three more minor witnesses, closing arguments would begin on Monday.

The last witness of the trial — Gary's last opportunity for rebuttal — would be Holly's old friend Robin Whitney. The judge would per-mit Harrington to put her on only if she was there that afternoon. Gary chartered a jet and promised to have her there by four. The jury was furious. It was noon; they were tired. Now they would have to come back at three-thirty for this kid. If she had something really significant to say, okay. "But she could have been faxed. She could have been videotaped," thought Yolanda as Robin Whitney, in a dis-pirited voice that expressed her awkwardness at testifying, spent ten minutes saying very little except that the Ramonas "seemed like a normal family." Beth and Tim felt she'd been brought in just to hurt

Holly. Nell and Yolanda were angered by Kurtock's "cheap shot" — putting Robin down for not knowing what a normal family was because her parents were divorced: "Robin's father didn't live at home, she was *envious* . . . Cruel bullcrap," Yolanda seethed. How dare he! Nell was more angry "that they manipulated me and wasted my time, bringing me down — driving fifty-four miles that day going back and forth, in the *rain,* for an eight-minute testimony." She wanted to wring Harrington's neck.

But Keith Himmelman was thinking, "She's the best of all the rebuttal witnesses, by far." He was impressed that Holly's closest girlfriend during the four years she was claiming abuse had seen and heard nothing, had felt absolutely no concern. The defense called no one. They'd been damaged, he felt. As Jean Sawday had feared.

As closing arguments were about to begin on Monday morning, Stephanie searched out a journalist and said urgently, "There's something I've got to tell you." The journalist was eager to listen. Would it be some eleventh-hour revelation? Some unrevealed proof, one way or the other, of Holly's abuse? "Gary said I didn't, but I did *so* use Tampax," she asserted. That was it. How had this trial so reduced her that this crude intimacy had become the most pressing thing this decent, private woman had to say that morning?

"Are we ready for our thirteen friends?" Snowden asked as the bailiff led the twelve jurors and single alternate in for closing arguments. The judge cautioned them: "What the attorneys say in argument is not evidence . . . Rely on your recollection of the evidence." Harrington began, with Kurtock, Miroglio, and Leonard to follow. This was the opportunity for each lawyer to reprise his themes and arguments and to try to sway any undecided jurors to his point of view. It was the final opportunity for damage control. Everyone knew what that meant for Harrington. But he would hold Gerner for now to deal with human damage.

"You heard from Garnet, Mrs. Ramona. The Ramona girls haven't talked to her since March 15, 1990 — she [Holly] ignored her grandmother's eightieth birthday, a very cruel and hard damage."

Harrington brought up the issue of money. "Sodium amytal is not a treatment for the problems Holly had . . . not for bulimia . . . not for depression. What it's a treatment for is a bank account that needs a little infusion." Citing the defendants' bills, the referrals to doctors who didn't treat Holly's base illnesses, and Isabella's staggering case-load, he charged, "Refer Holly to a psychiatrist or family practitioner, they would prescribe Prozac for Holly." Then Isabella would have lost a patient. "How can you keep adequate records for two thousand patients? Beats me. But with two thousand patients in three years, you have a *money machine!*"

In the hallway during the break, crying and hurt that Harrington had accused the girls of abandoning their grandmother, Stephanie told a journalist, "Garnet never called or wrote the girls — not ever . . . She's made no contact . . . There's so much they won't let us tell." However inconsistent and stumbling on the stand, Stephanie outside the courtroom was compellingly sincere.

On his second day of argument, Harrington returned to the theme of inconsistency. He wanted to leave, vivid in the minds of the ju-rors, the inconsistencies that had riddled the stories of Isabella, Rose, Stephanie, and Holly. It was a strong card for Harrington, for love him or hate him, Gary had scored as consistent.

Finally he faced "the Gerner issue." "Let me be direct, I'm embar-rassed by Dr. Gerner. It's my fault for calling him. He's not a bad man, but he did a bad thing in another case," Harrington confessed. Then, turning the disaster to his advantage, he added, "I'm sure Marche Isabella is a very nice person. But if she didn't do a professional job, she's below the standard of care — and responsible. She's supposed to help people. Here's Holly — happy, active, skis, [plays] tennis, riding. Before Marche Isabella, a GPA of 3.5; it fell to 1.7. She had friends at UC Irvine; now she has few friends. She used to do things with her dad . . . Now she never sees her family . . . Before Marche Isabella, Holly had a life. Now she's going to devote her life to being a survivor. This is not therapy; this is malpractice."

From what depth Harrington wrung his tears as he moved toward the close of his argument, who knew. But as he tried to convince the jury to make the award big enough to compensate the ravaged life he had described for seven weeks, he seemed to have reached the same ragged emotionality that pervaded the court. After explaining to the jury how Gary's total economic loss, past and future, added up to $8,583,645 — writing the numbers aggressively on his display board — he appealed to them to "add to that any allowance you . . . feel appropriate for emotional distress. That number should be signifi-cant." He paused, his chin quivering as he struggled to regain compo-sure. The room waited, hushed. His voice shaking with emotion but still bringing appropriate solemnity to a moment that could shape a man's future, he said, *"You know, fathers don't come in designer colors. What they do is the best they can . . ."* He paused again, crossed his arms, and slowly raised his eyes to look at the exhibit board holding the numbers, his silence seeming to say, "Mere numbers. How can they measure the loss?" *"That's what Gary Ramona did.* He didn't deserve to lose his family. And his marriage. And his job. And his reputation." His voice quavered. "We ask you to give him an award for that damage." The courtroom was hushed as he turned and walked to his chair and sat down. If his closing words had been calculated courtroom theater, he had achieved an actor's dream. He had moved the house to tears.

The defense began its arguments with the theme it had pounded throughout the trial: manipulation, control. "Why is Gary Ramona suing Marche Isabella and Richard Rose and Western Medical Center–Anaheim?" asked Kurtock. "He's doing it because he wants to control his daughter . . . to show that he can tell her what to think . . . can cut off the aid that she can get from other people."

Miroglio had practiced his closing argument in the shower a hundred times, and his parents and wife were in the courtroom. He knew he was dealing with a tired jury. In a loud and fiery voice he told them, "I do have good news for you . . . You're not on the hook. We're going to let you off the hook in three big ways. You don't have to decide this case based upon whether or not Mr. Ramona did it or not . . . Next, you don't have to get involved in the argument about whether repressed memories happen or whether they can be proved . . . Finally, folks, it's not your duty . . . to try to put the Ramona family back together based on the verdict. I submit to you, folks, you can't do that."

Stephanie thought Jeff Kurtock's closing had been outstanding. Now Bruce was doing really well. "I personally felt, 'Wow, things are finally turning in our favor. Maybe the jury's finally going to understand everything.'"

The lock was still one of the strongest emotional points for the jury. Would Stephanie have made up such an elaborate, detailed story if it wasn't true? *Had* Gary locked her out while he molested Holly? Miroglio exploited the unknowns. Holding one of the photographs of the door, he said, "Remember Stephanie said there was a lock inside, a deadbolt you could lock from the inside that didn't go through to the outside . . . Where do you put a security lock . . . or deadbolt? You put it up high." Gary's team went on alert. Security lock? Was he insinuating a chain lock, like those in hotels? With a dramatic flourish, Miroglio showed the jury the blown-up photograph Gary had taken. "The picture is cropped off. You couldn't tell . . ." What? Gary went ballistic. "That's just baloney," he whispered to Harrington. There was no security chain lock! Back at the house they had the original photograph showing the whole door, but they'd used the more visually effective blowup as evidence. It was too late to show the original to the jury, and Miroglio knew it. "I don't care what the judge said. You've got to get that picture into evidence," said Gary, who raced home at lunch to get it.

Miroglio struck another telling blow when he cast Gary as a possible perpetrator who could easily have deluded neighbors like Charlie Piazza. A perpetrator could be anyone. He was the man next door. ". . . Every single time some wacko goes and gets an AK-47 and goes into a post office and shoots a bunch of innocent people . . . there's a clip with a news guy standing [in] the neighbor's yard . . . saying he was the greatest guy." It was a shocking image that pushed the edge of good taste, but he moved quickly past it with a whispered, ". . . it doesn't happen in the front yard . . . You can't know unless you live with the terror yourself what it must be like to hear footsteps coming down the hall. It happens in secret, in shame."

Harrington had Gerner, but Miroglio's damage control lay with Prince and Holly's story of her grandmother's rape, for they posed Holly's most serious credibility gap. Like Gerner, they had to be faced. Miroglio's strategy was to lump these two bizarre events in with other suspicious mysteries. "I've got to address something Holly wishes I didn't have to. I wish I didn't have to. The dog. I don't know what happened . . . Holly's mental production of Gary telling her of her grandmother's rape by her brothers . . . I don't know what to make of it . . . I don't know what to make of somebody who takes pictures of his daughters, school pictures, and keeps them by a toilet in a *Playboy* magazine . . . who won't have sex with Stephanie for the last four years of their marriage, and instead satisfies himself by friction up against her body. But something's not Ward and June Cleaver about this guy and his 'normal' sex drives." Lifting a page from Terr, he combined a bunch of provocative but inconclusive images — images of events vigorously denied by Gary — into a cluster of symptoms and

signs. From separate ingredients, he created a whole dish, as he said
— "lasagna." Again, he offered the jury an easy escape from the mysteries: ". . . You can resolve this case . . . in a rapid fashion by believing
that Holly's story is believable, and in fact it happened."

Leonard was the last defense attorney. The jury was no longer
taking notes. Compared with Miroglio's impassioned thundering,
Leonard's closing argument lacked fire this late in the day, which
suited his continuing attempt to vanish, with his client, into the woodwork. He spoke the last words for the defense: "I would ask that you
don't allow Gary Ramona's distorted view . . . of this lawsuit and of
. . . the relationship with his family to allow him to control Holly
Ramona further. Remember, she can run, but she can't hide."

Vanished from these closing words was the assertive, stubborn,
and independent Holly seen on the stand, the Holly of "*my* memories
. . . *my* meeting . . . *my* mind." Was she running, scared and desperate,
or was she a young woman in firm control of her life? The jury was
left with this disturbing conflict as the defense closed with the call:
Save Holly from her father!

Harrington, though, had the final opportunity to speak. In response to Kurtock's theatrical effort to show that a friendless Gary
Ramona had been supported only by hired guns and the neighbors
he'd bought with his free wine and hors d'oeuvres, Harrington turned
the tables by flaunting the absence of Holly's friends on the stand.
"They criticize Gary for bringing Robin Whitney. She was Holly's
close friend at the very time that she now claimed she was being
raped." But why had the defense not called "Amy and Ann Sawday,
Nicole Maestas, Janice Brown? Where are the Diamond Bar neighbors?" he demanded. "None of them appeared to say that Gary was
anything other than a loving, affectionate, available father. Where
are Holly's junior high friends? Not here . . . The missing witnesses are
not from the *plaintiff's* side. The missing witnesses are from the other
side of the table."

Harrington had the last word, too, about the lock. Lloyd Jenkins
watched, trying to control his laughter, as Harrington pulled a sleight
of hand worthy of Houdini. Chatting to the jury to divert them, he
strolled to the clerk's desk and — out of the judge's view — deftly
pulled the small original picture from his pocket and slipped it underneath the stack of evidence on the desk. Then, pulling it out, he
walked toward the jury, displaying it close to the jury box. "Mr. Miroglio said this is obviously cropped. He has no way to know that," he

said with a note of triumph. Now this small original showed the entire door, with no security lock. This was not clever, it was *"cheating,"* Miroglio muttered angrily as he saw Harrington slip the photo from his pocket. The defense rose as one. "Your Honor. Your Honor!" "You know better than that, Mr. Harrington," the judge cautioned him mildly, "but I can understand . . ." Harrington gallantly apologized, but he had rung the bell. He then used the lock to segue into a rejection of the entire twenty-eight points on the T-graph. "We've shown you the photographs of the deadbolt, and it has a key on the outside . . . Mr. Miroglio has an imaginary security lock at the top of the door which was never testified to by anybody . . . *There's no evidence!"* There was no evidence, he reminded them, for any of the vignettes on the celebrated list. "Twenty-eight times zero is *zero!"*

"It was beautiful," Marty Cook whistled to himself. To Yolanda, "That was a Matlock moment."

Harrington, standing before the jury in his svelte blue three-piece suit for the last time, expanded on his great line of five days earlier. "If I order a ham sandwich and say, 'Hold the mayo,' I'm sex-abused? That's silly. *Sometimes a cigar is just a cigar."* Then he sent them to deliberate inspired by Hamlet. "'Someday perhaps we will look back even on these things and smile,'" he quoted. "Holly won't. She didn't just lose her childhood. It was taken from her. She has no father anymore. It was taken from her by this fraudulent sodium amytal procedure. Gary will never look back and smile." As Harrington closed, he explained to the jury what they must do. "Yes, I have the burden of proof that these are false memories. This is not a criminal trial in which I must prove something beyond a reasonable doubt. Preponderance of evidence" — he made his graceful hands two scales, balancing — "means that you're persuaded . . . that my witness and my case is slightly more probable than the defendant's side of the case . . . Gary actually can't win the case. Nothing can ever compensate him for the loss of his family and his life . . . But you can award him damages for what he's suffered by way of lost income . . . and for . . . emotional distress . . ." Harrington's voice cracked and faded as he spoke the last words of argument in the trial: "Make him whole . . ."

On Wednesday, May 11, the jury retired to deliberate. "How will we find out when they've reached a verdict?" a reporter called out. *"Be* here," said the judge, as the attorneys and spectators settled in for a wait that could be a day, a week, a month. The jury was armed with a sheet of formal instructions, telling them how to proceed in their deliberations to achieve a verdict. The burning questions they must answer — the eight questions that would decide *Ramona* — lay in the two-page Special Verdict. Every word of it had been battled out by the attorneys, who knew that even the subtle tone of a question might prejudice a juror's decision. This was the verdict that would be delivered to the judge and read to the court. But it was already late afternoon, so the jury only had time to elect a foreman. Each wrote a name on a piece of paper and threw it to the middle of the table. Tom Dudum won, with six votes.

That night, Shelley didn't sleep ten minutes. She kept thinking, "I'm going to be the only one thinking . . . he didn't do this." Beth, Tim, and Marty Cook didn't sleep either. Tim had always feared he wouldn't be up to it when the moment came. Marty had started getting nervous in the last days of the closing argument, as the job ahead became real. "We'd been having fun. Playing games . . . Then the atmosphere changed. It got quieter . . . Now we'd have to go to work, and that scared me." In the heat of it, he didn't feel wise enough to make this decision. None of them did.

Thursday, May 12. They sat in the jury room, paralyzed by nearly eight weeks of silence. Where could they suddenly begin? Tom Dudum knew the single word that would release the tension: "What about Gerner?" That's all it took. Gerner was the burst of air released from the bottle after seven weeks of building pressure. The jurors laughed, voices tumbling over one another, as they all spilled out their stored-up Gerner moments. Tom let them run; the tension had to come out.

The first question was by far the most daunting of the eight — the critical one from which the others unfolded: "Were any of the defendants negligent in providing health care to Holly Ramona by implanting or reinforcing false memories that plaintiff had molested her as a child?" Right out of the block, it forced them to decide: Were these false memories? And, by implication, did Gary do it? Miroglio had been dead wrong, in his closing argument, telling them that false memories — and Gary's guilt — were not their issues. They had to face it — they would have to play God. But how, when everyone in this trial on both sides, even Loftus, said you couldn't know for sure? The jurors were all struggling, personally, with Gary's guilt or innocence. Tom Dudum saw that "Gary was still an unsolved mystery. But unlike books or movies, no one was giving us the answer." He polled the jury to see where they stood. They needed nine to get a verdict.

If nine jurors said no, all three defendants — Rose, Isabella, and the hospital — were "not guilty." And everybody went home. If nine answered yes for even one of the three defendants, the jury must move on to the second question. The vote was 8–4 for a yes to the first question. Already, a majority for Gary. But it could go anywhere. The first poll was seat-of-the-pants, a product of emotion and confusion. The jurors themselves were shocked. It didn't break down along gender or even age lines. One of the four no votes was a man, Marty Cook, the banker, who had joined Becky, Beth, and Nell on Holly's side. Five women, all mothers, had voted yes, rejecting Holly's memories. The first poll, though, had revealed a pattern: three — Becky, Beth, and Nell — were, Keith observed early, "unswayable" against Gary.

Question Two, when they got to it, would take them to the confrontation: ". . . did that defendant cause plaintiff to be personally confronted with the accusation that he had molested Holly Ramona, or affirmatively act in the events leading to that confrontation . . . ?" If the jury said yes — if Isabella or Rose had caused Gary to come to the confrontation — they would then move on to the critical third question: Has plaintiff suffered damages that were caused by the negligence of any defendant? Had Gary been hurt? The rest of the questions posed details of relative guilt and size of damages.

The jury did not have to have absolute certainty of anything — of Gary's guilt, Holly's truth, or the defendants' role. They had only to decide what seemed "slightly more probable than not" on the balance scales. They must each seek and vote for the "evidence that has more convincing force than that opposed to it" — even a tiny bit more force.

They tacked sheets of poster paper on the walls around the room, putting one name — that of key witnesses, the three defendants, and Gary — on each sheet and started listing whatever they could recall that might help guide them to an answer to the first question. Were the memories false and, if so, negligently implanted or reinforced?

From the outset, it was hard for the jurors to separate their feelings about Gary from the issue of whether rape had actually occurred. They quickly broke down into two camps, with fence sitters. "Four of us felt that something did happen," said Marty Cook of himself, Nell, Becky, and Beth. At first, Yolanda feared, "Becky's too young — a little girl," as she watched her emerge as Holly's most ardent champion. Trying to hold her ground against the Gary faction, Becky felt the rest were picking on her "because my opinion was in the minority." Some saw Yolanda's outspokenness against Becky — and a comment she made about having some "abuse issue" in her family — as betraying a personal agenda. Guilty or not, Nell couldn't stand Gary. "My personal feeling — my honest-to-goodness belief — is that Gary screwed up his own life," said Tom. Yolanda perceived Gary as arrogant. "But okay," she argued, "so you don't like his attitude, his ego. It's who he is. It doesn't make him guilty."

Scribbling whatever seemed relevant under each name on the sheets of paper helped contain the chaos. "But each time they changed a point on one person's sheet, it changed all the others. Poor Marty was swinging back and forth. It was total confusion," Beth observed. It was hard to get beyond the powerful feelings driven by their own experiences. Marty's feelings as a father colored his feelings about Gary: Gary should have gotten involved, tried to help a troubled daughter. Tim struggled to put his empathy for Holly in balance. He identified with her feeling betrayed by a parent. When he was thirteen, he had watched his mother walk down the stairs and out the door as he cried for her not to leave. He still hadn't dealt with this abandonment. On the first vote, he was straddling the fence. "I wanted to believe . . . Holly had trauma from something." His sympathy for her was so strong, how could he ever vote against the therapists? But he knew it was his "responsibility to do just what the facts and evidence say and not take my feelings into account."

They had hoped they could look to the expert witnesses to lead them to answers. "They laid a useful foundation," Yolanda argued. Becky had found Terr interesting and helpful — until she got to the Black Plague. Oh, they had some good laughs over Ring Around a Rosy. But even the favorite witnesses, Loftus and Gutheil, "kind of cancel each other out," Marty observed. There was considerable cynicism that "they're being paid $50,000 to be biased," as Becky put it. Tom Dudum expressed it more strongly: "You can take all of the testimony from all those guys and throw it out the window, because it all didn't matter when it came down to it. It was a waste of money." At heart, he felt, it was a "he said, she said" — it came down to Gary's, Stephanie's, and Holly's credibility.

Just after lunch, tension rose among the lawyers in the courtroom when the jury asked for a readback of some testimony, then asked for several more. What did it mean? they whispered, trying to divine the jury's thinking.

Then the jury asked for a readback of Stephanie's testimony on the infamous lock scene at Diamond Bar. It confirmed what several jurors hadn't noticed, that Kelli was in the *front* yard. Marty Cook thought it was strange. "Why would you have your children locked out in the front yard?" It proved a major negative factor for Gary and swayed Tom back to her side a bit, Becky felt. But, on the other hand, Shelley pointed out, "When Stephanie comes home and finds the child out in the front yard, she never bothers to find where *Holly* is. She's only four or five . . . She grabbed her yellow towel and just went back to the beach!" They were listening to one another. "As every point was made," Shelley noted, "someone would say, 'Oh, I hadn't thought about that.'" Twelve minds were working together, Becky marveled. To Shelley Maynard, a psych technician, Stephanie's vignettes were riddled with enigmas: "She remembers a yellow towel but can't remember how many enemas?" "Everybody felt bad for her more than sympathetic," said Becky. "Even Nell and I, who were extreme on the defense side and most likely to make excuses for her, said, 'There are a lot of inconsistencies here. I mean, it's quite convenient that she forgets things.'"

By four-thirty, four readbacks had come and gone. After nearly a full day, the jury was still unable to get past the first question. Tom was frustrated. He felt that the question was written all wrong. How could they answer a compound question — false memories, implantation, and reinforcement — that should have been broken into three parts? But what really blocked them was the issue of Gary. At four forty-five, they sent their fifth message to the judge: "We need clarification regarding if we have to decide whether Gary molested Holly in reaching our verdict." The defense was shaken. The jury had not taken the swift route to a verdict — simply believing Holly. Kristina Flaherty, a reporter who'd covered the Orange County courts for seven years, said, "I think they're trying to find malpractice in Question One, and have to know if they can proceed to Question Two without finding that Gary did it." The judge's response left the jurors still in a quandary. They would find their answer, he said, by rereading the instruction about "preponderance of the evidence." The judge was ordering them back to the evidence to find which way the scales tipped toward Gary's guilt. Now they knew they could not escape a decision about Gary. Keith Himmelman, applying his businessman's logic, summed up his thoughts about Holly's memories: "If he didn't rape his daughter, they were false; if he did, they were true. You couldn't proceed to decide if the memories were false if you didn't make that decision." They didn't have to state it out loud or take a vote. They could still have doubts. But each would have to come up with a decision that either rape or innocence was "more likely than not."

Tom Dudum knew he had to get them focused on the evidence. On Friday morning, he printed two headings on the blackboard and underlined them: Evidence. Emotion. He knew he mustn't suppress the emotion; it needed an outlet. But they had to start separating the two. Tom told them, "Let's look at what the question says. Let's look at the therapist and doctors — look at what they did and said." Marty Cook began by putting his feelings as a father under Emotion. He went back through his notes. Critical analysis had started.

Tom stayed rigorously neutral, urging them over and over to weigh emotion against the evidence until they had caught the idea and made it their mission. They'd be talking about Mondavi, Becky noted, and "someone would say, 'Well, maybe he wasn't going to get fired,' and we'd all chime in, 'That's not evidence! That's not evidence!'" They took each name on the wall in turn and searched every note they'd written on that person to try to figure it out. "Does this have anything that's going to help us?" They took Gerner's testimony seriously, but thought his findings too extreme, too exaggerated, to be credible. Strike Gerner. They struck down witness after witness as contributing nothing substantive to the evidence.

They began a hunt for physical evidence. "The hardest thing for those with doubts about the repeated rape going on so long and so often was, *where's the evidence?*" Tom observed. "If Holly hadn't emphasized the multiple rapes, we would have found her more believable, and we wouldn't have been looking so strongly for that physical connection." All agreed that if rape had been repeated over and over, somehow something would have shown up in that pediatrics history . . . *"The only evidence was the pediatrics history."*

They counted enemas. Beth and Tim went through their notes to find the medical records of Dr. Lisbon, a pediatrician who'd seen Holly several times. "He took a history of Holly, and under history — not under recommendations — he put down 'enemas every four or five days,'" Tim noted. "No matter what we heard on the stand, there it was in black and white." That notation meant, to Tim, that those enemas were given. Every four or five days! His notes and memory reminded him that Stephanie had changed her story about how many enemas she remembered. Under cross-exam, she'd remembered *no* enemas. "That tells me she's being careful not to say that enemas could have caused the trauma," he suggested. Nell corrected him: "Stephanie said, 'Maybe one.'" "Whether it was one or twenty, Stephanie would have remembered the difference," Shelley maintained. Tim's sympathies for Holly were still, and would always be, powerful. But looking at the medical history, he was being reluctantly pulled away from her belief that her father raped her.

"It came down to the hymen" for Keith. "She's abused from five to sixteen in every orifice of her body and her ob-gyn says 'partially separated hymen.' I'm sorry. If this young girl had been raped that many times, the hymen would have been more damaged . . . or gone. It was the determining factor in my mind that there isn't a chance that Gary raped her."

Tom questioned them again and again to get each person's opinion, especially the shy jurors. At last the voting showed that an internal decision had been reached on Gary. The judge had told them they didn't have to be 100 percent sure that Gary did, or didn't, molest his daughter. There were huge doubts — there would always be doubts, Tom knew. "There was not a consensus. But there was enough feeling that he didn't do it to say that 'false memories' were more likely than not."

Now that they had moved past "the Gary decision" and decided on false, they could focus on the next parts of Question One: if Holly's memories were false, did the defendants implant them? "We didn't think they did," Beth said. Perhaps they were the "delusional intrusions" of depression and bulimia, as Dr. Hudson said. Or distorted memories of snakelike catheters. But had the defendants reinforced them? That would be an act of negligence. It was now late morning on Friday the thirteenth. As Marty Cook laughed later, "We spent a day and a half on the first question and a half day on the rest."

Marty hadn't slept, feeling the pressure of knowing that, the next day, his would be the swing vote on Question One. He felt that Becky, Beth, and Nell would vote no and were not going to change their minds. He turned back to his notes and examined Isabella's role. "Isabella's supposed to be treating her for bulimia, and there's never anything about bulimia . . . And Holly got worse." Why didn't Isabella bring Gary down to work out Holly's issues, as she did with Stephanie? In his notes, too, was Isabella's wanting to do the sodium amytal — a useless drug, as they'd heard for weeks. He looked at Rose. "Dr. Rose testified one way. But when you looked at what was written there in the records, it was different." Marty was seeing "reinforcement." So were the others. "I think the majority of us agreed there was no evidence that Rose and Isabella actually planted the thoughts, but they had been reinforced," said Tom. He took another poll. Marty switched. They now had a 9–3 vote for a yes on Question One. The jury had found malpractice.

The irony would haunt Tom. "The defendants were guilty, in a sense, of doing their job. We were told for seven weeks that reinforcing and reassuring your patient is part of therapy." Yet, according to the instructions, the reinforcement of false memories was negligence.

The wisdom circulating through the courthouse was that the jury would reach a verdict that day so that they could go home for the weekend. By early afternoon the courtroom was full, the tension heightening.

The man rumored to be psychotic by the trial's resident psychiatrists — the straggle-bearded man with the Willie Nelson bandanna headband who had restlessly roamed through the back rows, seat jumping, throughout the trial — made some people nervous. Would he be violent when the verdict came down? someone asked Dr. Stoer. "He's not the one I worry about," said the old psychologist. "It's the principals, the family."

On the first day of jury deliberations, Marian Dodds had gone back into combat clothes. But she arrived on Friday looking as smart as a TV anchorwoman. In a white satin shirt with lace appliqué, she sat beside Carolyn Thompson. Marian's blossoming, like the confidence of several of the other women who had come for confirmation of their memories, was fragile, dependent on a verdict she could not control.

In the jury room, Tom polled for Question Two: Had the defendants caused or participated in the confrontation? Here, the strong feelings that the confrontation between Holly and her father should never have happened — that it was the singular event that transformed Holly's problems from a family and therapy matter into the adversarial battle that destroyed the family — gathered into an almost unanimous yes vote. Beth was the only juror who voted no.

As Tom moved on to the third question — Did Gary suffer damage because of the defendants' negligence? — the jury gave its first unanimous vote: yes. Even those who disliked Gary's "selling himself too hard in the courtroom" — or Tom, who saw Gary Ramona's ego and ambition in his job as unrealistic — believed he had been damaged by the actions of the three. With that yes the Ramona jury made history. They gave a verdict of malpractice to the first nonpatient ever permitted to sue psychotherapists over recovered memories. The implications for the profession were enormous.

For Becky the pain was over; the rest was "the easy part." She felt new energy. They now had to determine who had caused the damage and how much, if anything, each of the defendants would pay. But there was a wrinkle in Question Eight that forced the jury to make a complex new decision. The final question invited the jury to assign any portion of the total negligence causing the plaintiff's injury to the plaintiff himself — Gary Ramona — or to "all other persons." A whopping 40 percent was placed on Isabella's shoulders, with 10 percent to Rose, 5 percent to the hospital, and 5 percent to Gary Ramona — censure for his failure to get more involved in Holly's problems, his refusal to see flaws in his life and his job, his arrogance and ego, his insensitivity to Stephanie. "He was not a molester," Tom thought, "but a bad parent."

But the tantalizing part of the verdict was the 40 percent burden of responsibility placed on the shoulders of "all other persons." The jurors were not required to name names publically, but among themselves they did. Stephanie. "Stephanie, we thought, was a big contributor. She's the one who let it leak out to everybody," said Marty Cook. Beth defended her: "I can see how she did it. She just got hysterical, probably, when she found out it was really true, and told her best friend." That's why the jury named the friends, too, in the 40 percent. Jean Sawday. Isabel and Dorothy Mondavi. Others. "They spread it all over the place," said Marty. The women friends had "tattled it all around. In doing so, got things to where they were," said Shelley. Barry Grundland was also named.

In casting 40 percent of the blame on "other persons," the verdict achieved its highest purpose. It did more than warn therapists; it cautioned gossips that they must not condemn and destroy without proof; it turned the responsibility back to America's families, to America's dinner tables. To us. Were we listening to our children, feeding their emotional hungers? The insurers and Gary would still pay 100 percent of any dollar award. But the jury had seized the chance to cast

a broader net for social responsibility. With a yes vote on that sym-
bolic 40 percent, an eighteen-year-old checkout girl, a cook, a nurse,
and a mother of seven had chastised the wives of the valley's most
powerful family and issued a statement about the standard of care we
must apply in our daily lives. Wagging fingers at wayward neighbors
to preserve the common good, the jurors had transformed Courtroom
B into an early American town hall.

The 40 percent would not banish gossip in Napa Valley and sup-
plant it with critical thinking. And it held personal risks. Yolanda
must face Jean Sawday three times a week at the Napa Valley Country
Club. But the jury did not falter in attributing blame to powerful
members of their community.

When they got to "the money part," the range of feelings and
doubts found concrete expression. Gary was asking for $8.5 million.
In the range of numbers they came up with, the jurors expressed the
ambiguity of feelings not expressed in a yes or no vote. At first Tim
was "definitely between zero and five million." Yolanda was pushing
for 3.5 million. "But five of us said zero," said Tim. Both Nell and Tim
wished later they'd been stronger for zero. It was going to be higher
than that, but nothing near the numbers Yolanda wanted.

After agreeing that Gary had suffered damage, the jury made a
stunning about-face on Question Four, which named a dollar award
for "discomfort, fears, anxiety." If Tom Dudum had his way, Gary
wouldn't get a cent for personal stress; it was minor, he thought. Others agreed. Over the objections of Yolanda and Martha Piccolo, they
voted Gary not a penny for emotional distress, granting him damages
for lost income only.

Marty Cook explained the rationale: "You can't find in his favor
and give him nothing . . . His psychiatrist said that he suffered from
posttraumatic stress, but it was minimal. He could function. He
started to consult. So we'll give him a little token. I could live with
that. I felt that even if he didn't do the extreme thing, he contributed
enough to the situation . . ." Even Beth admitted, "We have to agree,
he did lose money." It wouldn't be zero. But as the number shrunk,
Yolanda was "very disappointed. We had vindicated him." Martha
Piccolo, Keith Himmelman, and Yolanda Nash were left holding out
for a high award.

"I think our conflict was evident in the dollar amount we finally
decided to award," said Tom Dudum. It was he who negotiated the
final figure: half a million, a year's pay at Mondavi. "The half a mil-

lion dollars, it bothered me," said Yolanda. She was satisfied, though, with the two messages they were giving: "There was no proof that Gary molested his daughter" and "there were a lot of problems with the treatment that this family went through."

As they agreed on the dollar award, "people just wanted it to be over with," said Marty. Suddenly the bailiff and guards were going back and forth to the judge, and the jurors were being rushed to the courtroom. Nell had not felt this nervous since the first day, when they'd faced all the cameras. Beth's knees were weak. How would the public react to their verdict? Yolanda was so angry at the paltry award that she defiantly put on her sunglasses as the jury prepared to march in for their biggest moment. But they all believed in what they had done. Becky felt very good — they all felt good, she thought — that, even with a joke like Gerner, they hadn't disqualified his testimony. They'd based their work on the evidence. Tim had come with the high-minded hope that he could do his patriotic duty. He would go back to the kitchen at the Veterans Home on Monday content that he had done it.

The *Chronicle*'s Diane Curtis, one of three reporters the judge would call when a verdict was reached, was waiting for the ring from the cellular phone in her purse. But just before five P.M., word flashed through the hall like a bolt of lightning: there was a verdict. Someone had picked it up on Bay Radio from San Francisco. It would be delivered as soon as the judge could notify the lawyers and principals and get them into the courtroom. The bailiff, Larry Fontana, and a policewoman searched everyone, from chin to ankles, with an electronic wand at the courtroom door. Every purse and briefcase was searched. By five-fifteen, the courtroom was filled. The mood was electric.

For Gary, "All of a sudden, everything was on the line. It's all done. I'm just sitting there crying. But nothing can be changed." Suddenly he saw that, for all his involvement, he was ignorant of how the verdict worked. He was embarrassed but asked Harrington, "How will I know if I won the lawsuit? Tell me, I've got to know." The lawyer went through it again: "If it's *no* on the first one, it's over." He'd have lost. "If it's *yes* on the first one, we go to the second. If it's *yes* on the second, we go to the next, and the next, and the next . . ." It was *yes* Gary had to hear when the moment came.

"We're going to clear the building and lock the front door at this point," the judge said calmly, trying not to alarm people.

The two camps handled the final moments as differently as the stories both sides had told. Betty Nye hugged Marche Isabella and said, "You saved Holly's life." The defendants hugged their lawyers. "An early verdict is generally for the defense," an experienced TV reporter whispered to some of the media. Gary watched them "all giggly and real chipper, feeling that they had this thing," while Gary's camp was quiet and sober. Gary had no idea if he would win. "Is the building secure?" Snowden asked Fontana. "Yes, Your Honor." "A verdict has been reached . . . This is your last chance to get out . . . No one who is in the courtroom is going to be permitted to leave the courtroom until the jury has left . . ." The jury was coming. Gary Ramona "just couldn't believe it. I didn't know what to do. All of a sudden, I'm down to the moment that I spent four years for, to have my day in court." Through habit and will, he forced himself to stand and smile, hands behind his back, waiting to greet the jury for the last time.

At 5:33 P.M., a silent crowd watched the jurors file in for the verdict. As they took their seats the judge said, "Let the record reflect that the jurors are all present and in their places. Mr. Dudum, Deputy Fontana informs me that the jury has reached a verdict. Is that correct?"

"That's correct."

The courtroom held its collective breath. But Snowden was not to be rushed. Clasping his hands before him, he said, "I have a number of things I want to say to you before taking the verdict," and delivered the King Henry speech he had warned the room weeks earlier was coming. ". . . I don't know that I have ever had a case that has been as interesting, as difficult, as compelling as this one . . . as fascinating and terrible . . . Winston Churchill described Russia as 'a riddle wrapped in a mystery in an enigma.' And that thought has come back to me many times in the course of this trial . . . I don't think I've ever been as completely and totally sure that I don't know what a jury's verdict is going to be."

Sensing the tension, he asked "for your indulgence" as he addressed the jury. "What you have participated in, in such a magnificent way, is a process that is very, very old." From the feudal baronies of twelfth-century England came "King Henry and, more importantly, his son, the second King Henry . . . to create a more organized government . . . a system whereby when two people had disagreements with each other, a number of people from the community would be brought into a court . . ." He went on to trace the origins of the jury system, one of the few institutions that operates today "in essentially an identical fashion to the way it operated over eight hundred years ago. So that what you are doing runs very deep. There is some incredibly grand confidence that we, as people, have in the process which you have participated in."

"This is cruel and unusual punishment," Miroglio thought, and groaned. After four years of hell, to make them wait. Holly waited for word in Orange County. But Stephanie and Shawna sat still, faces straight ahead, clutching hands, Neil Shapiro beside them. "You have served for five bucks a day and fifteen cents a mile," the judge went on. But, phrasing the larger payoff in historic terms, he praised and thanked a jury that had participated in how "we as a society, in an organized and civilized way, resolve differences." The feelings were mutual. "The judge may have sometimes ignored the lawyers, but he never ignored us. He was great," thought Yolanda. Snowden praised and thanked "six excellent attorneys" who had worked "in the eye of the tornado . . . I commend you, all six of you, for the very big piece of your souls that you have committed to this litigation." "I wouldn't hesitate to hire any of those attorneys for myself," Keith Himmelman was thinking.

The attorneys rose as, at last, Snowden asked, "Mr. Dudum, if you would, please give the verdict form to the bailiff." Larry Fontana handed it to the judge, who, expressionless, scanned the first page and the second, then turned back briefly to the first and handed it to the clerk. Stephanie and Shawna squeezed hands. "Miss Larsen, would you . . . please read the verdict."

"Question Number One . . . Answer . . . 'Yes.'" Gary held his breath, aware of the stunning silence.

"Question Number Two . . . 'Yes.'

"Question Number Three . . . 'Yes.'"

That was it; the rest was details. Malpractice had been found. Several dozen cellular phones popped from pockets and the buzz began.

Once they got past the third yes, Gary Ramona "was on a high." His elation sunk for a moment as he heard the low award, but he thought he could figure it out: they really meant to give him a million, but they figured he'd already got half of it in his half-million-dollar settlement with Mondavi.

Jean Sawday reeled as she heard the verdict. She had sat waiting, confident it was "a slam-dunk deal. Gary will get zilcho . . . If they could have heard us and our children say what we saw and heard, I don't think Gary would've gotten one dime." "Why hadn't they believed Holly?" Betty Nye agonized. She wanted to kill Gary Ramona.

Stephanie broke into tears. "I've got to call Holly. I can't let her hear it on TV." Neil Shapiro handed her his phone. She cried to her daughter, "I'm sorry, Holly. It's okay, it's okay." Strain showing in the dark circles under her eyes, staring bleakly ahead, she held intertwined fingers over her mouth as she tried to compose herself to walk the gauntlet of press crowding at the door, waiting for her. Shapiro tried to shepherd her through, but, tears streaming, running her hand through her hair, she stopped and faced the lights. She declared with more ferocity than she had ever shown on the witness stand: "What my husband did was wrong. He raped my daughter. It's a mother's worst nightmare." Her voice was shaking with anger as she hurled her final statement at Gary: "He should not have received a penny for *raping his own daughter.*"

Carolyn Thompson was "numb," tears streaking her cheeks as she was washed along with the exiting crowd. Marian Dodds left quickly, beaten. For her, emotional problems had not been healed by someone else's lawsuit, by superficial bonding with women she would never see again — or by fickle media attention. For her, for Carolyn, them, Courtroom B had been unforgiving.

Right after the verdict, Gary had leaped up to bear-hug his team. He shook hands with the judge and thanked him and the court personnel. He thanked Larry Fontana and the clerks. He thanked Tom Dudum and the jury on camera, as the *Register* wrote the headline: GARY RAMONA WINS.

Confusion reigned in the halls as reporters shuttled up and down the elevators trying to find any jurors who would talk to them. Had Gary really won if he, himself, was 5 percent guilty of his own damage and if he had been awarded only one sixteenth of what he had asked? If Holly's memories were indeed false, yet only reinforced — not planted — by the defendants, where did they come from? What was the jury saying? What did the verdict mean? Had they said that Gary didn't do it? That was the bottom line for everyone, the first question every juror, every reporter, every observer, would be asked — for months and even years to come.

When Tom Dudum emerged from the jury's brief meeting with the attorneys upstairs, he was besieged by mikes and tape recorders. "The consensus was that it was slightly more probable that sex abuse did not occur. There was not enough evidence to support that it had happened . . . As far as hard evidence, there wasn't a whole lot."

But they had found negligence, negligence "shared by some parties that weren't even in the courtroom": the verdict was a message to therapists and to the healing professions. "We felt that there was nothing . . . malicious . . . They should have done some things differently . . . The medical community for the past hundred years has been thought of as an untouchable being." No longer. Emboldened by the Ramona verdict, accused parents across the country would be calling their attorneys. With new hope and energy, John Carver and dozens of accused parents would drive to Sacramento the next morning to argue in noisy and emotional hearings that the state make it tougher to get recovered memories into court.

Before the lawyers left the courtroom, there was a little exchange that expressed the ambiguity that would continue to haunt the case. Gary's team, Ed Leonard knew, had two stacks of press releases ready to hand out: one if they won, the other if they lost. The moment the judge released the jury, Harrington started handing one stack to the media. Leonard came up and asked his adversary with a chuckle, "Which one did you give out?"

Yolanda was so bothered by the low award that, when she got home, she made her girlfriend walk with her to the liquor store to buy some tequila. "This was going to be a serious drink." But she couldn't drink. She pushed back the furniture, put a tape in, and started exercising. "But my heart was just really burdened, so I started praying. All of a sudden, the name of Gary's wine business just popped into my head." She called Information, dialed Gary, and blurted out, "Mr. Ramona, I don't know what it is I want to tell you, but as long as there's breath in her body don't give up on what happened between you and your daughter. I'm praying for you." She had to tell him that not everybody agreed with the award.

"Can you be ready in about thirty minutes? I'll come and get you. You're joining us for dinner," Gary said and drove south to American Canyon.

"I was jumping around this house, my whole spirit was just jubilant. I was on my knees, like: 'Thank you, Jesus!'" Yolanda recalled. "Him and Barbara came right here and picked me up," whisking her off, as her seven children watched, bedazzled. Minutes later, wearing black stirrup pants and her husband's purple shirt, Yolanda was at a table at Bistro Don Giovanni with the Harringtons, Gary and Barbara, the Jenkinses, Scott Evans, Harrington's colleague Gail Saliterman, and the Mondavis. She told them everything. Yolanda told them the only time she felt truth come out of Holly's mouth was when Harrington gave her the cards she wrote her father. "You're my ride home," she joked as she told Gary what the jurors thought of him. "You're an arrogant, egotistical man. The other jurors thought that was something against you. But, okay, that's the way you are." She had some wine, but she was too excited to eat. Margrit sat silent, amused that Gary Ramona and Bob Mondavi had found somebody who could outtalk them. At the end, "everyone said I made their celebration. I didn't have a heaven or hell to put Gary in, but I was able to help him get on with his life." It was the best night of Yolanda's life.

Seven weeks of heartbreak over the Ramona family's failure to communicate had changed her. She used to go home on a Friday night, go to her room, and collapse. The Friday after the trial, she and the kids put on old clothes, big socks, tied their heads up in kerchiefs, and cleaned the kitchen. Moved everything out of the room. Poured water and soap on the floor; then, using their bodies as mopping rags, they slid all over the floor, laughing their heads off. They just slid and slid, and the kids talked away. Yolanda learned things she had never known. The boys had a secret hiding place, a clubhouse. The girls had feelings about things — friends, boys — she had had no idea of. "And I was listening."

Tim called his mother and took her to lunch in Walnut Creek, finally ready to talk to her about the day he watched her leave, thirteen years earlier, the day that had "kind of ruined my whole life." He discovered that she still suffered, too — "she feels she betrayed us." She knew and cared that he'd gone from being a straight-A student to getting in trouble with the wrong crowd when she walked out on her seven kids. The Ramona family would never be the same, he knew. But the trial left him feeling "like I should try staying as close to my family as I can . . . If you can hate just one less person . . ."

Lenore Terr sat with Holly on the set of the *Maury Povich Show*, amazed. "She's strong, forward, assertive. She hasn't been processed and trained for this one. She looks secure," Terr observed. Then Holly said something funny, "actually funny. She's getting a laugh out of the crowd . . . She's grown." But Terr was worried about the impact of *Ramona* on all the Hollys out there. "Therapists will bounce back . . ." They would make adjustments: be more cautious about quick confrontations, about sodium amytal, about their obligation to parents — the self-help folk might listen more to the professionals. "I'm more worried about patients. What really bothers me is that *Ramona* sets up a fear of therapists in those who really need therapy."

"She's wonderful," Neil Shapiro thought, watching Holly on *Maury Povich*. "I ought to send her flowers or something. No, what do flowers tell her? That she's a nice young lady? I'm going to send her a teddy bear because her father took away a lot of her childhood, and she can't get it back. I know what that's like."

In the wake of the trial, at home, Stephanie cried as she talked about Gary to Emelyn Cruz Lat, from the *Register*. "Yes, I loved him. He did everything for me — everything for me. I would have liked to have thought he did love me." But "he couldn't have loved me and have done what he did . . . If my daughter came to me today and said, 'Mom, I lied. It didn't happen,' I'd tell her she's the biggest liar on this earth because I've already got that piece of the puzzle and I know it took place . . . I believe my daughter. *A mother knows*."

Stephanie needn't have worried. Talking freely to reporters by phone from Orange County in the aftermath, Holly said, "He wants me to recant. I will never do that. To recant that would be a lie." The verdict had been "an incredible blow. Words can't say how much it hurt . . . to have twelve people basically say that they don't believe this happened. But I'm not going to let them have that much of an impact or let my father destroy me . . . I know what happened and nobody can tell me differently . . . I've come so far, I am going to continue." Marilyn Van Derbur and Eileen Franklin would take her under their wing when she joined them as a celebrity survivor, a spokeswoman for recovered memories and sexually abused children; Miss America would teach Holly to boogey-board at the Santa Monica beach. Planning to receive her master's from Pepperdine in July, "I want to start a private practice specializing in eating disorders and sexual abuse . . . The best judge of a false memory is another abuse victim because they *know* . . . If I turn out to be half the clinician my therapists are, I'll be very happy."

Ramona v. Isabella would officially become a precedent case, binding on all future cases, only if the verdict was confirmed by Califor-

nia's Court of Appeals. But the defense, already defeated by the appellate court five times in its four-year effort to kill *Ramona* before the
trial even began, did not appeal. The awards were low enough, the
insurers felt, and the risks too great. Still, from the moment the verdict
was read, *Ramona* became a landmark — and a catalyst: it would
soon be seen as the turning point in the recovered memory wars.
Freud's groundbreaking concept of repression had been humbled by a
father who fought back, and the repercussions would be felt for at
least the rest of the decade. On May 17, the *Wall Street Journal* named
the Ramona case "the first successful courtroom challenge to practitioners of 'recovered memory' therapy." Every subsequent story on
the phenomenon would refer to *Ramona*.

On May 31, Daniel Goleman's major *New York Times* story on
Dan Schacter's memory distortion conference at Harvard named the
Ramona verdict as one of the events that had made May "an epic
month for false memory . . ." and that gave "new ammunition for
critics of recovered memories." With his case so linked to the frontiers
of memory science, the influence that would flow from that single
conference was precisely what Gary Ramona had dreamed his lawsuit
would trigger. The case emboldened George Franklin's attorneys to
appeal his murder verdict, an appeal that would lead to the dismissal
of that trial in 1995 and plans for a new trial in 1996. *Ramona* would
lead insurers to scrutinize recovered memory therapy and the cascad-
ing awards against them. *Ramona v. Isabella* led directly to the dismissal of Holly's own lawsuit against her father by a Los Angeles
judge the December after the trial, a crucial setback to dozens of pending, and all potential, suits against accused parents — even though
later Holly, pleading for "her day in court," reinstated her case once
again. The size of the threat to the feminists' war on the patriarchal
system could be seen in Gloria Steinem's attack on the founders of the
False Memory Syndrome Foundation at the American Psychological
Association's annual meetings in New York the following summer.

For Gary, "the high was over Saturday morning. Everybody was leaving." With them was gone the intellectual stimulation, the camarade-
rie, the feverish weeks of work with the attorneys and experts. Harrington was leaving that morning with Gail Saliterman and Richard
Scheer. "It was the strange feeling of coming through after a war and
you look around and see all the debris," Gary says. The living room

was a high-tech graveyard — computers, a Xerox machine, the tangle of telephone wires, the metal stands that had held the mountains of documents. "There was a garage full of legal documents and blowups, projector, and depositions and videos and you name it." The house was showing the wear and tear of twenty-five people passing through, camping out, for two months. Lloyd and JoeAnna and Scott left on Sunday — as if a third family had abandoned him.

It pained Gary that the jury had paid him not a penny for his emotional distress. "How could the jury honestly look themselves in the mirror every morning and say that there was no emotional stress for this man? What do they think I am, Superman?" Meanwhile, the two people the jury had found guilty of causing at least 50 percent of his family's disaster were flying home to their families and their lives in Hawaii and Virginia. The insurers would pay every penny, and wouldn't even feel such a small amount, he feared.

Gary Ramona saw nothing but loss. He summed up his feelings in the *Chronicle*'s story after the trial, "The High Price of Victory": "The victory is only in the sense that these incompetent mental health people have been held responsible." But what had he won? His family was more hardened against him than ever. He was so deep in debt with legal costs, it could take him ten years to pay. He had his life to rebuild from the ground up. "There are no winners in this." But the salesman never stopped making the call. "I do hope and pray that one day I will reestablish a relationship with my daughters. Hopefully, they'll be able to see the truth of the matter."

The morning after the verdict, Bruce Miroglio had to do something to get *Ramona* out of his system. He impulsively drove down to a marble and granite works in Oakland and bought a twenty-pound chunk of white Carrara marble. Back in his workshop, he chipped at the marble for hours with a hammer and chisel until rough shapes began to emerge. It would take hours and weeks before you could see what they were: a father's hand holding a daughter's hand. It was the only way he could think of to wash the sadness from his soul. It helped, that night, to rejoin the clamor of four kids at the dinner table, all asking, "Please, can I say grace? Can I 'do my day' first?" Sitting in his special chair on the patio after dinner having a glass of Sangiovese with his cigar, Miroglio looked up and, high in the hills to the west, saw the gray slate roof of the Ramonas' dream house, almost hidden in the trees.

The Impact

I came to this book without any measurable knowledge of or attitude toward recovered memories. I knew Napa, of course — I'd lived there, off and on, for sixteen years. I knew the Mondavi family. But I had known nothing of the Ramona case until the front-page story in the *Register* on the eve of the trial. I drove over to the courtroom, five minutes from my home, to listen and learn. If I brought anything to Courtroom B those first days, it was an excitement over these strange memories, an eagerness to understand this extraordinary new power of the mind. Like everyone else I'd watched, fascinated, as these memories were unleashed in the Franklin murder trial to solve a twenty-year-old crime. After George Franklin's conviction in 1990, I had been intrigued enough, as a writer, to take the prosecuting attorney, Elaine Tipton, to lunch.

Something beyond her story captivated me. Simon Schama was currently arguing in his elegant books that history — beyond the inescapable objective facts — was given its shape and meaning in our cultural and national memories by the teller's point of view. In *Dead Certainties,* he showed how General Wolfe's death at the Battle of the Plains of Abraham was three very different histories — and Wolfe three very different men — in the hands of three storytellers: a painter, a foot soldier, a psychohistorian. Now this young prosecutor had been given a rare opportunity to reopen a page of history and bring new shape and meaning to the bloody death of little Susan Nason — and a jury had chosen her truth.

Careers were already being built on these memories, books and TV specials written and filmed. But I wrote nothing then.

Six years later, on July 3, 1996, I watched Elaine Tipton, in a raspberry red suit, stand in a San Mateo courtroom to say the single sentence that set George Franklin free: "The people move to dismiss for lack of prosecution." A damning body of evidence showed Eileen Franklin Lipsker to have lied about the source of her memories, about hypnosis, about her claims that she had "seen" her father commit two more murders. She stood discredited, accused of perjury, and, with her father's first trial already reversed a year earlier, the case against him was now fully dismissed. A montage of *Ramona* film clips on the evening news prefaced sound bites from Richard Harrington on the dubious future of repressed memory cases, as KRON-TV's reporter Anthony Moor declared, "It's the final nail in the coffin of recovered memories." By then I was in the final stages of writing my manuscript on the Ramona trial, armed with far more understanding, skepticism, and opinion than I had had in Courtroom B.

I had learned enough of the human outcome of courtrooms to be sad to see Holly Ramona making lawsuits a way of life.

Although the collapse of *Franklin* would make her case harder to win, the California Supreme Court had, in mid-1995, awarded Holly her day in court; she had hired Gloria Allred, a celebrity attorney in Los Angeles who had represented Nicole Brown Simpson's family in the O.J. trial. A sexual abuse survivor network — an informal alliance of lawyers, therapists, survivors, feminists, and advocates for abused children — was supporting her, running full-page ads for the Holly Ramona Appeal and Trial Fund. But Stephanie was nervous. "Recovered memories are taking a lot of hits, and I don't want Holly hurt anymore."

They were, indeed, taking hits in lawsuits from Pennsylvania to California. *Franklin* and *Ramona* confirmed that the courts would be the decisive forum for the memory wars. Completing its first legal survey by mid-1996, the FMSF reported conservative — and admittedly incomplete — numbers: seven hundred repressed memory suits at the trial level, another two hundred that had reached the appeals courts, and many settled out of court and filed in foreign countries from Israel to Australia. Fifty third-party suits against therapists were reported. Elizabeth Loftus was testifying in cases all over the country; Harrington had turned recovered memory cases into "a small cottage industry."

Since *Ramona* had not been appealed, it would never be a binding legal precedent. Few families had the war chest to mount a major lawsuit against therapists, as Gary Ramona had. But the Napa trial was proving to be "the darkest cloud hanging over the recovered memory movement," as Frederick Crews had predicted in his book *Memory Wars*. *Ramona* had a swift and dramatic impact. Its use of a powerful team of scientific strategists and experts to force recovered memories to a rigorous scientific test set the pattern for New Hampshire's *Hungerford* case, in which the defense hired a team that included Pope and Loftus, staged a major two-week pretrial hearing, the first using the Daubert test in a criminal trial, and — just a year after *Ramona* — won a decision from the judge to deny recovered memories their day in court. "Repressed memory *may* be validated in the future. . . . Only time will tell," said Judge Groff. But that uncertain future provides "no justification for the introduction of such evidence in a trial today under our system of criminal justice." For now, the memories were "not . . . scientifically reliable."

Next, Christopher R. Barden, an attorney and psychologist from Minnesota, seized on *Ramona* to sue therapists, launching ten lawsuits against a single St. Paul therapist, Diane Humenansky. Hiring a team of experts that included Loftus and Richard Ofshe and applying an aggressive new legal style he calls "science-intensive litigation," he won the first multimillion-dollar awards ever against psychotherapists: $2.6 million in the Hamanne case in August 1995 and $2.54 million in the Carlson case in January 1996. "*Ramona* alerted lawyers to the possibility that complicated psychotherapy negligence suits were even possible. It permitted lawyers like me to get huge law firms to invest in these cases — and to use the power of the legal system to try them."

Responding with the swiftest, surest pressure for the reform Gary Ramona sought, that same month, January 1996, a Texas insurer underwritten by Prudential denied insurance to any therapists who "use hypnotherapy to assist clients in recovering . . . repressed memories of possible abuse."

Within a year of *Ramona*, pretrial hearings testing memories by the Daubert and Frye rules for "scientific acceptability" had become standard. At a hearing in California in September 1995, the judge dismissed the memories as "junk science," while in Maryland a court of appeals encapsulated the trend in judicial thinking: "we are unconvinced that repression exists as a phenomenon separate and apart

from the normal process of forgetting." Several dozen courts had rejected the memories, increasingly at the state appellate and supreme
court levels, among them Texas, Rhode Island, Alabama, Arizona,
and Maryland. In May 1996, the memory wars reached the highest
court in the land: the U.S. Supreme Court upheld an appeals court
finding that abuse allegations in *Borawick v. Shay* were "fanciful . . .
far-fetched . . . uncorroborated."

One of the worst hits came on November 15, when the only jury
trial of 1996 that gave victory to an accusing plaintiff — a $750,000
award to a Salt Lake City woman, Cherese Franklin, who claimed
thirty-three-year-old memories of abuse by her cousin — was overrid-
den and reversed by the district judge, rejecting the techniques used to
recall the memories as "unreliable." By the end of 1996, appellate
courts in nearly three quarters of the states had considered recovered
memory cases; of the seventeen appellate decisions reached, all seventeen dismissed the plaintiff's charges of remembered abuse.

From Portland, Oregon, to Allegheny County, Pennsylvania, retractors and parents were winning their cases. In September 1996, a
father and his daughter would win a $1.9 million award against a
therapist, Virginia Humphreys, from a jury in San Diego. In November, the Rutherfords in Missouri won a $1 million malpractice settle-
ment from a church counselor for hypnotically planting memories of
rape, sodomy, and forced abortions in their daughter — whose medical records proved her to be a virgin. On February 5, 1997, Harrington filed for summary judgment to again dismiss Holly's case
against her father. Calling for a Kelly-Frye test of the admissability of
her memories, he and Gary would be back in court on April 10.

Any doubt that the battle was now focused in the courts was dispelled by the January 1996 issue of one of the most influential legal
forums in the nation, the *Harvard Law Review,* which ran a ninety-
six-page broadside against the Ramona case and third-party recovered memory lawsuits. This cannonade against a case that was not
even a precedent suggested the size of the threat it posed for "the other
side." The authors, two feminist law professors at Northwestern, argued a Gary Ramona–be–damned social policy: "In light of the other
remedies available to the person falsely accused, we conclude that the
interests of the victims and therapists outweigh the alleged abuser's
interests."

In what seemed a direct riposte, Sheila Taub, in the *Journal of
Legal Medicine* several months later, argued that this "delicate bal-

ance between protecting the rights of accusers and accused" must be addressed by a legal system that resists ideology and professional self-interest in the rigorous pursuit of the science of memory — it must "reflect the most accurate information that is currently available from scientific studies on the validity of recovered memories of child sexual abuse."

Events were "unbelievably positive," Pam Freyd told a meeting of accused parents in Marin County five days before Franklin was released. "We've won the intellectual battle . . . The issue now is *justice.*" Fighting the lobbying force of powerful mental health professional organizations, FMSF now extended its battlefield beyond courtrooms to legislatures, licensing boards, and — soon, Freyd hoped — congressional hearing rooms, all places where statutes, disciplinary action, licensing standards, and a nationally publicized congressional investigation into recovered memories could further tighten the vise on wayward therapists. Although the FMSF was restrained from lobbying directly for legislative change, there was an active drive, violently fought by the therapy profession, to install state laws to reform therapists' practices. Data were still being studied for what promised to be the most positive sign — a graph that showed a precipitous drop in lawsuits filed by accusers after 1994. After *Ramona.*

Freyd saw isolated legal setbacks: a pretrial hearing in *Shahzade* in Massachusetts, a federal case, had deemed clinical psychiatrists, not scientists, the appropriate judges of recovered memory's scientific acceptability — a triumph for the testimony of dissociation's champion, the psychiatrist Bessel van der Kolk. The U.S. Supreme Court had guaranteed confidentiality for therapists' records, making it more difficult to mount a legal attack against them. So far, state legislative initiatives to force therapists to adhere to tighter standards of practice had met with defeat; voicing the view of the opposition, Mary Williams, the California attorney who had spearheaded the state's survivor-friendly delayed discovery rule, condemned the legislative effort as "scapegoating therapists . . . killing the messenger . . . striking fear into therapists and . . . victims as well." Williams was gratified to see California, twice since 1994, uphold the delayed discovery rule as she had always intended it — to give women who had never repressed their abuse memories the right to sue as adults.

At the FMSF offices, they were still getting calls from accused parents; it was still happening. More than twenty thousand accused parents had now called. "But if we can get enough institutional change in place in three years — if we can get enough children back, FMSF can close its doors," Freyd said. The deeper cultural change would take longer. The numbers of retractors increased daily, as well as the numbers of a new category, returners, who went home without retracting their memories. The conflicting emotions surrounding the reentry of still-troubled daughters into families were creating a new and challenging stage, but one these parents would happily face. "Our children will come back," Freyd told the sad roomful of parents in San Rafael. "I didn't think it three years ago. But they *will* come back."

There were signs that therapists were chastened. In April 1995, the profession had been humbled by a two-part exposé on PBS's *Frontline,* "Divided Memories." Ofra Bikel, its producer, took viewers into therapists' offices and ruthlessly revealed some of the grotesque memory recovery techniques in use. Defending her belief in Holly's memories on the program, Stephanie Ramona said, "A mother has a gut feeling, and it's strong . . . Then you go with the symptoms and it all comes together." Bikel asked her, "You said you were happy for twenty-five years, so where was your gut feeling?" Stephanie stumbled for a response, but Bikel had turned the mantra "a mother knows" into a hollow shell.

Marche Isabella continued to be indignant. Appearing at an FMSF conference in Baltimore, she was outraged when she was refused equal time with the keynote speaker, Richard Harrington, to defend herself. In the role of the therapist wronged, she lectured to family therapists in San Francisco on how to protect themselves from lawsuits, warning, "Don't ever appear at a deposition without an attorney. It's the dumbest thing you can do." The day's speakers, Isabella and Kee McFarlane, whose suggestive interviewing of children in the notorious McMartin case had been widely condemned, continued to be invited to talk and given a place of honor — a slap in the face to damaged families, Freyd felt. Lenore Terr received a standing ovation from an overflow crowd of clinicians when she received the Child Advocacy Award at the APA's annual meetings shortly after the Ramona trial, and her lectures on PTSD and recovered memories were enthusiastically received at psychiatrists' conferences two years later in Vancouver and in San Diego, even as *Franklin* came down. Confidently dispatching the Franklin dismissal as "strictly constitutional objections . . . that had nothing to do with the matter of memory in the courtroom," she claimed that "new science supports all aspects of my balanced view."

But some family therapists were feeling remorse at their profession's fall from grace. At the *Family Therapy Networker*'s symposium in Washington, D.C., in March 1996, several confessed the damage they had done, their words an echo of the apology by one of Salem's young witch-hunters, Ann Putnam: "I justly fear that I have been instrumental, with others, though ignorantly and unwittingly, to bring upon myself and this land the guilt of innocent blood."

Asking the audience "to consider therapists' contribution to the breakdown of families and communities over the past decade," one therapist, Frank Pittman, said, "We've been encouraging people to do what, in the short or the long run, makes them feel self-actualized . . . We've urged people to leave home, to break off with their parents, their husbands and wives, and even their children, and to settle for nothing less than perfect relationships that are never going to interfere with their self-pitying narcissism." Another regretted the loss of trust the obsessive incest hunt had imposed between parents and children, making a father "afraid to rub lotion on my baby's sweet bottom for fear of the vice squad" or that those innocent acts could be skewed into memories of abuse years later.

Two men were in a unique position to get therapists' attention. Their largest insurance agent, Eric Marine, and the legal counsel to California's (now) twenty-five thousand MFCCs, Dick Leslie, were teaching risk management to any therapists who would listen. Marine could not force change simply by raising insurance rates — if he closed therapists down, he'd be out of business, too. But he offered a discount on their rates if they would come and hear how not to be sued. "You have to look out the office door at reality . . . The Ramona jury said it: the public doesn't like what you're doing. You've got to help clients get on with their lives," Marine cautioned, hopeful that therapists were, finally, "coming out of denial." Therapists bristled as Leslie lectured them to maintain "neutrality" with repressed memory patients, to pursue continuing education, to resist buying into "garbage" like alien abductions, and to be skeptical of claims that "80 percent of women with bulimia were abused as children." Sharing a podium with Marche Isabella, he pointedly warned, "Don't prematurely disrupt relationships . . . *read* about memory."

The reform Gary Ramona sought was also being seen in disciplinary action by state licensing boards; the first trickle of therapists

were being censured, their licenses suspended or revoked. At the end
of 1996, Leslie was relieved to see that no MFCCs had disciplinary action pending on repressed memories. But California's Medical Board
was pursuing charges of "gross negligence and repeated acts of negligence" against a Laguna Beach psychologist, Douglas B. Sawin, a
healer wounded, he told me, by his own abusive parents and by the
seven addictions from which he was recovering — among them alcohol, sex, drugs, sugar, caffeine, and an eating disorder. In an extraordinary two hours in which I invited him to treat our interview more like
a therapy session so that I could get a sense of his style, he revealed his
own pain and doubts to me in an emotional flood that drew me into
the maelstrom, eager to reciprocate with my own revelations, and left
me disturbed by how addictive and suggestive this climate of intense
confession could become. *Frontline's* "Divided Memories" alleged
that Sawin's six years of therapy with a gifted young singer, Kate
Rose, had led her to memories of satanic ritual abuse, twenty-seven
multiple personalities, self-mutilation, lawsuits against her parents,
mental hospitals as her family of choice, and a disabling dependence
on Sawin. Although the use of the state licensing boards as a tool
for reform was just beginning, the accountability that Yolanda Nash
continued to believe was the redeeming lesson from the Ramona trial
was reaching beyond Courtroom B into the profession and culture.

These events, in sum, seemed to be sounding the beginning of the
end of the victim culture and incest fixation that had strewn such
havoc through the decade. But the memory wars were not over. Many
on the front lines still struggled with their own ambivalence, an internal conflict that seemed personified in the hypnosis expert David
Spiegel, who had defended George Franklin in 1990 and now defended therapists. He still cautioned that hypnosis produced as much
false memory as true and believed that "the Ramona jury did the
right thing," yet shared the speaker's podium with the recovery movement gurus van der Kolk, Colin Ross, and David Calof. The biggest
and most powerful group of therapists, the American Psychological
Association, seemed paralyzed by ambivalence, unable to censure its
own transgressing therapists and give its members clear guidance. The
deep and persisting rift between clinical and research psychologists
was revealed in the 236-page statement on recovered memories finally
published in February 1996 by the APA's task force. For three years it
had struggled to hammer out a position that both sides could support.
But its report revealed only the smallest patches of common ground.

While American, Canadian, Australian, and British psychiatrists and physicians had released cautionary statements about recovered memories — the bold Canadian statement specifically discouraging Ramona-style confrontations — the APA document was an embarrassing public airing of the stubborn disagreements over memory and trauma, a waffling confession that the powerful psychology profession — a quarter-million Ph.D. psychologists in the United States — did not have the will to clean its own house and settle what Frederick Crews called the "war of succession" between Freud and Janet, between psychoanalytic and cognitive approaches to therapy, between what a clinician and a scientist call truth.

As the dispute turned personal and ugly, Elizabeth Loftus finally resigned from the APA, saying that it had moved "disturbingly far from scientific thinking." Since her set-to with John Briere in Toronto in 1993, the APA had been an increasingly hostile place for her. She had tried to bridge the intellectual chasms, even going on the conference circuit with Colin Ross, a multiple personality advocate, and writing an afterword for his book on satanic ritual abuse. But she felt crucified by ethics charges reportedly filed against her with the APA by two women who had won civil suits after recovering memories of sexual abuse, charges for what they claimed were misrepresentations Loftus had made about them in an article on memory in *Psychology Today*. Defending Loftus, the journal attacked the complaints as "baseless," made "because Loftus is a woman, a scientist, unshakable, and widely liked." A vitriolic posting on the Internet further attacked her; Web site postings were now the fastest weapon in the memory wars, spreading rumors, attacks, and wins and losses on both sides with the speed of light. At the annual meeting of the breakaway American Psychological Society in San Francisco in July, Loftus hugged a plaque she had just been awarded, clinging to the words the president had said when he called to tell her of the honor: "Your courage was also noteworthy to the committee."

The shape of the scientific battle over memory took a clear form by 1996. As Daniel Schacter and his colleagues Larry Squire and Joe LeDoux met for an informal summit during a break at the Cognitive Neuroscience Society meetings in San Francisco in March, they reviewed the gains and losses. Squire feared that many, perhaps most, psychologists still clung to the "deep myths" of memory — especially the idea, imprinted from earliest training and promoted by psycho-analysis, dreams, and hypnosis, that "it's all in there somewhere," waiting to be pulled back. LeDoux still recoiled as the myth of "body memories" of abuse from past and present lives persisted — the myth that "the body keeps the score," as van der Kolk expressed it. "The body doesn't have memories; the brain has memories," LeDoux reminded us.

At least some of the deep myths, however, had been dispelled by the broad public exposure to memory science since the controversy began. Memory distortion and the ease of creating false memories were now widely accepted by both sides, some of its causes better understood. Fewer therapists, they hoped, would now trust memories that rose from hypnosis or sodium amytal.

The three had seen Freud's cornerstone, repression, largely abandoned by the clinical side as the primary rationale for recovered memories. One child memory expert, Stephen Ceci, had witnessed the historic shift from inside the hostile APA task force as the three clinicians, finally cornered by the unrelenting demand for proof of massive repression by the three research psychologists, had shifted their support from repression to dissociation.

They had watched clinicians — as they abandoned repression — embrace the traumatic memory theory that had been consolidating for several years. Lenore Terr had given glimpses of its growing strength as, in the Ramona trial, she had made a PTSD diagnosis for Holly's memories. A composite of leading-edge science, leaps of faith, and speculation, the theory was spreading like a jungle vine; research into PTSD had exploded, as had the use of the diagnosis. "The term PTSD is now being bandied about so casually that it is in danger of becoming trivialized," the psychiatrist August Piper cautioned. "Originally, the diagnosis was intended for people who had suffered events not only truly beyond ordinary human experience, but also ones that provoked extreme fear and terror about threats to one's life or limb." *DSM-IV* had diluted the criteria to cover virtually any frightening event, and now it was being applied to a grab bag of minor symptoms purportedly caused by childhood sexual abuse. "If any diagnosis is stretched so widely that it applies to every event, it ceases to mean anything at all."

The three scientists still found no evidence for the dissociation theory's most basic claim: that unconscious traumatic memories seen only as symptoms could cross over to explicit memory and awaken

dormant memories of incest put to sleep by hippocampal shutdown
when the trauma occurred. The much-touted shutdown of the emotionally overloaded hippocampus held little promise for Squire that
reliable memories could blossom from it. He still saw no proof that
you could turn a partially encoded memory into a complete one. "You
have forgetting and you have dissociation, but what you don't have is
a mechanism for recovery." LeDoux agreed to the extent that "the
emotional memory can never be converted into a *memory* of the emotion." But with so little known about the subtle interaction between
the amygdala's emotional memory and hippocampal memory of the
emotional experience, "it is at least possible that the amygdala activation could facilitate the hippocampus . . . and could be a retrieval cue
that could make a hard-to-access memory more accessible."

These words warmed the hearts of memory advocates, who were
claiming further proof of the "hippocampal connection" in studies
showing that the hippocampus of sexually abused women was smaller
than in women who were not abused, studies that suggested that
trauma might cause hippocampal shutdown, shrinkage, or damage
that could explain lost memories of abuse. Though provocative and
promising, those studies were, so far, straws in the wind.

But they were part of an aggressive drive by the true believers to
argue that the memory debate had reached a middle ground where all
agreed that both false and real recovered memories were possible.
Lenore Terr defined that middle ground: "There are some entirely
true recovered memories, some true ones with false details, some false
ones with true details, and some entirely false ones." The *Family Therapy Networker* suggested that "the polarized black-and-white debate
is shading into gray." But claiming that scientist and clinician had now
moved toward a middle ground was to ignore that a wide range of
memory distortion and forgetting was old stuff to the scientists. And
in stretching that middle ground to include Terr's "entirely true recovered memories" — if they mean memories as massively dispatched
and then accurately recovered as was claimed for Holly Ramona's —
was to falsify the scientists' views. The *Networker* gave Schacter's
words an advocate's spin: "'There are corroborated cases that I accept as validated,' says Harvard University memory researcher Daniel
Schacter, whose book *Searching for Memory* argues for the existence
of both false and genuine recovered memories."

Schacter's fuller views are hardly an argument, but more an ordinary explanation, for recovered memories. "I don't think you need

any of this fancy neuroscience. You just need gradual forgetting, a little bit of conscious avoidance, and directed forgetting. Over time the memory decays. There's some of it left, and with appropriate cues you can recover it. I think that fits just about all of the evidence of documented cases — Ross, Cheit, Fitzpatrick." Yes, some people did remember abuse they had forgotten. But it was "lack of rehearsal" — not a complex dissociation theory — "that is probably involved in the true documented cases of recovered memory . . ." "But," Schacter added, "that doesn't get you to Holly Ramona." What relevant evidence scientists did have "is not going to change one's interpretation of the Holly Ramona–type case to believing that all this happened and was suddenly recovered."

Those who had spent their careers on the leading edge of memory research were still skeptical that the kind of repeated emotional traumas claimed in cases like Holly Ramona's could be banished from memory for decades. There was still agreement with Jim McGaugh's oft-repeated statement, "Strong emotional experiences tend to be strongly remembered."

In their preoccupation with winning "entirely true recovered memories" a respectable place on the continuum of memory, its advocates ignored the purpose of the quest for truth: justice for and protection of the innocent. Playing with semantics and shades of gray, they ignored the fundamental issue: that there were no grays in incest. It had happened or it had not. There were no grays in the destruction of Gary Ramona's life; it was absolute. I heard echoes of Sawin's comments to me that, in listening to his patients' truths, he had learned to "release the concept of objective reality . . . I don't disbelieve anything." Fine sentiments in a simpler time. But six years after Holly's first flashbacks, no responsible scientist would dare claim to know if, or how, her memories could be true. And as long as young women could send destructive thunderbolts from their fingertips based on a reality no scientist could verify — a reality that might be true, partly true, or as ephemeral as spectral evidence — that benevolent, relativist approach to truth was unacceptable.

Meanwhile, as a sinking movement grasped for credibility, it now risked diluting attention from the genuine horror of posttraumatic stress as it had already diluted attention from the very real horror of child abuse in America — the two issues the recovered memory movement had claimed to care about most. By January 1997 and the three-hundredth anniversary of Salem Village's Day of Contrition —

Salem's official shouldering of responsibility for the killings of innocents — there was no similar sign of willingness to take responsibility
for the damage done in late-twentieth-century America. The memory
wars went on.

By 1996, PET scans had become the wars' weapon of choice. Van
der Kolk was getting attention for a study that showed PET's bright
blobs of color "lighting up" sections of the brain where, he claimed,
traumatic memories were occurring that played by different rules than
other memories. The study, van der Kolk stated, could explain the
rape victim's "speechless terror" and showed "a possible mechanism
for dissociation."

"That study does not have any direct bearing on recovered memories of childhood sex abuse," Schacter retorted.

With his Harvard credentials to lay before a jury, van der Kolk had
become the most prominent champion of recovered memories and the
most influential courtroom witness. Schacter had faced him in public
debate as he found himself becoming a more prominent voice for
scientific skepticism.

At the Cognitive Neuroscience Society meetings in San Francisco,
Schacter unleashed his own new PET study. In a darkened room, he
flashed a "picture" of a false and true memory on a screen. His subjects had been given a simple test in which lists of true and false words
were read and recalled while PET scans had recorded brain activity.
The scans' eruptions of color — yellow, blue, green — showed that
both true and false words shared many regions, including one near the
hippocampus. Schacter had speculated that when a false memory was
mistakenly mixed with remnants of actual experiences, it could easily
give rise to the strong conviction that the memory was real. Here was
fascinating support.

Examining the scans, however, he saw, also, that true memories
activated one region of the brain, false memories another, suggesting
a means of distinguishing one from the other. The false word lit up
the frontal lobe, already implicated in false memories — the region,
he felt, that would lead to the next step in understanding recovered
memories. But Schacter made it clear, as his study was broadcast
across the country, that he was not claiming to have discovered the
long-sought litmus test for true and false memories of sex abuse. PET
data could change from one study to the next. These were lists of
words, not satanic ritual rape. Soon his own subsequent studies with
different techniques would show how different results could be ob-

tained, "underscoring the need to be cautious about extrapolating from the laboratory to the real world . . . at this early stage of research." But he and his colleagues held in their hands at least a tentative model of how the brain produces accurate and false memories. It was another shaft of light shed on the deep myths.

This use of PET scans — the ideologue reaching for dramatic scenarios from slim data, the skeptical scientist open to doubt and to new findings — summed up the difference between the two camps' approaches to resolving the memory wars.

In his final writings, Carl Sagan addressed the tortuous balancing act demanded by justice for both victim and accused. His familiar scientific rigor tempered by compassion, he cited in *The Demon-Haunted World* appalling statistics of rape and abuse of women in America and cried the reality of "ghoulish sexual predation by parents, or those acting in the role of parents. Compelling physical evidence — photos, for example, or diaries, or gonorrhea or chlamydia in the child — have in some cases come to light . . . The problem is real and urgent . . . On the one hand, callously to dismiss charges of horrifying sexual abuse can be heartless injustice. On the other hand, to tamper with people's memories, to infuse false stories of childhood abuse, to break up intact families, and even to send innocent parents to prison is also heartless injustice. Skepticism is essential on both sides. Picking our way between these two extremes can be very tricky."

Trials were theater. "They're a show," said Eric Marine, who had been to too many "shows" since recovered memory lawsuits began. The best science was seldom showy; the few experts, like Loftus, who could combine serious science with showmanship became courtroom superstars. On the stand, scientists tended to say, "I don't know." Yet scientists must become the principal gladiators in the memory wars if, as Arthur Miller wrote at the end of 1996, "today, as in Salem three centuries ago, the only defense against the depredations of others is a profound dedication to fact and evidence and the rule of law." If trials were theater, the lawyers who would be successful in the defense of justice in upcoming trials would be the ones who could capture and translate to the witness stand the excitement — the "fact and evidence" and honest doubt — the best scientists knew at the frontiers of memory.

*

Far from the front lines, the lives of those pulled into the wars by *Ramona* went on. Robert Gerner's ethics troubles escalated to the point of disciplinary action by the California Medical Board; its November 10, 1994, Action Report stated that Gerner's medical license had been revoked, though stayed for seven years' probation, and that Gerner had been suspended for sixty days for "gross negligence, repeated negligent acts and incompetence in engaging in sexual relations with a female patient in therapy . . ."

Bruce Miroglio, who had humiliated Gerner in court, had seen his name painted in gold on the law firm's doors on Main Street, promoting him to a full partner. Despite the verdict, its ambiguities made him feel that he had not lost *Ramona*.

The trial had not talked Carolyn Thompson out of her memories of molestation by her parents, as she had hoped it would. With Tom in prison, her children had little contact with their father, and her alienation from her own family was nearly complete. Survival was a daily struggle; she had chosen to go on welfare so she could be with her children and return to school. But since the trial, she had seen the miracle of a child springing back from abuse, had seen Aaron, now ten, grow into a sociable, empathic fifth-grader with a strong sense of justice; Alison was strong. Carolyn was still emotionally raw, but the outrage she had found and screamed from her journals was taking the form of a book. She was breaking the abuse cycle.

Holly had received her master's in psychology from Pepperdine and was doing therapy with adults at Charter Hospital in Orange County. She had completed her three thousand hours of internship in July of 1996, the final step before taking her exams as an MFCC. She had had several dates with men. When she went to Napa for Shawna's high school graduation, she broke Stephanie's conservative mold and turned up in slim blue jeans and a jeans jacket, with a "very L.A." head of tawny long hair. But Holly was uncomfortable in the valley that had rejected her memories, and she flew back to Orange County the next morning. In spite of the negative climate, she was still hoping to get a trial date scheduled against her father. "She's better," said Miroglio.

Stephanie had decorated the tree all by herself the previous Christmas at two in the morning. She was stronger during the day and even felt happy often now — perhaps because "the girls are fine and strong. Each is a wonderful person. They are so much more together than I am at nearly fifty-two." The friends were still staunch. Steph-

anie rented a house at Tahoe for two weeks in the summer and took
Betty gambling. She wished the world could see the sense of humor,
the fun the family of women had — "the loyalty and closeness that
nobody can break, not even Gary." She has some plans for her future,
but won't discuss them. "I've grown very private," even though she
finds herself falling into the old trap of trusting people. She has found
the strength to look inside at her own and her family's failings, if not
yet outside, at memory science. At times Stephanie was still as fragile
as the baubles she hung on the tree. "When I hear a child call its
mother, I always wonder, 'Did Holly call my name?'" She tries to help
people who call her with their abuse and their memories. The survivor
network — which is "stronger than ever," she says, since George
Franklin's release and still active in its defense of Holly — sends them
to her. "But I just can't . . . can't take it. Can't handle it." Alone at
night, she wakes up, punishing herself. "If I'd been a better mother —
if I'd paid attention, if I'd really talked with my kids." Napa Valley
had become hard for her. "The family's having a tough time. It's the
fallout. We feel vulnerable." The women cling tightly on an island
surrounded by growing doubt and disbelief.

Yet since the trial Stephanie's private voice has strengthened. The
witness stand was a cruel place for her. But there is no stumbling or
halting as the tiger in her unleashes its protective fury. At any hint of
skepticism — any threat of damage to her children, of challenge to
Holly's memories or to her actions — a mass of passion, anger, and
unshakable belief bursts from her, a cry from the heart:

"It's always 'poor Gary.' Why don't people see the damage done to
these kids! It's unbelievable — one man, one little tiny man could destroy so many lives, so many people . . . My children did nothing. No
one knows. *You* don't know. If only my children could tell you the
things they know. We were there. There'll never be proof — there
can't be with this . . . There *is* repressed memory. It exists! My daughter doesn't lie. I was there. I know. The scientists can say whatever. I
know more than any scientist. It happened. It's in God's hands . . .
with Gary."

Kelli was working as a private investigator in Boulder, Colorado.
Shawna had tried college in Colorado but went home at Christmas
and was working at an upvalley supermarket and taking a road trip to
Montana. Shawna had called Gary. She told her mother that she'd
been so young when it all began that she hadn't had a chance to deal
with her dad.

Yet, just after the trial, she arrived at insights about him that, interestingly, echoed the feelings he had always had about exclusion. "Dad was always . . . taking the pictures . . . It was like his only way to become part of the family was to live through the pictures he took and the memories that, like, *we* made, and to try to become part of them." Why hadn't her dad been able to join the family? she'd wondered. With Holly's memories, she thought she knew. "Not that he's sorry he did it, but he felt remorse — like, 'I know I'm wrong. But I'm hurt. And I want them to feel the hurt that I feel.' So then he'd, in a way, use the camera as his means of getting into us . . . of becoming the family that he saw all of us as." Now Shawna wanted closure.

Gary was buoyant with hope when she called. Still living in his Napa home with Barbara, he was pouring cement walkways and building patio arbors, just as in the days at Diamond Bar and Pinot Way. Still trying to rebuild his career, he was on the road marketing wine for his old friend Fred Franzia, still not making good money but hopeful as he set up a distribution network for a new brand. Bob and Margrit still invited him to the Christmas party, but he had to watch the winery from afar while it enjoyed the best performance in its thirty-year history. While Bob focused on creating an international center for wine, food, and the arts in Napa, Michael, now CEO, with Tim at his side, presided over a thriving empire. Despite the ravages of phylloxera, which had stressed some smaller wine growers to bankruptcy, Napa Valley's image was emerging intact. Responding to the grape shortage with characteristic bravura, the Mondavis were importing bulk wines from southern France, then bottling and marketing them as frankly French Vichon Mediterranean — gambling that their growing image as a global wine company would soften the shock waves.

Stephanie had gone to see Garnet after she had had a stroke, a sign of progress. But for Gary, reconciliation with the girls seemed remote. Even if Shawna still doubted his innocence, Gary hoped her call meant that perhaps they could forge a bond. They met at her place of choice, the Highway 29 Café at the south end of Napa next to the flea market, a "very laid-back little place" of fat-dripping platters of ham and eggs and chicken-fried steak. As Shawna ordered coffee and Gary orange juice and a muffin, he waited for the question none of the Ramona women had yet asked: Did you do it?

Instead Shawna said, "You know the ground rules."

"No, *what* ground rules?"

"You know." Confess, apologize to Holly, and get therapy. They had not changed since the confrontation six years earlier. Gary felt sick. Shawna must be under terrible pressure to stay loyal to Holly, he feared. But how could intelligent young women close their minds?

"Shawna, I didn't do it," he stated, as he had told Holly on that first day of confrontation. "If you want to believe the moon is made of green cheese, there's nothing I can do. But if you change your mind, Shawna, the door's always open."

Shawna went silent. The meeting was dead. "Do you want breakfast?" the waitress asked. Defeated, Gary asked for the check.

"No, I'll buy my coffee," Shawna insisted.

He wasn't going to win this little power struggle, he saw, so he joked, "Well, how about buying my o.j. and muffin?" She couldn't help smiling, then slapped down her dollar and rushed out.

But for Shawna it had, apparently, been closure. "Shawna's been able to sleep since then," Stephanie reported.

A little more than two years after the trial, seven of the jurors gathered at the courthouse, the word "justice" chiseled above them into the facade. "I think we made the right decision," said Yolanda, looking back from the pro-Gary side. "Yes, I stand by the decision I made," said Becky, from the anti-Gary side. Marty Cook, always the most ambivalent juror, said, "I still kind of struggle with it." "I don't think we answered all the questions," Tim added. But none would change the verdict. Becky still believed recovered memories could exist, but she, and this jury, had "followed the evidence."

The trial had inspired Becky and Tim. Becky still worked at the Vallejo Safeway while commuting to school in Sacramento, training to be a paralegal. But "what I want to do is behavioral psychology and get into jury picking, communications, stuff like that." Tim had been so impressed by the trained minds of experts equipped to go out and make a real difference in the world that he had gone back to college, upgrading his degree from dietetics to one in nutritional science; he would move on from mixing vats of cake batter at the veterans home to a career in research. Yolanda laughed as she reported that Jean Sawday now treated her like "a pal" at the country club and that she'd heard Holly had a boyfriend.

"I still think about what the Ramonas are doing now," said Keith

Himmelman. Reflecting on all that divided them, he added, "I don't think they could ever come together again."

"While there's a breath in the body, there's always a chance," Yolanda responded vigorously.

Beth nodded yes. "But there's years to go yet."

They've got to communicate, Marty urged. "Family's just too important to . . ." With the word "family," they were back in the deliberation room with the same spirited intensity. There had always been consensus on one thing.

"The fact remains," said Becky, "that the family was destroyed. Family is the most important thing in life."

If Becky is right, memory comes a close second. For a family *is* its memory. If we were to try to redefine family, as it is currently fashionable to do, perhaps it would be: a group that shares a common, intimate memory of the past and that transmits its story through the generations — a story that is continually restructured and embellished, but whose gist and values are the family's strength and identity. Without family stories, we cannot tap what Schama calls that "obstinately rich loam of memory . . . The sum of our pasts, generation laid over generation, like the slow mold of the seasons, that forms the compost of our future. We live off it."

Distortions of memory — a family's, a nation's — only became dangerous and obscene when they served and justified destructive goals: Hitler's consciously bending national memory to the myth of Teutonic superiority; village gossips exorcising their own demons by hurling unproven memories of incest at their neighbors. Young women so focused inward on their own personal healing from the wounds of memories, false and true, that they cannot turn outward to the rings of family and community that still encircle and love them.

The Ramonas' story has been cut short. A new story has tragically choked out the old — the one that merged Italian immigrants and Cherokees, the Midwest and California, and love that blossomed from its citrus groves and beaches. The story that tells Holly, Kelli, and Shawna who they are. Shawna met her father for coffee again just before Christmas 1996. Perhaps there is hope that the Ramonas may, one day, pick up their story and let it grow.

The Process

Since this is a story whose major theme and tension are a family's competing memories, I felt it was vital to find an approach and format that reflected that essential uncertainty over "what happened." It is a story of lives destroyed by allegations based on memories that cannot, by our best scientists today, be definitively proven true or false. There is, of course, an objective reality that cannot be denied. Gary Ramona raped, or did not rape, his daughter. His daughter's recovered memories of incest are, fundamentally, trustworthy or not. But the mists that surround objective truth in *Ramona* are like smoke over a battlefield, obscuring events and leaving the reader, like the jury, to match one truth against another and to come to personal conclusions: What were the sources of Holly Ramona's memories? Where does guilt for the tragedy truly lie?

This book, unlike my previous ones, was not the place for fully rounded reports of every scene, verified from two or three points of view — the conventional journalistic technique. There is safety in that approach, for it protects the writer from the accusation that she has unfairly skewed the story in one direction or another. I wanted to let the passions and biases of each major character speak directly, without a chorus of points of view diluting that strongly held "truth."

In searching for a format, I found my guides in two distinguished academics, the historian Simon Schama and the memory scientist Marcia K. Johnson, both of whom work with the disparate realities from which human history is fashioned. I have, humbly, followed their path in telling a "true story" that reflects the idea that "real history" is not neat and tidy; it is layer upon tangled, intertwined layer of ambiguous and inconclusive "truths."

"Past, present, and future are not discrete divisions among an orderly succession of life's events . . . They collapse onto each other, emerge from each

other, and constantly determine each other . . . The past . . . is an amalgama-
tion of 'nows,'" says Johnson, a leading expert in "reality monitoring," which
pursues the question: "How do we remain anchored in reality" when our
own reality is, at least partially, a distorted reconstruction? "What prevents us
from drifting into a world of fantasy pasts and futures . . . when, at any
moment, cognition (our awareness of events) is driven by vested interests that
affect how we seek out and sample information, how we interpret ambiguous
evidence and how we remember it or use it to predict the future. Some of this
mental activity is prompted by motives — our hopes, fears, desires, and needs
. . . Our recollection of the past is influenced by our current attitudes and our
current theories . . . In summary, there is no single truth about what was and
will be."

Like *Dead Certainties,* Schama's book on the battlefield death of General
Wolfe and the grisly murder of a Boston Brahmin, the Ramona family tragedy
is about "irreconcilable memories" — about the very different lives Gary,
Stephanie, and Holly Ramona claim to have lived under the same roof. To
capture and juxtapose these wild swings in perception, Schama lets alternative accounts compete for credibility, lets his stories "play with the teasing gap
separating a lived event and its subsequent narration," stories that "follow
the documented record with some closeness . . . but dissolve the certainties of
events into the multiple possibilities of alternative narrations." Thus his brilliant histories "end with accounts at odds with each other as to what has
happened . . ." As does *Ramona.*

For Schama, "this is not a naively relativist position that insists that the
lived past is *nothing* more than an artificially designed text . . . But it does
accept . . . that claims for historical knowledge must always be fatally circum-
scribed by the character and prejudices of its narrator." I agree.

Applying these principles in practical terms, I have often let a single eye
describe a scene. When the story arrives at an event that has high significance
for Stephanie, I let her tell it. I let Gary tell his most powerful moments. And
in those scenes the dialogue is his, or her, best reconstruction. In some cases, I
present the opposing memory of an event later. Just as often, however, the
other — Gary or Stephanie — has no memory of the event or denies it ever
happened. Throughout, I have tried to make it clear whose point of view is
being expressed and to identify those scenes that are subjective recapitulation.
What emerges for the reader, then, is the story like the one the jury heard —
opposing truths, half of which had to be untrue or only partly true. It is the
way history is created and transmitted at the level of individual experience. It
is the way wars and witch-hunts begin — in half truths fervently believed
without the "reality monitoring" of skepticism and openness to other
"truths." For this is a story, too, about witch-hunts.

As my seven weeks of observing the trial were augmented by subsequent
insights into the issues and the characters, I, too, became a storyteller.

Throughout the book, the author's voice joins other voices. The narratives draw from an immense body of research. I checked stories and quotations against a wide variety of source materials, especially several hundred hours of personal taped interviews, including a lengthy series of interviews with both Gary and Stephanie Ramona and a retelling of the trial by the jury taped at a gathering of most of the jurors at my home. Their story gave a rich perspective on the trial. My resources included daily trial notes that filled more than two dozen notebooks; depositions, trial transcripts, and court records; books, scientific and scholarly studies, magazine and newspaper articles, and many other original and secondary sources, most of them cited in the notes. I reviewed the court reporters' transcripts or audiotapes of every section of the trial depicted in the book. To root the family story in its larger history and the shifting uncertainties in a solid base of knowledge of the broader social issues, I extended my research to attend major and minor meetings and conferences of neuroscientists, both clinical and research psychologists, judges, MFCCs, accused parents, trauma and abuse survivors, skeptics, and critical thinkers; to interview the authorities and direct participants in the many aspects of the recovered memory wars; to be tutored in memory by the nation's most respected scientists; and to study all the relevant themes, from bestiality to legal theories of "duty." My interviews also reached far beyond the principal characters to include their friends and colleagues, courtroom observers, therapists, jurors, many of the witnesses, wine industry people, attorneys, insurers, and a broad spectrum of women involved in the key issues — retractors, those having flashbacks of abuse, multiple personalities, corroborated victims of child abuse, child protective services, and the survivor network.

Notes

PROLOGUE: THE MEMORY WARS

The opening scene in the Salem Memorial Park is drawn from a personal visit. "That poisoned cloud of fantasy," which describes spectral evidence, is from Arthur Miller's October 21/28, 1996, article in the *New Yorker*, "Why I Wrote 'The Crucible.'" Opening day of the Ramona trial is drawn from personal observation. I attended every day of the seven-week trial except for the three days of jury selection.

This summary of issues, events, and implications is a distillation of the author's thinking and research and incorporates many references that will be specifically cited in later chapters. Frederick Crews's quote comes from *The Memory Wars* (1995). The therapist quoted in "I am a therapist" is David Calof, in his article "Facing the Truth About False Memory," *Family Therapy Networker*'s Sept./Oct. 1993 issue.

The column was Kevin Courtney's in the *Napa Valley Register*, May 1, 1994. That recovered memories blossomed in America's most privileged neighborhoods is indicated by the False Memory Syndrome Foundation's (FMSF's) survey of forty retractors, published in the *Journal of Psychiatry & Law* (Fall 1995) — one of the few available profiles. The survey showed nearly half of the subjects (47.5 percent) self-reporting middle class and another 25 percent reporting upper-middle-class status; more than 90 percent had finished high school, half had their B.A., and nearly 20 percent had done graduate work; all were Caucasians. Some 35 percent reported an upper-middle-class socioeconomic level.

Judith Lewis Herman's quote "commonalities . . . between survivors . . ." comes from her 1992 book, *Trauma and Recovery*. Carol Tavris's "Beware the Incest Survivor Machine" appeared in the *New York Times Book Review* on January 3, 1993. The Anne Roiphe quote is from her 1996 book, *Fruitful*, a runner-up for the National Book Award. "It's like a novel . . ." was said by Bessel van der Kolk on the PBS *Frontline* documentary "Divided Memories, Part I," which aired April 4, 1995. UC Berkeley professor of social psychology, Richard Ofshe is credited with coining "robust repression."

I learned about the forms of evidence used in the Salem witch trials, especially "spectral evidence," from several sources, one of the most useful being *Salem Possessed,* the fascinating 1974 book by Paul Boyer and Stephen Nissenbaum.

Regarding memory and reality — the fundamental issues of this book — I have, throughout, applied the most current scientific understanding of memory as "malleable, reconstructive, suggestible, often unreliable, and easily implanted with false elements" in letting the characters tell their stories. Whether everything they say is true or not, it is the play of one reality against another that is the essential tension between Gary and Stephanie Ramona as their truths are ultimately tested in court. And competing "truths" are the principal expression of failed communication in the Ramona family.

The telling quote "We've deified our chefs . . ." is from the Napa psychologist Richard F. Mullins, Jr., whose comments to me on family dynamics were very helpful in the book's formative months.

1. A WORLD OF WOMEN

This chapter, Stephanie's story of her life until she moved to Napa Valley in 1979, is told primarily from Stephanie's point of view and draws on extensive personal interviews with her, on depositions, documents, hearings, and trial testimony from the divorce proceedings and the Ramona trial; on my personal interviews with and discovery testimony of Betty Nye, Jean Sawday, Karen Maestas, and Shawna, Kelli, and Holly Ramona; on an interview with Shary Quick; and on Holly's trial testimony. Gary's story, reported in Chapter 2, differs in some significant respects.

I also did research into post–World War II Southern California and San Gabriel Valley in the Glendora, Santa Ana, and Garden Grove libraries. The maxim regarding clothes, "Buy few items . . . ," was told to me by Gary Ramona, who claims to have heard it said many times by Betty Nye. Insight into Stephanie's stepfather, Walt Nye, was also gained from *The Spearheaders* (1960), written by a fellow Darby's Ranger, James Altieri, whose descriptions of Nye in battle suggest that, today, Walt Nye would have been diagnosed with posttraumatic stress syndrome.

The descriptions of Gary's motive for wanting to marry and of the early incidents of violence, marital conflict, and lies are predominantly from Stephanie: her recollections, her "truth." Alleged and described from the opening sentence of the first court documents filed in the divorce on March 14, 1990, through subsequent interviews, depositions, and testimony, the violence was

confirmed, in part, by Betty Nye and Holly, who both claimed some recollection of events. After pretrial evidentiary hearings in April 1993, Judge Snowden concluded that "evidence of plaintiff's outbursts of anger, including an
assault upon his wife, years ago, are not relevant to this case" and ruled by
Order In Limine on May 14, 1993, that they could not be offered as testimony.
Gary's description of this period often differs, and he denies all but one of the
violent or suspicious incidents: he confirms that he once hit her in the stomach.

Stephanie's description of the hours preceding Holly's birth is a classic
example of the wide divergence of their memories — or, at least, of the stories
Stephanie and Gary tell. The Ramonas' description of the Diamond Bar house
was augmented by my own visit to the house and a tour of an identical
neighboring house. The "lock" scene and the "washing sheets" scene at Diamond Bar, two of the most disturbing of Stephanie's memories, are a composite of personal interviews, Stephanie's T-graph entered into evidence in the
trial, depositions, and Stephanie's trial testimony. Stephanie and Shary Quick
remember Gary's presentation of the string of pearls differently; Shary recalls
its occurring at the graduation ceremony. I have used Stephanie's version.

Since this book inevitably became an examination of the suburban American family, several books I have long valued informed my understanding of
the Ramonas: *The Way We Never Were,* by Stephanie Coontz (1992), an
analysis of the American family over the centuries that debunks the myths and
assumptions about how families function. Donald Katz's *Home Fires* (1992),
a multigenerational study of a Brooklyn family that followed its post–World
War II dream to the new tract homes of Levittown, Long Island. And Robert
N. Bellah et al.'s *Habits of the Heart* (1985), whose point is that the founding
American struggle between the individual and the community, happily merged
in the "civil society" of the small town, has been skewed in favor of individu-
alism at the expense of community — an alienation largely created by separating the workplace from home and town.

Also useful was the May 15, 1995, *Newsweek* cover story, "Bye-Bye,
Suburban Dream," which argues that the suburbs have failed to fulfill their
promise of teeming life and human diversity, but instead have "promoted the
ideals of privacy and exclusivity," with suburban sprawl making the home
ever more isolated from the father's workplace. The safe cul-de-sac, a symbol of the Ramonas' dreams for family life, may be an endangered species
if *Newsweek*'s call is heard to "drop the cul-de-sac — a fancy term for 'dead
end.'"

2. THE BIRTH OF A SALESMAN

Gary Ramona's point of view dominates this chapter. My story of his
boyhood and life until the move to Napa comes from extensive personal
interviews with Gary, depositions, and trial testimony; from interviews with

Scott Evans, JoeAnna and Lloyd Jenkins, Maggie Haswell, and Margrit Biever. I visited all the sites of his boyhood, college, and Diamond Bar years — the Orange Grove Trailer Park, Mt. San Antonio College, and the neighborhoods in which he lived as a child and, later, with Stephanie. I visited the beaches both remember: Huntington Beach, Newport, Balboa Island. Wherever he recounts a conversation and another person is quoted, the quotation represents Gary's best memory of the event.

His recollections of their early years of marriage often contrast dramatically with Stephanie's. Their divergent memories of their sex life are important clues to the evolving family dynamics and as indicators (or not) of Gary's and Stephanie's sexual "normalcy," which became an issue during the trial when the sources of Holly's incest memories and her extraordinary sexual naiveté were debated.

Since Gary's career parallels the rise of Napa Valley to world rank as a premium wine area, in this and future chapters I have gone beyond my interviews in documenting that contemporary history. My reportage of the physical valley and its history, culture, and wine industry is based largely on my own long and deep association with Napa as a writer and resident. Arriving in 1978 to write the Napa Valley story for the *National Geographic*, I moved to the valley for two years and returned to live permanently in 1990. I know the Mondavi family — father, sons, and wives. Over the years, I've written numerous feature articles about the wine culture and the Mondavis and found them useful here. I've consulted a variety of other sources: articles, newspaper files, books, the Robert Mondavi Winery, depositions, and trial transcripts; I've had formal interviews and informal discussions, some off the record, with a number of people, including the former Mondavi public relations chief Harvey Posert, Margrit Biever, Greg Evans, and other Mondavi and wine industry people.

3. THE FAMILY TABLE

Here Stephanie's and Gary's stories begin to weave together, moving from his to her — to others' — memories of events. In each scene, I've tried to make the point of view clear. Generally, I stay in Stephanie's or Gary's eyes for several pages, but friends or other observers add to their accounts. The scene in the Westphalian lodge is an example, moving from Margrit Biever's to Gary's, to Stephanie's, then back to Gary's perspective.

The first wine auction is described from my *New West* profile of Robert Mondavi in August 1981. My principal source for the phylloxera story is the *New York Times Magazine* "What's Killing the Grapevines of Napa?" on October 17, 1993. The home movies shown at the trial gave me a vivid sense of the Ramona family from Holly's infancy through her departure for college, a family life fleshed out in interviews with neighbors, north and south.

Stephanie and Holly are the primary sources for the material on Holly's early history. Both testified on her weight and eating issues at trial and in depositions, and Stephanie discussed them in personal interviews. Holly also described her binging and purging episodes in the letter written to her father during her hospitalization, in Marche Isabella's therapy notes, and in an interview conducted during her psychiatric evaluation by Dr. Gerner, as well as at trial.

The Ramonas' empty dinner table in a valley that celebrates the table as the heart of the good life was a powerful irony I could not resist. As the theme of the family dinner table as metaphor for family strength grew to importance in the book, the *Journal of Gastronomy*'s special issue, "Taste, Health, and the Social Meal" (Winter/Spring 1993), provided rich sources in its excellent articles by Margaret Mackenzie, Leann L. Birch, and Margaret Visser. November 1995's Who's Who Among American High School Students' *Special Report on Teens and Their Families* revealed, as its most dramatic finding, "a strong relationship between close family activity such as eating dinner together and the students' sense of personal responsibility and emotional well-being." The family dinner table was the common thread among America's highest-achieving teens.

Gary's comments concerning Stephanie's figure and the cellulite on her leg are her best recollection of his words, as is his response to her question "Am I not attractive to you anymore?" and his assertion, in an Orange County hotel, that "there will be no therapy . . ." Shawna provided the scene with her father in New York in an interview.

The theory that "disordered eating" and depression could be caused by a daughter's conflict over her parents' roles — a high-achieving father, a frustrated homemaker mother — was proposed by Brett Silverstein and Deborah Perlick in *The Cost of Competence* (1995). "Holly would appear to be a classic case of their argument," the cultural psychologist Carol Tavris told me, "a conflict that has been played out for centuries . . . even in Elizabeth I and Lenin's daughter." The scene with Dr. Stiles in which the suggestion of molestation first appears is told from Stephanie's recollections and diverges from Dr. Stiles's testimony in trial.

The planning and building of the dream house was described to me by Gary, Stephanie, Margrit Biever, and the architect Sandy Walker.

4. FLASHBACKS

Stephanie's discovery of Holly's bulimia and the increasingly desperate events that unfold toward Holly's confrontation with her father are told primarily from Stephanie's perspective, as she interacts with Holly, Barry Grundland, and Marche Isabella. Gary's lack of concern for Holly's possible molestation and his angry words — to "leave it alone" — are Stephanie's recollection. Holly's story during the period of flashbacks comes primarily from testimony and trial materials, including Isabella's clinical notes and Dr. Gerner's psychological examination of Holly.

To protect her privacy, the neighbor who played "mother and father" with Holly is called by a pseudonym, "Kathy."

From the telephone conversation between mother and daughter when Holly confirmed that her father raped her through the stressful weeks until Holly's sodium amytal interview, the events and scenes are a mosaic of personal interviews, depositions, and the trial testimony of Stephanie, Holly, Isabella, Grundland, Gerner, and Richard Rose, who administered the sodium amytal.

Dr. Stephanie McClellan's pelvic exam of Holly comes from an interview at the Hoag Medical Center in Newport Beach, where she examined Holly, as well as from her deposition and trial testimony. Although McClellan was a witness for the defense, she has strong opinions on the case that she was not able to express on the stand. From the thousands of women she has seen in her busy Orange County practice, she says, "What the Ramona story meant to me was: How could a family that looked so good be so dysfunctional that they are here in court, playing out their relationship dramas in front of the entire world? What is important here is a young woman who so wholeheartedly believes she was raped by her father, though I can never prove it, that she had gone public with her entire life and violated every sense of privacy and decorum that women have in this area." Holly, she suspects, was "destroyed" even before she had memories; "abuse relationships with a father don't necessarily mean sexual abuse — indifference is a kind of abuse." She has seen too many families who "put on a happy face" rather than "fighting it out as a family . . . I've seen the beautiful lives and then I hear the secrets . . . the affluent trophy wives who, when they turn fifty, are lost." McClellan is disturbed by a strong trend she sees in her practice for young women to abandon their education and professions and "pour all their power" into domesticity, "to leave careers to go home and run families." An "incredibly busy" mother of three who sympathizes with the tug between children and career, she sees this trend denying daughters a role model of competence; the Ramona daughters "saw that powerfulness in the male and that helplessness in the female. Holly may have transposed that."

The court document quoted from in "to ascertain the truth . . ." was a Supplemental Declaration filed by Stephanie in the Ramonas' divorce case.

Gary's being notified of the March 15 meeting with Holly and his reactions were described by him in personal interviews.

The scene in which Stephanie and Gary drive to the new house in a pickup truck is entirely from Stephanie's memory. Gary remembers trips to the hilltop but has no specific recollection of this scene, which was full of such fear and significance for Stephanie.

5. CONFRONTATION

Stephanie, in personal interviews, gave her recollection of the scenes before flying south for the confrontation.

The sodium amytal interview — before, during, and after — is drawn from discovery and trial testimony of Dr. Richard Rose, Marche Isabella, Stephanie, and Holly and personal interviews with Stephanie. Holly's goals for the confrontation come from Gerner's interview with her.

The confrontation is told here from Gary's point of view; a merging of personal interviews with him and his depositions and trial testimony the events and dialogue are as he remembered them — a very different scene than the one described by Holly, Isabella, and Stephanie in later chapters. Current events of the day were published in the *Orange County Register* of March 15, 1990. I toured Western Medical Center–Anaheim to get the physical flavor and layout of the building.

6. A FAMILY FALLS APART

The aftermath to the confrontation is shown, first, through Stephanie's eyes, primarily from personal interviews. The Ramonas' divorce court records are the source of all specific references to court documents in this chapter.

Gary's view of the aftermath, including the meetings with Holly, Isabella, and Grundland is told mostly from personal interviews with Gary and Scott and Peggy Evans, with some reference to his and Richard Rose's depositions. The exchange between Stephanie and Gary at the car following his meeting with Holly and Isabella is Stephanie's recollection.

Mary Williams, the attorney who spearheaded California's extended statute of limitations and delayed discovery rule, gave me a good history of the dynamically changing legislative climate as California, and many other states, broadened its laws to protect alleged victims of childhood sexual abuse at a time when recovered memories were being uncritically accepted.

I was told by Bruce Miroglio about Rose's delay in writing his first discharge notes for Holly. Regarding "the Christian connection" in the recovered memory movement, New Life's brochures were deposition exhibits. Jeffrey Younggren, an ethics consultant for the state's licensing boards, considers unlicensed pastors "a major problem, a debate in the profession." Few, he says, have studied both divinity and psychology. "Most just take their seat-of-the-pants knowledge of religion and blend it with psychotherapy."

Sources for the Easter meeting in Southern California are Stephanie's, Shawna's, Kelli's, and Isabella's, discovery documents.

7. A MOTHER KNOWS

I conducted two personal interviews with Ephraim Margolin. The Wolf-gang Lederer material is drawn mostly from his trial testimony.

The charge of witch-hunt in my home valley is not made lightly, but I believe that it is appropriate and inescapable wherever damage to human lives is done by unproven and uncorroborated charges made on the basis of emotion, fear, and a lack of moral clarity and intellectual skepticism. In other words, it is, to me, a very simple and fundamental justice issue. Stephanie, Gary, and Bob Mondavi reported the spread of the incest rumor. Bob Mondavi gave his support of Gary's innocence at trial; Margrit Biever's position of "innocent until proven guilty" was confirmed to me in personal interviews. Greg Evans's comments come from a personal interview. The "bad boy" scene with Evans and Cliff Adams is from Gary's discovery testimony. This inside view of "the Gary issue" has been enriched by several informal conversations with people who shared that difficult time.

Given the malleability of cultural as well as individual memory and the ambiguous feelings of all concerned, the conscious or unconscious intent of the Mondavi board is, in itself, a worthy and subtle study of human motivation. As with the spread of the incest rumors, they appear to be an example of good people unwittingly doing bad things. The same could be said of Salem, where the horror of contemporary witch-hunts was vividly revealed to me by the presence, at the 300th anniversary of Salem's Day of Contrition on January 14, 1997, of several dozen people recently released from jail after serving years of multiple-lifetime sentences. They had been convicted of bogus charges of unimaginable sexual depradations growing from the preschool satanic sexual abuse hysteria of the late 1980s — charges that would be laughable to the sane person were their impacts not so tragic and were recurring paranoias not so impossible to vanquish, an inextinguishable part of the human condition.

The scene of the reading of the leave-of-absence letter to Gary is told from Gary's point of view, with personal interviews augmenting trial records.

8. THE CHRISTMAS PRESENT

Betty Nye's recollections are also from personal interviews. Holly's deteriorating condition is also documented in her own and Marche Isabella's accounts. The history of the legal tool of "delayed discovery" in California comes from personal discussions and written exchanges with Mary Williams, who was on the barricades. Stephanie's story is told here from personal interviews, depositions, and court documents. The declaration of expenses was *Declaration of Stephanie Ramona in Suppport of Request for Orders Pendente Lite.* The pleas for spousal support were contained in *Supplemental Memorandum of Points and Authorities Re Spousal Support Pendente Lite.*

The sealed affidavit filed on November 9 and announced in court on December 10, 1990, is *Supplemental Declaration #59720*. Sandra Musser declined to comment on her involvement in the Ramona divorce case, claiming attorney-client privilege.

The reports of bestiality in this chapter are from Isabella's notes. Gary gave me his response in personal interviews.

Robert Mondavi reported the Graebers' visit and the spread of rumors and growing opposition to Gary at the winery. Margrit Biever also reported her and Bob's views of the sons' and their wives' involvement in personal interviews.

A note on sodium amytal: from the first, "sodium pentathol" was widely and incorrectly used along with the correct term, "sodium amytal." To prevent confusion, I have used "sodium amytal" throughout.

9. THIS THING CALLED REPRESSION

The source of Eileen Franklin Lipsker's description of her first flashback of Susan Nason's murder is Lenore Terr's *Unchained Memories* (1994). The material relating to Terr and Elizabeth Loftus is drawn from my personal interviews with them, from their writings, and from *Franklin* legal documents and articles; several quotations and scenes are from Loftus's *Myth of Repressed Memory* (1994). Terr's words about her belief in repression, "Yes, I do . . . ," is from her trial testimony; her 1990 book *Too Scared to Cry* documents her Chowchilla research.

In this chapter, as elsewhere, a very useful source for the evolution of the recovered memory movement, in all its intersecting complexities, is Mark Pendergrast's rigorously researched *Victims of Memory* (1995).

Gary's growing sense of himself as a pariah and his isolation from Shawna comes from personal interviews and from the court Declaration of Gary Ramona #59720, February 4, 1991.

The precedent limiting the use of testimony derived from hypnosis or hypnotic drugs as admissible evidence, argued by Margolin before the California Supreme Court, is *People v. Shirley*, 31 Cal.3d 18 (1982). The Gary-Margolin scene is told from Margolin's perspective, from personal interviews; the scene where Gary meets Harrington is told from Gary's perspective, from his best recall of the dialogue and events. Richard Harrington is with the San Francisco law firm Chandler, Wood, Harrington & Maffly.

The section on Harrison Pope and Jim Hudson draws heavily on my personal interviews with them.

For Pope, one of the strongest arguments against the likelihood of bestiality in Holly's life came as he heard the nation's leading forensic psychiatrist, Park Dietz, testify on Gary's behalf in a deposition regarding the "implausibility of . . . her father having sex with the dog, which would have required him to insert his penis in the anus of the dog, since it's a male dog rather than the female she thought." Dietz had just examined the serial killer Jeffrey Dahmer — a monster who had committed sex with corpses and cannibalism among a host of unspeakable perversions. With an understated black irony, Dietz said, "I happen to know about people who do the most bizarre sexual things, and anal intercourse with a dog in the presence of your daughter would be a new one on me." He went on, "I think that it's unlikely it would be anal sex — unlikely that he would permit his daughter to watch — unless he were a sadistic man. And again, I don't see other evidence of sexual sadism." The source of Dietz's comments on bestiality is his deposition in *Ramona v. Isabella,* June 24, 1992.

Stephanie's perspective on the court hearings and her call to the *Napa Valley Register* are from depositions and personal interviews.

The section concerning MFCC therapists draws on information provided by the many state and national professional societies, associations, and boards that train, license, monitor, regulate, and promote the practice of psychotherapy in the United States, e.g., the American Association for Marriage and Family Therapy and the American Psychological Association. Of particular relevance are the state's licensing boards, which function within the state's Department of Consumer Affairs: the Board of Behavioral Science Examiners (MFCCs, LCSWs, and Educational Psychologists), the Medical Board (physicians and psychiatrists), and the Board of Psychology (psychologists). Helpful were personal interviews with Kathleen Callanan, Ph.D., then executive officer of the Board of Behavioral Science Examiners; Richard Leslie, legal counsel to the California Association of Marriage & Family Therapists (CAMFT); Jeffrey Younggren, an ethics consultant to California's licensing boards and vice-chair of the American Psychological Association's ethics committee; Dr. Martha Rogers, a forensic psychologist and clinician; Thomas O'Connor, executive director of the Board of Psychology; and Sherry L. Skidmore, the Southern California psychologist and MFCC who testified for Gary Ramona. The nonaccredited so-called approved schools are approved and regulated in California by its Council on Private, Post-Secondary and Vocational Education.

Napa Valley therapist Don Scully, president of the Redwood Empire chapter of CAMFT, made a good case for the appropriateness of the training and practices of *most* MFCC therapists in a letter to the editor, *Register,* April 18, 1994, and in a personal interview.

10. THE GATHERING OF EVIDENCE

Holly's psychiatric exam and interview were conducted by Robert H. Gerner, M.D., who appeared as an expert witness for Gary Ramona in the trial.

In addition to her depositions and trial testimony, I have also drawn, several times in the book, on a personal retelling of the Ramona case delivered by Marche Isabella to a therapists' conference at the Burlingame Marriott on November 16, 1994.

Edward R. Leonard of Harrington, Foxx, Dubrow & Canter in Orange, California, explained issues of "foreseeability" and "duty" in personal interviews.

A provocative overview of the volatile issue of third-party lawsuits against therapists and of the Ramona case in particular is Ralph Slovenko's "Duty of Therapists to Third Parties," a paper presented to the FMSF conference held in Baltimore in December 1994. Slovenko is a professor of law and psychiatry at Wayne State University Law School. The Molien case, which gave Gary Ramona a cause of action to sue therapists, is *Molien v. Kaiser Foundation Hospital,* 27 Cal.3 916, 616 P.2d 813, 167 Cal. Rpt. 831 (1980). The Tarasoff case is *Tarasoff v. Regents of the University of California:* Tarasoff I, 118 Cal. Rptr. 129, 529 P.2d 553 (1974), vacated, Tarasoff II, 17 Cal. 3d 425, 131 Cal. Rptr. 14, 551 P.2d 334 (1976).

Slovenko's paper also discusses a third key case in the evolution of third-party law, *Palsgraf,* one of the most celebrated torts cases dealing with the issues of duty and foreseeability. It is a seventy-year-old case involving an extraordinary chain of unlikely events — a passenger running to catch a train drops a package containing fireworks, which explodes when it hits the rails, causing a weight scale some distance away on the platform to fall, injuring a woman standing near the scale, Mrs. Palsgraf (*Palsgraf,* 248 N.Y. 339, 162 N.E. 99 [1928]).

Slovenko's conclusion that "in many circumstances, the duty of the therapist runs not only to the patient but also to others" is ominous for therapists, as expressed by Judith Lewis Herman at the American Psychiatric Association's 1994 annual meeting, speaking about the Ramona case: "The fact that a third party was given standing to speak on malpractice because he was not happy with the treatment of his daughter really opens the door to permit anyone who is dissatisfied with our treatment of any patient to lay claim against us." The opposing "survivor" movement's view of third-party lawsuits is fully presented in a *Harvard Law Review* paper discussed and cited in the Epilogue.

Eleanor Coppola did not know of the rumors and found Gary, if anything, "overqualified for our little winery."

Stephanie's strong words "I'm going to screw you royally . . ." are contained in Gary's March 4, 1991, Declaration. Gary's declining financial state is documented in his April 17, 1991, Post Trial Brief.

The garage scene, described from personal interviews with Jean Sawday and Gary Ramona, shifts from Jean's to Gary's point of view.

Richard Rose's move to Hawaii "for essentially personal reasons" was the explanation offered to me by his attorney, Bruce Miroglio.

A useful summary of the states' status as to credentialing and licensure of therapists at the time of the Ramona trial is a report by Kinly Sturkie and Wilbur E. Johnson, "Recent and Emerging Trends in Marital and Family Therapy Regulation," *Contemporary Family Therapy*, August 1994. It states that as of 1993, Virginia, Marche Isabella's new home, was not among the twenty-nine states that had "made statutory provisions for licensing, certifying, or registering marital and family therapists" but, instead, offered a subspecialty credential not formally recognized by the major national family therapy associations. Sturkie is president of the Association of Marital and Family Therapy Regulatory Boards.

Many of the scenes, quotations, and thoughts in this chapter are based on personal interviews with Stephanie, Gary, Scott Evans, Margrit Biever, Neil Shapiro, JoeAnna and Lloyd Jenkins, Bruce Miroglio, and John Suesans.

The scene in which Shapiro attempts to get Stephanie dismissed from slander charges is told from his point of view; Gary's words are Shapiro's best recollection.

11. THE GATHERING OF WITNESSES

Miroglio gave me his views of Gerner in personal interviews.

In an interview at McLean Hospital and in subsequent discussions, Pope and Hudson effectively presented their views from their scientific findings on the causes and treatment of eating disorders, as discussed in this chapter. They are impeccable methodologists. The issue, however, of what role is played in the cause and treatment of bulimia nervosa by medication, therapy, genes, and traumatic childhood sexual abuse inspires as much spirited debate as do recovered memories. Some interesting contributions to the debate are: the Oxford bulimia nervosa expert C. G. Fairburn's *Overcoming Binge Eating* (1995); the research on the pharmacological treatment of bulimia by Dr. Tim Walsh at Columbia Presbyterian Hospital and on the behavioral treatment of the disease by Stuart Agras at Stanford (W. S. Agras, "Nonpharmacologic Treatments of Bulimia Nervosa," *Journal of Clinical Psychiatry* 52, no. 10 [1991, suppl.]: 29–33); Kenneth S. Kendler et al.'s "Genetic Epidemiology of Bulimia Nervosa," *American Journal of Psychiatry* (December 1991), 148:12; G. Terence Wilson and Fairburn's "Treatment of Eating Disorders," in *Psychotherapies and Drugs that Work,* edited by Nathan & Gorman (in press), and S. L. Welch and Fairburn, "Sexual Abuse and Bulimia Nervosa: Three Integrated Case Control Comparisons," *American Journal of Psychiatry* (1994), 151:402–7.

Pope and Hudson's study of repression was published as "Can Memories of Childhood Sexual Abuse Be Repressed?" in *Psychological Medicine* in 1995. Citations for it, and for the four repression studies they evaluated, are in the selected bibliography.

A May 16, 1994, *New Yorker* profile on Park Elliot Dietz was a useful source. Although Dietz would not charm the jury as did several other expert witnesses, it is clear that attorneys and experts on both sides, as well as Gary Ramona, felt that they were in the presence of one of the great forensic psychiatric minds.

The scene of Gary reading the expert declarations to Stephanie is told from Gary's best recollection and reconstructed quotes. Isabella's attorney, Jeffrey Kurtock, is with Lewis, D'Amato Brisbois & Bisgaard. Stephanie's *Reply Trial Brief,* October 19, 1992, is the source of "for a highly unlikely . . . goal." Sources for Elizabeth Loftus are personal interviews, trial testimony, and *The Myth of Repression.* "Lost in the Mall" was published as E. F. Loftus and J. E. Pickerell, "The Formation of False Memories," *Psychiatric Annals* 25 (1993): 720–25. The Carol Tavris quotation from *Mismeasure of Women* has been slightly changed here from the one that appears in the book, at Dr. Tavris's request. American Professional Agency is, technically, a managing general agent that does everything an insurance company does except pay out claims. The primary source for Lenore Terr is my personal interview; Terr's notes on Holly's memories of bestiality are from her trial testimony. Stephanie reported to me her feelings about Musser and the end of her divorce; Miroglio reported to me his sense of Stephanie's distrust of men. Musser's lawsuit is referred to by Stephanie in a July 13, 1993, court declaration. Eric Marine's comments are from personal interviews.

Regarding abusers and pedophilia, I interviewed Dr. Fred Berlin by phone and Dr. Pierre Gagne by personal interview and telephone. In 1992, Linda Meyer Williams and David Finkelhor completed a much-quoted study of 118 admitted male perpetrators, a profile that identifies five types of incestuous fathers. Though never published, the report, "Characteristics of Incestuous Fathers" (1992), is available at the Family Research Laboratory, University of New Hampshire, Durham.

12. THE MEMORY LESSON

I drew on court records and personal interviews for the *In Limine* hearings for *Ramona v. Isabella* before Judge Snowden on April 23, 1993, in Napa Superior Court. Judge Snowden's quotes come from his courtroom statements and from his *Order In Limine,* signed and dated May 12, 1993. In the debate over "duty" and the viability of *Molien,* two cases significantly cited were *Burgess v. Superior Court* (1992) 2 Cal. 4th 1064 [9 Cal. Rptr. 2d 615]; and *Huggins v. Longs Drug Stores California, Inc.,* Supreme Court Case No. S030711 (which was pending a decision at the time of the hearing).

This chapter contains the book's major analysis of the current state of the art of memory science, with a focus on the new field of cognitive neuroscience, which marries biology to psychology and takes the brain systems approach to memory. I chose three scientists to represent the larger group — Harvard's Daniel Schacter, NYU's Joseph LeDoux, and UC San Diego's Larry Squire. I identified them first as comparatively uncontaminated with the ideological zeal that infects so many whose work touches the memory controversy; second, as scientists trained in psychology who had constantly to transcend tugs of sympathy for the humanistic, clinical psychotherapeutic tradition while applying the rigorous methodology of "pure science"; third, because their realms of memory research were at the heart of the mysteries of recovered memories: explicit, implicit, and emotional memory and the interactions between them; and, fourth, because their efforts to dispel the "deep myths of memory" are, I believe, a healthy contribution to the resolution of the memory wars and to the emotion- and resource-draining legal battles exemplified by *Ramona*. As I moved into the complex world of the hippocampus and amygdala, these three patiently worked with me to make sure I got it right.

Other scientists whose work and, in several cases, personal interviews contributed greatly to my education are Elizabeth Loftus, Stephen J. Ceci, and D. Stephen Lindsay (cognitive approaches to memory distortion, suggestibility); James McGaugh, Larry Cahill, and Michael Davis (emotional memory); David Spiegel (hypnosis, dissociation); Lenore Terr (childhood traumatic memory); Marcia K. Johnson (reality monitoring); Stephen Kosslyn (imagery); James McClelland (computer modeling); Endel Tulving (episodic encoding and retrieval cues, neuroimaging); John Kihlstrom (hypnosis, the cognitive psychology view); Michael Schudson (cultural and collective memory); Eric Kandel (long-term memory at cells, synapses level); Bessel van der Kolk (dissociation and trauma); Robert Sapolsky (stress effect on the hippocampus); Scott L. Rauch (neuroimaging of traumatic memory); Michela Gallagher (chemical and hormonal impact on memory); Martin Orne (hypnosis); and Barry L. Beyerstein (a Simon Fraser University research psychologist whose work combines psychology with neuroscience).

If, as I suspect, memory science is going to provide what Dan Schacter terms "the put up or shut up event" that will put to rest, confirm — or at least clarify — some of the competing theories for recovered memories, I suggest that the interested reader follow the unfolding memory story in several ways: by reading two excellent and accessible surveys of memory, Schacter's *Searching for Memory* and LeDoux's *Emotional Brain* (both 1996); by being alert to new findings in emotional memory, the impact of stress and trauma on memory, the interaction between explicit and implicit memory, and memory retrieval (little understood and in need of aggressive research), much of which may come from PET scan and other neuroimaging tools; read the proceedings of the Cognitive Neuroscience Society's annual meetings, where, in the same room, one finds Sapolsky, Damasio, Squire, Schacter, LeDoux, Tulving, Cahill, et al.

The Kandel article was "Flights of Memory," *Discover,* May 1994, by Minouche Kandel and Eric Kandel.

I reconstructed the Briere-Loftus debate at the 1993 APA annual meetings from the taped proceedings; I attended Briere's speech to the 1994 APA meetings in Los Angeles. The six members of the APA task force on recovered memories were three clinicians, Judith Alpert, Laura Brown, and Christine Courtois, and three research psychologists, Stephen Ceci, Elizabeth Loftus, and Peter Ornstein. Alpert and Ornstein were cochairs. It was finally released on February 14, 1996, as the "Working Group on Investigation of Memories of Childhood Abuse Final Report."

Citations for the three cases "eating away" at *Molien* are *Burgess v. Superior Ct.* (1992) 2 Cal 4th 1064; *Ochoa v. Superior Ct.* (1985) 39 Cal 3d 159; *Schwartz v. Regents of the University of California* (1990) 226 C.A. 3d 149.

The scene of Holly's hug is from a personal interview with Miroglio.

The two scenes that end the chapter — Salem and the Safeway parking lot — are Gary's recollections and quotes. My own visits to Salem augmented that scene.

13. COURTROOM B

I describe the trial and the cast of characters regularly in attendance partly as a direct observer who attended every day after jury selection. As in earlier chapters, I also let others tell the story from their own points of view. The account draws from personal interviews with other observers, including Marian Dodds and John Carver (both pseudonyms), Dr. Leo Stoer, Carolyn Thompson, and friends of Stephanie's and Gary's; with lawyers and witnesses; and from official trial transcripts.

The jury itself tells part of the story. Twice I gathered the jurors together, at my home shortly after the trial (June 19, 1994) and at the courthouse two years later (June 23, 1996) and conducted extensive taped interviews. I met with the following jurors: Rebecca Strunk, Tim Holewinske, Tom Dudum, Marcellous Cook, Michele Maynard, Beth Clark, Nellie Sweeney, Yolanda Nash, Keith Himmelman, and Kenneth Keri (the alternate). I conducted additional interviews with Holewinske, Nash, Himmelman, and Dudum. This enabled me to reconstruct their observations and feelings from the first day of jury selection through the entire trial, deliberations, and verdict, and to then have them reflect on their decision with the perspective of time. Permitting rare insight into the jury's thought processes and the dynamics of their deliberation, their "voices" throughout the trial come from transcripts of the interviews. The seriousness and discipline with which this disparate group of Napans contained their emotion and looked to the evidence have revitalized my faith in the jury system.

14. THE GREAT RECOVERED MEMORY DEBATE

Pope and Hudson's repression study is cited in the notes to Chapter 11. The "69 percent" Oppenheimer study is Oppenheimer, Howells, Palmer, and Chaloner, "Adverse Sexual Experience in Childhood and Clinical Eating Disorders: A Preliminary Description," *Journal of Psychiatry,* Res 1985.

Dr. Gerner's dénouement combines trial transcripts with Miroglio's and Leonard's description to me, and my own observation, of the scene. The Medical Board's disciplinary action against Dr. Gerner is reported in the Epilogue.

Kelli Ramona's letter to the editor appeared in the *Napa Valley Register* on March 31, 1994.

I interviewed Dr. Stephanie McClellan in her Newport Beach medical offices.

15. THE POWER OF SUGGESTION

In court, Robert Mondavi used the term "sodium pentathol." For consistency, I've used "amytal," the correct term, as noted earlier.

My interview with Dr. Sherry L. Skidmore gave me good insight into the Southern California MFCC environment in which Holly Ramona trained, works, and lives.

The freeing of Kelly Michaels was followed by a cascade of releases from prison, but Paul Ingram still sat in jail in Olympia, Washington, three years after the Ramona trial. In Northern California, awareness had been raised by a series in the *San Francisco Examiner* by Stephanie Salter and Carol Ness, "Buried Memories, Broken Families," April 4–9, 1993.

Miroglio gave me his recollections in interviews.

16. HOLLY'S DAY IN COURT

Personal interviews are the principal source for Neil Shapiro's comments on the trial, Lenore Terr's discussion with the *The Courage to Heal* authors regarding changes to the book, Stephanie's thoughts and reactions, Maggie Kelly's observations about the death of the family meal among her students, Richard Mullins on the abandonment of children, and Miroglio's preparation for and examination of Holly and Stephanie on the witness stand. The author's voice is heard, also, in describing and evaluating Holly's testimony. Ephraim Margolin quoted the pivotal *Courage to Heal* change in his article, "A Lawyer's View of Invented Memory: The Ramona Case," which appeared in *Champion* in August 1994. The Rose "castration" case scene on the courthouse steps is told from Miroglio's memory.

The Ceci and Bruck book *Jeopardy in the Courtroom* was published in 1995 by the American Psychological Association, but only after a fuss by clinicians, the majority of the APA's membership, forced the authors to disguise or delete some quotes from child interviews. The event is another eruption of the ongoing hostility and threat clinicians feel for and from research scientists like Ceci, whose work is reforming the inadequate child interviewing practices that have given us the McMartin, Little Rascals, and Kelly Michaels cases.

17. THE T-GRAPH

The defense's questions about Barry Grundland's lack of hospital privileges or board certification were not without substance. Although it is not uncommon for psychiatrists to eschew hospital privileges, it is virtually essential for any specialist who wishes to be considered a peer in Napa Valley's high-caliber medical community to have at least board certification.

In addition to my personal interview with Thomas Gutheil at his office in the Massachusetts Mental Health Center in Boston (a hybrid of a state hospital and Harvard's major psychiatric teaching hospital), I referred to his following articles: "True or False Memories of Sexual Abuse? A Forensic Psychiatric View," *Psychiatric Annals*, September 1993; "The Adversarial Game: Step by Step Strategy for the Expert," *Harvard Medical*, Spring 1987; and, on the Ramona case, "True Recollections of a False Memory Case; or, Two Gentlemen of Ramona," *Psychiatric Times*, July 1994, which appeared just after the trial.

Several scenes are drawn from personal interviews with Miroglio: his strategy and conduct of Stephanie's appearance on the witness stand, his asking Stephanie about the size of Gary's penis, and his thwarted hopes for a "home run" from Stephanie regarding Gary's modus operandi. From personal interviews, too, come Gary's whispered denials of the violence to Harrington, Lloyd and JoeAnna Jenkins's description of the intense scene at Gary's condominium after Stephanie's violation of the judge's order not to mention violence, and Gary's response to her reference to the "douching" episode. Stephanie's statements off the stand that she had not planned to leave Gary — that their sex life could be "fixed" by therapy — came from personal interviews.

18. THE DEBATE CONTINUES

JoeAnna Jenkins reported the scene in Bistro Don Giovanni.

The three precedents on the admissibility of novel scientific evidence are *Daubert v. Merrell Dow Pharmaceuticals,* 113 S. Ct. 2786, 125 L.Ed.2d 469 (1993); *Frye v. United States,* 54 U.S. App. D.C., 293 F. 1013 (1923), and, in

California, *People v. Kelly,* 17 Ca.3d 24, 549 P.2d 1240, 130 Cal.Rptr. 144 (1976). The standard new science must meet to be argued in court — of "general acceptance within the relevant scientific community" — was established with *Frye,* the 1923 landmark federal case, which was adopted in California in the Kelly case, giving the admissibility rule in California the name Kelly-Frye. The Daubert opinion, written by Justice Harry Blackmun, permits a broader interpretation of who that "relevant scientific community" might be; in the 1996 federal case *Shahzade v. Gregory* (see Epilogue), that community was deemed to be clinical psychiatrists, a decision that excluded the research scientists generally considered the relevant community qualified to evaluate a new science. Federally, *Daubert* has overruled *Frye.* But California courts, continuing to honor the old Kelly-Frye rule, have dropped the word Frye and applied to "novel scientific evidence" what is now called the Kelly test.

Every word in the long section of Lenore Terr's testimony has been checked against trial transcripts and personal interviews with Terr, the jurors, and Betty Nye. The new diagnosis in the *DSM-IV* is: V61.21 Sexual abuse of a child. The *New York Times Book Review* review of *Unchained Memories* was May 15, 1994.

19. VERDICT

For Jean Sawday's and Karen Maestas's thoughts and remarks, I drew on a personal interview and on my trial notes.

The "lock" scene in the closing minutes of the trial comes from interviews with Gary Ramona, Bruce Miroglio, Lloyd Jenkins, and from my own observation of events.

I reconstructed the jury's deliberations from my taped interview with nine of the jurors. The emotion and intensity they brought to the interview process gave me some indication of the intensity of the deliberations themselves.

Yolanda described to me the dinner with the Mondavis; the quotes are her best recollection. Regarding posttrial comments, Lenore Terr's are from our interview.

Jane Gross's stories in the *New York Times* early and late in the trial helped anchor *Ramona v. Isabella* in journalistic history. Goleman's story cited source amnesia as a possible explanation for false memory.

EPILOGUE

Because of the important links between *Franklin* and *Ramona,* I have followed events in *Franklin* closely since the Ramona trial. Richard Ofshe, a Pulitzer Prize–winning social psychologist, and Ethan Watters, in *Making Monsters* (1994), provide extensive insight into the gradual unraveling of Eileen Franklin Lipsker's credibility and her case against her father. They were

the first to propose the seminal role of recovered memory therapy and hypnosis in the creation of her memories of murder. In her concurrently published
book, *Unchained Memories*, Lenore Terr shows unabashed enthusiasm for
Lipsker's memories, a surprise from a scientist who had access at the time to
information that was already undermining Eileen's credibility (e.g., unsettling
defense evidence as well as Harry MacLean's skeptical 1993 book, *Once
Upon a Time)*. In a sensational finale in June 1996, Eileen's sister Janice
charged that both she and Eileen had lied and perjured themselves in court —
that both had undergone hypnotherapy and that Eileen's memories had
emerged there. The long-building portrait of Eileen as an opportunistic liar
now complete, next came behind-the-scenes revelations to the prosecution of
some extraordinary sleuthing by the defense that had turned up an airtight
alibi for George Franklin for one of several other murders Eileen had seen him
commit in her memories. Tipton had told me obliquely about the additional
murder memories when I lunched with her shortly after Franklin's 1990 trial.

It is true, as Terr reminds us, that the overturning of Franklin's conviction a year earlier was based on technical errors in the conduct of the trial —
that, as she pointed out on CBS radio at the time, recovered memories had not
been overturned. But that argument tumbled with the cascade of evidence
against Eileen's credibility that forced the prosecution, finally, to dismiss on
the grounds that it could not win its case. Terr told me, by faxed letter on
December 19, 1996, that had the Franklin retrial gone forward, "I would not
have willingly testified . . . because of the writings and talks I had already done
on the case (small differences in consistency could have been used by Franklin's defense to try and impeach my testimony)" — a gem of understatement.

Another Franklin-Ramona connection is the informal childhood sexual
abuse "survivor" network that continues to support both Eileen and Holly. As
Franklin was released on July 3, hovering in the hall was a Redwood City
psychiatric nurse, Suzanne McLennan, who states that *Ramona* "is one of the
things that created the network," which orchestrates moral support, protection, and funding to star "survivors" caught in recovered memory lawsuits —
Eileen, Holly, *The Courage to Heal* authors Bass and Davis. Eric Marine told
me he had met Holly, closely shepherded by McLennan, at a major abuse,
trauma, and dissociation conference in Austin, Texas, in September 1995.
Also, Lenore Terr is McLennan's therapist and monitor "of my psychological
well-being" while working with traumatized women. Talking to a reporter at
the Franklin dismissal, McLennan skillfully deflected questions on the issue of
Eileen's tarnished credibility and shifted to the movement's issue of choice:
child sexual abuse and incest as the root of most of America's psychopathology and family dysfunction. With Franklin back on the streets, she reported
Eileen as "devastated . . . She's very frightened for . . . her children's safety . . .
The man is obviously a molester and I believe he did murder." I am troubled
that McLennan and others cannot see that blind faith in fallen stars like Eileen

makes a mockery of the sickeningly real child abuse shown, for example, on network television the night of Franklin's release: the appalling sight of parents goading their two young children to fight as they videotaped them tearing murderously at each other with fists, teeth, screams, and rib kicks, cracking heads against the floor like coconuts until brother and sister were bloodied and insensible.

The quote "a small cottage industry" came from attorney Tim Reagan, who works with Harrington.

The FMSF is an excellent source of information on the legal action of the memory wars. Citations for the cases referred to are:

The "junk science" quote is *Engstrom v. Engstrom,* Superior Ct., Los Angeles Co., California, Case No. VCO16157, October 11, 1995. In his ruling at a Kelly-Frye hearing on September 7, 1995, the Honorable James M. Sutton said — several times, in several ways — that the purpose of these hearings was to distinguish between good science and junk science. Referring to recovered memory in his summing up, he said, "Again, I will refer to it in the pejorative term. In my term, this is junk science."

Borawick v. Shay, U.S. Ct. of Appeals, 2nd Circuit, Docket N.94-7584, (decision October 17, 1995).

For the reversal, a rare Judgment Notwithstanding Verdict (a JNOV) made on November 15, 1996, is *Franklin v. Stevenson,* 3d Judicial District Ct., Salt Lake Co., Utah, 94-9091779 PI.

Of great importance because it was a jury award in a third-party case, and a very large award, a San Diego jury found malpractice against the therapist Virginia Humphreys in October 1996 and awarded $1.9 million to a father on behalf of his eleven-year-old daughter, whose case is cited in the *1992 San Diego Grand Jury Report* (to protect a minor, the family was not named). The Rutherford case is *Rutherford v. Strand,* Circuit Ct., Greene Co., Missouri, 196-0C-2745.

The Shahzade case — *Shahzade v. Gregory,* U.S. Dist. Ct., Mass., Case N. 92-12139-EFH, Memorandum and Order (May 8, 1996) — is preparing for trial, with Christopher R. Barden and Harrison Pope's colleague Dr. Alec Bodkin expected to face Bessel van der Kolk again.

Citations for the Humenansky cases are: *Hamanne v. Humenansky,* Minn. Dist. Ct., Ramsey Co., No. C4-94-203, 8/1/95 and *Carlson v. Humenansky,* District Ct., Ramsey Co., Minnesota, Case No. CX-93-7260, 1/24/96.

The Hungerford case — *State of New Hampshire v. Hungerford,* Case No. 94-S-045 through 94-S-047 in the Hillsborough Co. Superior Ct., May 23, 1995 — is still on appeal as this book goes to press. Judge William Groff's Notice of Decision is a good summary of judicial thinking. Heartening to Hungerford was the decision by the American Civil Liberties Union to submit an amicus brief on his behalf, the first public stand the ACLU has taken against recovered memories. Summary judgment to dismiss Holly's case was filed in Los Angeles Superior Court in Pomona, with declarations by Dietz, Loftus, Hudson, Orne, and Richard Ofshe attached in support. Holly's deadline for trial against Gary Ramona is January 1, 1999.

The January 1996 *Harvard Law Review* article on the Ramona case, by Cynthia Grant Bowman and Elizabeth Mertz, stands as the classic example of skillful coopting of reputable science, social policy, and legal theory to make the political argument for recovered memory. I was dismayed to see survivor rhetoric replacing the academic rigor I expect of the *Harvard Law Review;* the authors admitted to reading no trial transcripts, relying "primarily upon the voluminous press coverage" of the Ramona trial, largely on a *Los Angeles Times Magazine* article by a writer who has demonstrated sympathy for the recovered memory side. Tapes of most of the testimony could easily have been acquired.

The state legislative initiative is the "Mental Health Consumer Protection Act," drafted by an attorney and clinical psychologist in Minnesota, Christopher R. Barden, who is also an active expert witness in recovered memory cases. Because it would impose restraints on all mental health practitioners, not just those employing questionable recovered memory techniques and practices, the act is being aggressively opposed by the professional organizations whose members would be affected: the psychological, psychiatric, and MFCC organizations. Although Barden's effort to enact the legislation has stalled, the goal has been won, he states. "What the bill requires is already being done by therapists as a practical necessity."

Pamela Freyd presented the graph of lawsuits filed by accusers at the Day of Contrition–Revisited convocation at Salem, Massachusetts, on January 14, 1997. The graph shows the numbers of lawsuits rising sharply to peak levels in 1992–1994, then dropping like a steep cliff. Given the time it takes to pursue a lawsuit and its appeals, however, the courts will be clogged with these cases well past the year 2000 — unless there is an epidemic of settlements and dismissals.

The therapists' conference Isabella addressed in San Francisco was on November 16, 1994, the conference also addressed by California MFCC's legal counsel, Dick Leslie. The FMSF meeting attended by Isabella was in Baltimore in December 1994; Terr received her award at the APA meetings in Los Angeles in August 1994.

The therapists who addressed the *Family Therapy Networker* symposium in Washington, D.C., were quoted in the magazine's May-June 1996 issue.

The charges made by Kate Rose's mother, Judy Norris, against the psychologist Douglas Sawin were prosecuted for the state's medical board at an administrative hearing by deputy attorney general Michael Sipe, with an ethics consultant, Jeffrey Younggren, testifying against Sawin; there was no decision by mid-January 1997.

See the notes for Chapter 12 for a citation on the APA's report on recovered memories. The material on Elizabeth Loftus is supplemented by personal interviews.

Frederick Crews's quotation comes from *The Memory Wars*. That book is a collection of his two-part review of recovered memory literature in the *New York Review of Books*, "The Revenge of the Repressed," November 17 and December 1, 1994; a selection of the vitriolic letters it inspired; plus his widely read essay "The Unknown Freud" (*New York Review of Books*, November 18, 1993). An anti-Freudian who petitioned the Library of Congress to reflect the full range of scholarly judgment in its planned show on Freud, he thrives at the heart of intellectual controversy, and his published exchanges make lively reading: see *Psychoanalytic Dialogues*, 6 (2), 1996, based on a symposium on the False Memory controversy, in which Crews takes on Adrienne Harris, Jody Messler Davis, and others.

Jill Neimark wrote the excellent memory article in *Psychology Today*'s January 1995 issue that incited ethics attacks on Elizabeth Loftus; she went to bat for Loftus in the March-April 1996 issue, "Dispatch from the Memory Wars."

A new study by Loftus reveals the dangers of therapists' facilitating the hunt for abuse memories by encouraging patients to imagine them. When Loftus asked subjects to imagine events, both true and false, she found, in later tests, that the act of imagining a memory strengthened the subjects' belief in its reality.

Perhaps the most exciting "memory" interview of my nearly three years of research was the meeting with Dan Schacter, Larry Squire, and Joe LeDoux on March 31, 1996, at San Francisco's Fairmont Hotel during the Cognitive Neuroscience Society's third annual meeting. It was a rare joint retrospective look by three elite scientists at the course and status of memory science and the memory wars.

August Piper is quoted on PTSD in the November 1996 *FMSF Newsletter*. The evolution of PTSD from ignored wartime stress symptoms, through its first appearance in *DSM-III* after Vietnam in 1980, to stardom in the diagnostic firmament today is well documented in Allan Young's *Harmony of Illusions: Inventing Post-Traumatic Stress Disorder* (1995). In his review of the book, J. Alexander Bodkin, assistant professor of psychiatry at Harvard Medical School, states that "since it is not required . . . even that the trauma can be *recalled*, it has become officially possible now to diagnose virtually anyone who suffers from a mood or anxiety disorder with PTSD if a clinician wishes to do so." Bodkin also states that for women suffering mood and anxiety symptoms believed to be caused by forgotten childhood sexual abuse, "PTSD is the usual diagnostic choice," with multiple-personality disorder a distant second and only for women with more severe illness.

Various new findings cast further doubt on claims concerning traumatic memory. For example, a study of Gulf War PTSD sufferers at the National

Center for Post-Traumatic Stress Disorder in New Haven (Southwick, Morgan, Nicolaou, and Charney, *American Journal of Psychiatry* 154 [Feb. 1997]: 173–77) found "inconsistent recall of combat trauma in the majority of veterans" and found that the greater the PTSD symptoms the more "amplification" of combat memories there was. The researchers concluded that "these findings do not support the position that traumatic memories are fixed or indelible." The *Harvard Mental Health Letter* (March 1997) reported on a 1996 study at the same center by Johnson, Rosenheck, Fontana, et al., which found that among Vietnam veterans with severe PTSD symptoms, four months of intensive treatment with a range of therapies "had no long-term effect on their symptoms." These findings call into question the widespread use of therapy to treat symptoms diagnosed as PTSD caused by sexual abuse.

In *Betrayal Trauma* (Harvard University Press, 1996), Jennifer Freyd posited that it is betrayal by a trusted parent that triggers the dissociation of incest memories. Yet the body of skeptical criticism grew. Alan A. Stone of Harvard, former president of the American Psychiatric Association, in "Where Will Psychoanalysis Survive?" *(Harvard Magazine,* Jan./Feb. 1997) indicted the grand Freudian enterprise. Stone observed that new memory research reveals that "much of what psychoanalysis considered infantile amnesia may be a function of the reorganizing brain rather than of the repressing mind," making reconstruction of meaningful individual histories a daunting task. He concludes, "If there is no important connection between childhood events and adult psychopathology, then Freudian theories lose much of their explanatory power. If memory cannot be trusted to construct a self-description, what does one do in therapy?" The survival of therapy, he proposes, lies in helping a patient "deal with his ordinary human suffering."

Van der Kolk's argument is contained in his 1995 paper "Dissociation and the Fragmentary Nature of Traumatic Memories," which he used as the basis of his court testimony. See the entry for Rauch et al. in the Selected Bibliography for the referenced PET scan study.

Some of the "hot" areas of research related to recovered memories are: work on "hippocampal shutdown" by stress-released hormones by Robert Sapolsky; on PTSD by the psychiatrists Roger Pitman and Scott Rauch, whose PET studies are causing attention; on the mapping of the amygdala by Joe LeDoux; on the effects of stimulant hormones on memory by James McGaugh and Larry Cahill and of opiate hormones by Michela Gallagher; and on the connection between trauma and reduced hippocampal size by Dennis Charney at Yale and Roger Pitman at Harvard.

The grape shortage that drove Napa Valley's gamble to market French wine "was driven primarily by demand, not phylloxera," says Mondavi's Greg Evans. But, admittedly, phylloxera did have the effect of reducing wine volume and raising wine prices. Importing from the Languedoc region, the Mondavis were one of numerous Napa Valley wineries that imported French wine during the mid-1990s. But Mondavi protected the sanctity of its "blood line" and image by not commingling a drop of French wine with Napa's under the Robert Mondavi label. The Mondavi's "global wine company" has been established with joint ventures, and winery and vineyard operations in France, Italy, Chile, and Australia.

The meeting between Shawna and her father was described to me by both Stephanie and Gary. The quotations from their meeting are Gary's reconstruction.

I was able to gather seven members of the jury at the courthouse on June 23, 1996, for a portrait and for a review of their feelings about the verdict more than two years after the trial.

Simon Schama's quotation is from his *Landscape and Memory* (1995), a long but brilliant book that, like my art school training, teaches a new way to see the world; Schama shows how we bring layers of deeply ingrained cultural memory to our perception and interpretation of the everyday landscapes in which our lives are set.

THE PROCESS

Johnson's quotes are from "Constructing and Reconstructing the Past and the Future in the Present," which is Chapter 14, *Handbook of Motivation and Cognition: Foundations of Social Behavior* (New York: Guilford Press, 1990), by Marcia K. Johnson of Princeton University and Steven J. Sherman of Indiana University.

Selected Bibliography

This list reflects my effort to read broadly on all sides of the issues. More sources are cited in the text and the notes.

American Medical Association. "Report of the Council on Scientific Affairs," CSA 5-A-94.

American Psychiatric Association. "Statement on Memories of Sexual Abuse," December 12, 1993.

American Psychological Association. "Working Group on Investigation of Memories of Childhood Abuse. Final Report, " February 14, 1996.

Armstrong, Louise. *Rocking the Cradle of Sexual Politics: What Happened When Women Said Incest.* New York: Addison-Wesley, 1994.

Bass, Ellen, and Laura Davis. *The Courage to Heal: A Guide for Women Survivors of Child Sexual Abuse.* 3rd ed. New York: HarperPerennial, 1994.

Bellah, Robert N., et al. *Habits of the Heart.* Berkeley: University of California Press, 1985.

Berendzen, Richard, and Laura Palmer. *Come Here: A Man Overcomes the Tragic Aftermath of Childhood Sexual Abuse.* New York: Villard Books, 1993.

Birch, Leann L. "Children's Eating: Are Manners Enough?" *Journal of Gastronomy* (Winter/Spring 1993), 7 (1).

Bowman, Cynthia Grant, and Elizabeth Mertz. "A Dangerous Direction: Legal Intervention in Sexual Abuse Survivor Therapy." *Harvard Law Review,* 109 (3), January 1996.

Boyer, Paul, and Stephen Nissenbaum. *Salem Possessed: The Social Origins of Witchcraft.* Cambridge, Mass.: Harvard University Press, 1974.

Briere, John N. *Child Abuse Trauma: Theory and Treatment of the Lasting Effects.* Newbury Park: SAGE Publications, 1992.

————, and J. Conte. "Self-reported Amnesia for Abuse in Adults Molested as Children." *Journal of Traumatic Stress* (1993) 6: 21–31.

Butler, Katy. "A House Divided: The Mixed Message of Napa Valley's Repressed-Memory Trial." *Los Angeles Times Magazine,* June 26, 1994.

Ceci, Stephen J. "False Beliefs: Some Developmental and Clinical Considerations." *Memory Distortion: How Minds, Brains, and Societies Reconstruct the Past.* Edited by D. L. Schacter. Cambridge, Mass.: Harvard University Press, 1995.

————, and Maggie Bruck. *Jeopardy in the Courtroom: A Scientific Analysis of Children's Testimony.* Washington, D.C.: American Psychological Association, 1995.

Coontz, Stephanie. *The Way We Never Were: American Families and the Nostalgia Trap.* New York: Basic Books, 1992.

Costin, Lela B., Howard Jacob Karger, and David Stoesz. *The Politics of Child Abuse in America.* New York: Oxford University Press, 1996.

Courtois, Christine A. *Healing the Incest Wound: Adult Survivors in Therapy.* New York: W. W. Norton, 1988.

Crews, Frederick. "Demonology for an Age of Science." Speech presented on January 14, 1997, at the "Day of Contrition-Revisited Convocation," convened by the Justice Committee in Salem, Mass.

———— et al. *The Memory Wars: Freud's Legacy in Dispute.* New York: New York Review of Books, 1995.

Daubert v. Merrell Dow Pharmaceuticals. 113 S. Ct. 2786, 125 L.Ed.2d 469 (1993).

Diagnostic and Statistical Manual of Mental Disorders (DSM-IV). Washington, D.C.: American Psychiatric Association, 1994.

Eberle, Paul, and Shirley Eberle. *The Politics of Child Abuse.* Secaucus, N.J.: Lyle Stuart Inc., 1986.

Fairburn, C. G. *Overcoming Binge Eating.* New York: Guilford Press, 1995.

Fredrickson, Renee. *Repressed Memories: A Journey to Recovery from Sexual Abuse.* New York: Simon & Schuster, 1992.

Freud, Sigmund. *The Major Works of Sigmund Freud.* The Great Books of the Western World (no. 54). Chicago: Encyclopaedia Britannica, 1990.

Frye v. United States, 54 U.S. App. D.C., 293 F. 1013 (1923).

Gardner, Richard A. *True and False Accusations of Child Sex Abuse.* Cresskill, N.J.: Creative Therapeutics, 1992.

Gilligan, Carol. *In a Different Voice: Psychological Theory and Women's Development.* Cambridge, Mass.: Harvard University Press, 1982.

Goldstein, Eleanor, with Kevin Farmer. *Confabulations: Creating False Memories, Destroying Families.* Boca Raton, Fla.: SIRS Books, 1992.

The Handbook of Forensic Sexology: Biomedical & Criminological Perspectives. Edited by James J. Krivacska and John Money. Amherst, Mass.: Prometheus Books, 1994.

Herman, Judith Lewis. *Trauma and Recovery.* New York: Basic Books, 1992.

————, with Lisa Hirschman. *Father-Daughter Incest.* Cambridge, Mass.: Harvard University Press, 1981.

————, and Emily Schatzow. "Recovery and Verification of Memories of Childhood Sexual Trauma," *Psychoanalytic Psychology* (1987) 4 (1).

Human Sexuality: An Encyclopedia. Edited by Vern L. Bullough and Bonnie Bullough. New York: Garland Publishing, 1994.

Johnson, Marcia K. "The Origins of Memory." *Advances in Cognitive-Behavioral Research and Therapy,* vol. 4. New York: Academic Press, 1985.

————, and Steven J. Sherman. "Constructing and Reconstructing the Past and the Future in the Present." *Handbook of Motivation and Cognition: Foundations of Social Behavior,* vol. 2. Edited by E. T. Higgins and R. M. Sorrentino. New York: Guilford Press, 1990.

Johnston, Moira. "A Magnificent Obsession." *New West,* August 1981.

————. "Napa, California's Valley of the Vine." *National Geographic,* May 1979.

————. "A Very Civil War." *California,* January 1989.

Katz, Donald R. *Home Fires: An Intimate Portrait of One Middle-Class Family in Postwar America.* New York: Aaron Asher Books, 1992.

Kosslyn, Stephen M. *Image and Brain: The Resolution of the Imagery Debate.* Cambridge, Mass.: A Bradford Book, MIT Press, 1994.

Kramer, Peter D. *Listening to Prozac: A Psychiatrist Explores Antidepressant Drugs and the Remaking of the Self.* New York: Viking Penguin, 1993.

LeDoux, Joseph. *The Emotional Brain: The Mysterious Underpinnings of Emotional Life.* New York: Simon & Schuster, 1996.

————. "Emotional Memory Systems in the Brain." *Behavioural Brain Research* (1993) 58, 69–70.

————. "Emotion, Memory and the Brain." *Scientific American* (June 1994), 50–57.

Loftus, Elizabeth F. *Eyewitness Testimony.* Cambridge, Mass.: Harvard University Press, 1979.

————, and Katherine Ketcham. *Witness for the Defense: The Accused, the Eyewitness, and the Expert Who Puts Memory on Trial.* New York: St. Martin's Press, 1991.

————, and Katherine Ketcham. *The Myth of Repressed Memory: False Memories and Allegations of Sexual Abuse.* New York: St. Martin's Press, 1994.

————, S. Polonsky, and M. T. Fullilove. "Memories of Childhood Sexual Abuse: Remembering and Repressing." *Psychology of Women Quarterly* (1994), 18: 67–84.

Mackenzie, Margaret. "Is the Family Meal Disappearing?" *Journal of Gastronomy* (Winter/Spring 1993), 7 (1).

Masson, Jeffrey Moussaieff. *The Assault on Truth: Freud's Suppression of the Seduction Theory.* New York: Farrar, Straus, 1984.

McClelland, James L. "Constructive Memory and Memory Distortions: A

Parallel-Distributed Processing Approach," in *Memory Distortion: How Minds, Brains, and Societies Reconstruct the Past*. Edited by D. L. Schacter. Cambridge, Mass.: Harvard University Press, 1995.

McGaugh, James L. "Emotional Activation, Neuromodulatory Systems, and Memory," in *Memory Distortion: How Minds, Brains, and Societies Reconstruct the Past*. Edited by D. L. Schacter. Cambridge, Mass.: Harvard University Press, 1995.

Miller, Alice. *Banished Knowledge: Facing Childhood Injuries*. New York: Doubleday, 1990.

———. *The Drama of the Gifted Child: The Search for the True Self*. New York: Basic Books, 1990.

Miller, Arthur. *The Crucible*. New York: Penguin Books, 1976.

Molien v. Kaiser Foundation Hospital, 27 Cal. 3 916. 616 P.2d 813, 167 Cal. Rpt. 831 (1980).

Money, John. *Lovemaps: Clinical Concepts of Sexual/Erotic Health and Pathology, Paraphilia, and Gender Transposition in Childhood, Adolescence, and Maturity*. New York: Irvington Publishers, 1986.

———. *Venuses Penuses: Sexology, Sexosophy, and Exigency Theory*. Buffalo: Prometheus Books, 1986.

Nathan, Debbie, and Michael Snedeker. *Satan's Silence: Ritual Abuse and the Making of a Modern American Witch Hunt*. New York: Basic Books, 1995.

Ofshe, Richard, and Ethan Watters. *Making Monsters: False Memories, Psychotherapy, and Sexual Hysteria*. New York: Scribner's, 1994.

PBS *Frontline*. "Divided Memories." Part 1, April 4, 1995. Part 2, April 11, 1995. Ofra Bikel, producer.

Pendergrast, Mark. *Victims of Memory: Incest Accusations and Shattered Lives*. Hinesburg, Vt.: Upper Access Books, 1995.

People v. Kelly, 17 Ca.3d 24, 549 P.2d 1240, 130 Cal.Rptr. 144 (1976).

Pope, Harrison G. *Psychology Astray: Fallacies in Studies of "Repressed Memory" and Childhood Trauma*. Boca Raton: Social Issues Resources Series, 1997.

Pope, Harrison G., Jr., and James I. Hudson. "Can Memories of Childhood Sexual Abuse Be Repressed?" *Psychological Medicine* (1995), 25: 121–26, 1995.

———. "Is Childhood Sexual Abuse a Risk Factor for Bulimia Nervosa?" *American Journal of Psychiatry* (1992), 149: 455–63.

———. *New Hope for Binge Eaters*. New York: Harper & Row, 1984.

Posner, Michael I., and Marcus E. Raichle. *Images of Mind*. New York: Scientific American Library, 1994.

Ramona v. Isabella et al. Napa Superior Court Case No. 61898, Napa, Calif., 1994.

Rauch, Scott, et al. "PET Imagery: Positron Emission Scans of Traumatic

Imagery in PTSD Patients." Paper presented at the annual meeting of the International Society of Traumatic Stress Studies, Chicago, November 1994.

Repression and Dissociation: Implications for Personality Theory, Psychopathology, and Health. Edited by Jerome L. Singer. Chicago: University of Chicago Press, 1990.

Robinson, Enders A. *The Devil Discovered: Salem Witchcraft 1692.* New York: Hippocrene Books, 1991.

Roiphe, Anne. *Fruitful: A Real Mother in the Modern World.* Boston: Houghton Mifflin, 1996.

Russell, Diana E. H. *The Secret Trauma: Incest in the Lives of Girls and Women.* New York: Basic Books, 1986.

Sagan, Carl. *The Demon-Haunted World.* New York: Random House, 1995.

Sapolsky, Robert. "Can Stress Damage the Brain?" Speech presented April 1, 1996, at the third annual meeting of the Cognitive Neuroscience Society, San Francisco.

Schacter, Daniel L. "Memory Distortion: History and Current Status," in *Memory Distortion: How Minds, Brains, and Societies Reconstruct the Past.* Edited by D. L. Schacter. Cambridge, Mass.: Harvard University Press, 1995.

————. *Searching for Memory: The Brain, the Mind, and the Past.* New York: Basic Books, 1996.

————, and John F. Kihlstrom. "Functional Amnesia." *Handbook of Neuropsychology,* vol. 3. Edited by F. Boller and J. Grafman. Elsevier Science Publishers B. V. (Biomedical Division), 1989.

Schama, Simon. *Dead Certainties.* New York: Knopf, 1991.

————. *Landscape and Memory.* New York: Knopf, 1995.

Silverstein, Brett, and Deborah Perlick. *The Cost of Competence: Why Inequality Causes Depression, Eating Disorders, and Illness in Women.* New York: Oxford University Press, 1995.

Slovenko, Ralph. "The Duty of Therapists to Third Parties." Paper presented at the False Memory Syndrome Foundation conference, Baltimore, December 1994.

Spiegel, David. "Hypnosis and Suggestion," in *Memory Distortion: How Minds, Brains, and Societies Reconstruct the Past.* Edited by D. L. Schacter. Cambridge, Mass.: Harvard University Press, 1995.

Spiegel, David, and Paul McHugh. "The Pros and Cons of Dissociative Identity (Multiple Personality) Disorder." *Journal of Practical Psychology and Behavioral Health* (September 1995): 158–66.

Squire, Larry R. "Biological Foundations of Accuracy and Inaccuracy in Memory," in *Memory Distortion: How Minds, Brains, and Societies Reconstruct the Past.* Edited by D. L. Schacter. Cambridge, Mass.: Harvard University Press, 1995.

————, and Pablo Alvarez. "Retrograde Amnesia and Memory Consolidation: A Neurological Perspective." *Current Opinion in Neurobiology* (1995), 5: 169–77.

————, B. Knowlton, and G. Musen. "The Structure and Organization of Memory." *Annual Review of Psychology* (1993) 44: 453–95.

Starkey, Marion L. *The Devil in Massachusetts: A Modern Enquiry into the Salem Witch Trials.* New York: Anchor Books, 1989.

Taub, Sheila. "The Legal Treatment of Recovered Memories of Child Sexual Abuse." *Journal of Legal Medicine* (June 1996), 17:183–214.

Tavris, Carol. "Beware the Incest Survivor Machine." *New York Times Book Review,* January 3, 1993.

————. *The Mismeasure of Woman.* New York: Simon & Schuster, 1992.

————, and Carole Wade. *Psychology in Perspective.* New York: HarperCollins, 1995.

Terr, Lenore. "Childhood Traumas: An Outline and Overview." *American Journal of Psychiatry,* 148:1, January 1991.

————. *Unchained Memories: True Stories of Traumatic Memories, Lost and Found.* New York: Basic Books, 1994.

Trevor-Roper, H. R. *The Crisis of the Seventeenth Century: Religion, the Reformation and Social Change.* New York: Harper & Row, 1968.

Van der Kolk, Bessel A. and Rita Fisler. "Dissociation and the Fragmentary Nature of Traumatic Memories." *Journal of Traumatic Stress* (1995) 8 (4).

Visser, Margaret. "On Having Cake and Eating It." *Journal of Gastronomy* (Winter/Spring 1993) 7 (1).

————. *The Rituals of Dinner: The Origins, Evolution, Eccentricities, and Meaning of Table Manners.* New York: Grove Weidenfeld, 1991.

Welch, S. L., and C. G. Fairburn. "Sexual Abuse and Bulimia Nervosa: Three Integrated Case Control Comparisons." *American Journal of Psychiatry* (1994) 151: 402–7.

Williams, Linda Meyer. "Adult Memories of Child Sexual Abuse: Preliminary Findings from a Longitudinal Study." *American Society for Prevention of Child Abuse Advisor* (1992), 5: 19–20.

————. "Recall of Childhood Trauma. A Prospective Study of Women's Memories of Child Sexual Abuse." *Journal of Consulting and Clinical Psychology* (1994) 62 (6): 1167–76.

Wilson, G. Terence, and Christopher G. Fairburn. "Treatment of Eating Disorders," in *Psychotherapies and Drugs That Work: A Review of the Outcome Studies.* Edited by P. E. Nathan and J. M. Gorman. In press.

Wright, Lawrence. *Remembering Satan: A Case of Recovered Memory and the Shattering of an American Family.* New York: Knopf, 1994.

Yapko, Michael D. *Suggestions of Abuse.* New York: Simon & Schuster, 1994.

Yool, George Malcolm. *1692 Witch Hunt: The Layman's Guide to the Salem Witchcraft Trials.* Bowie, Md.: Heritage Books, 1992.

Acknowledgments

I would like to thank my husband, Lee Block, who first encouraged me to sit in "for at least a day or two" on the Ramona trial and encouraged me through three years of intense work.

An extraordinary team has worked with me on this project. As in previous books, Sheilagh Simpson has brought her extensive skills and experience as general editorial assistant, editing, transcribing, doing research, and orchestrating the daunting job of fact-checking. I am blessed to have had Kristina Horton Flaherty, an experienced reporter who covered the Ramona trial for the *San Francisco Examiner,* as my principal research assistant and invaluable brainstormer. Christie Johnston, a photojournalist in New York, took over the task of photo editor and contributed a number of pictures. Jeanne Miller and Wendy Fairley ably transcribed tapes, and Charlene Avery tenaciously acquired trial transcripts from the court reporters. Michael Harris did research in Southern California. George Martin provided trial tapes. Keith Hezmalhalch's Kaleidoscope Productions copied all my interview tapes. Bruce Miroglio graciously took the brunt of my requests for trial material and information because he lives nearby. The research staff of the Napa City and County Library was wonderful. During the weeks of trial, several media women were heartening friends and a helpful "reality check," especially Elizabeth Mullen, Diane Curtis, Kristina Flaherty, and Jodi Roth.

There could have been no book without the nearly one hundred personal interviews and several hundred hours of audiotape that, with the trial, form the basis of *Spectral Evidence.* I am deeply indebted to Stephanie and Gary Ramona, who each met with me many times, going through the pain again to tell me their stories. I thank Shawna Ramona. The jurors' willingness to relate their experience has added an invaluable, rich dimension. The names of interview subjects appear throughout the book. Some do not appear by their choice or by editorial decision — such people as Joanne Yates, Ilona Rosson, and Tia O'Rear. But they know their contribution and my gratitude. Napa

Valley's community of therapists and educators were generous participants, particularly Don Scully, Sarah Boggs, Richard Mullins, Anne Evans, Maggie Kelly, and Charlene Steen, who permitted me to attend a group session with her multiple personality patients.

With my appetite for the science of memory whetted by the trial experts Elizabeth Loftus and Lenore Terr, I subsequently gained an education not only from them but also from interviews with half a dozen of the top memory scientists in the field and from the publications of many more, cited in the notes and bibliography. Dr. Thomas Gutheil was helpful on the intersection of psychiatry and the law. Many people helped to expand my understanding of the practice and theory of psychotherapy; the process of recovering memories of abuse; the experience of never-forgotten child abuse; the unmapped emotional path of retractors and returners; eating disorders; pedophilia; and the legal issues of duty and of admissible scientific evidence. Pamela Freyd and the staff of the False Memory Syndrome Foundation always responded promptly to requests for information. Several clinicians who believe in repressed memories of childhood sexual trauma, among them John Briere, Douglas Sawin, and Lenore Terr, gave me the clinicians' perspective; Briere made the important point that child sexual abuse should not be focused on at the expense of attention to the many kinds of child abuse that exist. From the abuse survivor network, social policy activist and attorney Sherry A. Quirk was helpful. I was privileged to hear and chat with the late Dr. Carl Sagan on the issues at a Skeptical Inquirer conference in Seattle in the fall of 1994.

I wish to thank all those who shepherded the book through its dramatic history at Houghton Mifflin. John Sterling, then editor in chief, was the first to give this book life and helped enormously in developing its themes and structure. Chris Coffin, the managing editor, moved this project forward in a thousand fine ways. Luise Erdmann did a splendid job as manuscript editor. Publicity director Rina Ranalli's enthusiasm and skill are greatly appreciated. Christine Corcoran was an expert coordinator. Thanks, too, to Peg Anderson, Betsy Peterson, and Glenn Kaye for their excellent advice. Finally, I thank David Brewster, who, as Houghton Mifflin's editorial director, became the book's champion and participated at every stage.

I am lucky to have, simply, the best agent in the business, Michael Carlisle of the William Morris Agency, a valued friend as well.

My dear friends and family are my support and strength. Phyllis Sarasy and Joan Blum did an early "read" and made useful comments. The flood of loving interest, good humor, and professional help I received from family is staggering: from my husband, the physician–lawyer–textbook author Alvin Lee Block, and all the Blocks; my mother, Christie Harris, Canada's distinguished author of children's books; my children, Donald and Christie Johnston; my sister, Sheilagh Simpson, and my brother Michael Harris; and my nieces Wendy Fairley and Patricia Simpson.

Index